Brain Drain and Brain Gain

Reports for the Fondazione Rodolfo DeBenedetti

Ageing, Health, and Productivity: The Economics of Increased Life Expectancy
Edited by Pietro Garibaldi, Joaquim Oliveira Martins, and Jan van Ours

Brain Drain and Brain Gain: The Global Competition to Attract High-Skilled Migrants
Edited by Tito Boeri, Herbert Brücker, Frédéric Docquier, and Hillel Rapoport

Education and Training in Europe
Edited by Giorgio Brunello, Pietro Garibaldi, and Etienne Wasmer

Immigration Policy and the Welfare System
Edited by Tito Boeri, Gordon H. Hanson, and Barry McCormick

Structural Reforms Without Prejudices
Edited by Tito Boeri, Micael Castanheira, Riccardo Faini, and Vincenzo Galasso

The ICT Revolution: Productivity Differences and the Digital Divide
Edited by Daniel Cohen, Pietro Garibaldi, and Stefano Scarpetta

The Role of Unions in the Twenty-first Century
Edited by Tito Boeri, Agar Brugiavini, and Lars Calmfors

The Ruling Class: Management and Politics in Modern Italy
Edited by Tito Boeri, Antonio Merlo, and Andrea Prat

Women at Work: An Economic Perspective
Edited by Tito Boeri, Daniela Del Boca, and Christopher Pissarides

Working Hours and Job Sharing in the EU and USA: Are Europeans Lazy? Or Americans Crazy?
Edited by Tito Boeri, Michael Burda, and Francis Kramarz

Brain Drain and Brain Gain

The Global Competition to Attract High-Skilled Migrants

Edited by
Tito Boeri,
Herbert Brücker,
Frédéric Docquier,
and Hillel Rapoport

With

Sascha Becker, Simone Bertoli, Giovanni Facchini,
Anna Maria Mayda, Franco Peracchi, Giovanni Peri,
Antonio Spilimbergo, and Alessandra Venturini

OXFORD
UNIVERSITY PRESS

OXFORD

UNIVERSITY PRESS

Great Clarendon Street, Oxford, OX2 6DP,
United Kingdom

Oxford University Press is a department of the University of Oxford.
It furthers the University's objective of excellence in research, scholarship,
and education by publishing worldwide. Oxford is a registered trade mark of
Oxford University Press in the UK and in certain other countries

Published in the United States of America by Oxford University Press
198 Madison Avenue, New York, NY 10016, United States of America

British Library Cataloguing in Publication Data
Data available

Library of Congress Cataloguing in Publication Data
Data Available

ISBN 978-0-19-965482-6

Jacket illustration: © Digital Vision

Acknowledgements

Both studies were originally prepared for the eleventh European conference of the Fondazione Rodolfo Debenedetti, held in Pisa in May 2009. This book draws much on the discussion in Pisa, which involved a qualified audience of academicians, managers of academic institutions, professional economists, representatives of unions and employers associations, and policymakers. Needless to say, we are very much indebted to all those who attended that conference and contributed actively to the discussion.

In particular, we wish to express our gratitude to Maria Chiara Carrozza and Riccardo Varaldo, respectively Director and President of the Scuola Superiore Sant'Anna of Pisa for their warm welcome to their university and active contribution to the policy debate. We are also indebted to Fabio Benfenati (Director, Department of Neuroscience and Brain Technologies, Italian Institute of Technologies, Genoa), Giovanni Dosi (Scuola Superiore Sant'Anna), Ugo Montanari (Deputy Director, IMT Alti Studi Lucca and University of Pisa), Pietro Reichlin (LUISS Guido Carli, Rome), and Daniele Terlizzese (Director, Einaudi Institute for Economics and Finance for their insightful comments in the final panel session.

We are most grateful to Carlo De Benedetti who allowed the Fondazione to exist and made possible this event, to which he also contributed with particularly insightful opening remarks.

Finally, special thanks go to Tommaso Colussi, Matteo Duiella, Roberta Marcaletti and Paola Monti who assisted us in the organization of the conference and worked hard and skilfully in preparing the background material for this volume.

The editors

Contents

Contents

Part II *Quantifying the Impact of Highly Skilled Emigration on Developing Countries*

By Frédéric Docquier and Hillel Rapoport

Contents

List of Figures

List of Tables

List of Boxes

List of Contributors

Sascha Becker (University of Warwick)

Simone Bertoli (CERDI, University of Auvergne)

Tito Boeri (Università Bocconi, Italy)

Herbert Brücker (IAB, Germany)

Frédéric Docquier (Université Catholique de Louvain, Belgium)

Giovanni Facchini (University of Milan)

Anna Maria Mayda (Georgetown University, USA)

Franco Peracchi (University of Tor Vergata, Rome)

Giovanni Peri (University of Davis, California)

Hillel Rapoport (Bar-Ilan University, Israel)

Antonio Spilimbergo (International Monetary Fund)

Alessandra Venturini (University of Turin)

Introduction

By Tito Boeri

The worldwide race to attract talents is getting tougher and tougher. So far the global winner has been the USA, capable of attracting PhD candidates and graduates not only from emerging countries, but also from the European Union. The percentage of immigrants with a PhD coming from Europe is up to ten times larger than the proportion of PhDs in the US population (Saint-Paul, 2008) according to the last available US Census data. Moreover, the USA has managed to keep many of these PhDs in universities, research centres, and laboratories located in its territory. This means that it has benefited from the knowledge spillovers typically associated with the work of these talents.

In tennis, it would be a 6–0 score in the first set of a USA vs Rest of the World match. However, the second set may be different. There are indeed indications that the Great Depression and the changes taking place in the worldwide geography of growth are also affecting the profiles of winners and losers in this race. Some emerging economies are now successfully attracting highly skilled migrants, while they continue to experience significant outflows of medium- and low-skilled workers. Europe may continue to be the land of missed opportunity, unable to attract the talent that is going either to the USA or to the new leaders of world growth. Once more, it may fail in improving its 'brain balance'.

The reason why the race is so tough and why the skill profile of migration is receiving so much attention from policymakers is that skilled migration is a way out of a policy dilemma facing many governments. It makes immigration not only economically advantageous, but also politically acceptable. Immigration contributes to the economic growth in the recipient country insofar as it increases the share of skilled workers in the population. By improving its per capita human capital endowments, the immigration country can support stronger growth *rates*, rather than simply experiencing a once-and-for-all, *level*, increase in GDP. The trend increase of education premia in most advanced economies suggests that the supply of highly educated workers is falling short of demand. Countries are just not increasing their

1

stock of tertiary educated individuals fast enough. Selective immigration can reduce this skill shortage.

Skilled migration is also politically more acceptable as inflows of skilled workers tend to reduce earning inequalities in the host country. Furthermore, more educated migrants generally have a faster integration in the labour market and assimilate in the society without creating major tensions within the native population. This faster integration also magnifies the economic benefits of migration. Indeed, the permanent effects of migration on growth rates originate from knowledge spillovers, via skill acquisition and learning-by-doing of native workers, as well as the competitive pressures on the latter to acquire more skills. Finally, skilled migrants do not compete with unskilled natives in their access to the welfare state or to subsidized childcare and other public services. Thus, skilled migration does not raise native concerns about the fiscal burden associated with migration.

These concerns are mounting in public opinion and drive negative perceptions about migration (Dustmann and Preston, 2005; Boeri, 2010). Low-skilled migration is an easy scapegoat for politicians wishing to place blame for their failures on someone else. Here are some quotes of popular politicians around the EU. According to Claus Hjort Frederiksen, former Danish Minister for Employment and Minister of Finance, 'if immigration from Third World Country were blocked, 75 per cent of the cuts necessary to maintain the welfare state would be unnecessary'. Heinz-Christian Strache, leader of the xenophobic FPO, carried out the triumphal campaign in the municipal elections in Vienna in 2010 stating that 'social housing, family allowances and child subsidies should become a citizen's right only and should not be given easily to immigrants'. The book by Thilo Sarazzin, former member of the board of the Bundesbank, is a bestseller in Germany and has plenty of statements of the kind: 'Germany is digging its own grave by admitting waves of immigrants who are spongers, welfare cheats, and sub-intelligent beings.' According to Roberto Maroni, Italian Minister of the Interior in the Berlusconi IV cabinet, 'migrants are a negative resource; we should not build houses (and religious sites) for them; it is outrageous that migrants acquire the same rights of Italians while only the latter pay'. In the words of Siv Jensen, leader of the Norwegian Progress Party, 'There is a large number of immigrants living on welfare and they have been in this condition for a very, very long time,' a statement echoed recently also by Catherine Megret, member of the French Mouvement National Républicain: 'there are simply too many immigrants, who knows how many children they send to the streets and then claim welfare'.

Skilled migration is another issue. And highly skilled migration cannot be used as a scapegoat even by the most xenophobic movements. The reason is that natives' perceptions about the role of migration improve with an increase in share of highly skilled immigrants. The more people with at least tertiary education in the migrant population, the better the overall 'grading': the evaluation of the role of immigration among natives (Boeri, 2010).

Not only a matter of migration policy

So far the race for talents has been run mainly through adjustment of migration policies. Starting from the late 1960s a growing number of countries adopted immigration policies specifically aimed at selecting and attracting highly skilled workers (Boeri, Hanson, and McCormick, 2002). A point-based system (PBS) was introduced in Australia, Canada, and New Zealand. In Europe, Switzerland and the UK are gradually introducing a PBS or planning to do so. The Dutch and German governments are also very seriously considering this option. In new large-scale immigration countries, like Italy and Spain, a point-based system is not in the pipeline, but a skill-selective mechanism for allocating quotas is being considered in the endless debate over the right type of migration policies. In a PBS, each application is allocated a score based on explicit criteria which typically reward educational attainment, experience, and language abilities. 'Bonus points' can also be given for employment in occupations and regions where there is a shortage of workers.

It is not obvious that migration policy is the best policy instrument to be activated in the race for talents. Is the skill content of migration responding to the design of migration policies or to other incentives? Other institutions, such as tertiary education, may have the potential to make a given location more palatable to highly skilled workers. A merit-based university system rewarding scientific achievements both in the recruitment of professors and in their pay (as well as in the allocation of the teaching workload), may be more successful than a PBS in attracting high-quality researchers. The USA, the winner so far in the global race for talents after all, does not have a PBS in place. Collective bargaining institutions, affecting wage dispersion and hence premia on education, are also likely to play a very important role in affecting the skill composition of migration, as highlighted by Roy's pioneering 1951 model (Roy, 1951).

It is even less obvious that the skill effects of migration on growth can work symmetrically in the sending and receiving countries. It cannot be said a priori that human capital acquisition via brain gain necessarily involves a human capital loss via brain drain in another country. Knowledge and entrepreneurial ideas can also flow without requiring the physical mobility of persons. They can return back home even without the persons who originated them. There is evidence that citations of patents are higher in locations where the cited inventor was living prior to being issued the patent in question (Agrawal,

Cockburn, and McHale, 2003). And there can be positive spillovers also from outflows of skilled migrants. For instance, the option for the most skilled to migrate and get rich abroad may encourage human capital investment in the country of origin (Beine, Docquier, and Rapoport, 2001; Cinar and Docquier, 2004). The returns to education in a developing country are often relatively small as these countries typically specialize in low-skilled production originating in a limited demand for highly skilled workers. This clearly discourages human capital investment. However, if, by studying more, one also acquires the right to legally migrate to a rich nation, then there is also an option value associated with human capital investment at home. Moreover, by studying more, one can better interact with highly skilled natives returning back home after some work experience abroad. This means that the social returns to human capital investment in the relatively poor countries may not be so much lower than the private returns.

Skilled migration and the ruling class

Return migration is substantial among highly skilled migrants and can contribute to the creation of political elites in developing countries. A recent work by Antonio Spilimbergo (a contributor to this volume) drawing on records from the American Fullbright Program indicates that some 200 heads of national governments, mainly in developing countries, were trained in the USA (Spilimbergo, 2009). Thus, the social returns to education in the sending country can be further enhanced by the possibility of improving the selection of their ruling class. And the country receiving and contributing to the human capital investment of these talented immigrants can hope to also obtain some political or diplomatic dividend from this migration flow.

These potential benefits associated with the training of very highly skilled migrants are not always fully understood. The Italian ruling class badly needs an educational upgrade. As documented in previous volumes of this series, the share of Italian MPs with a tertiary education declined substantially in the last 60 years (just at the time when their earnings were skyrocketing). Ignorance about the trickle-down effects of talents and a very strong political myopia may contribute to explaining why Italy is not investing at all in its small stock of foreign PhDs. A survey carried out by the Fondazione Rodolfo Debenedetti among the population of Italian PhD students with foreign passports in April–May 2009 is quite revealing in this respect. We received answers from about 450 students out of a population of 2,000. Most of them reported very serious problems with having a legal status in Italy. Two-thirds of them reported delays in receiving residence permits (and some of them had received the permits after the expiration date), four out of ten reported difficulties in interacting with the administrative offices dealing with migrants (apparently the officers did not speak English). Almost eight out of ten had to wait for at least three months before gaining an appointment with the local authorities in charge of regularization. These delays in obtaining residence permits prevented one PhD student out of four from travelling abroad to present their work in academic seminars (which means obtaining very useful comments and suggestions for future research) and four out of ten from spending their holidays abroad as they feared not being readmitted to Italy afterwards, due to their irregular status.

There was an open question in the survey about the problems met in dealing with migration. The answers do not require any comment. Here is a selection: 'the first time I received my permit in 9 months, the following time in 11 months and this time it is going to be more than a year'; 'the most frequent expression I heard from Italians was *"non lo so"* (I don't know) ...'; 'every person I've met at Questura had a different interpretation on what I was supposed to do to renew my permit of stay'; 'I am now doing an internship in Singapore. I got the stay permit within 3 hours of submission of my application. In Italy it took 22 months. [...] I am too much desperate with Italian bureaucracy. After finishing my studies I will run away from Italy'; 'I was planning to work in Italy, but the procedure to immigrate is very complicated and difficult, especially for my relatives, so I gave up this idea'; 'I have studied in 4 universities before coming to Italy and worked in different parts of the world. I found Italy one of the places where a foreigner does not feel comfortable. I found that Italy is losing capacity to integrate foreigners to its culture and this will have a strong impact on the quality of students it will be able to attract.'

Unsurprisingly, most of these students are not planning to remain in Italy after the completion of their studies. In particular 88 per cent of those having already decided what to do afterwards (almost 50 per cent of the interviewees declared to have made up their mind) reported the intention to leave Italy upon attainment of the PhD.

The example of Italy points to potential vicious cycles in the race for talents that prevents some advanced European countries from competing. An inward-looking and poorly educated ruling class does not realize the benefits of attracting highly skilled migrants and therefore treats them just like all other migrants. This in turn, prevents migration from contributing to the skill upgrading and internationalization of the ruling class. The chains may also work the other way round: 99 per cent of the members of the US Congress have received at least college education and two-thirds of them come from the Ivy League. This may explain why the USA is cherry picking PhDs from Europe and has a very high retention rate of those obtaining post-graduate educational attainments in an American university.

Brain flows and the Great Recession

As argued above, the crisis may quite radically change the profile of winners and losers in the race for talents. Many advanced countries are facing a public debt crisis and are forced to cut down on public spending, including some research and tertiary education programmes. This is bound to have some impact on the demand for talents in some of the traditional brain gainers, including the USA. For emerging countries, such as Brazil, China, and India, the Great Recession has merely been a parenthesis. They experienced a short break, in 2009, in their two-digit growth rates and, with the partial exception of India, do not seem to have come out of it with larger fiscal imbalances than before the crisis. Their exchange rate is appreciating and they are more and more involved in the global race for talents. Brazilian and Chinese universities, in particular, were very aggressive in the job market for economists in 2010 and 2011.

The Great Recession has also affected the supply of migrants. Credit constraints make it more difficult to finance the costs of migration (Rotte and Vogler, 2000). As pointed out by Hatton and Williamson (2009), typically a 10 per cent rule applies to migration in downturns, whereby every 100 jobs lost in a high-immigration country results in 10 fewer immigrants. This 10 per cent rule seems to describe pretty well the evolution of gross migration inflows in countries like Australia, Canada, and Italy during the Great Depression, and applies to other periods too. Return migration and lower inflows contribute to containing the rise of unemployment during cyclical downturns. During the severe 1890s depression in the USA, for instance, net immigrant exits reduced the unemployment rate by about 1.6 percentage points. The elasticity of migration against the unemployment rate in the country of destination is generally stronger for illegal migrants who do not have access to unemployment benefits and social assistance of the last resort.

All the available data and the anecdotal evidence in this book suggest that some decline in migration inflows and increase in return migration have occurred for all types of migrants. But how about the relative decline of skilled and unskilled migrants? How has the Great Recession affected the skill mix in countries of destination and origin?

Unfortunately reliable data on the skill composition of migrants after the crisis are not yet available. Thus, we should confine ourselves to some speculative reasoning. Skilled migrants are typically regular workers who have access to social transfers. They are also often favoured in terms of family reunification, which reduces even further their willingness to return. However, there is evidence that the very highly skilled are very sensitive to their cultural environment, notably to the degree of acceptance of migrants in the countries of destination. They want to put their children into schools and neighbourhoods where xenophobic attitudes are absent. Declines in inflows of skilled migrants were reported in Germany after increases in the share of votes going to xenophobic parties. Any severe slump tends to negatively affect natives' perceptions of migrants. Kessler and Freeman (2003) showed that right wing populism increased under adverse economic conditions in Europe. A 2009 Harris survey suggested that the share of natives agreeing with the statement that 'unemployed migrants should be made to leave' had doubled since the beginning of the recession and was close to 80 per cent even in relatively open societies like the UK.

Such changes in popular attitudes tend to affect short-sighted politicians seeking re-election. This contributes to explain why, in February 2009, the USA enacted a law imposing strict restrictions on the hiring of skilled immigrant workers by companies receiving government bailout money. In Spain, the Zapatero government has decided in the face of rising unemployment to offer all non-EU immigrants a chance to cash in their unemployment benefits; in exchange, they must leave the country and agree not to return for at least three years. As one would expect, this policy failed miserably: as of June 2009 there had been only 5,000 applications. The Czech Republic implemented a similar programme in February 2009, also for non-EU immigrants, with the same prospects of success. Malaysia and Saudi Arabia directed companies to lay off foreign workers first if they needed to downsize, and Ireland is apparently in the process of reconsidering its liberal immigration laws which have allowed massive levels of immigration to sustain the country's economic growth from the late 1990s. In Italy, the Berlusconi government passed (in May 2009) very strict legislation to fight illegal immigration.

These protectionist policies mostly affect the labour market prospects of the unskilled migrants rather than the market for talents. However, to the extent that they use migrants as scapegoats backing popular hostility with respect to migrants, they may discourage highly skilled migration and divert the flow of brains elsewhere.

A serious risk associated with such short-sighted reactions to mounting negative sentiments vis-à-vis unemployed migrants is to postpone recovery and create long-lasting social tensions even in countries that so far have not faced major problems with integration of migrants. The issue is that there may be a substitution of those migrants who have lost their job during the recession with other migrants who are less integrated. This may, in turn, increase even further negative public attitudes towards immigration.

This volume

The very key issue highlighted by these policy responses to the Great Recession is that migration policy is a long-term policy tool. Using migration restrictions to address short-term problems can have many unintended and undesirable consequences.

This volume contributes to placing policies affecting the international flow of talents in the right context, as a long-term problem of individual countries and of global governance.

As with previous volumes of this series, it reviews the most recent research on brain drain and brain gain, producing new and original results by the means of data sources specifically assembled for this study, and addressing several key policy issues. It draws on contributions from two teams of leading scholars in the field and on an important data gathering effort undertaken by the Fondazione Rodolfo Debenedetti.

Part I presents the contribution of the first team, which was coordinated by Herbert Bruecker (Institut für Arbeitsmarkt und Berufsforschung, Germany) and included Simone Bertoli (CERDI, University of Auvergne), Giovanni Facchini (University of Milan, Italy), Anna Maria Mayda (Georgetown University, Washington DC, USA), and Giovanni Peri (University of Davis, California, USA). The focus of this part is on brain gain, that is, it takes the viewpoint of the recipient country.

Part II is devoted to the consequences of brain drain, taking the viewpoint of the sending country. It collects the report of the second team, involving Frédéric Docquier (Université Catholique de Louvain, Belgium) and Hillel Rapoport (Bar-Ilan University, Israel), two pioneers in studies of human capital flows from developing to developed nations.

The study in Part I indicates that immigration restrictions are becoming increasingly selective in OECD countries as governments realize the desirability of skill-selective immigration policies from the point of view of aggregate welfare. It also documents that the stock of highly skilled migrants residing in this 'rich countries club' has increased significantly over time, reaching the remarkable level of 20 million, more than one-tenth of the highly skilled population in the destination countries. However, a few English-speaking OECD countries, notably the USA, Canada, and Australia, absorb the overwhelming share of these highly skilled migrants while the other OECD countries are net senders of highly educated individuals.

What drives the decisions of highly skilled migrants as to where to locate? The econometric analyses performed by the authors of this report indicate that it is mainly the labour market that is the key to attract talents. Wage premia on education are crucial: increasing the wage premium for education by US $10,000 has the potential to increase the share of the highly skilled in the immigrant population between 20 and 40 per cent relative to its initial value. Research and development spending also induces more inflows of highly skilled migrants, while generous welfare benefits and strict employment protection end up attracting more unskilled workers. This is hardly surprising as low-skilled workers face a higher than average risk of job loss.

With the notable exception of the USA, all countries that have so far been most successful in attracting highly skilled migrants have adopted a PBS in screening applicants for work permits. And the study documents strong gains from immigration of highly skilled migrants. Why then have only a few countries so far opted for a PBS? The answer provided by the authors calls the political power of the highly skilled natives into play. This political power goes far beyond the share of skilled natives in the electorate. This outcome can be explained more in terms of pressure groups than of preferences of the median voter. Governments appealing directly to voters could win in this political opposition.

There is, however, a potential drawback of the point system—its negative effects on growth, via the so-called brain drain and income distribution in the sending country. The 'brain drain', as its name suggests, is the assertion that migration tends to strip the sending nation of all its best workers.

However, as suggested by the study in Part II of this book, selective immigration policies increase individual incentives to invest in human capital in the sending countries, so that the impact of migration on human capital formation in the country of origin may not be so strong. In some cases, it may even turn out to be positive. Since migration to Europe is mainly temporary, human capital acquired in the country of destination could be subsequently transferred to the country of origin promoting growth in the sending region. Remittances, return migration, network effects favouring international transactions and technology diffusion, as well as brain gain channels, may more than compensate the sending countries for their loss of human capital.

Whether net benefits of brain drain are positive or negative is a matter of sound empirical work. The study by Docquier and Rapoport in Part II of this volume provides for the first time a measure of the net global impact of the brain drain on sending countries. This is done in various steps. First, a set of original indicators documenting the magnitude of highly skilled migration is provided. Then, based on a new data set on skilled migration developed by the authors within this project, the extent of brain drain overall and in specific professions, e.g. among scientists and health-care professionals, is measured. The next step is to test the theoretical mechanisms at work in compensating this brain drain, and the links between brain drain and remittances. Finally, using numerical experiments and empirical studies, an estimate of the net costs of the brain drain is offered for a number of developing countries. The results indicate that most developing countries experience a net gain from skilled emigration. Adverse overall impacts are found to be limited to a subset of countries exhibiting very high skilled emigration rates.

A number of policy recommendations are also offered to increase the benefits of brain drain, such as investment in the quality of public education, the opening up of the higher education market to private education providers, reliance on aid and development programmes (e.g. of the 'training and return' type) for obtaining the professional skills needed. The countries that are net losers may also want to consider, according to the authors, the redeployment of public resources to primary and secondary education and to post-secondary education for a few professions such as teachers and other civil servants with intermediate skills.

What type of global governance?

Are the recommendations developed in the two parts of the book mutually compatible? When we started working on this project, we were not at all sure that the research carried out by two independent groups of experts, taking such different viewpoints as those of immigration and emigration countries, could converge to a consistent set of policy recommendations. Did we succeed in achieving this convergence? The reader will judge by comparing the policy implications of the two parts of this volume. In these final sections of the introduction let me then just point out where potential conflicts of interest may arise and highlight the scope for international policy coordination.

Among the potential conflicts of interest: is the proposal of extending PBS to most advanced economies consistent with the goal of supporting growth in the sending regions? For most developing countries the answer provided in this volume is positive: PBS, by making more explicit the role played by education in the issuance of work permits, could strengthen incentives to human capital accumulation in the country of origin, increasing the benefits over the costs of brain drain. In other words, while competition in attracting talents is tough, there does not seem to be a conflict of interest between senders and recipients of migration flows in the case of many bilateral flows.

This is not the case, however, of the pool of countries generating most outflows to continental Europe, which are for the most part already experiencing at this stage an excessive brain drain. Here more fine-tuning of selective migration policies may be required so as not to harm the countries of origin of migrants. But this fine-tuning is possible only if there is some coordination among recipients, preventing a 'race-to-the-top' in encouragement of highly skilled migration being set in motion.

This book therefore provides powerful support to arguments in favour of stronger coordination among advanced economies, perhaps even more than that between developing and advanced economies in the governance of migration flows.

How can this coordination be achieved? The first step is to strengthen regional economic integration, extending its scope from product to labour markets. Immigration policies by definition involve cross-country spillovers and therefore there is a strong case for international policy coordination in this area.

It is often very difficult to agree upon a common immigration policy for economically highly integrated areas, such as the European Union, where a single market for labour does not exist as yet. The issue is that national voters are very concerned about delegating authority over migration policy to supra-national bodies.

Politicians have failed so far to convey to voters the message that without international policy coordination it is impossible to govern migration. They have not explained that an uncoordinated race for talent across the EU could negatively affect growth prospects in sending countries, and may end up inducing more unskilled migration. The outcome could be a race to the bottom in welfare provisions in an attempt to push unskilled migrants somewhere else.

Regional integration in migration policies would be a very important step. But it is also very important to strengthen coordination at the global level.

The economic rationale for migration policies is to induce some gradualism in flows that could otherwise occur in large waves inducing sizeable negative externalities in both receiving and sending nations. Migration in the long run can arbitrage huge cross-country differences in productivity, increasing global GDP. Globalization is quite advanced for goods and capital but still very imperfect for labour mobility. Partly due to this asymmetry in the extents of globalization at different margins, the potential gains from even a small liberalization of international migration are orders of magnitude higher than, say, a full liberalization of trade in goods and services, a comprehensive full debt relief programme, or a doubling of official development aid (Pritchett, 2006, 2010). For example, a recent World Bank study (Walmsley, Winters, and Ahmed, 2009) developed a bilateral migration model to simulate the welfare gains from an increase in South–North migration representing 3 per cent of the former's labour force and being filled by workers from developing countries in proportion to their traditional supplies to each developed economy. According to their computations, this modest liberalization of international migration would increase global GDP by US$288 billion, a surplus shared more or less equally between the migrants, home country residents, and host country residents thanks to the induced remittances. This can be compared to a previous study by the same authors where the gains from full liberalization of trade increase world output by just US$65 billion.

These immense potential gains associated with international migration can be realized only if migration flows are not distorted by asymmetric and beggar-my-neighbour policies. By levelling the playing field, migrants would go where their knowledge can best be used. The experience of Eastern enlargement of the EU, with the introduction of asymmetric transitional arrangements concerning the mobility of workers from the new member states, does suggest that migration flows can be greatly diverted by uncoordinated migration restrictions across neighbouring states (Boeri and Bruecker, 2005). This lack of coordination also makes the migration policy less effective as enforcement issues are magnified when common borders do not protect a single market for labour. Asymmetric policies mean having more borders to take care of. Finally a common policy can deliver a stronger message to those investing in human capital in the countries of origin. The famous Bangalore computer experts are unlikely to react to priority being given to highly skilled migrants in a small EU country, while they could look at Europe as a potential destination for their entrepreneurial ideas if the Union as a whole provided preferential access to them.

References

Agrawal, A.K., Cockburn, I.M, McHale, J. (2003), 'Gone But Not Forgotten: Labor Flows, Knowledge Spillovers, And Enduring Social Capital.' NBER WP 9950.

Beine, M., Docquier, F., Rapoport, H. (2001), 'Brain drain and economic growth: theory and evidence.' *Journal of Development Economics* 64 , 275–89.

Boeri, T. (2010), 'Immigration to the land of redistribution'. *Economica*, 77,651–87.

Boeri, T., Bruecker, H. (2005), 'Why are Europeans so tough on migrants?' *Economic Policy* 44,629–704.

Boeri, T., Hanson, G., McCormick, B. (2002), *Immigration Policy and the Welfare System*, Oxford: Oxford University Press.

Cinar, D., Docquier, F. (2004), 'Brain Drain and remittances: implications for the source country.' *Brussels Economic Review* 47(1), Special issue on skilled migration, 103–18.

Dustmann, C., Preston, I. (2005), 'Is immigration good or bad for the economy? Analysis of attitudinal responses.' *Research in Labor Economics* 24,3–34.

Hatton, T. J., Williamson, J. G. (2009), 'Emigration in the long run: evidence from two global centuries.' *Asian-Pacific Economic Literature* 23(2),17–28.

Kessler, A., Freeman, G. (2003), 'Beyond Fortress Europe? Public Opinion Immigration and Asylum in the EU.' Paper presented at the annual meeting of the American Political on Science Association, Philadelphia Marriott Hotel, Philadelphia, PA, Aug 27, 2003.

Pritchett, L. (2006), 'Let Their People Come. Breaking The Gridlock On Global Labor Mobility.' Center for Global Development, Brookings Institution Press, Washington, D.C.

Pritchett, L., Fanjul, G. (2010),'Goldilocks Globalizations: Soft Solutions to a Hard Problem.' Working Paper, Centre for International Development, Harvard University.

Rotte, R. Vogler, M. (2000), 'The effects of development on migration: theoretical issues and new empirical evidence.' *Journal of Population Economics* 13(3),485–508.

Roy, A. D. (1951), 'Some thoughts on the distribution of earnings.' *Oxford Economic Papers* 3,135–46.

Saint-Paul, G. (2008), 'Brain drain: some evidence from European expatriates in the United States.' *CESifo Forum* 3,19–27.

Spilimbergo, A. (2009), 'Democracy and foreign education.' *American Economic Review* 99(1), 528–43.

Walmsley, T. L., Winters, A. L., Ahmed, S. A. (2009), 'The Impact of the Movement of Labour: Results from a Model of Bilateral Migration Flows.' mimeo, University of Sussex.

Part I
Understanding Highly Skilled Migration in Developed Countries

The Upcoming Battle for Brains

by
Herbert Brücker
Simone Bertoli
Giovanni Facchini
Anna Maria Mayda
Giovanni Peri

Introduction

'I want to emphasize that to address the shortage of scientists and engineers, we must do both – reform our education system and our immigration policies. If we don't, American companies simply will not have the talent they need to innovate and compete.'

Bill Gates, Testimony at the US House of Representatives
Committee on Science and Technology on 12 March 2008

International migration into OECD countries and other high-income destinations in the Gulf region has increased during the last decades. About 20 million immigrants with tertiary education resided in the OECD at the beginning of this decade, representing about 11 per cent of the total highly skilled population living there. Although highly skilled workers are more internationally mobile than less skilled ones (OECD, 2008), skilled migration is still a small phenomenon compared to other facets of globalization. Essentially, as has been suggested by many authors, what we are experiencing is a wave of globalization that includes 'everything but labour' (Freeman, 2006; Pritchett, 2006). Besides its general low level, the incidence of highly skilled migration is heterogeneous across high-income countries. In fact English-speaking destinations, and especially those which have pursued an active skill-selective immigration policy, receive many more foreign highly skilled workers than all other OECD destinations. In addition, several OECD countries are even net senders of highly skilled workers.

OECD governments are becoming more and more aware of the potential gains of adopting skill-selective immigration policies. Highly qualified migrants can bring valuable skills which are in short supply, new entrepreneurial spirit, and they can also be a booster to local welfare systems. Thus, more and more countries are redesigning their immigration systems to make them more skill-selective. The recent introduction in the UK of a point-based system is just an example, and the recently adopted EU 'blue card' is another. Still, in many destinations countries domestic pressure groups have so far been very successful in limiting the inflow of foreign skilled workers (Facchini, Mayda, and Mishra, 2008). This means that while a 'Battle for Brains' is now starting, it is a long way from showing its full effects.

There are good reasons to believe that the contest for talent will intensify during the next few decades. Skill-biased technological change and, perhaps to a lesser extent, the growing specialization of developed countries in human capital-intensive activities will raise the demand for highly skilled labour. Ageing and the resulting pressures on the welfare states may also involve an increasing demand for highly skilled immigrants who create a net gain for public finances in destination countries (e.g. Boeri, Hanson, and McCormick, 2002; Boeri, 2009; Bonin, Raffelhüschen, and Walliser, 2002). Large and persistent earning differentials and declining transport and communication costs are likely to result in growing migration flows between rich and poor countries, even if the current financial crisis may lead to a short-term reduction.

Today, about 50 per cent of the highly skilled immigrants in the OECD originate from other OECD countries. However, the share of foreign talents originating in OECD countries has been declining over time. Thus, it is to be expected that the majority of future highly skilled immigrants will come from middle- and low-income countries, which are characterized by relatively poor human capital endowments. The increasing competition for highly skilled labour will hence affect the allocation of talent both among developed countries and between developed and less developed countries.

New theoretical models and richer data sets have greatly enhanced our ability to analyse the effects of skilled migration both on destination and source countries during the last decade. As discussed by Docquier and Rapoport (2009), recent developments have mainly focused on the question whether there is a *brain drain* from the sending-country perspective (e.g. Mountford, 1997; Stark et al., 1997; Vidal, 1998; Beine et al., 2001). The effect of skilled immigration in receiving countries and the competition of different destinations for highly qualified immigrants have received less attention in the academic literature, even though a few papers have started to analyse several important issues. For example, several studies have examined the impact of immigrants of different skill levels on wages (e.g. Borjas, 2003; Ottaviano and Peri, 2006) and unemployment (e.g. Brücker and Jahn, 2008; D'Amuri, Ottaviano, and Peri, 2008), or the different implications of highly and less skilled immigration on the welfare state (e.g. Boeri, Hanson, and McCormick, 2002; Bonin, Raffelhüschen, and Walliser, 2000). Moreover, several studies by international organizations have documented the scale of highly skilled immigration and the evolution of several policy issues (e.g. OECD, 2006; Kuptsch and Pang, 2006). Finally, other recent contributions have described the patterns of highly skilled emigration and immigration in individual countries of the OECD (e.g. Becker, Ichino, and Peri, 2004; Saint-Paul, 2004; Hunt, 2009). Nevertheless, a comprehensive analysis of highly skilled migration and the forthcoming contest for skill—which takes into account the interaction between immigration policies and potential outcomes—is still missing.[1]

The purpose of this study is to examine the causes and consequences of skilled migration from the point of view of the receiving countries. In particular we plan to address the following questions:

- What do skill-selective immigration policies in the receiving countries look like? Which strategies are pursued to attract highly skilled immigrants? What have been the main policy changes during the last decade?

- What are the main features of highly skilled immigration into developed countries? Which countries and regions tend to gain and which countries tend to lose human capital through the international mobility of highly skilled individuals?

- Which economic, legal, and institutional factors—including skill-selective immigration policies—determine the migration of highly skilled individuals?

- What is the impact of the immigration of highly skilled workers on output, capital accumulation, total factor productivity, and employment compared to the average impact of immigration?

- Do receiving countries also benefit from the immigration of highly skilled workers in an economic downturn?

- Why do so few countries adopt policies to attract highly skilled immigrants, given that the overall economic effects are beneficial? Can political economy forces help explain this apparent puzzle?

- What are the likely consequences of a widespread shift towards selective immigration policies? Is the Battle for Brains going to produce losers among the destination countries, and which is its impact upon the countries of origin?

Our argument is developed as follows. We start with a description of skill-selective immigration policies and of the main trends of highly skilled migration, which lays the background for further analyses. What are the policies towards highly skilled immigrants currently deployed by the destination countries? Chapter 1 outlines the different approaches selecting highly skilled immigrants in the main destination countries of the OECD and identifies the

---

[1] One interesting recent contribution in this area is the forthcoming volume by Bhagwati and Hanson (2009).

major shifts in policies which have occurred over the last decade. It also discusses the approach of the EU in entering the contest for talent, particularly the recently adopted 'blue card' initiative. We find that only few countries in the OECD pursue a consistent immigration policy which systematically selects highly skilled migrants by human capital criteria. These findings are supported by a cross-country survey of government officials carried out by the United Nations suggesting that only about one quarter of the countries in the sample has policies in place to attract highly skilled workers. This result is surprising in light of the widespread sentiment that highly skilled immigrants have beneficial effects on the destination country's economy.

Chapter 2 provides an overview of highly skilled migration into OECD countries. Using recently collected data on the number of immigrants with tertiary education in the OECD, we describe the main trends in the immigration of highly skilled individuals from the receiving-country perspective. Furthermore, the use of census data for selected OECD countries allows us to look at patterns of immigration at the very top of the skill distribution. We then analyse the development in the global pool of highly skilled individuals in the origin countries. Our data enable us to assess which OECD economies tend to gain and which tend to lose human capital through the migration of highly skilled individuals. Moreover, we address specific issues such as the international mobility of students, which plays a growing role in the mobility of foreign talents. Finally, we discuss the extent to which highly skilled immigrants are able to adequately employ their human capital in host country labour markets.

Building on this descriptive analysis, Chapter 3 examines the economic, legal, and institutional determinants of highly skilled migration in detail. Drawing on Ortega and Peri (2009) and Grogger and Hanson (2008), a scale equation and a selection equation are derived from a simple migration model. Using a panel data set which comprises 74 sending and 14 OECD destination countries over the 1980 to 2005 period, we explain the scale and the skill-selectivity of immigration using a large set of variables which are derived from economic and political considerations. *Inter alia*, we focus on wage levels and the wage premium for highly skilled labour, skill-selective and other immigration policies, the generosity of welfare benefits, labour market institutions, and research and development (R&D) expenditures. While there are some issues of omitted variables and reverse causality that cannot be fully resolved with aggregate data, the estimates reveal a robust and significant correlation between skilled immigration flows on the one hand and destination-country wages and immigration policies on the other.

Using the same data set, Chapter 4 addresses the impact of highly educated immigrants on employment, productivity, capital accumulation, and output in the receiving countries. Using an aggregate production function framework akin to growth accounting, we decompose the migration effects into a total immigration effect and the effect of the 'brain gain', which is measured as the share of tertiary educated individuals in the immigrant population. The empirical analysis exploits the variance in total immigration and its skill composition in 14 OECD countries during the 1980–2005 period for identification. In order to isolate the supply-driven changes in total immigration flows and their skill composition we use the push-factors—identified in the analysis of the determinants of migration in Chapter 3—as instruments. While there are still some concerns that some unobserved shocks affect push-factors and receiving countries at the same time, invalidating the instruments, we think our identification strategy is an interesting step forward with respect to the current literature. This analysis provides new insights concerning both the total effect of immigration and the immigration of highly skilled individuals in particular. Against the background of the current global downturn, we also analyse whether these effects differ between 'normal' and 'bad' economic times.

The findings in Chapter 4 suggest that total immigration is beneficial for employment, capital accumulation, and total output, and that these gains increase with the share of highly skilled individuals in the immigrant population. Nevertheless, most receiving countries restrict immigration and are reluctant to implement immigration policies that systematically select highly skilled immigrants. Chapter 5 focuses on this puzzle. Building on a political economy framework, we first analyse the factors that affect public opinion, since this represents one of the main forces driving immigration policy. Next, we empirically examine the determinants of individual attitudes towards highly skilled immigration. We consider two main channels through which immigration of highly skilled individuals affects public opinion—the labour market and the welfare state channels. In the following step, we analyse how individual attitudes are aggregated in democratic societies. In particular, we consider two alternative frameworks, which capture different political forces at play: the median voter model and the interest groups model. In the final step we assess the ability of the alternative frameworks to explain actual policy outcomes both for main European destination countries and for the USA.

While Chapter 5 provides a positive analysis, which helps understand why skill-selective immigration policies are not yet as widespread as one might expect, Chapter 6 adopts a more long-term view and addresses the possible implications of the contest for talents from a normative perspective. It explores—political economy forces against skilled migration notwithstanding—what would happen if developed countries compete more actively for highly skilled labour in the future. What will be the effect of this growing competition on the welfare in both the destination and source countries? We address this question in a three-country setting, which takes into account the strategic interaction between different destinations. Although increased emigration of the highly skilled undermines incentives of sending-country governments to invest in education, destination countries can achieve their objective of attracting more talented migrants with the adoption of selective immigration policies, but this policy shift can have adverse consequences for social welfare at origin.

Finally, Chapter 7 summarizes our main findings and draws some policy conclusions.

1

Selecting the Highly Skilled: An Overview of Current Policy Approaches

'The benefits of migration pay for its costs. The UK's thoughtful migration policy
and flexible, efficient work permit process are significant competitive advantages
for its businesses and economy. By allowing the UK to draw from the global talent
pool, migration has contributed significantly to London's success as a top global
financial centre, as well as making it one of the most dynamic, culturally diverse,
stimulating cities in which to live and work.'

Goldman Sachs International, 2005[1]

Selecting migrants according to the skills needed in the labour market is
becoming an increasingly widespread practice among developed countries—
although in many countries the recognition of degrees earned in foreign
universities and/or the portability of pension and health-care benefits are
still important unresolved issues.[2] These policies have a long history in traditional destinations, particularly Australia, Canada, and New Zealand, and, to a
lesser extent, the USA.[3] Conversely, most European countries have either
recruited manual workers from abroad or have not pursued skill-selective
immigration policies at all for decades. Increasing concerns that Europe may
lose the talent contest and, as a consequence, may see its long-term economic
growth prospects decline, has resulted in policy reforms both at the levels of
the EU and of its member states.

---

[1] Response to the consultation document on the introduction of the new point-based migration
system in the UK, 2005 (cited in Home Office, 2006, page 5).

[2] For an interesting example of how complex procedures to recognize foreign degrees might
result in significant barriers to the migration of medical professionals, see Glied and Sarkar (2009).
For an overview of the portability of pension and health-care benefits, see Holzmann et al. (2005).

[3] Interestingly, skill-selective policies have been introduced mainly following the elimination of
explicitly discriminatory policies, based on the immigrant's country of origin, in the early to mid
1960s.

The goal of this chapter is to provide a brief overview of skill-selective immigration policies in the main destination countries and of the major shifts in these policies which have been recently observed. We proceed via the following steps: first, we outline the main approaches to selecting highly skilled immigrants. Second, we describe the main features of these approaches in countries which have a long tradition of selecting highly skilled immigrants, that is Australia, Canada, New Zealand, and the USA. Third, we describe the approach of the EU in entering the talent contest, particularly the 'blue card' recently adopted by the European Council. Fourth, we discuss the changes in the immigration policies of some of the main destination countries in the EU. Finally, we present the results of a survey of government officials on the use of skill-selective immigration policies carried out by the United Nations.

1.1 A classification of skill-selective immigration policies

Countries like Australia, Canada, New Zealand, and the USA employ different types of policy tools for the selection of highly skilled migrants, which can be broadly classified as 'immigrant driven' or 'employer driven' (Chaloff and Lemaitre, 2009). Under the former, an immigrant is admitted into the country without necessarily having a job offer and is selected on the basis of a set of desirable human capital attributes. Under the latter, an employer has to make a job offer in order to grant admission to a highly skilled foreign worker.

'Immigrant driven' systems typically use a 'point assessment' to determine the desirability of a foreign national. This type of framework was first introduced in Canada in 1967, followed by Australia in 1989 and New Zealand in 1991. More recently, the UK introduced a similar scheme in 2001, and the blue card initiative, which has been adopted by the EU Commission in May 2009, also incorporates some features of the point system (EC, 2009a, b).

Point systems are used to select individuals on the basis of characteristics that make them 'desirable'.[4] The selection involves the identification of a 'pass rate' and, typically, point systems attribute substantial weight to five criteria: occupation; work experience; education; destination-country language proficiency; and age. A second set of criteria, which can be included in point systems, is also relevant. This includes: employer nomination/job offer; prior work in the destination country; education obtained in the destination country; settlement stipulations; presence of close relatives; and prior earnings.

Broadly speaking, we can distinguish two different economic models that underpin the attribution of 'points' in the first set of criteria. On the one hand,

---

[4] An interesting proposal for the construction of an 'optimal' point-based system has been recently put forward by McHale and Rogers (2009).

we have a short-term stance, in which emphasis is placed on the need to fill gaps in the destination country's labour market. In such a model, the applicant's recent occupation and work experience are particularly highly rewarded. On the other hand, we can identify a long-term perspective, which is inspired by an earnings or human capital economic model. In this context, education, age, and official language proficiency are instead the main focus.

In 'employer driven' skilled immigration systems—like the US H1B visa system—employers are the key players. They sponsor the application for the admission of a foreign worker and typically need to carry out a 'labour market' test. The purpose of the test is to establish that the vacancy for which an immigrant is requested cannot be filled by a local worker, and the stringency of the labour market test varies substantially across countries.

1.2 Skill-selective immigration policies in traditional immigration countries

It is useful to briefly review the salient features of the different systems to get a better sense of how they work in practice, keeping in mind that many actual migration systems blend facets of both employer- and immigrant-driven frameworks.

1.2.1 *Canada*

The point system for the 'independent' (or economic) class was introduced in Canada in 1967 and, since then, it has been used as the core criterion to determine which individuals will gain access to the country as skilled migrants. The economic class was expanded to include a 'business' class of immigrants in 1986, but its numeric importance has been limited and it has not exceeded a few percentage points of the total. In 2007, approximately 98,000 individuals, or 41 per cent of the total, have been admitted under the skilled worker programme as either principal applicants or spouses and dependants (CIC 2008), down from an average of around 50 per cent for the period 2000–06.

The working of the system has changed substantially over time, with new criteria being introduced and others being removed. The 'pass rate' has also varied over time, ranging from 50 points (out of a total of 100) in 1967, to 70 in 1986. The system's evolution is illustrated in Table 1.1. In the first 20 years from its introduction, the focus was on the occupational need of the economy at any given point in time. Since the 1990s the focus has changed, and now Canada implements a migration policy towards the skilled, which is no longer based on a 'gap filling' strategy but rather on an earnings/human capital perspective.

Table 1.1. The Canadian point system.

	1967	1978	1986	1996	2009
	Maximum number of points				
Experience	-	8	8	9	21
Specific vocational preparation	10	15	15	-	-
Occupational demand	15	15	10	-	-
Labour market balance	-	-	-	10	-
Education	20	12	12	21	25
Language proficiency	10	10	15	21	24
Age	10	10	10	13	10
Arranged employment or designated occupation	10	10	10	4	10
Personal suitability/adaptability	15	10	10	17	10
Levels adjustment factor	-	-	10	-	-
Relatives	5	5	-	5	-
Destination	5	5	-	-	-
Total	100	100	100	100	100
Pass mark	50	50	70	*	67

Sources: Green and Green (1999) and Citizenship and Immigration Canada. 'Pass mark' denotes the number of points that are required for admission.
* The pass mark varies by skill group. The pass marks are: professional 52; skilled administrator, 52; technical, 47; trades, 45.

The main goal of the new policy is to favour the immigration of individuals that are more likely to adapt successfully and thus assimilate faster. In many ways, the Canadian experience with the point system is particularly interesting, as it represents the evolution of a short-run migration model, focused on contingent labour market shortages, to a long-run framework where the focus is on adaptability of the immigrants to the destination country.

1.2.2 *Australia*

Most immigrants to Australia today enter under one of three categories: skilled workers, family reunification, or humanitarian. In 2005–06, over 50 per cent of the immigrant total was made up of skilled workers, whereas only 25% had received a visa based on the family reunification programme, and less than 10 per cent had been accepted as humanitarian applicants (Linacre, 2007). By comparison, in 1985 well over 50 per cent of new permanent settlers entered through the family reunification programme, and just over 10 per cent entered through the skilled worker programme.

This important change is the result of a series of initiatives introduced throughout the 1980s, which culminated in the 'points test' formally introduced in 1989. Under this regime, every year the Minister for Immigration not only sets the overall target for permanent settlers to be admitted in the country, but also fixes the numbers of individuals to be allowed in for family reunification and as skilled workers. Whenever a category requires a 'points test', the government also announces the 'pass mark'.

Table 1.2. The Australian skilled migration system, 2009.

	Maximum number of points
Occupation	60
Occupation in demand	20
Age	30
English language proficiency	25
Specific employment	10
Australian employment	10
Australian qualifications	25
Designated language	5
Studying and living in regional Australia	5
Partner's skill	5
State/territory government nomination	25
General skilled immigration pass mark	120
Employer nomination scheme pass mark	100

Source: Australian government (http://www.immi.gov.au/skilled/general-skilled-migration). 'Pass mark' denotes the number of points which are required for admission.

Skilled immigrants can enter either through a 'general skilled migration' scheme, or through an 'employer nominated' scheme. Under the former, individuals can apply provided that their occupation is listed in the Skilled Occupation List (SOL) and the relevant assessing authority has certified that they possess the required qualifications. Under the latter, an employer must have nominated the immigrant to fill a position in an occupation that appears in the Employer Nomination Scheme Occupation List (ENSOL). The SOL and ENSOL largely overlap, but the 'pass mark' is generally lower for 'employer-nominated' migrants than for 'general skilled migrants'. The lists are updated very frequently, based on labour market conditions.[5] Table 1.2 provides information on the allocation of points in 2009, together with the 'pass mark' for both the general skilled immigration scheme and the employer-sponsored one. In contrast to the Canadian point system, the Australian one is largely driven by the short-term needs of the local labour market.

1.2.3 New Zealand

The 'point system' for the general skill category of immigrants was introduced in New Zealand in 1991 and, until 2003, underwent only minor changes (Table 1.3). The main innovation in the early phase of the programme—in 1995—was a change in focus from qualifications as a sign of employability to a job offer, together with the introduction of additional points for settlement factors. A major change was introduced in 2003. As a result, a much greater emphasis is now placed on short-term occupation characteristics than on

---

[5] The 'pro-skill' bias of the immigration laws in Australia and Canada has increased in the recent past. See the discussion in Section 1.3.2.

Table 1.3. The New Zealand point system.

	1994	2001	2009
	Maximum number of points		
Skilled employment (current NZ/offer NZ)	3	5	60
Skilled employment bonus points	-	-	35
Relevant work experience	10	10	30
Relevant work experience bonus points	-	-	40
Qualifications	15	12	55
Qualifications bonus points	-	-	30
Family ties/settlement factors	7	9	10
Age	10	10	30
Total	43	46	290
Pass mark	20–31	24–25	100*

Sources: OECD (2003b) and New Zealand Immigration Service (http://www.immigration.govt.nz/). 'Pass mark' denotes the number of points which are required for admission.

general educational qualifications. Importantly, initial applications ('expression of interest' in the current jargon) meeting the minimum 'pass rate' will not automatically entitle the applicant to admission in the country, but rather lead to inclusion in a 'pool', in which they will remain for up to 6 months. Those ranking at the top of the pool (in terms of points obtained) will then be 'invited to apply' for residence, at a bi-weekly frequency. Thus, the New Zealand system has evolved into a model where entry is granted on the basis of very short-term labour market considerations, and little attention is paid to the long-term consequences of immigration policy.

1.2.4 The USA

The USA remains one of the main destinations for highly skilled immigrants, even if the country has not put in place a point system to select prospective foreign workers based on their qualifications. Currently, the main instrument for admitting skilled workers is represented by the H1B visa category, which was introduced in the 1990 Immigration Act, and is reserved for workers to be employed in a 'specialty occupation', defined as requiring theoretical and practical application of a body of highly specialized knowledge in a field.[6] Under this programme, 65,000 visas are issued annually,[7] and the minimum skill requirement is a Bachelor's degree. Visa requests need to be sponsored by the prospective employer, and a Labour Condition Application needs to be

[6] As documented in Chapter 2, a second important potential channel of entry for skilled workers is represented by the F1 visa category, which is used by foreign students acquiring higher education in the USA. This visa category allows the students to also complete a post-graduation period of optional practical training.

[7] The actual number changed several times at the end of the 1990s. For more information on this, see Congressional Research Service (2006).

submitted to ensure that the foreign workers do not displace or adversely affect wages or working conditions in the USA.

The H1B visa does not fall under the 'immigrant visa' category, that is it does not automatically result in the conferral of a permanent resident status. At the same time, it is one of the few visa categories allowing a worker to apply for permanent residency. The H1B visa category is a typical example of an 'employer driven' system. Beyond the H1B visa, there are other visa programmes for highly skilled workers, reserved for intra-company transferees (L1), internationally recognized athletes and entertainers (P), workers of extraordinary ability (O), and so on (Facchini, Mayda, and Mishra, 2008).

Importantly, as has been suggested by Beach et al. (2006), the absence of a specifically designed point-based system may play a key role in explaining the comparatively lower skill level of immigrants into the USA than those of immigration countries with point-based systems like Canada or Australia (see Chapter 2, Table 2.1).

1.3 Skill-selective immigration policies at the EU level

The immigration policies of the EU have been traditionally characterized by a fundamental dualism. On the one hand, internal labour mobility is one of the fundamental freedoms of the Common Market and hence subject to EU level jurisdiction, while the immigration of third-country nationals remains in the national policy domain of each member state. The free movement of workers within the Common Market is by definition not skill-selective. However, the EU also endorses the mobility of highly skilled individuals within the Common Market through its education policies, and in particular through the harmonization of study programmes under the umbrella of the 'Bologna process' and the mutual recognition of university degrees.

Regarding third-country nationals, most EU member states mainly recruited manual workers from abroad during the 1960s and early 1970s, and then pursued heavily restrictive immigration policies after the first oil price shock of 1973 (Zimmermann, 1995). Concerns that the EU may fall back in the global contest for highly skilled workers and that labour shortages will become widespread over the course of demographic change have meanwhile triggered several new policy initiatives at the EU level. At the 1999 Tampere (Finland) meeting of the European Council, the leaders of the EU set out the elements for a common EU immigration policy, and attracting highly skilled individuals was an explicit goal. As a result, the EU has started to interfere in immigration policies vis-à-vis third-country citizens through a series of initiatives of the European Commission, namely the Green Paper on an EU approach to managed immigration (EC, 2004) and the Policy Plan on Legal Migration (EC 2005), which outline a strategy for attracting particularly skilled and highly skilled migrants. For the selection of highly skilled immigrants, two initiatives are particularly relevant: two directives of the European Council regulate the admission of students (European Council 2004) and researchers (European Council 2005) from third countries. Both directives had to be adopted by national law in 2007 and have eased entry to the EU of third-country nationals as students and researchers, and facilitated their mobility across EU member states once they have been admitted by one member country.

1.3.1 *The EU blue card initiative*

A second important initiative is the European Council Directive on 'the conditions of entry and residence of third-country nationals for the purpose of highly qualified employment', which was adopted on 25 May 2009 (European Council 2009a, 2009b). This initiative represents the EU wide attempt at drafting a common policy for highly skilled foreign migrants, leading to the issuance of a temporary work permit (the so-called 'blue card'). While the introduction of a point-based system was explicitly considered, unless the points are set at the EU level, immigrants would continue to face very different admission criteria. Setting the points at the EU level has been ruled out though, as this would violate the subsidiary principle.

The initiative is limited to a common definition of the criteria to qualify for admission under the highly skilled migration programme (the existence of a work contract, professional qualifications, and a salary above a minimum level set at the national level), and it contains a provision limiting the access of the 'blue card' holder to only the receiving country's labour market for the first 18 months after arrival. More freedom of movement is contemplated after this period, including the possibility of the migrant gaining access to a second member country's labour market. Ample margins of discretion are retained by each member country. In particular, no coordination is envisaged as far as the actual migration quotas are concerned.

1.4 Skill-selective immigration policies in a group of EU member countries

Although the competencies of the EU in the area of immigration policy have steadily increased over the past ten years, the core decisions continue to fall in the domain of national governments. Thus, to assess the actual selectivity of immigration policy in Europe it is necessary to look at the policy changes at the national level.

1.4.1 *The UK*

The UK government published a document in 2006 (Home Office 2006), which contained the blue print for an important overhaul of the country's immigration policy framework. The document laid out a new strategy, which identifies five different categories of immigrant to be admitted under a point-based system, the first two of which focus on highly skilled immigrants. Under the Tier 1 programme, highly skilled workers can apply for an entry permit, without needing an existing job offer. The so-called Tier 2 scheme is instead reserved for medium- and highly skilled workers who have already received a job offer. Table 1.4 below summarizes the current allocation of points for the Tier 1 programme.

The requirements in place are in many ways more stringent than in other point-based systems and, if they are met, they give the applicant only temporary admission into the country. One interesting and important difference between the UK initiative and the other systems which we have reviewed so far consists of its reliance upon previous earnings as a measure of expected labour market performance of the perspective migrant. Importantly, previous earnings are to be assessed using the rates prevailing in the country of emigration (and this will surely pose important challenges when the system is fully implemented).

1.4.2 *Germany*

Germany stopped the active recruitment of third-country nationals —along with many EU countries—following the first oil price shock in 1973. As a result, family reunification, humanitarian immigration, and the immigration of ethnic Germans (the so-called 'Spätaussiedler') became the main channels of entry. However, immigrant workers can be admitted if employers are able to prove that the position cannot be filled by a German or another EU citizen.

Table 1.4. The UK point-based system (Tier 1).

	Maximum number of points
Qualifications/academic degree	30–50
Age	5–20
Language proficiency	10
Maintenance	10
Recent earnings	5–45
UK labour market experience	5
Total	140
Pass mark	95

Source: UK Border Agency (http://www.ukba.homeoffice.gov.uk). Pass mark denotes the number of points required for admission.

Against the background of low skill levels in the immigrant population in Germany and an increasing shortage of highly skilled labour, the Schröder government launched a reform with the immigration act of 2005, which explicitly targeted highly skilled workers. Two groups are perceived as highly skilled: the first comprises scientists and teaching personnel with excellent qualifications (i.e. university professors), outstanding sportsmen, and artists. The second refers instead to managers and specialists whose income is at least twice the ceiling of health insurance in Germany, that is it is above €85,000 p.a. as of 2008, though the 2009 amendment of the immigration act reduced this ceiling to €66,500. Both groups are entitled to permanent residence permits. Moreover, a residence permit is granted to individuals who are self-employed if they invest €500,000 and employ at least five persons.

In quantitative terms, this reform was a failure: only 466 residence permits were granted for the two groups of highly skilled individuals in 2007, and only 115 of these were granted to new arrivals. It is unlikely that 2009 will have changed the picture substantially, since the €66,500 income ceiling is still well above the average income level of individuals with a university degree, particularly in the age groups below 40. Altogether, the reforms of the immigration legislation in Germany did not fundamentally change the conditions for the entry of highly skilled individuals.

1.4.3 *Italy*

Italy has a long history as a source of emigrants, and until 1986 its immigration policy was based on public order legislation dating back to 1931, which left many issues to administrative discretion. In 1990 the so called 'Martelli' law (Law 39/90, 28 February 1990) introduced a provision for a quota system to limit the inflow of immigrant workers from outside the EU, which *did not* target highly skilled workers. The quota system is mainly employer driven, and a labour market test requires the employer to list the job vacancy through the Public Employment Service. This provision is *pro-forma* though, as no application has ever been rejected due to a successful referral by the Public Employment System (Chaloff and Lemaitre, 2009). Work visas are initially for a limited period (two years in the presence of an open-ended contract), but they can be renewed and converted into a residence permit after five years of legal stay.

The quota system grants privileged access to citizens from countries that have signed an immigration agreement with the Italian government. Up to 44,600 workers from these countries will be admitted in Italy according to the 2008 legislation, and they will face no restriction as far as their sector of employment is concerned. The second category is represented by citizens of other countries with which Italy does not have an agreement on immigration.

Up to 105,400 foreigners will be admitted under this grouping, but they will be allowed to work only as *domestic helpers* or *care workers*.

Altogether, the Italian quota system and other immigration policies do not consistently target highly skilled workers.

1.4.4 *Spain*

Like Italy, Spain has been for most of the past century a country of emigration (OECD, 2003a). The first piece of legislation introduced to regulate foreign immigrant flows, the Foreigners Law of 1985, was the result of Spain's need to align its policies to those of the EC bodies, rather than being a policy response to growing immigration pressure. According to this framework—known as the 'general regime'—the entry of a labour migrant was based on employer request and the admission was left essentially to administrative discretion (Bruquetas-Callejo et al., 2008). A key discriminate was a labour market test whose criteria were only vaguely defined.

To create a new channel of legal entry, an immigration quota was introduced in 1993 for which no individual labour market test had to be performed. The latter was replaced by the government's identification, on a yearly basis, of those sectors/occupations with labour shortages and by its determination of the overall number of work permits to be issued. The total quota was kept very low though, and fluctuated around 20–40,000 permits per year. The return of the Socialist party to power in 2005 marked the reintroduction of the general regime, with the purpose of allowing more flexibility for employers.

While the quota system could have been used to introduce selective immigration policies, its actual effects have been rather limited (Bruquetas-Callejo et al., 2008). More generally, its purpose has been defied by the sheer scale of the illegal flows. Spain carried out six major regularization processes after 1985 (specifically in 1986, 1991, 1996, 2000, 2001, and 2005), and 98 per cent of those foreigners obtaining a residence permit in Spain did so from illegal immigration (Dolado, 2007). In other words, the official Spanish government policies towards legal migrants have only played a very limited role in shaping the current composition of the immigrant population.

In conclusion, some EU member states have started to reform their immigration policies both to increase the number of foreign workers and to attract more highly skilled workers. Nevertheless, these reforms have been very cautious and can only be regarded as incremental steps rather than major shifts towards a skill-selective immigration policy.

1.5 Present and future policies to attract highly skilled immigrants: evidence based on UN data

The patterns we have identified in our analysis are confirmed when we look at recent, comprehensive cross-country data. Since 1974 the United Nations has carried out a survey of government officials to elicit their views on the overall level of immigration and to document their policies towards immigration. An additional question was introduced in 2007, with a specific focus on governments' policies towards highly skilled workers. Table 1.5 reports summary statistics for this variable, by each country's income level.

Officials in only five countries (Bhutan, Botswana, Jordan, Saudi Arabia, and the United Arab Emirates) report policies in place to reduce the arrival of highly skilled workers. On the other hand, 25 per cent of governments declare policies aimed at increasing the number of skilled migrants. In the majority of countries (59 per cent of the 143 countries in the sample), the government's goal is to maintain unchanged the level of highly skilled migration. Finally, in the remaining 18 countries, governments do not intervene with regard to highly skilled workers. What these summary statistics show is a strong status quo bias. While some countries are actively engaged in increasing the flow of skilled migrants and very few are trying to curtail their number, most governments' policies are aimed at maintaining as constant the skilled migration flow. In other words, while the competition for talent has already begun, it seems to be still in its early phases.

Table 1.5. Governments' policy on highly skilled immigrants by income group, 2007.

Income group	Policy on high-skilled workers				
	Lower	Maintain	Raise	No intervention	Total
	Figures in brackets denote percentages				
High-income countries	2	18	20	5	45
	(4.44)	(40.00)	(44.44)	(11.11)	(100.00)
Upper-middle-income countries	1	24	9	2	36
	(2.78)	(66.67)	(25.00)	(5.56)	(100.00)
Lower-middle-income countries	2	29	4	2	37
	(5.41)	(78.38)	(10.81)	(5.41)	(100.00)
Lower-income countries	0	13	3	9	25
	(0.00)	(52.00)	(12.00)	(36.00)	(100.00)
All countries	5	84	36	18	143
	(3.50)	(58.74)	(25.17)	(12.59)	(100.00)

The table presents frequencies and row percentages by income, size of migration inflow, and size of migration rate. *Policy on high skilled workers* is the government's policy on the migration of highly skilled workers. The possible values on *Policy on high skilled workers* are: the government has policies in place to lower, maintain, or to raise the immigration of highly skilled workers; the government does not intervene with regard to the migration of highly skilled workers (or it does not know whether the government intervenes). Data for migration is for 2005. The migration rate is defined as the migration inflow divided by the population of the destination country.

Source: United Nations.

Table 1.5 shows that richer countries are more likely to have policies in place to increase the migration of highly skilled workers. In particular, 44 per cent of high-income countries have active skilled migration policies, as opposed to 25 per cent of upper-middle-income countries and 11 per cent and 12 per cent, respectively, of lower-middle-income and lower-income countries.

1.6 Conclusions

Altogether, we can conclude that immigration policies are characterized by a strong status quo bias. Only a few small and medium-sized countries (Australia, Canada, New Zealand) pursue an 'immigrant driven' approach which consistently selects highly skilled individuals. But, even in these countries, no more than 40 per cent of immigrants are selected by human capital criteria. Still, the likelihood that family reunification will tend to reproduce the skill structure of selected immigrants will give rise to a 'multiplier' effect, through which skill-selective policies are likely to produce long-lasting effects.

The main destination of immigrants in the world, the USA, regulates part of its immigration by an 'employer driven' approach, that is by specific visas for occupations, which are in short supply (H1B visas). However, the absence of a point system and the relatively small share of immigrants entering on an H1B visa may explain why the average skill level of the immigrant population in the USA is well below that of Australia, Canada, and New Zealand.

In Europe, most countries throughout their history have not pursued a skill-selective immigration policy. During the last decade, though, we have observed incremental policy shifts both at the EU level and at that of its member states. At the former, several action plans and the introduction of the 'blue card' initiative are attempts to attract highly skilled individuals from third countries and to facilitate the mobility of third-country nationals once they have been admitted to an EU member state. Nevertheless, the scope of these efforts is limited, given that immigration policies vis-à-vis third-country nationals continue to remain by and large in the national domain. At the national level, several countries such as the UK and Germany have launched reforms aimed at attracting highly skilled individuals. While they are important steps, they fall far short of being radical policy shifts.

2

Global Trends in Highly Skilled Immigration[1]

The objective of this chapter is to provide an overview of highly skilled migration into developed countries. In particular, we look at the balance of highly skilled migration within the OECD and between the OECD countries and other countries of the world. Recent progress in the collection of data on the educational attainment of migrants facilitates the analysis of highly skilled immigration in receiving countries. Building upon the work of Carrington and Detragiache (1998), several new data sets on the skill structure of immigrants have been established: Docquier and Marfouk (2006), Beine, Docquier, and Rapoport (2007), Dumont and Lemaitre (2005) and Defoort (2009) have constructed comprehensive data sets from population censuses on the educational level of immigrants in the OECD by country of origin, which enable us to outline the skill structure of the foreign-born population in the developed world. These data sets can be linked to the skill composition of the native population in the destination and sending countries, which in turn allows us to characterize the skill selectivity of migration both with respect to the population in the receiving and in the sending countries (Section 2.1). Moreover, we can analyse the development of the pool of highly skilled workers in both developed and less developed countries, which forms the battlefield of the contest for talent (Section 2.2).

Although the data sets described above enable us to draw a comprehensive picture of the mobility of highly skilled individuals, they suffer from a series of shortcomings, which limit in various ways the scope of our descriptive analysis. One important drawback is represented by the fact that the definition of highly skilled worker refers to tertiary educational attainment only, which represents a rather broad category ranging from individuals with practical and technical education degrees (e.g. nurses) to PhD holders. To get a more detailed picture, we supplement the data collected by Docquier and Marfouk

[1] We thank Paola Monti, Valentina Jung, Alexander Raatz, Markus Wilhelm, and Michael Zibrowius for their help with the data and for providing excellent research assistance.

(2006) and others with information on individuals with PhD degrees and completed university degrees in a selected number of countries from the population censuses. Moreover, we analyse how many migrants are represented in top management and professional occupations in receiving countries in order to shed some light on the question of whether the battle for talent affects the recruitment of elites in the private and public sectors (Section 2.3).

The admission of foreign students has become an increasingly important gateway for highly skilled immigration. A substantial part of the college graduates immigrating to Australia, Canada, the USA, and the UK move there to attend graduate study programmes. Many countries have eased the access of foreign students to their university systems, and enhanced opportunities for working in host countries after the completion of the degree. In the EU, the Bologna process—among other measures—was specifically designed to encourage the cross-border mobility of students. We therefore examine whether and to what extent the international mobility of students has increased at different levels of tertiary education (Section 2.4).

Not all the human capital of highly skilled immigrants acquired in the sending or receiving countries can be transferred into the host country labour markets. Analysing the phenomenon of the downgrading of skills and of the assimilation of highly skilled foreigners is beyond the scope of this study. Instead we provide some data from the USA and Canada on the wage levels of immigrants and natives at the top of the skill distribution as a first indicator (Section 2.5). Finally, Section 2.6 concludes.

2.1 Highly skilled immigrants in the OECD

2.1.1 *Sources and limitations of the data*

The analysis in this section is based on the data set compiled by Beine, Docquier, and Rapoport (2007), which is an updated version of Docquier and Marfouk's (2006) data set. Since the data set is based on decennial censuses, the latest information available refers to the year 2001 for most countries. This data set distinguishes the immigrant population aged 25 and above by its educational attainment (tertiary, secondary, primary, or less) and by country of origin, which makes it possible to approximate both the stock of highly skilled labour that has been attained from abroad in the receiving countries, and the stock of highly skilled labour which has moved abroad in the sending countries. The host country information is derived from national censuses, which usually take place every ten years. The source country information has been taken from the Barro and Lee (1993, 2000) data set which, however, does not cover all source countries. In the case of missing countries, the skill distribution has been extrapolated from neighbouring countries with the closest human development index. The Beine, Docquier, and Rapoport (2007) data set refers to the 1990 and 2000 censuses. To complement this cross-sectional information we use in addition a data set compiled by Defoort (2009), which provides for six destinations in the OECD information from 1975 to 2000 in five-year intervals, which enables us to describe the development of highly skilled immigration in the major destinations among OECD member states.

Although these data sets are an important step forward in providing comprehensive information on the skill structure of immigrants residing in the OECD, a number of caveats apply. First of all, the available information does not enable us to distinguish between education that has been acquired in the home or in the host country. Beine, Docquier, and Rapoport (2007) try to circumvent this problem by providing information on the age of entry, which shows that recent arrivals have similar or higher education levels compared to those who have resided already for longer periods in the host country. Nevertheless, an accurate measure for the human capital acquired through immigration cannot be derived from macro data—this can only be taken from individual survey data (see Rosenzweig, 2005, for a discussion). Second, the distinction between tertiary, secondary, and primary education levels is rather rough. In particular, the category of tertiary education includes individuals with practical and technical education degrees; university degrees as well as those at the top of the skill distribution (see UNESCO, 1997, for a description of the ISCED classification which we adopt here). Moreover, since educational systems differ greatly across countries, the information is not entirely comparable. We therefore provide in the later sections of this chapter detailed information on the top of the skill distribution. Third, human capital acquired in other countries may not be entirely transferable. The issue of the so-called 'skill-downgrading' will therefore be discussed at the end of this chapter. Fourth, and finally, these data refer to the stock of foreign residents and thus provide no information on return and circular migration, which is however particularly important in the case of highly skilled immigration. Again, this information can only be derived from micro data sets which follow migrants in host and home countries over time. However, it is worthwhile noting that the stock data used here covers both permanent and temporary migrants, albeit we are not able to distinguish these types of migration here.

2.1.2 *The stock of highly skilled immigrants*

Based on this data set, the stock of highly skilled immigrants in the OECD can be estimated at about 20 million individuals in 2000/2001, where we define highly skilled by tertiary educational attainment (i.e. academic or professional diploma beyond high school degrees). More than 50 per cent of those reside in the USA, another 22 per cent in Australia, Canada, and New Zealand, that is the traditional immigration countries which pursue highly selective immigration policies. About 24 per cent reside in the EU and other Western European countries, most of those in the UK (6 per cent), Germany (5 per cent), and France (3 per cent). The Southern European countries attract only moderate shares (Spain: 1.4 per cent, Italy: 0.7 per cent). Altogether, the English speaking countries attract about 80 per cent of immigrants with tertiary educational attainment in the OECD (Table 2.1).

Not surprisingly, the share of immigrants in the population with tertiary educational attainment is extremely high in those countries which pursue a highly skill-selective immigration policy. The share of foreign-born individuals in the population with tertiary education amounts to 43 per cent in Australia, 24 per cent in Canada, and 21 per cent in New Zealand. However, there are also some other destinations for which immigrants represent a large proportion of the skilled population: Switzerland (35 per cent), Iceland (25 per cent), and Ireland (25 per cent). In the USA, the share is at about 11 per cent, and this is due—at least partly—to the high share of individuals with tertiary educational attainment among the native population there and to the large inflows of illegal immigrants from Mexico. In Europe, the share of immigrants in the highly skilled population is— beyond Iceland, Ireland, and Switzerland—relatively large in the UK (16 per cent), Sweden (14 per cent), and Austria (12 per cent), while skilled immigration is much less important in Italy and the other Southern European countries.

The data set compiled by Defoort (2009) allows us to analyse the long-term trends in highly skilled migration for selected OECD countries. Note that these countries cover more than 85 per cent of the highly skilled immigrant population in the OECD.[2] As Figure 2.1 shows, the stock of highly skilled immigrants has increased by a factor of 5 in the USA, from 1.8 million in 1975 to 9 million in 2000, while in the other traditional immigration countries (Canada, Australia) the increase has been only relatively moderate, as the stock of highly skilled immigrants has grown there only by a factor of 2. The European destinations played only a negligible role in the 1970s, but the stock of highly skilled has grown by a factor of 5 there until the 2000s.

---

[2] Note that the Defoort (2009) data set is due to different data sources and methodologies not entirely comparable to the Docquier, Beine, and Rapoport (2007) data set employed in Table 2.1.

Table 2.1. Immigrants with tertiary education in OECD countries, 2001.

	Stock of highly skilled immigrants[1]				(Self-)selection indicators	
	persons	in per cent of			share of high-skilled in immigrant population relative to share of highly skilled in	
		all OECD-30 highly skilled immigrants	host country highly skilled population	host country immigrant population	host population[2]	home population[3]
Australia	1,638,052	8.02	43.76	40.27	1.35	4.47
Austria	103,211	0.51	11.77	12.65	0.84	0.96
Belgium	99,770	0.49	7.05	18.34	0.93	1.90
Canada	2,724,095	13.34	24.83	58.77	1.11	8.24
Czech Republic	46,988	0.23	na	11.45	na	0.85
Denmark	39,635	0.19	4.91	17.29	0.80	1.77
Finland	21,511	0.11	2.59	23.77	1.02	1.99
France	608,985	2.98	8.18	16.42	0.89	2.62
Germany	1,020,755	5.00	9.67	21.77	1.24	2.35
Greece	64,784	0.32	6.17	15.00	1.10	1.11
Hungary	12,545	0.06	1.50	11.61	0.97	0.36
Iceland	6,560	0.03	24.46	31.06	2.00	2.76
Ireland	115,721	0.57	25.59	41.15	2.12	3.00
Italy	142,418	0.70	2.27	15.44	1.05	1.65
Japan	267,370	1.31	1.21	28.05	1.17	3.87
Korea	45,971	0.23	0.88	38.13	1.48	4.49
Luxembourg	21,772	0.11	na	21.72	na	1.60
Mexico	81,954	0.40	1.56	44.87	3.97	2.62
Netherlands	393,891	1.93	16.16	21.97	1.00	2.55
Norway	63,904	0.31	8.46	28.69	1.16	3.07
New Zealand	217,854	1.07	21.36	40.89	0.98	4.33
Poland	103,496	0.51	3.80	13.96	1.26	1.10
Portugal	27,488	0.13	3.08	18.56	1.47	4.37
Slovakia	5,913	0.03	na	15.17	na	0.90
Spain	294,040	1.44	6.38	18.54	1.14	1.53
Sweden	195,869	0.96	13.66	25.69	1.11	2.53
Switzerland	280,075	1.37	33.98	18.60	1.16	1.52
Turkey	148,689	0.73	5.18	21.49	2.53	1.38
United Kingdom	1,233,421	6.04	15.93	34.95	1.83	7.08
United States	10,400,000	50.91	11.27	42.62	0.85	5.74
OECD-30	20,426,737	100.00	10.45	35.06	1.31	3.37

1) Share of highly skilled individuals, i.e. individuals with attained tertiary education (ISCED 5A, 5B, 6) in 25+ aged population. 2) Ratio of share of highly skilled individuals in immigrant population to the share of highly skilled individuals in host country population. 3) Ratio of the share of highly skilled individuals in immigrant population to the share of highly skilled individuals in home country population weighted by the number of migrants from the respective home country.

Sources: Data sources Beine et al. (2007), Defoort (2009); own calculations of shares and indicators.

2.1.3 Are immigrants favourably selected with respect to observable skills?

As a first hint to the skill bias in the immigrant population, we have computed the share of highly skilled individuals among the immigrant population (see the fourth column of Table 2.1). Again, this share is extremely high in destinations which pursue a selective immigration policy (Australia, New Zealand,

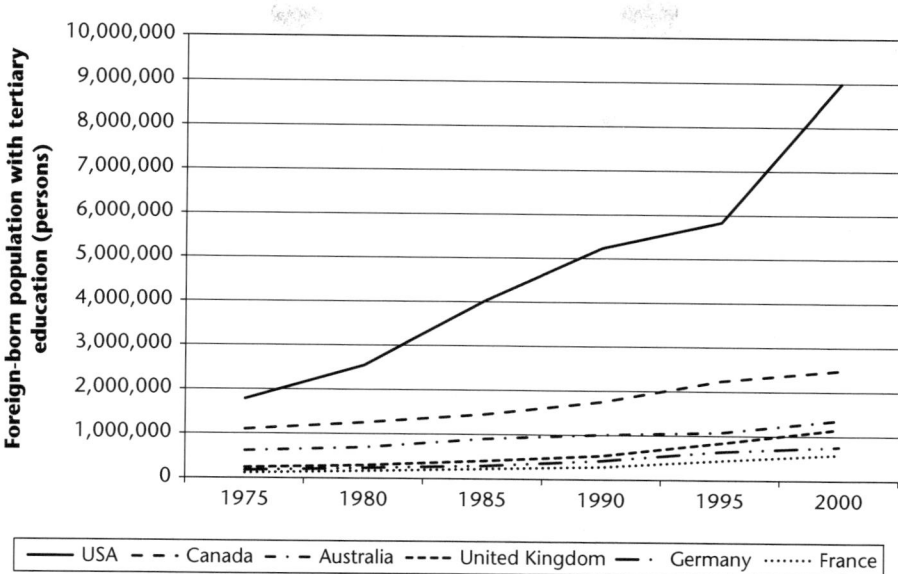

Figure 2.1. Foreign-born population with tertiary education attainment in selected destination countries, 1975–2000

Sources: Data source Defoort (2009); own calculations.

and Canada) or at least some skill-selective immigration policies (USA, Ireland, and the UK). Some of the relatively poor destination countries in the OECD (Mexico, Korea) also achieve relatively high shares of highly skilled individuals in the immigrant population, while those shares are rather low in the Southern European countries (Italy, Spain, Greece, and Portugal).

We present below two indicators to describe the skill selectivity of the immigrant workforce in some further detail. The first indicator, I_1, divides the share of highly skilled individuals in the immigrant population by the share of the highly skilled in the native population:

$$I_1 = \frac{S_m^h}{S_n^h},$$

where S_m^h is the share of highly skilled individuals in the immigrant population aged 25 and above in the host country, and S_n^h is the share of highly skilled individuals in the native population in the same age group. This first indicator gives us information on whether immigrants are positively selected on observable skills with respect to the host country population.

The second indicator, I_2, divides the share of the highly skilled in the immigrant population by the share of the highly skilled in the sending-country population and weights these shares by the share of a sending country in the immigrant population of a certain destination:

$$I_2 = \sum_{i=1}^{N} m_i \frac{s_{m,i}^h}{s_{n,i}^h},$$

where $s_{m,i}^h$ is the share of highly skilled individuals in the immigrant population aged 25 and above from sending country i, $s_{n,i}^h$ the share of highly skilled individuals in the same age group in sending country i, and m_i the share of immigrants from sending country i in the total immigrant population of the host country. Finally, $i = 1, 2 \ldots N$ denotes the sending-country index. Thus, the second indicator measures the skill bias of the immigrant population relative to the source country population. In both cases, an index above 1 indicates that the immigrant population is positively selected relative to the host country or the source country population, while an index below 1 indicates a negative selection bias.

We find that the share of the highly skilled among the immigrant population is higher than that of the native population of the OECD in the aggregate and much higher than that of the native population in the sending countries, as the last two columns of Table 2.1 show. However, aggregates may hide interesting differences across countries. We observe a positive selection bias relative to the destination-country population in some but not all countries which pursue a highly selective immigration policy (Australia, Canada), in countries which have relatively recently attracted large numbers of immigrants (Ireland, Iceland, the UK) and in some countries where the share of the highly skilled is relatively low in the native population (e.g. Germany). A negative selection bias relative to the destination country's population is found instead in some continental European countries (Austria, Belgium, France), and, interestingly enough, in the USA. In the latter case this can be traced back inter alia to the high share of highly skilled individuals in the native population.

The last column of Table 2.1 shows a strong skill selection of immigrants in the OECD relative to the home country population. On average, the share of highly skilled individuals in the immigrant population of the OECD exceeds that in the source country population by a factor of 3.4. The selection bias is particularly high in Canada (8.2), the UK (7.1), the USA (5.7), and Australia (4.5), while it is low in some continental European countries such as Austria, Belgium, and Germany.

Interestingly enough, the skill composition of the immigrant population in the OECD is extremely balanced by gender. Among the 20.4 million immigrants with tertiary educational attainment, almost 50 per cent are females. This also holds true for most destination countries in the OECD. Substantially larger shares of males in the highly skilled immigration population can be observed in Germany, France, Austria, Belgium, and Mexico, that is destinations which receive a high share of immigrants from sending countries with strong gender discrimination in higher education. In contrast, Italy, Spain, the Netherlands, and Japan receive larger shares of females, which can be attributed, *inter alia*, to the fact that females are better represented in the educated population of the source countries there.

2.1.4 Where do highly skilled immigrants come from?

Almost two-fifths of the highly skilled immigrants in the OECD come from other high-income countries. Table 2.2 groups the source countries by their income level and Table 2.3 by regional groups of source countries, using the classifications of the World Development Indicators from the World Bank (2008).

According to this classification, only 9 per cent of the highly skilled immigrant population in the OECD is born in low-income countries, 27 per cent in lower-middle-income countries such as China and India, 26 per cent in higher-middle-income countries such as Mexico, Northern Africa, and Russia, and 38 per cent from high-income countries in the OECD and other high-income countries such as the oil-producing countries in the Middle East (Table 2.2).

Beyond the high-income countries, the largest sending region for highly skilled immigrants is Latin America and the Caribbean (17 per cent), followed by East Asia and the Pacific (15 per cent), and Eastern Europe (10 per cent). In contrast, the share of Sub-Saharan Africa is, at 4.6 per cent of all highly skilled immigrants in the OECD, negligible (Table 2.3).

The importance of high-income countries as a source of highly skilled immigrants has been substantially declining in the six main receiving countries of the OECD over the past four decades: while two-thirds of the highly skilled immigrants in Australia, Canada, France, Germany, the USA, and the UK were born in high-income countries in 1975, this share had declined to less than 40 per cent by 2000. At the same time, the share of the low-income countries has increased from 9 to 17 per cent, and that of the middle-income countries from 28 per cent to 44 per cent (see Figure 2.2). In particular, the stock of highly skilled immigrants from lower-middle-income countries in South and East Asia has surged during the last decade.

2.1.5 The Battle for Brains across OECD countries: who wins, who loses?

The OECD countries are at the same time important destinations for, and origins of, highly skilled migrants. Table 2.4 reports estimates of both the highly skilled immigrant population which each country receives from other OECD countries, and the highly skilled emigrant population from this

Table 2.2. Source countries of highly skilled immigrants in the OECD by income level, 2001.

		Stock of highly skilled immigrants[1]			
		home country group share by income level[2]			
	all home countries	high	upper middle	lower middle	low
	persons	*in per cent*			
Australia	1,638,052	53.85	17.57	20.87	7.72
Austria	103,211	46.14	37.40	15.40	1.06
Belgium	99,770	71.72	8.58	14.23	5.46
Canada	2,724,095	45.17	20.01	26.66	8.16
Czech Republic	46,988	63.92	18.78	14.23	3.07
Denmark	39,635	52.98	16.14	23.92	6.96
Finland	21,511	37.48	46.37	11.29	4.87
France	608,985	39.65	14.73	32.39	13.23
Germany	1,020,755	38.72	37.05	18.10	6.14
Greece	64,784	26.88	19.07	51.78	2.26
Hungary	12,545	64.78	35.22	0.00	0.00
Iceland	6,560	68.95	12.37	10.19	8.49
Ireland	115,721	80.81	7.27	6.98	4.94
Italy	142,418	38.19	21.56	34.20	6.06
Japan	267,370	49.67	9.80	37.39	3.14
Korea	45,971	45.63	8.39	35.08	10.90
Luxembourg	21,772	86.93	6.44	4.81	1.82
Mexico	81,954	63.75	26.44	9.24	0.58
Netherlands	393,891	46.82	17.16	32.01	4.00
Norway	63,904	61.07	12.04	18.71	8.18
New Zealand	217,854	64.54	14.33	18.03	3.10
Poland	103,496	14.02	42.44	42.70	0.84
Portugal	27,488	45.36	25.80	22.27	6.57
Slovakia	5,913	7.14	77.41	12.68	2.78
Spain	294,040	39.02	34.17	24.96	1.85
Sweden	195,869	43.48	25.73	25.89	4.91
Switzerland	280,075	68.51	17.42	11.00	3.08
Turkey	148,689	36.94	50.68	10.84	1.54
United Kingdom	1,233,421	46.21	14.06	19.30	20.43
United States	10,400,000	28.67	30.29	31.11	9.93
OECD-30	20,426,737	37.72	25.69	27.40	9.20

1) Share of high-skilled individuals, i.e. individuals with attained tertiary education (ISCED 5A, 5B, 6) in 25+ aged population. 2) Income levels of home countries are classified by using the income classification of the World Development Indicators.

Sources: Data sources Beine et al. (2007), own calculations.

country which lives in another OECD country. Interestingly enough, only seven OECD countries are net recipients of highly skilled individuals in the OECD: the USA (+ 3.4 million), Australia (+ 708,000), Canada (+ 643,000), Switzerland (+ 97,000), Belgium (+ 60,000), Sweden (+ 20,000), and Luxembourg (+ 8,000). Thus, not only the relatively poorer OECD member states like Mexico and Turkey, but also most Western European countries, are net senders of highly skilled labour to other OECD countries, particularly to the USA. In some cases the net losses are sizeable, like the UK (–970,000), Korea

Table 2.3. Source countries of highly skilled immigrants in the OECD by region, 2001.

	Stock of highly skilled immigrants[1]							
	home country group share by region[2]							
	high income[3]	Latin America, Caribbean	Eastern Europe, Central Asia	East Asia, Pacific	South Asia	Middle East, North Africa	sub-Saharan Africa	unknown
	in per cent of all highly skilled immigrants							
Australia	51.95	2.17	7.00	17.11	8.39	4.41	4.68	4.30
Austria	45.32	1.22	37.13	2.62	1.30	9.45	0.85	2.11
Belgium	71.75	2.51	5.76	2.76	1.40	8.87	6.91	0.04
Canada	45.22	8.97	11.45	14.99	9.48	5.81	4.09	0.00
Czech Republic	63.28	0.58	28.49	2.93	0.54	2.18	0.89	1.11
Denmark	52.74	2.74	16.54	4.59	4.12	14.74	3.81	0.70
Finland	35.89	1.53	44.22	3.19	1.64	5.30	3.67	4.57
France	39.66	3.77	7.77	5.48	2.66	28.70	11.95	0.02
Germany	39.70	3.36	30.70	4.42	4.22	15.46	2.13	0.00
Greece	26.89	0.76	61.23	1.26	0.88	6.88	1.94	0.07
Hungary	32.48	0.00	17.66	0.00	0.00	0.00	0.00	49.85
Iceland	68.93	2.20	22.47	2.00	1.33	1.17	1.88	0.03
Ireland	77.95	0.41	4.18	3.84	3.18	1.16	5.75	3.54
Italy	38.27	10.51	23.41	6.28	3.66	12.38	5.38	0.11
Japan	49.39	11.56	0.45	33.60	3.58	0.43	0.43	0.57
Korea	39.97	0.00	0.00	38.51	9.12	0.00	0.00	12.40
Luxembourg	86.69	1.57	4.95	1.42	0.38	2.70	1.98	0.31
Mexico	63.38	30.45	2.72	1.08	0.44	1.14	0.21	0.58
Netherlands	47.25	10.04	7.94	22.60	2.10	6.85	3.22	0.01
Norway	61.10	3.36	10.66	6.72	5.98	7.28	4.85	0.05
New Zealand	63.76	0.62	2.63	12.07	11.26	1.57	6.80	1.29
Poland	13.51	0.00	80.86	0.93	0.00	1.03	0.00	3.67
Portugal	45.37	19.45	18.52	0.91	0.93	1.06	13.77	0.00
Slovakia	5.74	0.63	69.53	1.71	0.63	1.41	0.64	19.71
Spain	38.22	39.65	6.36	1.54	0.65	9.68	1.85	2.05
Sweden	42.61	5.30	23.37	3.33	2.51	17.64	3.08	2.16
Switzerland	64.98	4.34	12.26	2.73	1.77	5.72	2.56	5.63
Turkey	36.56	0.00	55.95	0.28	0.42	4.46	0.00	2.33
United Kingdom	46.22	4.80	3.06	4.44	17.29	4.95	19.23	0.00
United States	28.56	27.20	7.70	19.32	8.85	4.49	3.29	0.60
OECD-30	37.49	17.11	10.27	15.21	8.17	6.19	4.62	0.94

1) Share of high-skilled individuals, i.e. individuals with attained tertiary education (ISCED 5A, 5B, 6) in 25 + aged population.— 2) Regions of home countries are classified by using the definitions of the World Development Indicators (WDI).— 3) High-income regions comprise high-income OECD and other high-income countries, e.g. Gulf countries. Sources: Beine et al. (2007); own calculations.

($-594{,}000$), Germany ($-370{,}000$) and Italy ($-340{,}000$). Interestingly enough, New Zealand, a country which pursues a highly skill-selective immigration policy, and usually perceived as one of the winners of the Battle for Brains, also sends to other OECD countries more highly skilled individuals than it receives from them.

Nevertheless, these losses can be compensated by the immigration of highly skilled individuals from other origin countries. Indeed, according to our data

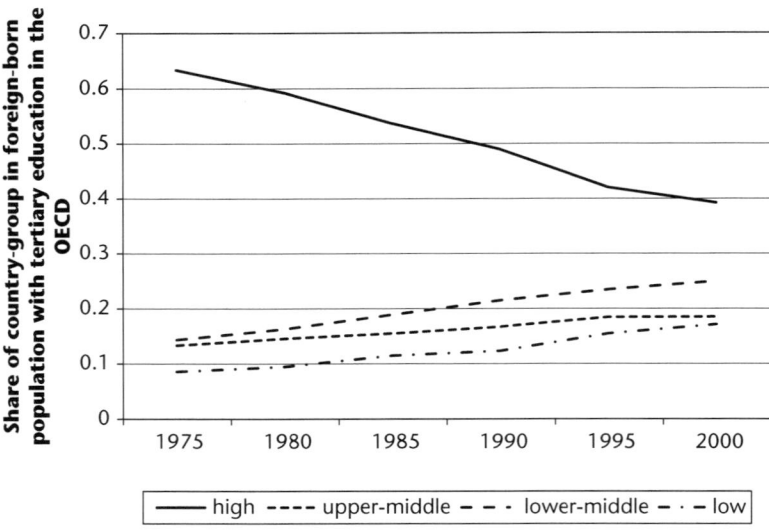

Figure 2.2. Share of source countries in highly skilled immigrant stock by income level, 1975–2000.

Sources: Data source Defoort (2009), own calculations.

about 11.9 million highly skilled individuals from non-OECD countries resided in the OECD in 2001. However, 9 million of these reside in Australia, Canada, and the USA, that is in those countries which are the main net recipients of highly skilled migrants in the OECD anyway. Consequently, even if we consider the highly skilled immigrant population from non-OECD countries, 17 out of 30 OECD countries send more highly skilled individuals to other OECD countries than they receive from OECD and non-OECD countries (Table 2.4).[3]

To sum up, the global contest for talent is not won by the OECD or the high-income countries as such. The real winners are the USA and some other English-speaking countries that pursue highly selective immigration policies, such as Australia and Canada. The UK, some continental European countries, and Korea are instead the main losers. Moreover, relatively poor countries in the OECD at the periphery, such as Mexico and Poland, are important net senders of highly skilled migrants.

---

[3] Unfortunately, we cannot properly calculate the difference in the stock of highly skilled immigrants from abroad and of highly skilled natives residing in other countries since data on highly skilled migrants from OECD countries residing in non-OECD countries are unavailable.

Table 2.4. Immigrant and emigrant population with tertiary education in OECD countries, 2001.

	Stock of highly skilled immigrants[1]			Memo item:
	from OECD-30 in country	from country in OECD-30	difference	stock of other highly skilled immigrants in country
Australia	826,301	117,865	708,436	811,751
Austria	64,537	130,146	−65,609	38,674
Belgium	73,914	13,738	60,176	25,856
Canada	1,166,275	523,461	642,814	1,557,820
Czech Republic	6,345	70,449	−64,104	40,643
Denmark	23,612	67,889	−44,277	16,023
Finland	8,300	72,594	−64,294	13,211
France	240,867	310,751	−69,884	368,118
Germany	566,185	936,520	−370,335	454,570
Greece	15,575	161,667	−146,092	49,209
Hungary	2,950	123,289	−120,339	9,595
Iceland	4,270	7,125	−2,855	2,290
Ireland	90,668	228,141	−137,473	25,053
Italy	57,515	395,229	−337,714	84,903
Japan	132,097	278,268	−146,171	135,273
Korea	18,375	612,937	−594,562	27,596
Luxembourg	13,987	6,419	7,568	7,785
Mexico	51,235	949,330	−898,095	30,719
Netherlands	170,422	254,730	−84,308	223,469
Norway	41,265	44,067	−2,802	22,639
New Zealand	135,201	174,870	−39,669	82,653
Poland	14,957	454,557	−439,600	88,539
Portugal	12,197	145,765	−133,568	15,291
Slovakia	3,436	24,097	−20,661	2,477
Spain	111,450	154,650	−43,200	182,590
Sweden	100,706	80,553	20,153	95,163
Switzerland	189,274	92,554	96,720	90,801
Turkey	53,683	174,687	−121,004	95,006
United Kingdom	511,030	1,478,474	−967,444	722,391
United States	3,804,292	426,099	3,378,193	6,595,708
OECD-30	8,510,921	8,510,921	0	11,915,816

1) Share of high-skilled individuals, i.e. individuals with attained tertiary education (ISCED 5A, 5B, 6) in 25+ aged population.

Sources: Data source Beine et al. (2007); own calculations.

2.2 How large is the global pool of highly skilled labour?

A Battle for Brains can unfold only if the pool of highly skilled labour is supply-constrained. To analyse this issue, once again we define individuals as highly skilled if they have attained a tertiary education level. As Table 2.5 shows, the worldwide supply of individuals with tertiary education amounts to 338 million: 191 million or 56 per cent of those reside in high-income countries, 17 per cent in upper-middle-income countries, 24 per cent in lower-middle-income countries and 3.5 per cent in low-income countries (Table 2.5).

Table 2.5. Total population and immigrants with tertiary education by country groups, 2001.

	Pool of highly skilled 25+ population			Highly skilled immigrants in OECD-30	
		in per cent of			in per cent of
	thousand persons	global stock of highly skilled population	home population	thousand persons	home country stock of highly skilled population
	by income groups				
High-income countries[1]	190,728	56.41	29.09	7,706	4.04
Upper-middle-income countries	55,889	16.53	11.56	5,200	9.30
Lower-middle-income countries	79,761	23.59	4.90	5,475	6.86
Low-income countries	11,729	3.47	2.82	1,862	15.88
Total	338,107	100.00	10.62	20,435	6.04
	by region				
High-income countries[1]	190,728	56.41	29.09	7,706	4.04
Latin America and Caribbean	29,978	8.87	12.05	3,485	11.63
Eastern Europe and Central Asia	28,174	8.33	11.37	2,092	7.43
East Asia and Pacific	42,174	12.47	4.23	3,096	7.34
South Asia	28,073	8.30	4.31	1,663	5.92
Middle East and Northern Africa	11,793	3.49	8.41	1,260	10.69
Sub-saharan Africa	7,187	2.13	2.96	941	13.09
Total	338,107	100.00	10.62	20,435	6.04

1) High-income countries comprise the high-income OECD countries and other high-income countries according to the WDI classification.

Sources: Data sources Beine et al. (2007); Defoort (2009); Barro/Lee (2000); own calculations.

This pool has been increasing over time. The global number of individuals with tertiary education has grown from 93 million in 1975 to 319 million in 2000, or by a factor of 3.4 in 25 years. During the same period of time, the world population grew from 4 to 6 billion people, that is by a factor of 1.5.[4] In the high-income countries, the labour supply of the highly skilled has grown at a factor of 2.9 less than proportional during this time span. In contrast, it has grown in the lower-middle-income countries by a factor of 6.3, in the upper-middle-income countries by a factor of 4.5, and the low-income countries by a factor of 3.8. The growth of the highly skilled

[4] Own calculations based on Defoort (2009) and Barro/Lee (2000). Small differences to the figures by Beine et al. (2007) occur due to differences in the methodological approach.

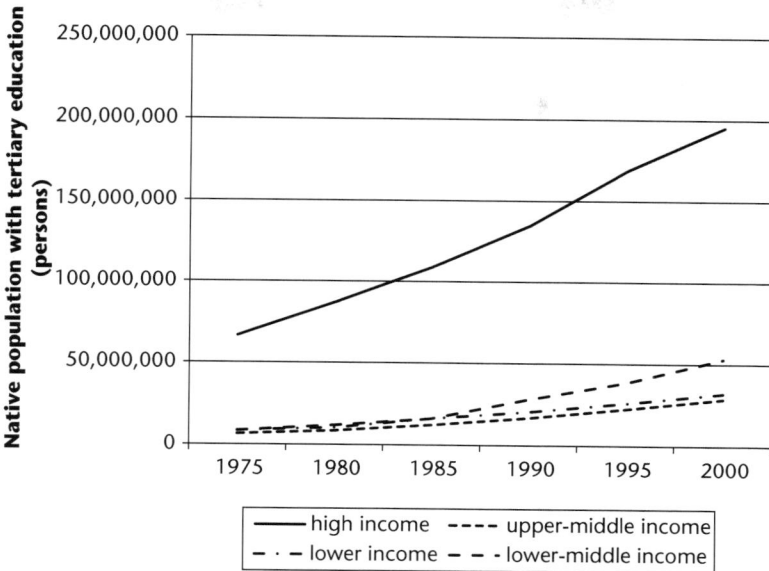

Figure 2.3. 25+ population with tertiary educational attainment, countries classified by income, 1975–2000.

Sources: Data sources Barro/Lee (2000); Defoort (2009), own calculations.

labour supply has accelerated especially in the lower-middle-income countries during the last decade—making this country group the second largest source of highly skilled labour in the world. It is thus reasonable to expect that the role of the lower-middle-income countries in South and East Asia as suppliers of highly skilled labour will further increase during the next decades (Fig. 2.3).

Of course, only a minority of the highly skilled population is willing to migrate or has the legal, economic, and social opportunities to do so. In 2001, about 6 per cent of individuals with a tertiary education belonged to the immigrant population. The share is particularly high among the low-income countries (16 per cent) and the upper-middle-income countries (9 per cent), while it is rather low among the high-income countries (4 per cent) and the lower-middle-income countries (7 per cent) (Table 2.5).

These rather moderate emigration shares refer, however, to aggregates, which conceal differences across countries. In fact, in some upper- and lower-middle-income countries the share of emigrants exceeds 30 per cent of the highly skilled population, which suggests that the pool of highly skilled labour is largely exploited there.

However, at the global level, the rather moderate shares of emigrants among the highly skilled population suggest that the pool of potential immigrants with tertiary education is far from exhausted. This may be traced back to the fact that only a minority of OECD countries (Australia, Canada, and New Zealand) actively recruit highly skilled immigrants at present, while the largest destination, the USA, pursues a mixed immigration policy which grants only a limited amount of visas to highly skilled immigrants. For the supply constraint to bind, a major policy shift is required, that is the introduction of an active and highly skill-selective immigration policy in both the EU and in the USA.

2.3 Looking at the top of the skill distribution

So far, we have focused on the broad category of tertiary education, which covers a wide range of qualifications. This section provides a closer look at the upper end of the skill distribution for the OECD and some selected non-OECD countries wherever the relevant information is available.

2.3.1 *High concentration of immigrants in population with academic degrees*

Table 2.6 displays the number of foreigners holding a PhD degree in Canada, Germany, Spain, and the USA. Interestingly enough, the share of foreigners is increasing at the upper end of the skill spectrum compared to the group which has attained tertiary education. The share of foreign-born in the total population that have acquired a PhD amounts to 51 per cent in Canada, to 27 per cent in the USA, to 10 per cent in Spain, and to 5 per cent in Germany. The rather high shares of individuals with a PhD among the foreign-born population which stays for less than 1 year in the host country suggests that a substantial number of these acquired their PhD abroad, although we have no information in the census on the country where the PhD was attained. Information from selected European countries (France, Germany, and Switzerland) suggests that about one-third of the foreign-born students are 'educational inlanders' (Kuptsch, 2006), that is individuals who have obtained their educational degrees in the destination country.

While the structure of the foreign-born population with tertiary education in the OECD was balanced by gender, the structure of the foreign-born population with a PhD degree is not. The share of males with PhD degree exceeds that of females by a factor of 2.5 in the foreign-born population, while it exceeds that in the native population by a factor of 2.

Table 2.6. Immigrant and native population with a PhD degree, 2001.

	Natives	Foreign-born		
			by year since arrival	
		all	less than 1	1 to 4	more than 4
		persons			
Canada	51,123	52,428	n.a.	12,376	40,052
Germany	397,429	20,300	714	5,857	13,714
Spain	143,600	16,600	1,440	4,340	10,780
USA	1,058,671	390,023	6,963	61,756	321,000
OECD-4	1,650,823	479,351	9,117	84,329	385,546
	in per cent of 25+ population of respective group				
Canada	0.41	1.47	na	2.67	1.29
Germany	1.06	0.93	2.66	2.04	0.74
Spain	0.69	1.16	1.08	1.08	1.20
USA	0.85	1.69	2.69	2.09	1.62
	in per cent of total 25+ population with PhD degree				
Canada	49.37	50.63	na	11.95	38.68
Germany	95.14	4.86	0.17	1.40	3.28
Spain	89.64	10.36	0.90	2.71	6.73
USA	73.08	26.92	0.48	4.26	22.16
OECD-4	77.50	22.50	0.43	3.96	18.10

Data sources: Integrated Public Use Microdata Series—International (IPUMS International), Version 4.0, Minnesota Population Centre, Minneapolis, 2008; Statistics Canada; Federal Statistical Office Germany, National Institute of Statistics Spain, Bureau of Census, USA; own calculations.

A larger number of OECD countries report data on the number of immigrants who have completed university with a degree.[5] Again, we see that the concentration of foreign-born is higher at the upper end of the skill-spectrum compared to the tertiary education level. The share of foreigners in the population with a completed university degree reached 43 per cent in Canada, 25 per cent in the USA, and 8.5 per cent in Spain in the year 2000. These shares have considerably increased over time in all receiving countries. Moreover, the share of foreign born individuals who have obtained a university degree is in most countries similar to that in the native population or even exceeds it, particularly in Canada (see Table 2.7).

2.3.2 How are immigrants represented in top occupations?

The formal level of educational attainment as reported in the previous section can serve only as a hint to the actual human capital of the immigrant

---

[5] Note that the category of tertiary education covers also college education and technical and other professional education levels beyond high school.

Table 2.7. Immigrant population with a completed university degree in selected OECD countries, 1970–2005.

	1970[1]	1980[2]	1990[3]	2000[4]	2005
Foreign-born with completed university degree (persons)					
Canada	160,000	496,000	772,000	1,310,026	na
France	236,720	319,620	599,064	na	na
Netherlands	23,281	na	na	23,281	na
Spain	na	27,227	90,082	164,820	na
UK	na	na	na	325,300	na
USA	717,051	1,636,959	3,172,215	5,868,732	7,699,884
Foreign-born in per cent of 25+ population with completed university degree					
Canada	39.41	35.87	35.43	42.95	na
France	15.16	16.29	18.05	na	na
Netherlands	8.39	na	na	1.32	na
Spain	na	5.30	5.49	8.48	na
UK	na	na	na	14.48	na
USA	7.31	9.20	12.34	17.68	20.64
individuals with completed university degree in foreign-born 25+ population in per cent					
Canada	8.09	19.72	24.93	34.76	na
France	6.79	8.77	14.17	na	na
Netherlands	6.24	na	na	20.61	na
Spain	na	10.21	19.73	11.43	na
UK	na	na	13.35	na	na
USA	11.92	18.72	22.34	25.42	29.44
individuals with completed university degree in native 25+ population in per cent					
Canada	5.48	14.93	19.12	24.32	na
France	7.46	8.91	13.52	na	na
Netherlands	5.04	na	na	22.76	na
Spain	na	3.00	8.70	9.33	na
UK	na	na	8.88	na	na
USA	11.77	18.07	22.71	26.74	27.90

1) Canada and Netherlands 1971; France 1975. 2) Canada and Spain 1981; France 1982. 3) Canada, Spain, and the UK 1991. 4) Canada, Netherlands, Spain, and the UK 2001.

Data sources: Integrated Public Use Microdata Series—International (IPUMS International), Version 4.0, Minnesota Population Centre, Minneapolis, 2008; Statistics Canada; Federal Statistical Office of Germany, National Institute of Statistics, Spain, Bureau of Census, USA, own calculations.

population. Educational degrees may be hardly comparable across countries and immigrants may lack complementary skills such as language or cultural knowledge which are needed to transfer the human capital acquired abroad to the labour markets in destination countries. Looking at how immigrants are represented at the top of the occupational distribution therefore provides a good approximation of how the human capital acquired by highly skilled immigrants is valued in host countries' labour markets. To this end, we analyse the absolute numbers and shares of immigrants at the ISCO 1 and ISCO 2 occupation level. ISCO 1 covers top management positions in public

Table 2.8. Immigrants with tertiary education in key management and highly skilled professional positions, 2006.

	Total stock of immigrants (25+)			Share of occupational group in total stock			
				immigrants		natives	
	key management occupations[1]	high professional occupations[2]	all occupations	key management occupations[1]	high professional occupations[2]	key management occupations[1]	high professional occupations[2]
Australia	211,777	396,263	1,997,517	0.11	0.20	0.11	0.17
Austria	32,594	35,667	516,391	0.06	0.07	0.09	0.08
Belgium	54,730	65,298	382,057	0.14	0.17	0.11	0.19
Denmark	1,678	17,919	159,863	0.01	0.11	0.02	0.12
Finland	1,010	8,810	48,000	0.02	0.18	0.03	0.15
France	184,181	267,539	2,071,134	0.09	0.13	0.07	0.11
Greece	22,892	37,176	556,606	0.04	0.07	0.10	0.13
Hungary	10,853	23,472	108,375	0.10	0.22	0.08	0.12
Ireland	31,002	39,048	195,234	0.16	0.20	0.14	0.14
Luxembourg	5,317	11,240	78,825	0.07	0.14	0.06	0.12
Mexico	16,861	26,186	117,974	0.14	0.22	0.02	0.08
Netherlands	61,825	122,644	761,095	0.08	0.16	0.12	0.17
New Zealand	44,580	59,592	338,943	0.13	0.18	0.12	0.13
Norway	8,590	17,692	126,144	0.07	0.14	0.09	0.10
Poland	11,502	24,684	113,892	0.10	0.22	0.06	0.13
Portugal	26,456	57,386	395,816	0.07	0.14	0.07	0.08
Spain	74,203	103,269	1,093,927	0.07	0.09	0.08	0.12
Sweden	13,380	62,170	445,545	0.03	0.14	0.06	0.17
Switzerland	55,680	80,491	930,822	0.06	0.09	0.09	0.11
United Kingdom	379,892	411,481	2,327,892	0.16	0.18	0.14	0.12
USA[3]	2,750,000	3,280,000	23,580,000	0.12	0.14	0.12	0.16
OECD-21	3,787,226	4,751,764	36,346,052	0.10	0.13	0.10	0.14

1) Legislators, senior officials, and managers (ISCO 1). 2) High professional occupations (ISCO 2).

Sources: Data sources OECD (2009); own calculations of shares and indicators.

administration and private business,[6] ISCO 2 includes highly skilled professionals and academics in engineering, natural sciences, social sciences, medicine, law, media, and arts (ILO 2009).[7]

In order to get a hint of whether immigrants are particularly affected by a skill downgrading, that is whether immigrants are employed below their education level, we present in Table 2.8 the number of immigrants with tertiary education in key management and top professional occupations and the shares of these two groups in the total immigrant and native population with a tertiary education degree. Interestingly enough, at the level of the entire OECD, these shares are strikingly similar: 10 per cent of the immigrants and the natives with a tertiary education degree fill top management occupations according to the ILO classification, and 13 per cent of the immigrant and 14 per cent of the native population with a tertiary education degree are employed in highly skilled professional occupations (Table 2.8).

However, these rough data do not control for the field of study and do not distinguish between advanced and less advanced tertiary education degrees, such that the figures have to be taken with a grain of salt. Nevertheless, these figures do not suggest that skill downgrading largely affects the potential human capital gain of the receiving countries. In Section 2.5 we review the econometric evidence on whether immigrants can transfer their skills into host country labour markets in some detail.

2.4 The competition for foreign students

Foreign students are an important source of highly skilled immigration. The incentives for moving abroad are high since studies in foreign countries are well rewarded in the labour market even if the students return to their home countries. Receiving countries can benefit from the immigration of foreign students by acquiring human capital which is well adapted to the host country labour market (Kuptsch, 2006). Even if the receiving countries cannot completely recover the costs of the studies by tuition fees, they may benefit later through the productive use of human capital in the labour market. More and more destination countries have therefore facilitated the immigration of foreign students by adjusting their immigration laws and easing access to the labour market for foreigners who have completed their studies in the country.

---

[6] Leading positions in public administrations, ministers, members of parliament, entrepreneurs, top management positions in private businesses, business consultants, auditors, tax consultants etc. Note that this category covers also entrepreneurial activities.

[7] Engineers, academics in natural sciences and mathematics, social sciences, medical doctors, university and other teachers, legal persons, journalists, artists.

Triggered by concerns that Europe may fall back in the contest for talent, the EU has harmonized study programmes under the umbrella of the Bologna process, and it encourages intra-European flows of students. However, many countries have increased the share of university education costs to be born by students, and many discriminate against foreign students through higher tuition fees (e.g. Australia, Netherlands, Switzerland, and the UK). Altogether, these processes have increased incentives for destination countries to attract foreign students, even if they cannot recover the entire costs of their studies in the short term.

The available data on foreign student flows reflect these trends. Again, information on foreign students has to be interpreted with care, since a substantial number of the foreign students have grown up in the host countries and are therefore 'educational inlanders' Kuptsch (2006).

Nevertheless, the available data suggest that the number of foreign students has increased substantially. In advanced research programmes (ISCED 6), that is study programmes which are completed with a publishable thesis or disser-tation, the share of foreign students has grown in the eight years from 1998 to 2006 from 11 per cent to 22 per cent, while the enrolment of foreigners in all tertiary education programmes has increased from 4 per cent to 5.4 per cent during the same period of time (Figure 2.4).

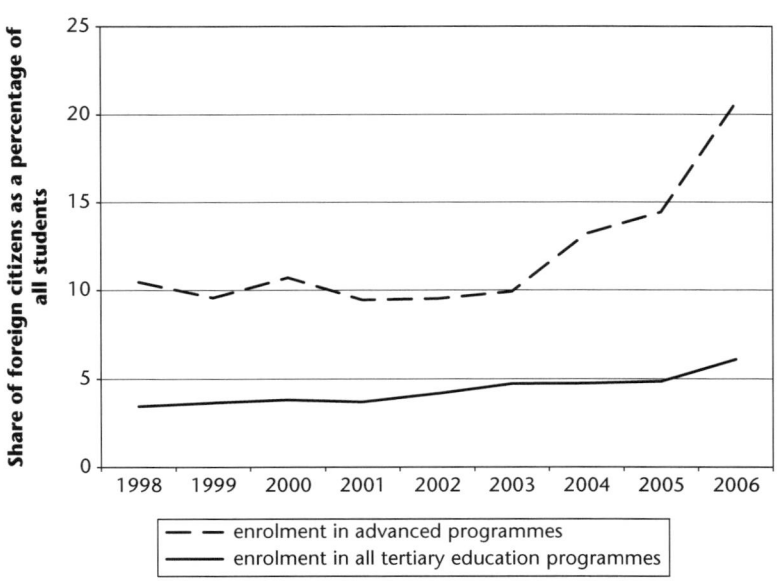

Figure 2.4. Participation of foreigners in tertiary education and advanced education programmes in the OECD-27, 1998–2006.

Sources: OECD (2009), own calculations.

In general, it is important to note that foreign students are heavily concentrated at the upper end of the tertiary education programmes: In 2006, the share of foreign-born individuals in the total enrolment of practical and technical education programmes (ISCED 5B) was only 3.8 per cent, but it reached 8.1 per cent in theoretical programmes (ISCED 5A) and 22.4 per cent in advanced research programmes (ISCED 6). Foreign participation in advanced research programmes and theoretically based programmes is particularly high in Switzerland, the UK, Norway, and Luxembourg. In the largest destination, the USA, foreign participation in advanced research programmes and theoretically based programmes is also well above the OECD averages, at 26 per cent and 29 per cent respectively (see Table 2.9). Similarly, Kerr and Lincoln (2008) report on the basis of census data that 24 per cent and 47 per cent of the US workforce in science and engineering with bachelor and doctorate degrees are foreign citizens compared to a 12 per cent immigrant share in the US workforce.

The education of immigrants and natives differs also with respect to their specialization. The OECD educational database provides some information on specialization patterns of enrolled foreign and native students. In our analysis we distinguish between technical and practical and theoretically based programmes (ISCED 5) on the one hand, and advanced research programmes (ISCED 6) on the other hand. The latter category comprises PhD and equivalent programmes.

The most striking fact is that foreigners are more than proportionally represented in sciences, and this specialization pattern is even sharper if we consider the participation in advanced research programmes: 11 per cent of the foreign students in the OECD which participate in ISCED-5 study programmes are enrolled in sciences, compared with 6 per cent among the native students. Moreover, 27 per cent of the foreign students in the OECD which are enrolled in advanced research programmes study sciences, compared with 13 per cent of the native students (see Table 2.10).

Interestingly enough, in most other programmes, such as engineering, social sciences, law, and business administration, the specialization patterns of foreign and native students are very similar. A notable exception are health- and welfare-related studies which also comprise medical doctorates, where we find a higher share among native students (25 per cent) compared to foreign students (17 per cent) in the advanced research programmes.

Whether foreign students contribute to the human capital endowments of the receiving countries depends on whether these countries are able to retain them. While many countries, such as Germany, don't even grant work and residence permits to foreign students after the finalization of their studies, more and more countries have realized that foreign students are an important source for highly skilled labour. A recent survey from Italy, however, suggests

	Foreign students (persons)				Foreign students in per cent of total students			
	total tertiary education[1]	advanced research programmes[2]	theoretically based programmes[3]	practical and technical programmes[4]	total tertiary education[1]	advanced research programmes[2]	theoretically based programmes[3]	practical and technical programmes[4]
Australia	217,055	11,988	192,987	12,080	20.87	29.66	22.96	7.60
Austria	39,329	3,520	35,809	na	15.54	20.93	16.86	na
Belgium	40,607	2,321	24,518	13,768	10.30	31.02	13.41	6.75
Canada	148,164	13,302	134,862	na	14.60	38.26	13.76	na
Czech Republic	21,395	1,807	19,267	347	6.34	7.98	6.80	1.09
Denmark	19,123	912	15,264	2,947	8.35	19.20	7.80	10.33
Finland	8,955	1,663	7,292	na	2.90	7.51	2.54	na
France	247,510	24,997	196,794	25,719	11.24	35.80	12.33	4.80
Germany	261,363	na	248,149	13,214	11.42	na	12.70	3.93
Greece	16,558	414	14,171	1,973	2.54	1.84	3.67	0.81
Hungary	14,491	642	13,720	129	3.30	8.06	3.38	0.52
Iceland	715	19	691	5	4.55	12.18	4.55	1.29
Ireland	na	na	na	na	na	na	na	na
Italy	48,766	1,926	45,980	860	2.40	5.03	2.33	6.18
Japan	130,124	12,586	88,176	29,362	3.19	16.78	2.90	3.03
Korea	22,260	2,024	14,697	5,539	0.69	4.66	0.74	0.47
Luxembourg	1,137	na	na	na	42.24	na	na	na
Mexico	na	na	na	na	na	na	na	na
Netherlands	35,374	na	35,374	na	6.10	na	6.18	na
Norway	67,699	2,278	47,935	17,486	28.47	42.78	28.35	27.60
New Zealand	14,297	1,127	12,952	218	6.66	22.33	6.24	11.17
Poland	11,365	942	10,409	14	0.53	2.88	0.50	0.06
Portugal	17,077	1,570	15,257	250	4.65	7.65	4.45	5.91
Slovakia	1,733	77	1,641	15	0.88	0.72	0.89	0.53
Spain	51,013	14,783	27,057	9,173	2.85	19.18	1.84	3.82
Sweden	41,410	4,414	36,077	919	9.80	20.65	9.47	4.51
Switzerland	39,415	7,626	25,917	5,872	19.23	44.25	17.04	16.47
Turkey	19,079	872	17,135	1,072	0.81	2.68	1.05	0.16
United Kingdom	418,353	40,193	318,937	59,223	17.91	42.68	18.44	11.57
United States[6]	572,509	78,884	396,285	na	3.31	26.34	29.41	na
OECD-27	2,526,876	230,887	1,997,353	200,185	5.42	22.42	8.12	3.75

1) All tertiary education comprises the ISCED 6, ISCED 5A and 5B level. 2) ISCED 6 level. Advanced research programmes are concluded with a publishable thesis or dissertation, which qualify *inter alia* for a faculty post or research position in the private sector. 3) ISCED 5A level which comprises studies which cover also theoretical qualifications. 4) ISCED 5B level, which comprises education programmes with technical and practical occupational qualifications. See UN (2006) for a description of the ISCED classification. 5) All tertiary 2005; advanced and theoretical programmes. 6) All tertiary 2001.

Sources: OECD STAT database; own calculations of shares and indicators.

Table 2.10. Field of study of foreign and native students (ISCED 5 and ISCED 6), 2006.

	Foreign students				Native students			
	science	engineering, manufacturing and construction	health and welfare	social sciences, business & law	science	engineering, manufacturing and construction	health and welfare	social sciences, business & law
share of study field among all immigrant and native students in ISCED-5 programmes[1]								
Australia	0.12	0.15	0.14	0.26	0.08	0.10	0.16	0.23
Canada	0.13	0.19	0.13	0.32	0.09	0.12	0.16	0.34
Czech Republic	0.05	0.30	0.09	0.19	0.06	0.30	0.09	0.20
Denmark	0.20	0.03	0.06	0.06	0.19	0.02	0.05	0.03
Finland	0.05	0.26	0.15	0.24	0.04	0.22	0.17	0.34
Greece	0.09	0.16	0.13	0.23	0.09	0.15	0.12	0.27
Ireland	0.10	0.09	0.10	0.14	0.10	0.08	0.08	0.14
Mexico	0.05	0.18	0.09	0.30	0.05	0.16	0.07	0.31
New Zealand	0.11	0.20	0.16	0.23	0.07	0.24	0.16	0.21
Norway	0.14	0.06	0.19	0.20	0.07	0.12	0.19	0.23
Slovakia	0.03	0.24	0.09	0.14	0.04	0.27	0.06	0.18
Spain	0.00	0.27	0.12	0.28	0.00	0.30	0.12	0.29
Sweden	0.08	0.16	0.20	0.21	0.05	0.14	0.22	0.21
OECD-13	0.11	0.18	0.13	0.28	0.06	0.18	0.12	0.28
share of study field among all immigrant and native students in ISCED-6 programmes[2]								
Australia	0.36	0.12	0.23	0.06	0.35	0.06	0.26	0.05
Canada	0.35	0.18	0.12	0.17	0.27	0.07	0.13	0.24
Czech Republic	0.21	0.24	0.11	0.15	0.26	0.28	0.11	0.11
Denmark	0.31	0.09	0.00	0.20	0.29	0.10	0.00	0.23
Finland	0.19	0.24	0.19	0.12	0.22	0.19	0.21	0.17
Greece	0.16	0.13	0.20	0.17	0.19	0.15	0.24	0.16
Ireland	0.35	0.06	0.10	0.08	0.40	0.05	0.08	0.07
Mexico	0.11	0.09	0.22	0.20	0.07	0.08	0.37	0.18

New Zealand	0.21	0.08	0.15	0.26	0.17	0.06	0.14	0.31
Norway	0.33	0.07	0.22	0.10	0.20	0.19	0.22	0.12
Slovakia	0.11	0.19	0.14	0.15	0.14	0.18	0.14	0.17
Spain	0.00	0.22	0.27	0.27	0.00	0.30	0.25	0.24
Sweden	0.30	0.16	0.22	0.12	0.24	0.20	0.28	0.12
OECD-13	0.27	0.15	0.17	0.17	0.13	0.16	0.25	0.19

Figures do not add up to 1 since only selected study areas are considered. 1) ISCED refers to technical and practical study programmes. 2) ISCED 6 refers to advanced and theoretical study programmes.

Sources: Data sources OECD (2009); own calculations of shares and indicators.

that particularly continental European countries have a problem retaining foreign students due to poor job and career opportunities: 88 per cent of the PhD students who have already decided (47 per cent of the interviewees) what they will do upon completion of their PhD course say that they will leave Italy. Note that 85 per cent of the foreign PhD students receive a grant (mostly from the hosting Italian university), and that the availability of a grant is one of the major driving forces behind the choice of coming to Italy. Hence, Italy pays for their education (and this contributes to attracting foreigners), but is then unable to retain the students, who report on the high quality of the educational system, but poor career opportunities. About 75 per cent of these PhD students are enrolled in scientific and engineering faculties, that is are specialized in fields which promise high economic and social returns (Colussi et al., 2009).

2.5 How do highly skilled immigrants assimilate into host labour markets?

The effects of highly skilled immigration as well as the incentives for highly skilled individuals to migrate depend on whether they are able to transfer their human capital into the labour markets of host countries. There exists a large literature building on Chiswick (1978), Carliner (1980), Borjas (1987) Jasso and Rosenzweig (1985; 1990), and others which examines the 'assimilation' of immigrants into host country labour markets, that is the age–earnings profile of immigrants relative to the native population, controlling for the year of entry and cohort effects (see Chiswick and Miller, 2007; Epstein and Gang, 2009. Venturini and Villosio, 2008, for recent contributions). While the overwhelming share of these studies focuses on the returns to education in general, some of them directly address the labour market performance of highly skilled individuals.

These studies find that (i) highly skilled immigrants have a lower probability than natives of similar education levels of obtaining highly skilled jobs (see Mattoo, Neagu, and Özden, 2008, for the USA, Green, 1999, for Canada, Kler, 2006, for Australia); (ii) have higher unemployment risks (see Chiswick et al., 1997, for the USA, Cheung and Heath, 2007, for the UK); and (iii) receive lower wages than natives (see Brekke and Mastekaasa, 2008, for Norway, Clark and Drinkwater, 2008, for the UK, Friedberg, 1996, for Israel, Wadensjö, 2009, for Sweden, Kerr, 2006, for Australia). Clark and Lindley (2009) however find for the UK that highly skilled individuals entering the country through the educational system perform better in terms of both wages and employment opportunities than natives, while immigrants who enter the country through the labour market channel perform worse.

The evidence on whether wages and other labour market outcomes of highly skilled immigrants converge to—or even overtake—those of natives is mixed.

Many studies find no evidence for the convergence of wages (e.g. Brekke and Maastekaasa, 2008; Epstein and Gang, 2009. Constant and Massey, 2003), while others find mixed or rather weak evidence for wage convergence (Kler, 2006; Friedberg, 1996). In contrast, the findings of Chiswick and Miller (2007) indicate that the share of immigrants who obtain a job above their skill level increases with the length of stay in the host country, and Chiswick et al. (1997) show that unemployment risks decline with the length of stay.

Recently, Hunt (20011) examined the performance of highly skilled immigrants who have graduated in the USA using the 2003 wave of the National Survey of College Graduates. Interestingly enough, immigrants who graduated in the USA have significantly higher wages than native graduates, are more likely to start up a firm and be granted a patent, and author more academic papers. Similarly, Peri (2007), Hunt and Gauthier-Loiselle (2008), and Kerr and Lincoln (2008) find that a higher number of immigrant college graduates or a higher number of temporary student visas raises patents per capita significantly. However, these effects may disappear once the analysis controls for the field of study and the census region: immigrants are over-represented in fields with high returns in the labour market, that is computer sciences and mathematics, engineering and physical sciences, and in high-wage regions. While highly skilled immigrants earn 2.9 per cent more than natives without controls, they earn 8.2 per cent less if all covariates are considered (Hunt, 2011).

An in-depth analysis of the earnings of highly skilled immigrants and other aspects of their labour market performance is beyond the scope of this chapter. We rather provide here some descriptive data on the wages of full-time employed highly skilled immigrants by age group for the USA and Canada.

Figures 2.5 and 2.6 and Annex Table A2.1 display the age–earnings profiles for foreign-born and native PhD graduates in the USA and Canada. Interestingly enough, the two countries show different assimilation patterns. In the USA, PhD graduates receive similar wages as natives until they achieve the 40–44 age bracket, and higher wages in the age brackets above 44. In contrast, foreign-born individuals in Canada receive in all age brackets lower wages than natives except for the 60 to 64 age group.

Interestingly enough, a similar analysis for individuals with highly skilled professional occupations shows that foreign-born may outperform natives if we control for occupation: foreign-born individuals in professional occupations (ISCO 2) receive substantially higher wages than natives in the USA in all age brackets (Fig. 2.7 and Annex Table A2.2). In contrast, wage levels of foreign-born individuals in ISCO 2 occupations are in most age brackets below those of natives in Canada (Fig. 2.8 and Annex Table A2.2).

A similar picture emerges if we carry out the same analysis for the age–earnings profile of foreign-born and natives in ISCO 1 occupations and if we control for gender (not displayed here).

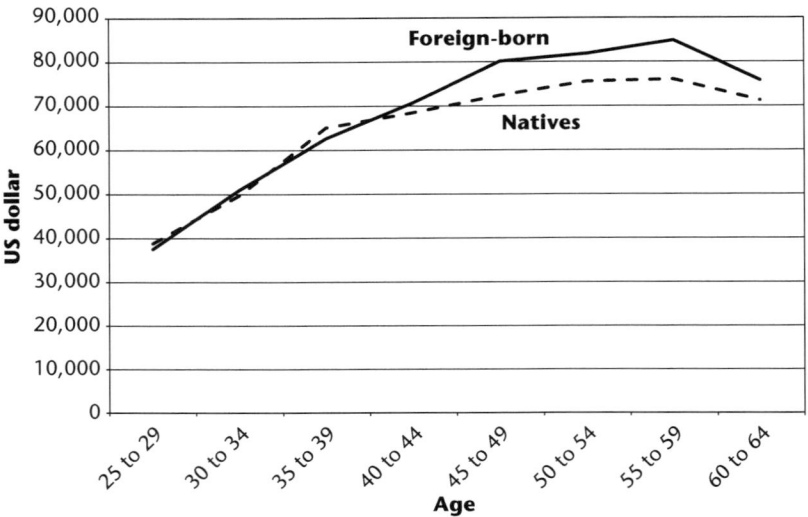

Figure 2.5. Annual wage incomes of PhD graduates in USA, 2000.
Sources: IPUMS international, own calculations.

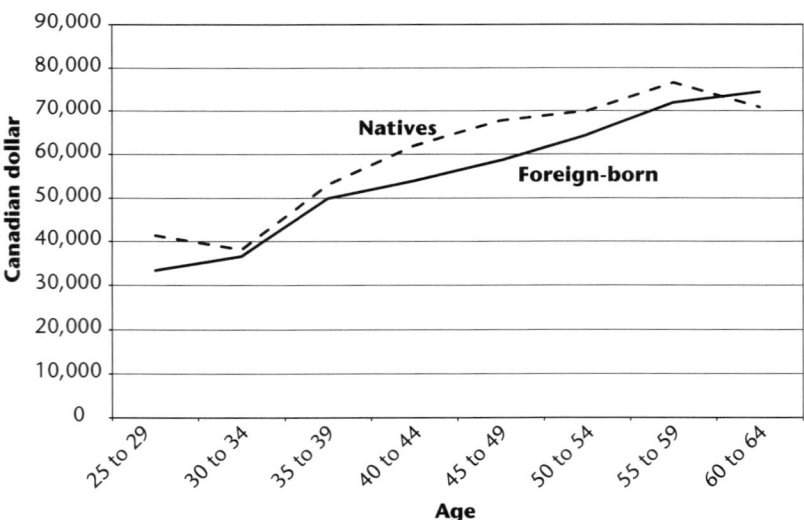

Figure 2.6. Annual wage incomes of PhD graduates in Canada, 2001.
Sources: IPUMS international, own calculations.

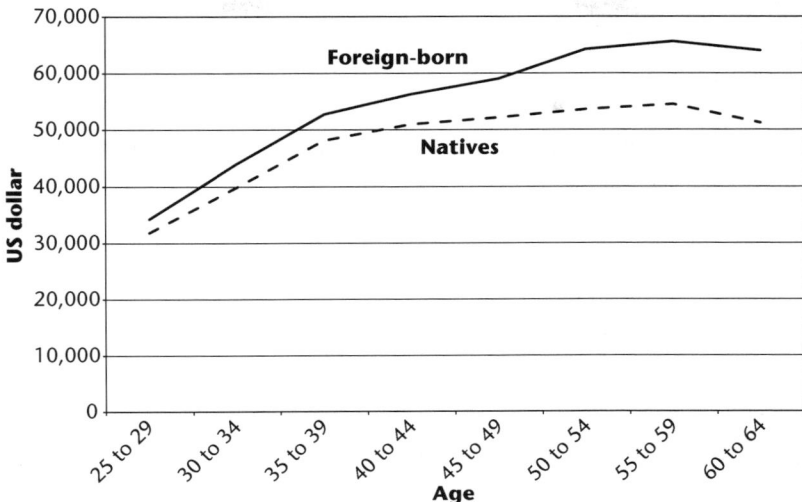

Figure 2.7. Annual wage incomes of highly skilled professionals (ISCO 2) in USA, 2000.
Sources: IPUMS international, own calculations.

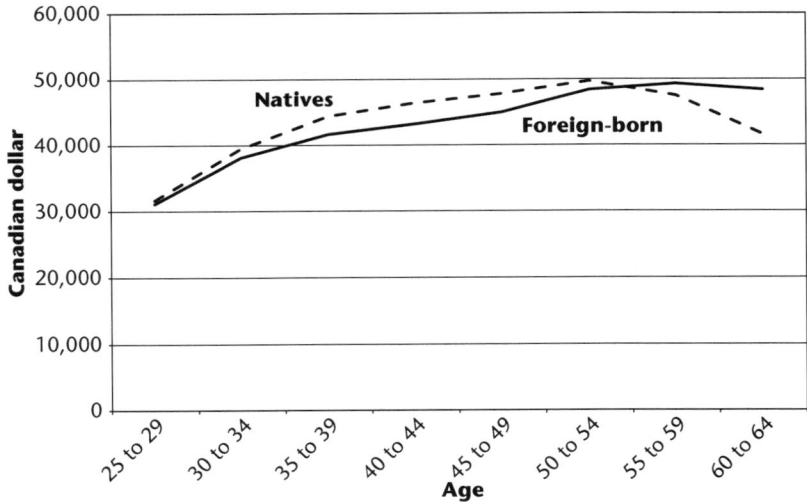

Figure 2.8. Annual wage incomes of highly skilled professionals (ISCO 2) in Canada, 2001.
Sources: IPUMS international, own calculations.

2.6 Conclusions

The descriptive analysis provided in this chapter suggests that only a minority of the high-income countries benefit from a net inflow of highly skilled migrants. The available data indicates that the global pool of highly skilled labour consists of about 320 million individuals, and 190 million of them reside in high-income countries. The stock of highly skilled immigrants in the OECD can be estimated to be about 20 million, 50 per cent of these coming from high-income countries. Interestingly enough, only a minority of OECD countries are winners in the contest for talent, in the sense that they obtain more highly skilled individuals than they send abroad. While the USA and countries with a highly skill-selective immigration policy (Australia, Canada) are net winners, Europe is a net sender even if we consider the inflows from non-OECD countries. The picture within Europe is mixed: particularly rich countries such as Luxembourg, Switzerland, and Sweden benefit from a net inflow of highly skilled labour, while most other countries lose.

Data on immigration at the top of the skill distribution are scarce. The available evidence suggests that the concentration of foreign-born individuals among the population with a PhD degree is significantly larger than that among the population with a tertiary education degree. Moreover, foreign students are heavily over-represented in advanced research programmes (ISCED 6) and theoretically based programmes (ISCED 5A). In these programmes, they specialize more than native students in sciences and similar fields, which may explain the fact that increasing the number of foreign college graduates raises the number of patent applications per capita significantly. Again, the USA, Canada, and Australia benefit more than proportionally from the immigration of individuals at the top of the skill distribution.

The available data suggest that the share of individuals in top professional occupations (ISCO 2) and top management occupations (ISCO 1) among the immigrant population is very similar to that of natives in selected OECD countries. At first glance, this suggests that skill downgrading does not heavily affect highly skilled immigrants. Our descriptive data indeed indicates that immigrants with a PhD degree and immigrants in ISCO 1 and ISCO 2 occupations have similar or higher earnings than natives with the same educational or occupational level in the USA. However, the age–earning profile of immigrants is well below that of natives in all age brackets in Canada. Microeconometric evidence suggests that distinct differences between highly skilled immigrants and natives exist in earnings and other labour market outcomes if we control for covariates such as field of study, other human capital characteristics, and regions of residence.

Annex Table

Table A2.1. Wage income by selected skill groups in USA and Canada, 2000/01.

Age	USA		Canada	
	Natives	Foreigners	Natives	Foreigners
	in US $		in Canadian $	
		PhD		
25 to 29	38,870	37,580	41,340	33,410
30 to 34	49,780	50,990	38,110	36,580
35 to 39	65,090	62,650	53,030	49,930
40 to 44	68,500	70,750	61,900	53,950
45 to 49	72,410	80,090	67,700	58,580
50 to 54	75,540	81,800	69,980	64,320
55 to 59	75,980	84,800	76,560	71,950
60 to 64	71,250	75,760	70,910	74,430
		completed university degree		
25 to 29	35,200	37,630	32,090	28,730
30 to 34	46,670	47,930	42,760	35,680
35 to 39	58,300	55,570	50,310	40,000
40 to 44	61,530	57,580	53,520	41,650
45 to 49	60,260	58,620	54,020	43,780
50 to 54	61,210	61,230	55,450	48,100
55 to 59	62,250	62,510	51,080	47,940
60 to 64	57,720	57,240	44,350	46,430

US figures for 2000, Canadian figures for 2001
Sources: IPUMS international, own calculations.

Table A2.2. Wage income by selected occupations in USA and Canada, 2000/01.

Age	USA		Canada	
	Natives	Foreigners	Natives	Foreigners
	in US $		in Canadian $	
		ISCO 01		
25 to 29	34,670	33,870	33,840	32,840
30 to 34	45,790	45,050	44,260	40,480
35 to 39	56,040	55,610	52,320	45,310
40 to 44	61,290	58,800	56,500	45,780
45 to 49	64,090	61,860	57,420	48,210
50 to 54	66,560	64,430	58,910	51,770
55 to 59	65,750	64,490	52,770	50,650
60 to 64	60,350	59,020	47,880	46,800
		ISCO 02		
25 to 29	31,870	34,300	31,660	31,110
30 to 34	39,880	44,030	39,510	38,130
35 to 39	48,160	52,700	44,360	41,660
40 to 44	50,980	56,280	46,380	43,180
45 to 49	52,150	59,040	47,800	44,950
50 to 54	53,600	64,250	49,710	48,370
55 to 59	54,500	65,640	47,470	49,300
60 to 64	51,190	64,030	41,570	48,370

US figures for 2000, Canadian figures for 2001
Sources: IPUMS international, own calculations.

3

The Determinants of Highly Skilled Migration: Evidence from OECD Countries 1980–2005

Highly educated individuals tend to be more internationally mobile than less educated ones, as shown by the evidence provided in Chapter 2. This higher mobility can be related to better incentives to move—determined by the wage structure at destination—to lower costs of moving, and to better opportunities to do so. In this latter respect, as Chapter 1 demonstrates, some major destination countries grant exceptions to their tight immigration policies for the highly educated. In particular Table 1.5 shows that high-income countries during the recent decades have adopted policies aimed at raising the number of highly educated immigrants. This is due to a shared sentiment that highly educated workers can positively contribute to the economy of the recipient country by bringing valuable skills, stimulating investment and growth, promoting innovation, and raising productivity. The goal of this chapter is to analyse how geographical, legal, institutional, and economic factors affect the scale of immigration and the skill composition of the immigrant population. Chapter 2 provided descriptive evidence that the countries—such as Australia, Canada, and New Zealand—which have consistently adopted skill-selective immigration policies are net receivers of talented immigrants, and the multivariate analysis we present in this chapter allows us to isolate the effects of immigration policies from those produced by potential confounders.

We analyse the determinants of the scale migration flows towards OECD countries, and their skill composition. A deeper understanding of the determinants of migration and of the skill selection of international migrants was limited for a long time by the lack of comprehensive data on the skill structure of international migrants and by the lack of information on institutional variables. Recent progress in the collection of data on immigration stocks and flows by education levels of migrants and across countries—see the data sets by Docquier and Marfouk (2006), Docquier, Lowell, and Marfouk (2009), and Defoort (2009) discussed in Chapter 2—has opened up new analytical opportunities. Interesting insights on the selection of international migrants by skill level are provided in recent papers by Belot and Hatton (2008), Grogger and Hanson (2008), and Brücker and Defoort (2009).

Three distinct features set this chapter apart from the recent contributions in the literature. First, we focus on the determinants of the migration of the highly educated workers, compared to the determinants of the scale of immigration. By estimating a total migration equation and then an equation that explains the differential movement of high- and low-skill migrants, we can characterize more thoroughly the effect of economic, legal, and policy variables in promoting total and selective immigration. Second, we correlate total immigration and the skill selection of the immigrant population with a rich set of economic and institutional determinants. We include variables that capture the main institutional features of immigration laws, variables that capture labour market institutions and the generosity of welfare, as well as variables mostly influencing the career prospects of skilled immigrants like the host-country spending on research and development. As several of these variables are rather collinear, we use the strategy of including them in the regressions a few at a time, keeping only those that are statistically significant in most specifications. Third, in contrast to most other papers which employ either cross-sectional data (Belot and Hatton, 2008; Grogger and Hanson, 2008) or only a small sample of destination countries (Brücker and Defoort, 2009), we use a novel panel data set which comprises 14 countries of destination and 74 countries of origin and includes all the major sources and receivers of migrants in the world. This data set enables us to identify the impact of different institutional and economic characteristics in the destination and the sending countries and to control, with a very rich set of dummies, for unobservable factors which may play an important role in the estimation of macro migration equations.

We are mainly interested in the differences in total immigration and its skill intensity across receiving countries, and not so much on the volume of migrants relative to those who stay. In particular, we intend to identify the effects of wages, laws, institutions, and economic variables in the receiving country on the total flow of immigrants and the share of tertiary-educated relative to primary-educated immigrants.

Following Ortega and Peri (2009), who in turn draw on Grogger and Hanson (2008), we estimate two empirical equations, one for the scale of total migration and one for the skill selection of the immigrant population. Such a simple empirical framework is derived, as shown in Annex 3.1, from a simple theoretical framework based on utility maximization by heterogeneous individuals, who differ by schooling level and account for skill-specific migration costs. Differently from Grogger and Hanson (2008) we include in both equations (scale and skill-selection) a set of country of origin by year effects that fully absorb sending-country-specific factors, and we allow those dummies to differ by skill group. This implies that we are not omitting any relevant sending-country variable, while we focus on the relation between receiving-country variables and migration flows and their skill composition.

Focusing on the receiving countries, while controlling for sending-country effects, we find that after-tax wages are a key determinant of the selection of highly skilled immigrants as well as of total immigrants. The wage premium for education strongly increases the share of the highly skilled in the immigrant population and is thus the main economic factor which affects the skill composition of this group. Similarly, changes in the immigration legislation which favour highly skilled immigrants relative to the less educated have a positive and strongly significant impact. These two effects are robust across specifications. Generous welfare benefits and labour market regulations like stronger employment protection also increase the total inflow of migrants including the highly skilled, but reduce the favourable skill-selectivity of the immigrant population. Finally, R&D expenditures have a strong positive impact on selecting the highly educated. These last two effects, however, are not very robust to different specifications.

The remainder of this chapter is structured as follows. First, we present the main equation used in our empirical analysis. Second, we describe the construction of our data set and the relevant data sources and we preview very briefly some features of the data. Third we discuss the estimation results. Finally, the main conclusions are drawn.

3.1 The empirical model

Migration and the selection of immigrants with respect to their education levels are driven by economic factors such as wage and other income differentials as well as by institutional variables which affect the returns to migration in the receiving country and the costs of migration.

The basis of our empirical analysis is equation [3.1] below. Assume that we observe, with some measurement error n_{odt}, the number of people born in country o and residing in destination country d for a set of countries of origin O, destinations D, and for different year t. The log of the migration flow from o to destination d is given by

$$\ln n_{odt} = D_{ot} + D_d + \beta_1 W_{dt} + \beta_2 X_{od} + \beta_3 Y_{dt} + e_{odt}, \qquad [3.1]$$

where the term D_{ot} is a set of country-of-origin by time effects that absorbs all the characteristics of each country of origin that vary over time (including wages) and affect either wages or costs in those countries. D_d are destination-country dummies absorbing time-invariant features of the receiving country that affect migration costs. Y_{dt} captures time-varying institutional and economic variables in the destination countries and e_{odt} is a zero-mean disturbance term. We are allowing for time-invariant, destination-specific migration costs (through dummies) and we include time-varying ones via Y_{dt}, which proxies for changes in the tightness of immigration laws or in other policy variables. Finally, X_{od} captures the bilateral time-invariant migration costs which include the size of the initial network of immigrants from o in d that certainly affect the propensity for that particular channel of migration. This would make specification [3.5] consistent with those theories that attribute a large importance to networks in affecting migration costs. At the same time including a set of bilateral dummies allows us to control for special bilateral trade relationships (common markets, currency unions, trade agreements) that may affect trade and correlate with migration flows.[1] Notice also that the specification obtained is founded in a simple optimization framework (described in Annex 3.1) and it is similar to a 'gravity' equation explaining the logarithm of migration flows as a function of origin and destination factors and of bilateral fixed costs. This empirical specification is very broadly used to analyse total trade flows.

The specification of the migration equation in [3.1] thus considers country-specific heterogeneity by fixed effects, which capture national differences in culture, climate, geography, and other time-invariant factors relevant for migration decisions. However, we impose the restriction of uniform slope parameters on the coefficients. One might argue that estimators which allow for heterogeneity not only in the intercept but also in the slope parameters, such as the mean group estimator proposed by Pesaran and Smith (1995), or shrinkage estimators are more appropriate if heterogeneity across countries matters. However, comparative studies of macro-migration models find that standard fixed effects estimators outperform heterogeneous estimators in terms of forecasting accuracy (see Brücker and Siliverstovs, 2006). Similar results are obtained in other studies which compare the forecasting performance of fixed effects and heterogeneous estimators in other contexts (Baltagi and Griffin, 1997; Baltagi et al., 2000). Ultimately the trade-off between the number of parameters to estimate and the precision of the estimate of each parameter convinced us to capture the heterogeneity across countries of origin via fixed effects.

---

[1] The existing literature finds that the empirical positive correlation between migration flows and trade flows stems from two channels. First, both flows are affected by distance, contiguity, and other determinants of bilateral transport costs. Second several studies have found a trade-creation effect of migrants who decrease information costs of exports (e.g. Rauch and Trinidade, 2002; Head and Ries, 1998). Theoretically trade can also be a substitute for migration, but no empirical evidence of a negative correlation has been found.

The derivation of equation [3.1] from a utility maximization model relies also on the assumption of the independence of irrelevant alternatives (IIA), that is it assumes that other destinations do not affect bilateral migration flows. IIA arises from the assumption that the disturbances in equation [3.1] are i.i.d. across countries. This assumption might be violated if migrants perceive two or more destinations in our data set as close substitutes. As Hausman and McFadden (1984) have demonstrated, the estimation coefficients should be stable across choice sets if IIA is satisfied, that is if we drop countries from the sample. For a similar data set Grogger and Hanson (2008) prove that the coefficients are indeed stable, and we tested that the same holds for our sample.[2]

On the basis of the empirical model [3.1] it is straightforward to derive an equation which explains the selection of highly skilled migrants by destination-country characteristics. Consider two types of potential migrants, highly educated ones, labelled by H, and less educated ones, labelled by L. For each type of migrant we can derive a migration equation similar to [3.1]. Subtracting each side of these two equations one from the other yields:

$$\ln n^H odt - \ln n^L odt = D'ot + D'd + \beta'1(w^H dt - w^L dt) + \beta'2X_{od} + \beta'3Ydt + e'odt, \quad [3.2]$$

where the superscripts H and L refer to the characteristics of 'highly' and 'less' educated migrant flows.

Equation [3.2], which we call the selection equation, explains the selectivity of migrants with respect to their skills. More precisely it states that the logarithmic difference of high- and low-skilled migration flows, $(\ln n^H_{odt} - \ln n^L_{odt})$ depends, among other things, on the difference of the wage for highly and less skilled labour in the country of destination, $(W^H - W^L)$, on the time-variant characteristics of the immigration laws in the receiving country, Y_{dt}, on fixed receiving-country characteristics D'_d, on fixed bilateral migration costs, X_{od}, and on a full set of origin by year dummies D'_{ot}. We thus assume that the institutional framework for immigrants and other institutional conditions in the destination country, such as labour market institutions or the generosity of welfare benefits, as well as bilateral migration costs may affect migration decisions of different education groups differently. By estimating how wage, institutions, and policy variables affect total immigration, on the one hand, and its skill-intensity, on the other, we can emphasize their different roles and the response of highly educated immigrants relatively to the rest.

---

[2] We checked that the estimates of the coefficient b_1 are stable to omitting one receiving country at the time.

3.2 Data

Estimating equations [3.1] and [432] requires a data set which distinguishes migration flows by skill levels. Drawing on Ortega and Peri (2009)[3] we constructed a data set which comprises migration flows for a panel of 14 receiving countries in the OECD and 74 origin countries over the period 1980–2000. We have complemented these data by a rich set of explanatory variables, which can be classified into legal variables capturing the immigration laws at the countries of destination, wages, and other economic variables which may affect the returns to human capital in the destination countries, and other institutional variables such as the regulation of labour markets and the generosity of welfare benefits.[4]

3.2.1 *Migration flows*

For the calculation of the annual bilateral migration flows we used two data sets. For the years 1995 to 2005, we obtained the flows of migrants from the International Migration Dataset (IMD) provided by the OECD. For the period 1980–1995 we used a data set collected and organized by Mayda (2010), which is based on OECD data.[5] Since the data source and the methods of data collection are the same, we merged these two data sets obtaining a balanced and consistent panel when we select 14 OECD destination countries[6] and 74 countries of origin.

The data are based on population registers and residence permits, which can be considered as relatively accurate measures for the legal entry of foreign nationals. While the OECD makes an effort (especially since 1995) to maintain a consistent definition of immigrants across countries, there are some differences between destination-country definitions. An important one is that some countries define immigrants on the basis of the place of birth and others on the basis of nationality. While this inconsistency can make a pure cross-country comparison inaccurate, our analysis focuses on changes within destination countries over time. Therefore it should be exempt from large mismeasurement errors due to this classification problem.

The migration flows have then been decomposed for each bilateral pair into three groups: those with tertiary, secondary, and primary education. Since

---

[3] We thank Francesc Ortega for allowing us to use the data.

[4] More details on the data can be found in Ortega and Peri (2009).

[5] We refer to Mayda (2009) for specific descriptions of the data relative to the 1980–1995 period. The source (OECD International Migration Data) and the definitions, however, are the same as those provided by the OECD for the statistics relative to the 1995–2005 period. Hence, we simply merged the two series.

[6] Australia, Belgium, Canada, Denmark, France, Germany, Japan, Luxembourg, Netherlands, Norway, Sweden, Switzerland, the UK, and the USA.

direct measures of the education level of immigrant flows are not available, we used the Docquier et al. (2008) data set on the education levels of the stocks of immigrants in 1990 and 2000 to construct the educational structure of migration flows by specific bilateral pair. More specifically, we use the 1990 data for the flows prior to 1990, we interpolated the 1990–2000 education composition of stocks and attribute them to the flows in the intermediate years, and finally we attribute the 2000 stock composition to the post 2000 flows. As the education composition of emigrants from a specific country is relatively stable over time, and the relatively large variance in the skill level of the immigrant population is caused by shifts in the country of origin mix, this method should capture most of that variation from the receiving-country perspective.

If we look at the total immigration rates (i.e. the total annual number of immigrants divided by the population of the receiving-countries) in the 14 destination countries of the OECD, two facts are evident. First, we see the overall immigration rate in the OECD has increased substantially from about 0.25 per cent in the early 1980s to 0.4 per cent in the 2000s, with a peak triggered by the fall of the iron curtain in Europe and surging immigration in the USA around the year 1990 (see Fig. 3.1). Second, we see that differences across destination countries matter since we observe no common trend

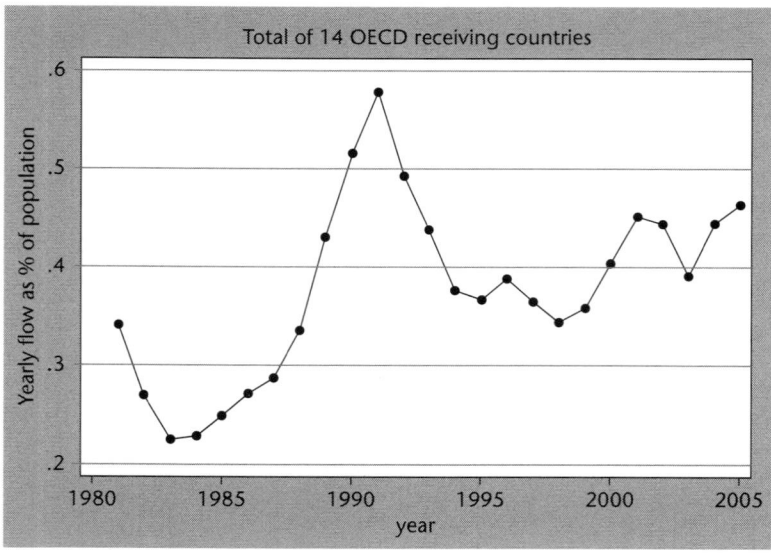

Figure 3.1. Annual inflows of immigrants into the OECD-14 as percentage of population, 1980–2005.

Note: The source of the immigration flow data is the OECD International Migration Database. The population data are from the Penn World Tables, 6.2.

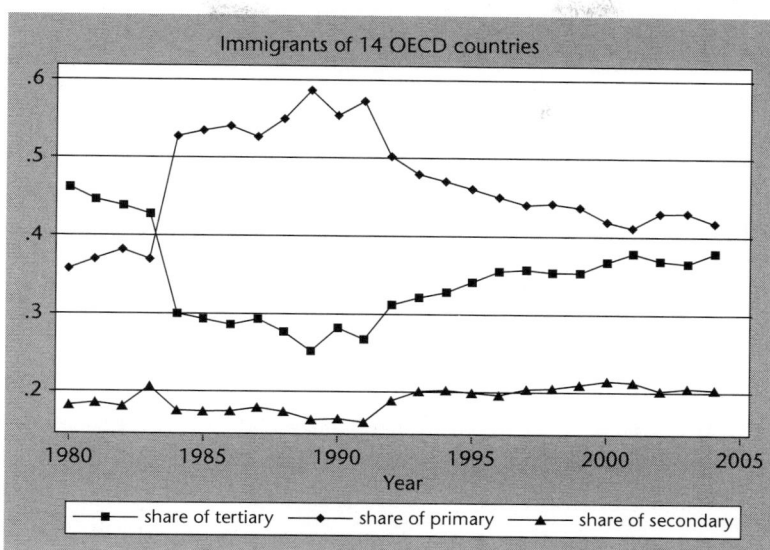

Figure 3.2. Average composition of immigration flows into the OECD-14 by education, 1980–2005.

Note: The source of the immigration flow data by education group is our calculations. We impute the share of immigrants from country *o* to country *d* by education group from the share in the stock of immigrants from country *o* in country *d* in the closest year available. Then we aggregate the flows for all countries of origin and obtain the composition of immigrants by education in the country of destination.

growth of immigration in the OECD destination countries and a lot of idio-syncratic fluctuation there (Panel A3.1 in the Annex).

An examination of composition of immigration flows by skill level yields two main trends. First we see a bipolar concentration of immigration at the upper and the lower end of the skill spectrum. While both the group of individuals with tertiary and primary education account for 40 per cent of total immigration flows, the group of secondary educated individuals only accounts for about 20 per cent. Second, the period of fastest increase in the immigration flows (1984–1990) also corresponded to a period of a significant increase in the share of less educated while the subsequent slow-down in flows (1991–2000) corresponded to an increase in the share of more educated (Fig. 3.2). It is also important to notice that the incidence of highly educated among migrants (almost 40 per cent in 2005) was much higher than their incidence in the population (about 25 per cent), confirming the fact, already reported in Chapter 2, that the highly educated have a much greater propen-sity to migrate than the less educated.

An important limitation of our data set is that accurate information on illegal migration is not available. This affects not only the level of immigration flows, but also the skill composition in some countries: only at the time of regularization is the information on undocumented immigrants revealed. For instance the significant increase of the less skilled in the period before 1990 might be traced back to the regularization of illegal migrants in the USA in 1986, while the latter increase in the share of medium- and highly skilled immigrants might be the result of the East–West migration in Europe.

The individual country trends are reported in Annex Table A3.2. Similar to our analysis in Chapter 2, we see that Australia and Canada achieve the highest shares of highly skilled immigrants, followed by the USA (Table A3.2).

3.2.2 Immigration legislation

The second novelty in the data set used here refers to the variables which capture different features of the immigration laws (see Ortega and Peri, 2009 for a detailed description). We use and update two data sets: the Mayda and Patel (2004) data set and the Social Reforms database of the Fondazione Rodolfo DeBenedetti (FRDB) (2007). The Mayda and Patel (2004) data set documents the main characteristics of immigration policies in several OECD countries (between 1980 and 2000) and the years of changes in their legislations. The FRDB Social Reforms Database collects information about social reforms in the EU-15 countries (except Luxembourg) over the period 1987–2005. We merged and updated these two data sets obtaining the complete set of immigration reforms in the period 1980–2005 relative to all the 14 OECD countries considered, for a total of more than 240 laws. The method is described in Ortega and Peri (2009), although we use a different classification of the laws here.

For each variable we classify the changes in the legislation beginning in the year 1980 (standardized to 0). Depending on certain criteria, we classify each law by + 1, −1 or 0 depending on whether it contributes positively, negatively or it is neutral with respect to a certain criterion. We construct the following five variables:

- 'Requirements for Entry': captures how cumbersome the visa application and entry process is in terms of fees, time, and documents and how stringent immigration quotas are.

- 'Requirements for Residence': measures how cumbersome the process of acquiring permanent residence or citizenship is in terms of fees, waiting time or degree of family relation with a citizen.

- 'Restriction from Benefits': measures how restricted the access to welfare benefits which are granted to native citizens is for immigrants and whether the access is subject to extra requirements (such as duty of registration, or limitation of their movement) relative to native nationals.

- 'Undocumented': measures how strict the laws against undocumented immigrants are (such as border control, legal rights granted to undocumented, and possibility of regularization).

- 'Asylum' measures how strict the requirements for political asylum are and how cumbersome it is to apply for asylum.

- 'Pro-skilled': captures the cumulated value of all laws which favour highly educated (or skilled) immigrants against the less educated one way or another.

The first five variables share the feature that an increase in their value increases what is considered the 'tightness' of immigration laws, presumably increasing the cost of immigration, while a decrease in their value 'relaxes' immigration laws, probably reducing immigration costs. The last variable is calculated as the cumulative value of all one-unit increases triggered by changes in laws which affect the skill selection of immigrants in one direction or another. An increase in this variable shifts the immigration costs, reducing them for highly educated and increasing them for less educated.

There are a few laws (4 out of 240) that are less than clear in their contribution to a specific criterion or that may change some more vague features of immigration laws (such as those stating generic measures for promoting immigrants integration or appointing a committee to deal with some immigration issues). In those cases we have attributed to the laws a 0 contribution to each criterion.

It is interesting to comment on a few features of the six variables capturing immigration laws. As each variable for each country is set equal to 0 in 1980 the variable should be thought as capturing the change in policy stance over the considered period. Hence, for instance, a country such as Australia whose 'Requirements for Entry' increased from 0 (in 1980) to 2 (as of 2005) experienced a tightening of its entry policies while a country such as the USA, whose variable 'Requirements for Entry' decreased from 0 to –2 in the same period, experienced a loosening of its entry policies.

Figure 3.3 provides an idea of the average evolution of each of the six policies over time, averaging over the 14 OECD countries which are weighted by their population. The variables that experience the largest change over time (positive in all cases) are Pro-skilled, Restriction from Benefits, and Undocumented. Between 1980 and 2005 each of the considered countries enacted on average two laws reducing the access of immigrants to benefits available to citizens, and about 2.5 laws tilting the preference towards skilled immigrants and against undocumented immigrants. Conversely, Requirements for Entry, Requirements for Residence, and Asylum were, overall, slightly loosened. The most important fact, for our purposes, is the clear trend to pass immigration laws favouring educated immigrants. Canada,

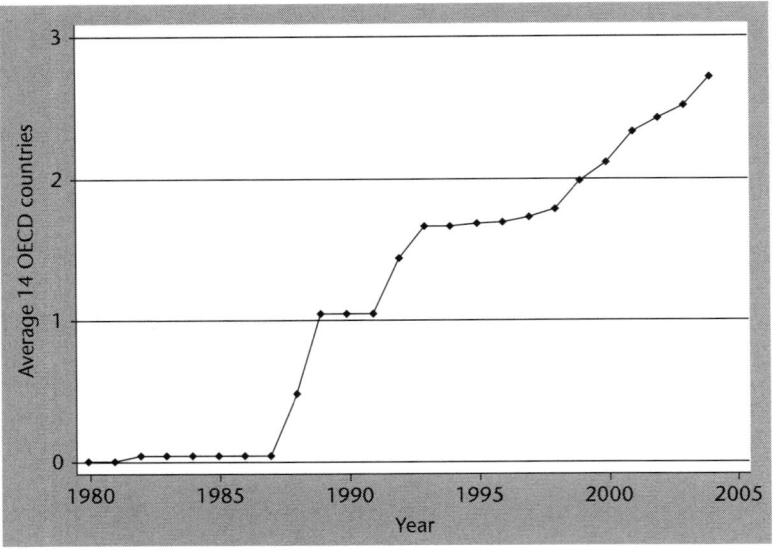

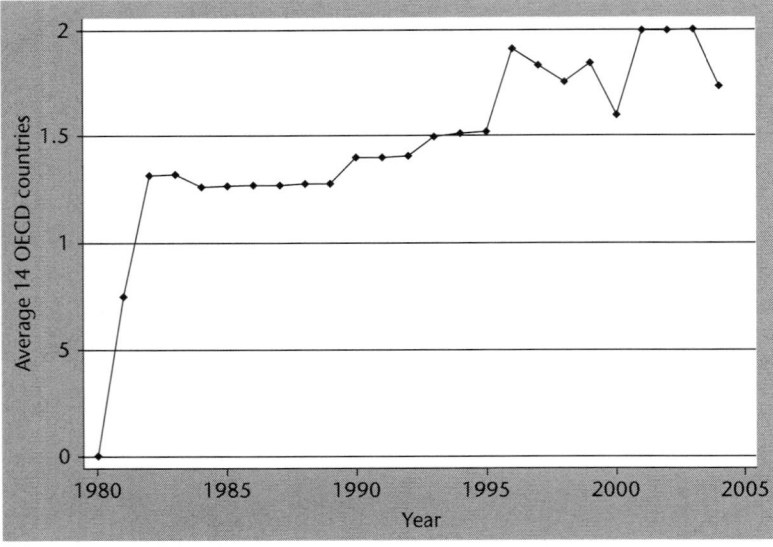

Figure 3.3. Average behaviour of the Immigration laws: 14 OECD countries, population weighted.

Note: Each variable is described in the text. It is obtained by cumulating the changes with respect to each criterion from 240 immigration laws enacted in the considered OECD countries between 1980 and 2005.

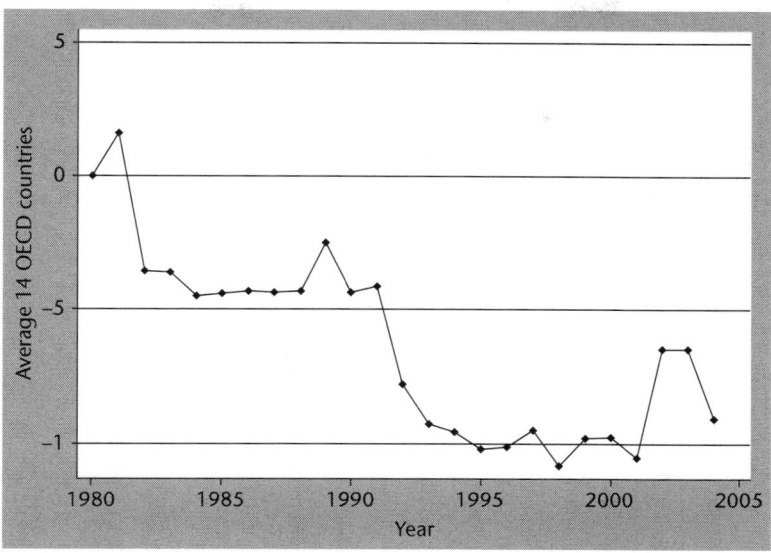

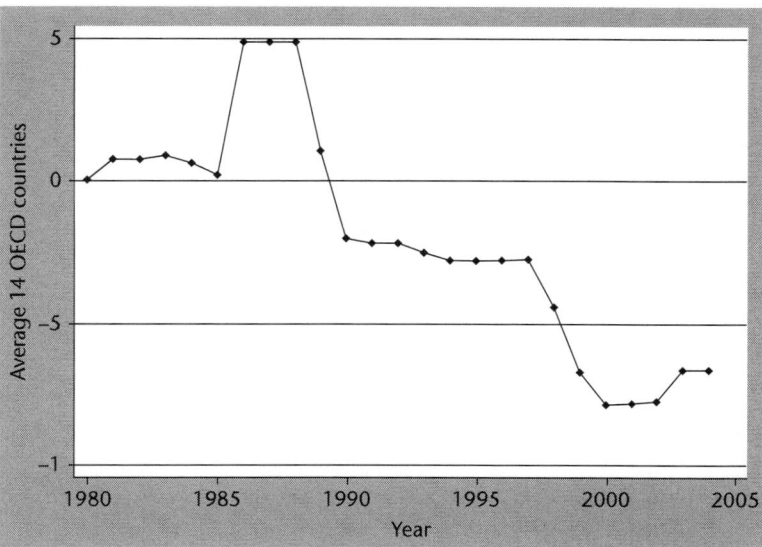

Figure 3.3. Continued

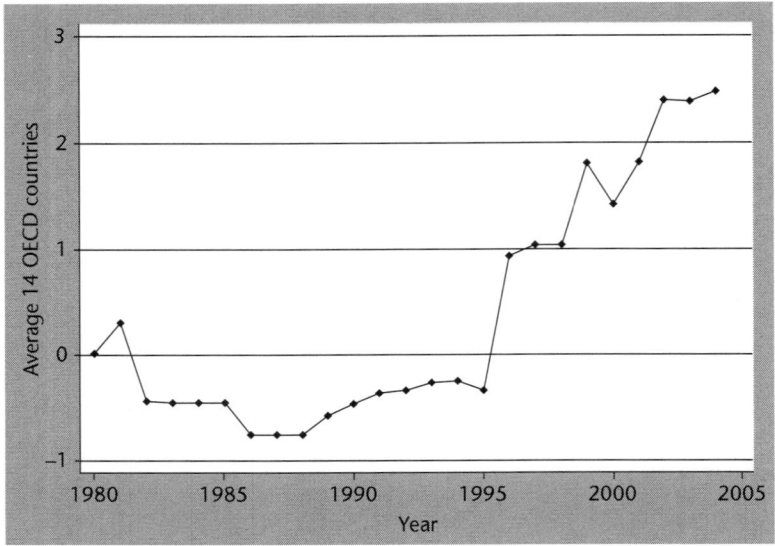

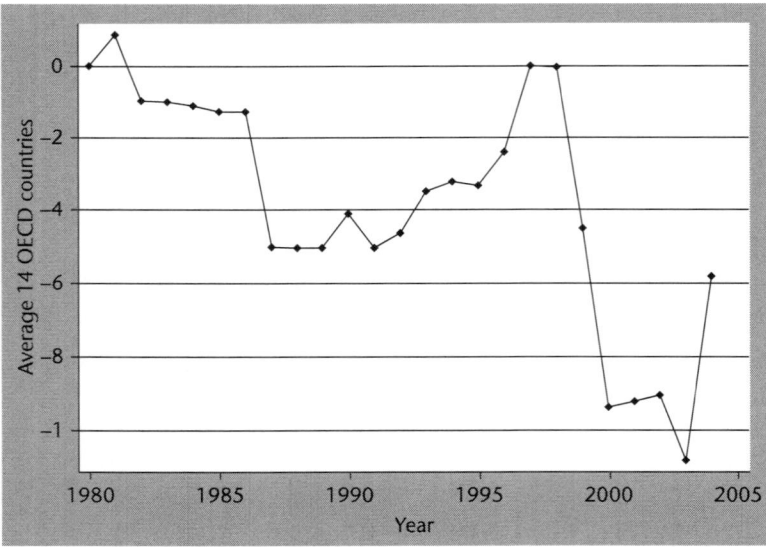

Figure 3.3. Continued

Japan, and Australia in the 1980s and 1990s led the trend of pro-skilled immigration reforms.

The correlation matrix between the six policy variables (reported in Table A3.3) provides a preliminary idea of whether these policies moved together across countries over the considered period (positive correlation). Interestingly, in general there is not a large positive correlation among the variables, indicating that countries did not move uniformly to tighter policies across the board. Countries that tightened their Requirements for Entry, in general did not restricted the access of immigrants to benefits. Similarly, countries that were tougher on undocumented immigrants did not restrict the access of immigrants to benefits. This may indicate that by tightening the entry of documented and undocumented immigrants the receiving countries accepted a selected and smaller group of immigrants (the lucky few) that could be allowed to participate in larger measure to the benefits allowed to the citizens.

3.2.3 *Wage variables*

Harmonized wage data are not available for our panel of countries during the 1980–2005 period. We follow therefore the macro-migration literature (e.g. Hatton, 1995; Mayda and Rodrik 2005; Pederson, et al. 2006) and use the average GDP per person in the country of destination as a measure of the average wage, W_d, in order to implement equation [3.1] empirically. However, to implement regression [3.2] we need a measure of the wage in the receiving country for the representative highly educated (tertiary schooling) and for the representative less educated (primary schooling) individual. To construct these wages we proceed as follows. From the World Income Inequality Database, 2008 (V2.0)[7] we obtain the Gini coefficient for each receiving country. We select only 'high quality' observations (those ranked 1 and 2) from that data set.[8] Then, using the Gini coefficient, the average GDP per person and the assumption of log-normal distribution of income per person in each country and year, one can calculate the income per person at any percentile of the distribution.[9]

---

[7] Available at http://www.wider.unu.edu/research/Database/en_GB/database/.

[8] If there is more than one value per country and year we average them. There are some missing years for some countries that we fill by linear interpolation. We also use the value in the closest (latest or earliest) available year to complete the series backwards (to 1980) and forward (to 2004). This way, the 14 receiving OECD countries have a complete series 1980–2004.

[9] If per capita income y in a country is distributed according to the lognormal distribution then the relationship between the Gini coefficient G and the standard deviation of the lognormal distribution is: $\sigma = \sqrt{2}\Phi^{-1}((G+1)/2)$ where ϕ is the CDF of a Standard Normal distribution (N(0,1)). Then, defining as $Z^x = \phi^{-1}(x)$ the x percentile of the N(0, 1) distribution and as $\bar{y}$ the average per capita income, the income at the x percentile of the distribution is given by the following formula: $y_X = \bar{y}e^{(\sigma Z_x - \sigma^2/2)}$.

We then use the Barro and Lee (2000) data set that provides the share of population, 15 years and older, with primary, secondary, and tertiary education for years 1980, 1985, 1990, 1995, and 2000. We interpolate those data to obtain yearly shares and we extend the 2000 share to 2005. We also assume that the income per person of people in the country correlate exactly with their education. This implies that the bottom part of the income distribution is occupied by individuals with primary education, the intermediate section contains individuals with secondary education, and the top part of the income distribution contains those people with tertiary education. By doing this we identify, for each country and year, at which percentile of the income distribution is the median primary-school-educated and at which percentile is the median tertiary-school-educated. For instance, if the percentage of individuals with primary, secondary, and tertiary schooling in a country are 50 per cent, 30 per cent, and 20 per cent, respectively, we infer that the person at the 25th percentile (from the bottom) is the median primary educated individual, and the person at the 90th percentile of the income distribution is the median tertiary educated. Using the formulas to calculate the individual income at any percentile (described above) we impute the wage of median high- and less-educated person in each receiving country and in each year. Those wages are, respectively, W^H_{dt} and W^L_{dt} that we use in the regressions below. Grogger and Hanson (2008) show in a cross-sectional analysis that the estimates of the wages for high and less skilled are very similar to those derived directly from the percentiles of the wage distribution.

We also calculate the after-tax wage income that may be a more appropriate measure of available income (incentive to migrate) and could differ significantly across countries if the degree of progressivity of the taxes with income is different across countries. To calculate after-tax wage we use the data on the average income tax rate from the OECD Tax Database (2008). Such rates, for each country, are relative to year 2000 and we apply them to the whole period. In particular we apply to the median, primary educated individual the rate for a single worker with no dependents whose earnings are 67 per cent of the average workers' earnings. To the median tertiary-educated worker, we apply the rate for a single worker with no dependents whose earnings are 167 per cent of the average workers' earnings.[10] Tax rates do not vary over time. However the very different degree of progressivity of tax systems across countries interacted with a changing income distribution may produce variation in after tax income. For instance, the average rate on the highly educated group is 35.3 per cent for the USA and 53.5 per cent for Germany.

---

[10] In both cases the tax rate includes income taxes net of benefits plus the employer and employee payroll taxes.

3.2.4 *Other variables*

For the generosity of welfare benefits we use data on welfare spending per person (in thousands of 1995 US $) obtained from Mayda (2007). These data include the welfare spending for elderly and survivors (both in cash and services), the benefits for families (in cash and services), the benefits for injury, illness, and disability and the benefits related to labour market hardship (such as unemployment benefits and active labour market policies).[11]

For the labour market protection in the destination countries we use two measures: the ratio of minimum to median wage (Minimum Wages) and an index measuring the degree of employment protection in the country (Employment Protection Laws) that combines measures of stringency of firing laws, dismissal laws, hiring laws, and unemployment benefits. That index ranges between 0 (minimal protection) and 4 (maximum protection) with a standard deviation across countries around 1. The idea is that higher values of these variables imply stronger protection and bargaining power of employees. Both variables have several missing values and they only cover the period 1980–2000.[12] The variables are from Mayda (2007) who in turn follows the definitions of Elmeskov, Martin, and Scarpetta (1998).

Finally, we consider the amount of intra-mural R&D spending per person (in thousands of 2000 US $) in our estimates, from the OECD-STAN database.

3.3 Regression results

We expect that the effect of wages is positive on total immigration and that the wage skill premium has a positive and significant impact on highly skilled immigrants. At the same time we expect that the variable Pro-skilled, which captures immigration laws which favour highly skilled immigrants relative to others, to have a positive sign, while the Welfare Generosity variable should be more important in attracting less skilled immigrants and hence can shift the selection of immigrants towards the less educated. Similarly, protective labour market institutions should be more relevant to attract less skilled immigrants (hence possibly increasing total inflow but worsening the selection), while R&D intensity should increase the skill intensity of immigrants with no clear effects on total immigration. Using our data and the empirical specifications in [3.1] and [3.2] we set to find out whether these expectations are supported by the analysis. As we are identifying the effects of destination-country variables on immigration flows using the variation over time only,

---

[11] These variables only cover the 1980–2000 period and have some missing values.
[12] Notice the reduced number of observations in Table 3.4.

and as some of these variables moved together or did not change much, there are some issue of collinearity and large standard error when we include many of these variables together. Hence our strategy is to begin with the variables found to be more relevant by the literature (wages, after tax wages, immigration laws) and then include different sets of variables one at a time, keeping those that are significant in most subsequent specifications.

3.3.1 Wages and geography

Table 3.1 shows the coefficient estimates for the basic specification of the total migration equation [3.1] and for the selection equation [3.2].

Specifications (1)–(3) in Table 3.1 report the estimates of the coefficients on average wages in the destination country and on some bilateral characteristics that potentially affect migration costs.[13] The dependent variable is the natural logarithm of the total annual migration flow between country o and country d. The bilateral variables included are a Land-Border dummy, a dummy for sharing the same official language (Language), a dummy for having had colonial relations (Colonial), and the natural logarithm of distance between the two countries.[14]

Specifications (4)–(6) report the estimated wage coefficient for the selection equation as well as the effect of the bilateral characteristics on selection. The dependent variable of this regression is the logarithmic difference in the flow of immigrants with tertiary and those with primary education.

The total immigration specifications confirm the findings in Ortega and Peri (2009). The average wage (income per person) in the destination country is a very important determinant of total migration. An increase of the average wage difference between the destination and the sending country by US $1,000 (in 2000 PPP) would increase the migration flow by about 6 per cent.

Among the geographic and cultural distance variables we find that colonial ties have a positive and significant effect and the logarithm of distance has a negative and significant effect on total immigration, supporting our expectations. The other two variables are not significant, confirming the findings of Ortega and Peri (2009). The estimates obtained using average wage (1), median wage (2), or after tax median wage (3) are rather similar and the coefficient on the wage variable in the total immigration equation is around 0.06.

More interesting, however, for the purposes of this chapter, are the effects of the explanatory variables on the selection of immigrants. While

---

[13] Notice that while the total immigration regression includes the 0 cells the selection regression can be estimated only using the non-zero immigration flows. Hence columns (4)–(6) are estimated on a reduced number of observations relative to columns (1)–(3).

[14] These bilateral data are from Glick and Rose (2002).

Table 3.1. Basic specifications: effects of average wage and wage premia on total immigration and the selection of immigrants, 14 OECD receiving countries, 1980–2005.

Regression:	Total immigration: dependent variable log of total immigrant flows			Selection: dependent variable log difference immigration tertiary–primary education		
Specification:	(1) Average wage	(2) Median wage	(3) After-tax median wage	(4) Wage differential	(5) After-tax wage differentials	(6) After-tax wage differentials, country pair dummies
W_{Ave} destination	0.051** (0.001)	0.063** (0.014)	0.06** (0.012)			
W_{TER}-W_{PRI} destination				0.01** (0.004)	0.025** (0.005)	0.04** (0.02)
Land Border	−1.55 (0.99)	−1.57 (0.97)	−1.57 (0.97)	−0.04 (0.26)	−0.11 (0.27)	n.a.
Language	0.48 (0.53)	0.57 (0.51)	0.56 (0.51)	0.74** (0.19)	0.77** (0.19)	n.a.
Colonial Ties	3.80** (0.54)	3.56** (0.53)	3.55** (0.53)	−0.86** (0.24)	−0.85** (0.24)	n.a.
ln(distance)	−2.21 (0.22)	−2.21** (0.21)	−2.22** (0.21)	0.67** (0.07)	0.58** (0.07)	n.a.
Country-pair dummies	No	No	No	No	No	Yes
Observations	22,662	22,662	22,662	5,486	5,486	5,486

Note: Specification (1)–(3) analyse the determinants of total migration flows. The dependent variable is the log of the bilateral flow of migrants between country i and j. Specification (4)–(6) analyse the determinants of immigrant selection between education levels. The dependent variable is the log difference of the bilateral flows of tertiary educated and primary educated migrants. Observations are weighted by the population of the receiving country. All regressions include a set of (74X25) country-of-origin by year dummies and 14 destination-country effects. Robust standard errors clustered by country-pairs are reported in parentheses. **, * imply significance at the 5%, 10% level.

the wage-premium effect is significant in all specifications, it is significantly larger when we consider after-tax wages. In the specification using after-tax wages and controlling for a full set of country-pair dummies (specification 6) the coefficient is 0.04, implying that an increase in the tertiary–primary premium by US $1,000 (in PPP, 2000) would increase the difference in flows of tertiary relative to primary educated by 4 per cent.

This is not a small effect. For instance, an increase in that premium by US $18,000 (which equals the average increase for the destination countries between 1980 and 2000) would increase the share of the tertiary educated (at a given share of primary educated immigrants) from 30 percentage points to 50 percentage points in the total immigration flows. This corresponds to 72 per cent of the initial value. As the imputation procedure used for wages is likely to introduce a large measurement error, such estimates can have a non-trivial bias down. Hence the effect of the skill-premium on selection could be even larger.

The other specifications find a smaller effect (between 1 and 2 per cent increase for each increase in the skill-premium by US $1,000). The estimated coefficient on the wage premium is in general smaller than the estimated wage coefficient for the total migration regression. This may be due to some attenuation bias in the selection equation. As we are taking differences between two imputed wages both the imputation mechanism, as well as the difference between wages, certainly add measurement error to the wage premium. We also confirm the findings of Grogger and Hanson (2008) that the after-tax wage differentials (specifications 5 and 6) have a more significant coefficient than the pre-tax differential (specification 4) in explaining selection.

The coefficients on the geographic variables should be interpreted as the differential effect on the flow of highly educated, relative to the flow of less educated immigrants. Hence a positive coefficient implies an increase in the relative selection of highly educated. First, sharing the same language significantly increases the selection of the highly educated among immigrants, while the presence of colonial ties significantly decreases it. These results make sense as highly educated immigrants are usually employed in occupations where knowledge of the local language is important while the less educated work in more manual and physical types of jobs. Hence language differences are more costly for highly than for less educated migrants. This may be one important reason why English-speaking countries are very attractive to highly educated migrants. At the same time colonial ties may be linked to preferential immigration policies towards the less educated. Distance is positively related to selection, as on average the highly educated tend to migrate to farther countries because of their better knowledge of career opportunities and international professional networks. Finally sharing a land border has no significant additional effect on the selection of migrants, once we account for the distance effect.

It is also interesting to comment on the estimates of the fixed receiving-country effects, obtained when estimating specifications (1) and (4) in Table 3.1. Those fixed effects (estimated relative to Australia whose dummy is set to 0) are reported in Table A3.4. Column 1 reports the effect on total flows that capture the time-invariant ability of a country to attract immigrants (once we control for wage differential, geography, and sending-country characteristics). We notice that the Anglo-Saxon off-springs (Australia, Canada, and the USA) have the largest values. The coefficient of Canada is not significantly different from Australia (0) and the one of the USA is the only one that is significantly positive. Conversely, all the EU countries have a significantly negative fixed effect, which is largest for Luxembourg. In part this is a scale effect (as the attraction of immigrant increases with size); in part it is probably due to an overall more open policy and attitude towards immigrants in Australia, Canada, and the USA relative to Europe. The second column of coefficients in Table A3.4 identifies the specific country-effect in selecting highly educated immigrants. The countries that have the largest fixed-effect in attracting skilled immigrants are the USA, Australia, and Canada. For the first country this effect (on top of the wage-premium) can be due to its R&D and high-tech intensive sectors that employ many foreign scientist and engineers. On the other hand, Canada and Australia have immigration laws that are very pro-skilled which may explain part of their specificity.

3.3.2 Immigration laws

In the next step we analyse the effects of different legal immigration policies on total migration and on the selection of highly educated immigrants. Table 3.2 reports the estimates of the coefficients in equations [3.1] and [3.2] once we include the six variables capturing different features of the immigration laws. Specifications (1) and (2) include all the immigration-law variables while specifications (3) and (4) only include those that turn out to be statistically significant. As usual in each regression (both for total immigration and selection) we include a full set of country-of-origin by year dummies to capture all the push-factors and their differential impact on more and less educated migrants and 14 destination-country dummies. Looking at the impact of laws on the total inflow of immigrants we find that most of them have the expected qualitative effect but not all of them are significant. Requirements for Entry, Requirements for Residence, and Undocumented do not have much of an impact on total immigration flows (or on its skill intensity). The first two variables capture some procedural features that may not much affect the cost of migrating. The last variable may discourage

Table 3.2. Effect of immigration laws on total immigration and selection by education.

Dependent variable:	All immigration laws		Only statistically significant laws	
	(1) Total immigration	(2) Selection	(3) Total immigration	(4) Selection
W_{Ave} destination	0.054** (0.020)		0.051** (0.019)	
$(W_{TER}-W_{PRI})$ destination, after tax		0.015* (0.004)		0.016** (0.005)
Requirements for Entry	0.01 (0.03)	-0.01 (0.03)		
Requirements for Residence	-0.04 (0.05)	-0.01 (0.03)		
Restrictions from Benefits	-0.07** (0.03)	0.08** (0.02)	-0.08** (0.03)	0.08** (0.03)
Asylum	-0.09** (0.04)	0.02 (0.02)	-0.09** (0.04)	
Undocumented	-0.02 (0.02)	-0.02 (0.02)		
Pro-skilled	-0.08 (0.05)	0.11** (0.02)		0.12** (0.02)
Bilateral Controls	Yes	Yes	Yes	Yes
Observations	22,662	5419	22,662	5419

Note: Specification (1) and (3) analyse the determinants of total migration flows. The dependent variable is the log of the bilateral flow of migrants between country i and j. Specification (2) and (4) analyse the determinants of immigrant selection between education levels. The dependent variable is the log difference of the bilateral flows of tertiary educated and primary educated migrants. The explanatory variables are lagged one year. Observations are weighted by the population of the receiving country. All regressions include a set of (74X25) country-of-origin by year dummies and 14 destination-country dummies. Robust standard errors clustered by country-pairs are reported in parentheses. **, * imply significance at the 5, 10% level.

undocumented immigration. Since we focus on legal immigration, this variable may have little effect on documented immigration flows.

To the contrary, a significantly negative impact is associated with Restriction from Benefits and Asylum. These two variables may signal more substantially the policy stance of a country towards immigration. In particular, restricting the access of benefits to immigrants and imposing some extra requirements (of registration and limited mobility) may imply less favourable conditions for them and long-term costs that discourage their inflow. Moreover a tough stance on political refugee (asylum), as it has a large international visibility, may strongly signal the policy stance of the receiving country on immigrants in general. The provisions restricting access of immigrants to benefits may be more likely to affect immigrants in the low-income range (primary educated). The positive and highly significant coefficient on the Restriction from Benefits variable in the selection equation confirms this expectation strongly. Reducing the access to benefits significantly changes the composition of immigrants towards more tertiary educated individuals.

The only other immigration law that has a significant impact on the selection of immigrants is the Pro-skilled variable which explicitly captures immigration policies favouring immigration of highly educated. On average, passing a Pro-skilled law resulted in the increase of the share of highly educated relatively to less educated immigrants by 12 per cent (for instance from 30 to 33 per cent of the total).

Laws increasing the tightness of entry, of residence requirements, the tightness of procedures to obtain asylum, and tightness towards the undocumented do not seem to have much of an effect on the selection of immigrants. Again, these laws may be affecting procedures for immigration but not altering the substantial cost of immigration for potential migrants. On the contrary, Restriction from Benefits may have a strong real (and perceived) effect in discouraging less educated immigrants, hence resulting in a negative overall effect and a positive selection effect.

All in all, in terms of the immigration of highly educated we can say that Pro-skilled immigration laws seem to have a noticeable positive impact on their inflow and laws restricting the benefits of immigrants also promote selection of highly educated. These last types of restrictions, however, also discourage total immigration so that the actual volume of highly educated immigrants may not increase.

3.3.3 *Welfare generosity*

A very common worry, especially in Europe where the generosity of the welfare state is greater than in the USA, is that immigrants are attracted by larger welfare transfers. Moreover, among them, less educated immigrants should be more subject to the attraction of a generous welfare state. We check here whether these claims are founded.

We first enter, in equations [3.1] and [3.2], the variable 'welfare spending per person' as the total of all its component specifications (1) to (4) and then we enter separately four components, divided into 'old age benefits', 'family-related benefits', 'disability and injury benefits', and 'labour market related benefits'. Our goal is to analyse the impact of such spending on the total immigration and on the selection, controlling or not for immigration laws.

Column (1) and (2) in Table 3.3 identify the effect of welfare spending on total immigration (+ 0.77) and on the selection (−0.20). Both effects are significant, implying that more welfare spending attracts larger flows of immigrants and a larger share of the less educated. While the effect on total flows is robust to the inclusion of immigration laws, the selection effect is not. It disappears (coefficient of −0.02 with a standard error of 0.08) when we control for the significant legal immigration variables. This implies that welfare generosity is generally not associated with countries which have pro-skilled immigration laws in place.

When we decompose the welfare spending into its categories we see that the unemployment/labour market spending and the old age welfare spending are the most relevant variables for increasing immigration (as well as increasing the share of the less educated). Protection against labour market uncertainty and for old age may thus be particularly valuable to immigrants and may reduce some of the costs associated with residing aboard. Notice also that the inclusion of welfare variables does not decrease (possibly it increases) the importance of average wages in affecting total immigration and the selection of immigrants.

3.3.4 *Labour market institutions*

Table 3.4 presents our findings on how labour market institutions and employment protection in the receiving country affect total immigration and its composition. We analyse the impact of labour market protection on total immigration and on its selection by estimating the usual specifications [3.1] and [3.2] including, alternatively, only the labour market laws (specification 1 and 2), those laws and average welfare spending per person (specifications 3–4), and those two sets of variables plus immigration laws (in specifications 5–6 that do not report, however, the coefficient on immigration laws). Recall that we use two measures for labour market protection, the ratio of the minimum to the median wage (minimum wage) and the tightness of the employment protection legislation (employment protection laws).

Interestingly enough, the results show that stronger labour market protection (high minimum wage and high value of the index for employment

Table 3.3. Effect of welfare generosity on total immigration and selection by education.

	Total welfare spending		Controlling for immigration laws		Welfare spending by category	
	(1) Total immigration	(2) Selection	(3) Total immigration	(4) Selection	(5) Total immigration	(6) Selection
W_{Ave} destination	0.09** (0.02)		0.09** (0.02)		0.08* (0.03)	
(W_{TER}-W_{PRI}) destination, after tax		0.03** (0.008)		0.02** (0.008)		0.02** (0.007)
Welfare spending per person	0.77** (0.26)	-0.20** (0.08)	0.73** (0.16)	-0.02 (0.08)		
Old age spending per person					0.98** (0.37)	-0.67** (0.15)
Unemployment/labour market spending per person					0.83* (0.46)	-0.89** (0.18)
Spending for family welfare per person					-0.06 (0.34)	0.16 (0.17)
Spending for disability per person					0.60 (0.68)	0.24 (0.34)
Bilateral controls	Yes	Yes	Yes	Yes	Yes	Yes
Observations	8662	5419	8662	5419	8662	5419

Note: Specifications denoted with 'Total' report the effect of the variables on the log of total bilateral flows. Specifications denoted as 'Selection' report the effects of the variables on the logarithmic difference of immigrant flows of tertiary and primary educated. Welfare spending is in 1995 PPP US dollars. The source of the data is OECD (2001). Observations are weighted by the population of the receiving country. All regressions include a set of (74X25) country-of-origin by year dummies and 14 receiving-country dummies. Robust standard errors clustered by country-pairs are reported in parentheses. **, * imply significance at the 5, 10% level.

Table 3.4. Effect of labour market regulation on total immigration and selection by education.

	Labour market laws		Labour market laws and welfare		Controlling for immigration laws	
	(1) Total immigration	(2) Selection	(3) Total immigration	(4) Selection	(5) Total immigration	(6) Selection
W_{Ave} destination	0.08**(0.02)		0.09**(0.02)		0.08(0.03)	
$(W_{TER}-W_{PRI})$ destination after tax		0.02*(0.006)		0.01(0.006)		0.01(0.07)
Minimum wages	−4.33**(1.09)	0.88(0.75)	−3.55**(1.10)	1.44**(0.65)	−2.88**(1.40)	1.64**(0.69)
Employment protection laws	−0.36*(0.20)	−0.57**(0.07)	0.47(0.41)	−0.55**(0.08)	0.10(0.33)	−0.54**(0.09)
Welfare spending per person			0.42(0.31)	−0.08(0.09)	0.41(0.31)	−0.08(0.09)
Bilateral controls	Yes	Yes	Yes	Yes	Yes	Yes
Observations	6544	2376	6486	1689	6387	1689

Note: Specifications denoted with 'Total' report the effect of the variables on the log of total bilateral flows. Specifications denoted as 'Selection' report the effects of the variables on the logarithmic difference of immigrant flows of tertiary and primary educated. The variable 'Minimum Wage' is the ration of the minimum wage to the median wage in the receiving country for each year. The variable 'Employment Protection Laws' is an index that captures the extent of pro-employee provisions in the labour market laws, including how hard it is to fire or dismiss a worker and how generous the unemployment system is. The source of the data is Mayda (2007). Observations are weighted by the population of the receiving country. All regressions include a set of (74X25) country-of-origin by year dummies and 14 country of destination dummies. Robust standard errors clustered by country-pairs are reported in parentheses. **, * imply significance at the 5, 10% level.

protection) are associated with lower immigration flows when those variables are included by themselves. Employment protection laws also show a negative impact on the selection by education, while that of the minimum wage is insignificant. Wage levels still have the usual very significant effect. Countries that increased the protection of insiders in labour markets (with higher minimum wage or more protective laws) are likely to provide worse employment opportunities to immigrants than countries with less protective and more competitive markets, hence the negative effect on total flows. At the same time, stronger employment protection may be relatively more important for the less educated, hence the negative selection effect of this variable. The effects of labour market institutions, however, are not very robust. Including the welfare spending as a control eliminates the effect of employment protection laws on total immigration, while the minimum wage variable becomes positive and significant in the selection equation. Controlling for immigration laws further reduces the effect of labour market institutions on total immigration.

Overall, however, we estimate a significant negative effect of minimum wage on total immigration in all regressions and a negative selection effect of employment protection laws. The qualitative result emerging from these coefficients is that stronger bargaining power of labour in the receiving country discourages immigration and at the same time makes the share of the less educated among immigrants larger.

3.3.5 R&D spending

Finally, we enquire into the effect of research expenditures in the receiving country on the selection of immigrants. As many occupations that employ highly educated workers are in the high-tech sectors, and research and development in recent decades has produced innovations that are 'skill-biased' we expect countries with large R&D spending to produce more opportunities and provide more jobs for highly educated immigrants. While part of the skilled-biased nature of technology in a country is captured by the wage premium (always controlled for in the selection equation), R&D spending may directly generate scientists and engineering type jobs or endow them with better conditions and resources. For instance, the world-class quality of many universities and laboratories in the US and UK have been for a long time an extremely strong factor for attracting international talent. R&D resources may generate incentive for talented individuals to immigrate and create jobs that employ more of them.

Hence, we include in our basic regressions the amount of intra-mural R&D spending per person (in thousands of 2,000 US dollars) and we estimate its effect on total immigration and selection. Specifications (1) and (2) of Table 3.5 show that higher R&D spending is associated with lower total

Table 3.5. Effect of R&D intensity on total immigration and selection by education.

	Including R&D spending per person		Controlling for immigration laws	
	(1) Total immigration	(2) Selection	(5) Total immigration	(6) Selection
W_{Ave} destination	0.07** (0.02)		0.07** (0.02)	
$(W_{TER}-W_{PRI})$ destination		0.03** (0.005)		0.01 (0.006)
R&D spending per person	-2.43** (0.83)	1.29** (0.33)	-2.33** (0.86)	0.23 (0.35)
Tightness of access to benefits for immigrants			-0.03 (0.04)	0.05 (0.04)
Tightness of asylum			-0.11** (0.04)	
Pro-skilled preference				0.19** (0.02)
Bilateral controls	Yes	Yes	Yes	Yes
Observations	20,335	5320	20,335	5320

Note: Specifications denoted with 'Total' report the effect of the variables on the log of total bilateral flows. Specifications denoted as 'Selection' report the effects of the variables on the logarithmic difference of immigrant flows of tertiary and primary educated. The variable R&D spending per person is in 2000 PPP US Dollars. The source of the R&D data is OECD STAN database. Observations are weighted by the population of the receiving country. All regressions include a set of (74X25) country-of-origin by year dummies. Robust standard errors clustered by country-pairs are reported in parentheses. **, * imply significance at the 5, 10% level.

immigration and stronger selection of the highly educated. The effect on selection is very large: increasing R&D per person by US $100 would increase the share of immigrants with tertiary education (given the share with primary education) by 12.9 per cent of its initial value. This effect, however, is not robust to the inclusion of the immigration legislation. The effect of the pro-skilled immigration laws ends up absorbing most of the effect of R&D spending per person such that the R&D variable becomes insignificant in specification (4). This may signal that those countries with higher research spending have also been more aggressive in pursuing pro-skilled immigration policies, so that once we control for the second, the first variable is not very significant. Interestingly enough, the negative effect of R&D spending on total immigration stays significant even after controlling for immigration laws.

3.4 Discussion and conclusions

Our exploration into the determinants of the international flows of highly educated migrants has been pursued by way of estimating a total immigration equation and a selection equation. The panel structure of our data set enabled us to employ a full set of country of origin by year effects which absorb time and sending-country-specific factors as well as receiving-country fixed effects. Our analysis of a rich set of explanatory variables allowed us to make some progress in the important determinant of total flows and selection of immigrants in destination countries. On the other hand the aggregate nature of the data, the need to impute wages in the destination country and the imperfect measures of migratory flows that do not include undocumented immigrants and return migration imply that our results should be taken with a grain of salt. In particular measurement error of different kinds can induce biases in the estimates. While we have provided several specifications and robustness checks the possibility of lingering biases still exists.

We find that the average after-tax wage difference between the receiving and the sending country heavily affects the overall scale of migration, while the after-tax wage premium for the tertiary educated is quantitatively the main economic determinant for the selection of highly educated individuals. An increase of the skill premium for tertiary education by US $10,000 increases the share of tertiary educated immigrants between 20 and 40 per cent of its initial value.

Moreover we find consistently that the changes in the immigration legislation which favour high-skilled immigrants relative to less educated ones are among the most important and robust correlates which affect the positive selection of immigrants. Interestingly enough, we also find that laws limiting the access of immigrants to welfare benefits and increasing the restrictions for residence permits or the requirements for political asylum are associated with lower immigration, in particular of the less educated, producing a smaller total inflow of immigrants and a stronger selection bias of the immigrant population towards the highly educated.

We then directed our attention to three types of variables that may have an important impact on the selection of high-skilled immigrants: the generosity of welfare benefits, the degree of employment protection and labour market regulation, and the intensity of R&D spending in receiving countries. On the one hand, we find some evidence that more generous welfare transfers increase the number of total immigrants and increase the share of less educated among them. This would be consistent with the idea that some of the less educated immigrants are attracted by the generous welfare transfers of some receiving economies but the more educated are not. On the other hand, higher labour market protection reduces immigrants overall and has only a mixed impact on immigrant selection. Both effects, moreover, are not very robust. In particular, they tend to disappear if we include the immigration law variables into the regressions. Finally, countries with higher R&D spending per person attract more highly educated immigrants. Throughout the analysis, the average wage (in determining total immigration) and the wage premium (in determining the selection) have a positive and significant effect.

Thus, we can conclude that the after-tax wage premium and immigration policies which favour highly skilled immigrants relative to others seem to be strongly correlated with the share of highly skilled individuals in the immigrant population. This turned out to be robust in many specifications of our estimation model. Less robust are the findings with respect to the generosity of the welfare benefits, the level of the minimum wage and of employment protection, as well as the level of R&D spending, although they seem to affect the skill-selection of the immigrant population also in the expected ways.

Due to the aggregate nature of the data and to the possibility of omitted variable bias one would want to interpret our results with caution. However, the effects of wages, of the education premium, and of immigration laws, as they confirm our priors, have a reasonable magnitude, are quite robust, and may truly reveal a causal effect on immigration flows.

Annex 3.1 Optimization model behind the estimated migration equations

The theoretical framework underlying the estimated equations [3.1] and [3.2] includes heterogeneous agents who derive migration decisions across multiple destinations from a static optimization problem. Potential migrants choose a destination country in order to maximize their utility net of migration costs.

First, from the decision of an average (representative) agent who maximizes his or her utility across multiple destinations, we derive a scale equation for the total migration flows. Second, applying the same framework to two agents with different levels of education (high and low), we derive a selection equation, which explains the size of the flows of immigrants with tertiary education relative to those with primary education. The latter equation enables us to analyse the impact of economic and .institutional variables on the skill selectivity of migration flows, which is the main purpose of this chapter.

Consider an average agent i who lives in the origin country $o \in O = \{1,...,O\}$ and decides whether to stay in o or to migrate to any of $d \in D = \{1,...,D\}$ potential destination countries. The utility from a given destination d depends on the migrant's expected permanent value of labour income in that country and on the costs associated with migrating to d. Specifically, individual i's utility (net of costs) associated with migrating from country of origin o to country d is given by:

$$U_{odt} = \delta_{od} - v_{odi} = f(W_d) - g(C_{od}) - v_{odi,} \qquad [3A.1]$$

where δ_{od} is a country-pair-specific term, capturing migration benefits and migration costs and shared by all individuals migrating from the same origin to the same destination, and v_{odi} is an individual-specific cost term. The term δ_{od}, in turn, is assumed to be an increasing function f of permanent expected earnings, W_d, assumed to be identical for any individual who moves to country d^{15}, and a function g of costs of migration, C_{od}, which may include destination-specific terms and bilateral costs that vary by country pair and also are common among individuals.

Equation [3A.1] is based on the assumption that the benefits and costs of migration are separable. We also assume that the average expected income in the country of destination W_d can be approximated by the GDP per capita in the country of destination. We explicitly allow migration costs to depend on specific destination-country factors ϑ_d (such as immigration laws), and on specific bilateral country factors X_{od} (such as geographical or cultural distance).

Without loss of generality, we normalize the average expected utility from not migrating (staying in o)—which equals $f(W_o)$—to zero. Obviously, migration costs are zero for individuals who choose to stay in the country of origin. Similar to Grogger and Hanson (2008) and Ortega and Peri (2009), we assume that the functions f and g are (approximately) linear and increasing. Hence, we can rewrite equation [3A.1] as:

---

[15] Such an assumption rules out the possibility of selection of immigrants based on unobservable characteristics and, while common in the literature, may induce error or bias.

$$U_{odi} = f_1 W_d - g_1 \vartheta - g_2 X_{od} - v_{odi}, \qquad [3A.2]$$

where f_1, g_1, and g_2 are positive constants.

The idiosyncratic term v_{odi} captures any individual, unobservable characteristic that affects costs and hence is important to migration decisions. Under the assumption that v_{odi} are independent identically distributed random shocks following an i.i.d. extreme value distribution, the migration problem considered resembles exactly the standard discrete choice Logit model discussed in McFadden (1974). In particular such a model implies that the utility (net of costs) associated with migration decisions is equal to the logarithm of the proportion (probability) of individuals that migrate to each destination, relative to those who stay in the country of origin. Namely,

$$\ln s_{od} - \ln s_{oo} = f_1 W_d - g_1 \vartheta_d - g_2 X_{od}, \qquad [3A.3]$$

where $s_{od} = n_{od}/n_o$ (is the proportion of people born in o who migrate to $d - n_{od}$ – in the total population born in o, denoted as n_o), while s_{oo} is the share of those who stay in o (n_{oo}) among all those born in o. Note that if we do not normalize the utility from staying at home to zero, we would have instead of equation [3A.3]

$$\ln s_{od} - \ln s_{oo} = f_1 W_d - f_2 W_0 - g_1 \vartheta_d - g_2 X_{od}, \qquad [3A.3']$$

Since we are interested in the role of destination-country determinants, we keep our normalization such that the coefficient f_1 measures the effect of an increase in the gap of expected wages between the origin-destination pair of countries, keeping the wage in the country of origin fixed.

We substitute the definition of the shares into equation [3.3] and solve for $\ln n_{od}$, that is the logarithm of the migrants which move from o to d, and note that the population which stays in the country of origin, n_{oo}, as well as the wage in the country of origin, W_o, are constant across all destinations d and hence can be subsumed into a country of origin effect. This enables us to rearrange [3A.3] into

$$\ln n_{od} = D_o + f_1 W_d - g_1 \vartheta_d - g_2 X_{od}, \qquad [3A.4]$$

where the D_o is a set of fixed effects that collects all terms that do not vary by destination d (in equation [3A.3'] they include $f_2 W_o$ and $\ln s_{oo}$). *Adding the time dimension and assuming that the cost ϑ_d depends on bilateral invariant characteristics and on time-varying ones such as policies, immigration laws, and economic conditions we obtain equation [3.1] in the text.*

Annex Figures and Tables

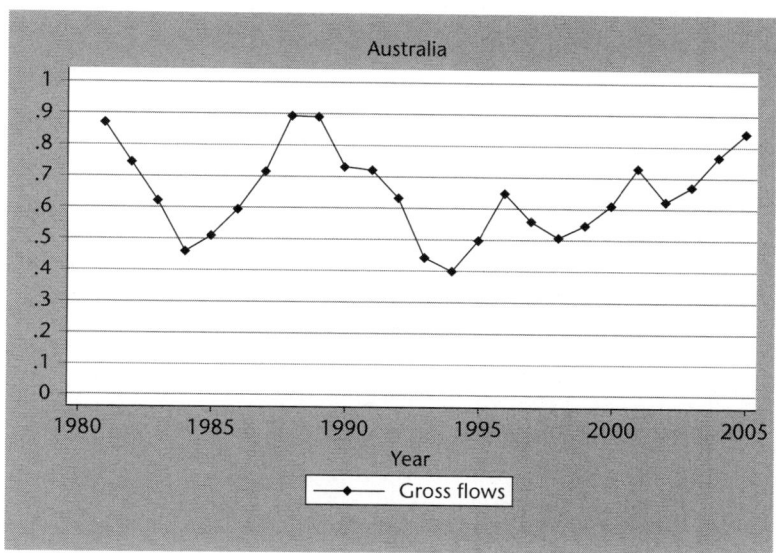

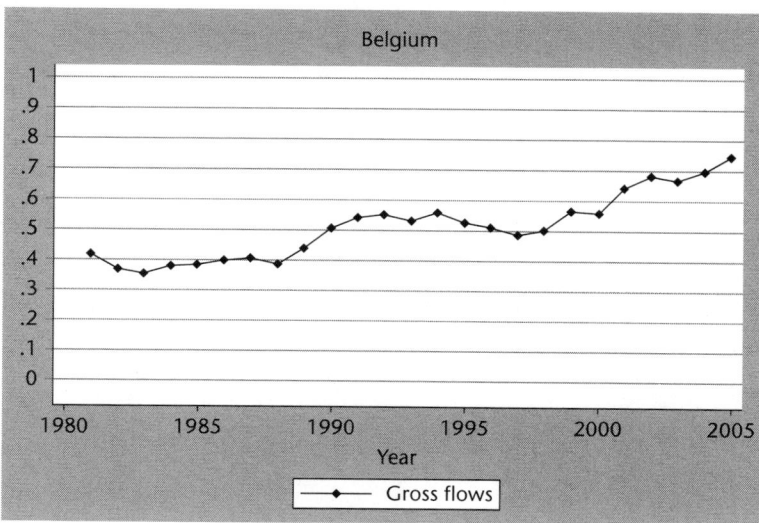

Figure A3.1. Immigration rates 1980–2005.

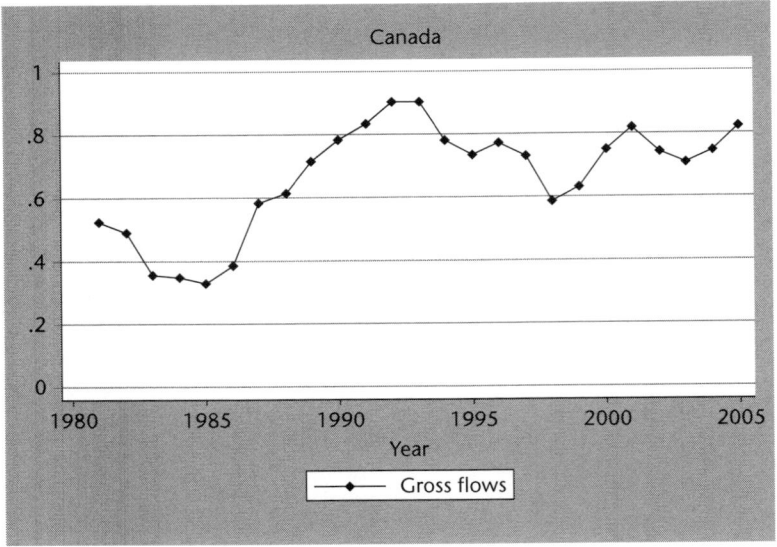

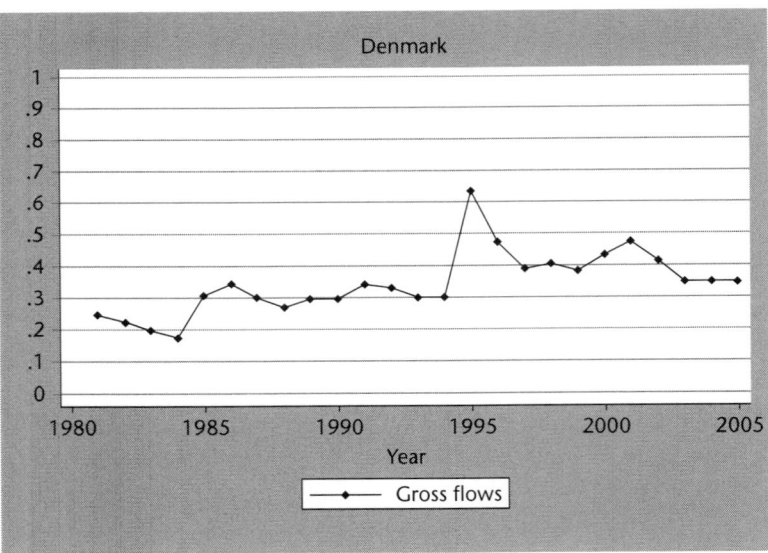

Figure A3.1. Continued

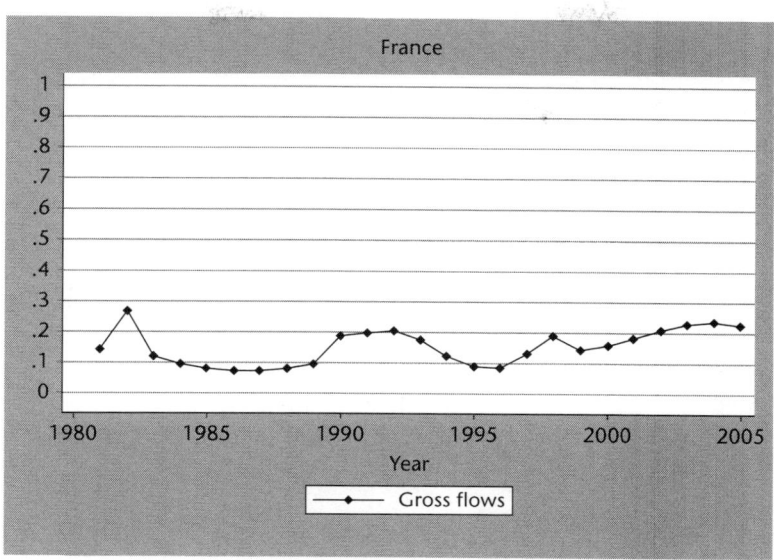

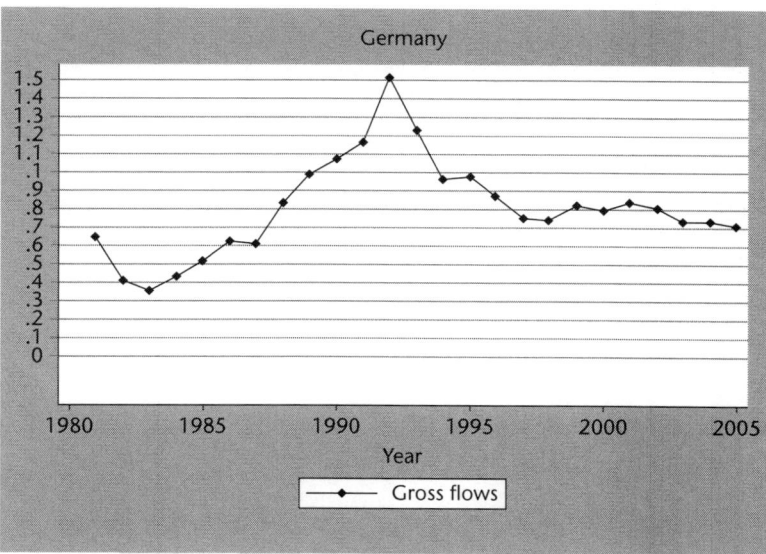

Figure A3.1. Continued

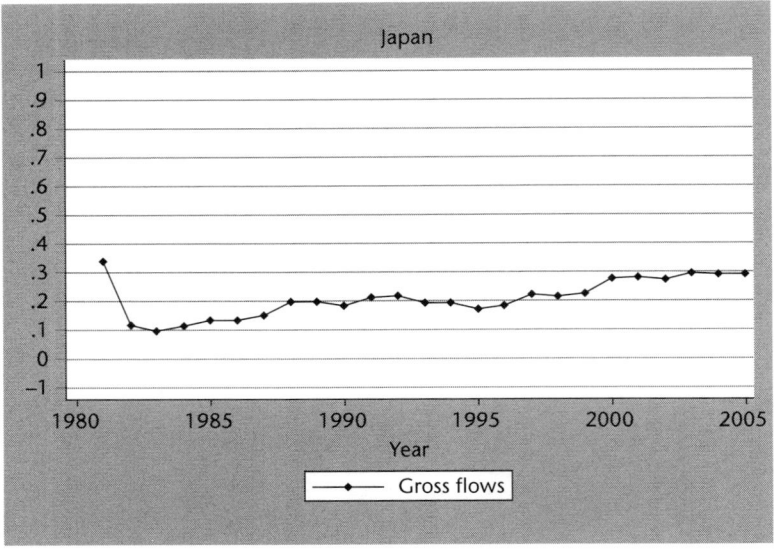

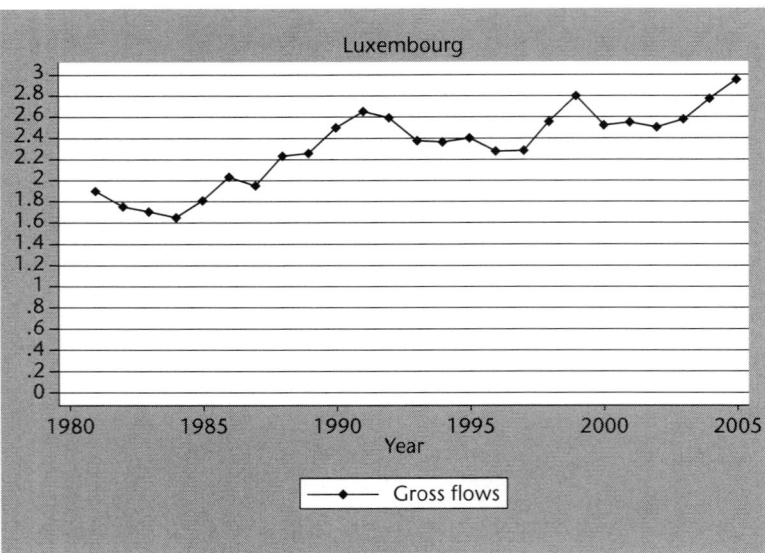

Figure A3.1. Continued

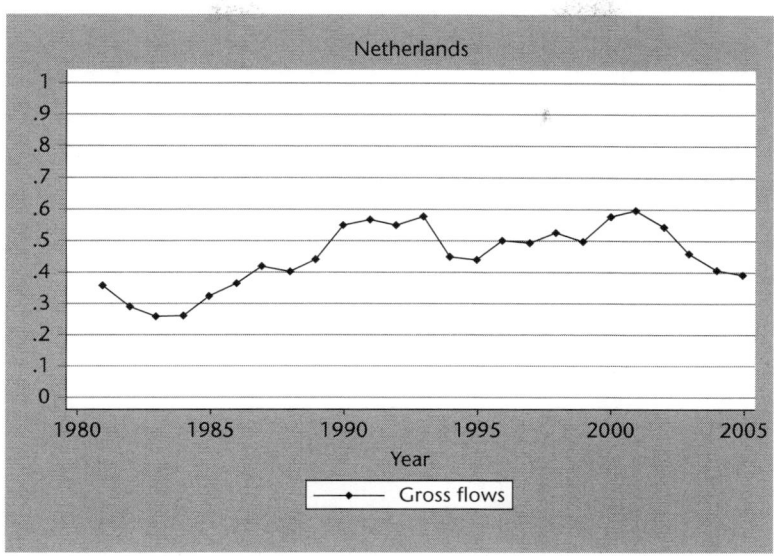

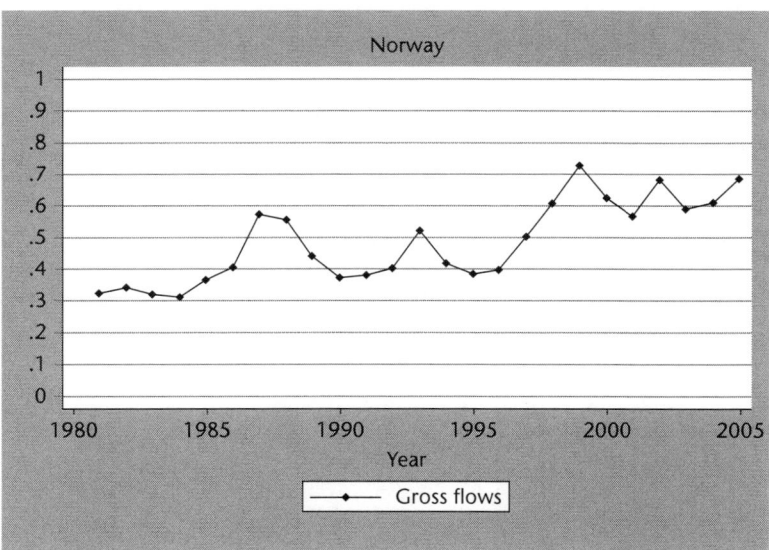

Figure A3.1. Continued

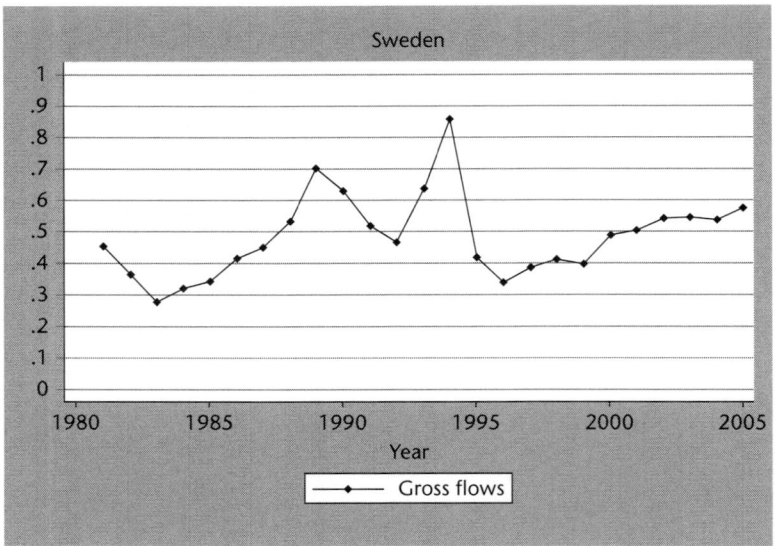

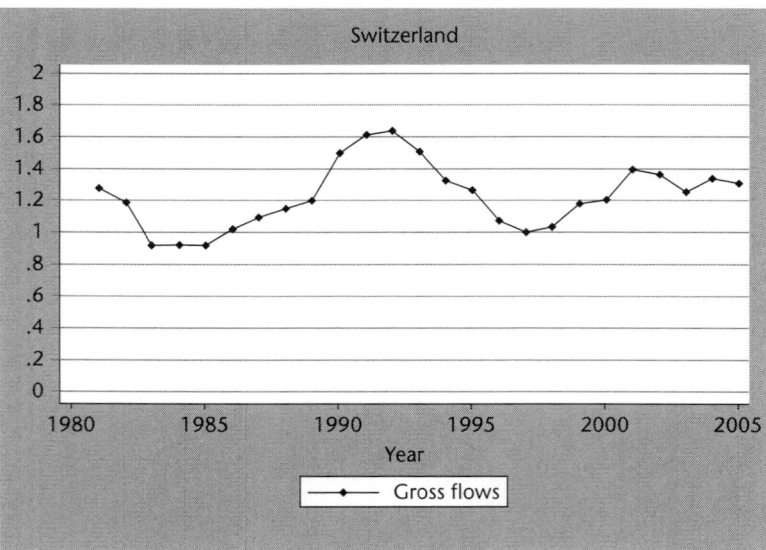

Figure A3.1. Continued

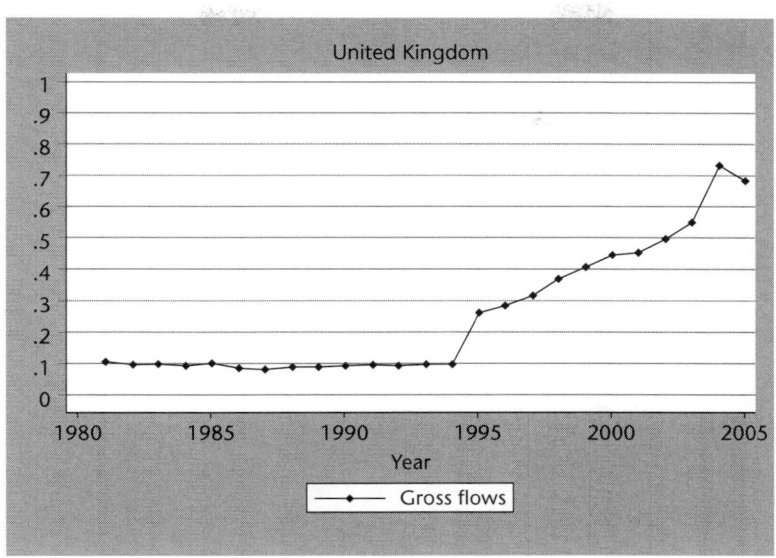

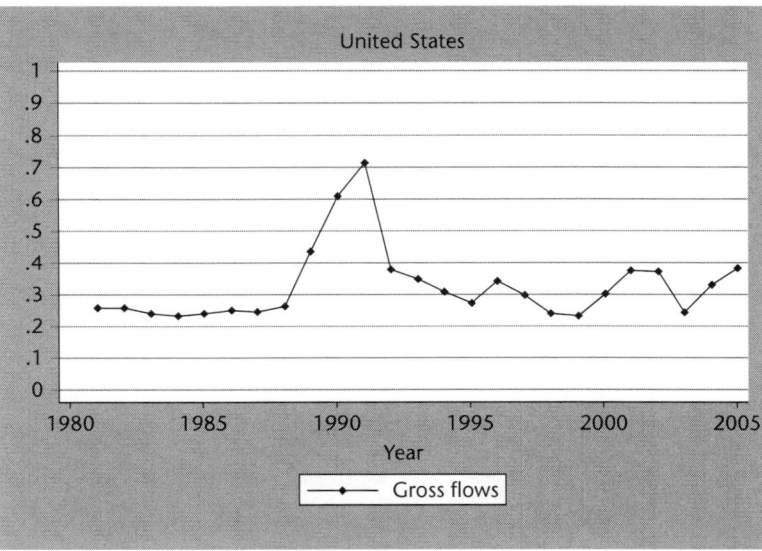

Figure A3.1. Continued

Table A3.1. List of the countries of origin of migrants for the bilateral migration data.

Countries of origin		
Algeria	Ghana	Nigeria
Australia	Greece	Norway
Austria	Guatemala	Pakistan
Bangladesh	Guyana	Peru
Belgium	Haiti	Philippines
Bosnia-Herzegovina	Honduras	Poland
Brazil	Hong Kong	Portugal
Bulgaria	Hungary	Romania
Cambodia	Iceland	Russian Federation
Canada	India	Slovenia
Chile	Iran	Somalia
China	Iraq	South Africa
Colombia	Ireland	South Korea
Croatia	Italy	Spain
Cuba	Jamaica	Sri Lanka
Cyprus	Japan	Suriname
Denmark	Kenya	Sweden
Dominican Republic	Laos	Thailand
Ecuador	Lebanon	Tunisia
El Salvador	Malaysia	Turkey
Ethiopia	Mexico	UK
Fiji	Morocco	USA
Finland	Netherlands	Vietnam
France	New Zealand	Zaire
Germany	Nicaragua	

Table A3.2. Percentage of immigrants with tertiary education, 14 OECD countries 1985, 1995, and 2005.

Country	1985	1995	2004
Australia	49%	52%	58%
Belgium	5%	19%	23%
Canada	54%	61%	63%
Denmark	12%	17%	22%
France	6%	21%	19%
Germany	6%	22%	29%
Japan	38%	36%	33%
Luxembourg	21%	20%	22%
Netherlands	17%	17%	24%
Norway	24%	25%	29%
Sweden	19%	23%	30%
Switzerland	16%	21%	25%
UK	25%	35%	42%
USA	44%	44%	44%

Note: The percentage of immigrant with at least some tertiary education is calculated by imputing to each inflow of migrants from a specific country of origin the educational composition of the stock of migrants in the receiving country from that country of origin. The original data on the education of the stock of immigrants in 1990 and 2000 is from Docquier (2007) and the data on the total inflow of immigrants for each origin-destination pair by year are from the OECD International Migration Database.

Table A3.3. Correlation matrix for the immigration laws (14 countries, 1980–2005).

	Requirements for Entry	Requirements for Residence	Restrictions from Benefits	Undocumented	Asylum
Requirements for Residence	−0.15				
Restrictions from Benefits	−0.44	−0.06			
Undocumented	0.29	−0.22	−0.43		
Asylum	0.24	0.05	−0.27	0.13	
Pro-skilled	−0.27	−0.20	0.32	−0.05	−0.20

Note: Each immigration law variable is standardized to be 0 in each receiving country in 1980.

Table A3.4. Country-specific effects in attracting immigrants and in selecting highly educated.

Country	Estimated fixed effect in the total immigration equation	Estimated fixed effect in the immigrant selection equation
Australia	0 (0)	0 (0)
Belgium	−2.77** (0.55)	−2.38** (0.54)
Canada	−0.49 (0.48)	−0.52 (0.47)
Denmark	−2.57** (0.48)	−2.67** (0.49)
France	−3.09** (0.54)	−2.86** (0.54)
Germany	−2.26** (0.55)	−2.25** (0.55)
Japan	−0.80 (0.50)	−1.02* (0.49)
Luxembourg	−6.70** (1.02)	−4.31** (0.78)
Netherlands	−2.32** (0.53)	−2.17** (0.52)
Norway	−2.90* (0.56)	−2.48** (0.52)
Sweden	−1.74** (0.54)	−1.87* (0.55)
Switzerland	−3.50** (0.57)	−3.44** (0.56)
UK	−1.74** (0.53)	−1.95** (0.53)
USA	1.15** (0.50)	1.72* (0.44)

Note: The reported estimates and t-statistics are the fixed destination-country effects obtained from estimating equation in specification (1) of Table 3.1 and specification (4) in Table 3.1. The values are relative to the estimated fixed effect for Australia (set equal to 0). *, **, significant at the 5%, 1% Level

105

4

The Effects of Brain Gain on Growth, Investment, and Employment: Evidence from OECD Countries, 1980–2005

Chapter 3 provided evidence that selective immigration policies are effective in influencing the skill composition of incoming migration flows, while Chapter 1 showed that the adoption of these kind of policies has been, to date, the exception rather than the rule among OECD countries. The limited adoption of this effective policy tool represents a puzzle, given the widespread perception that an improved skill composition of the immigrant population can bring additional economic benefits for recipient countries.

This chapter examines the impact of the immigration of highly educated workers on employment, productivity, and capital accumulation in the recipient countries, to see whether the presumed positive impact of highly educated immigrants is actually confirmed by aggregate data analysis. Building on Ortega and Peri (2009)[1] we use a production function framework to identify the migration effects in a cross-country setting. Our approach is based on the idea that the aggregate production function of the destination country (and hence its income per person) is influenced by the inflow of immigrants and by their skill mix in at least three ways. First, immigrants increase the total labour supply and may at the same time either crowd out some natives or attract them into employment, if they provide complementary skills to those of the natives and stimulate specialization. Hence, we first estimate the total impact of immigrants on employment. Second, they may trigger higher investment as the marginal product of physical capital increases due to the increase in the labour supply. Moreover, as highly educated immigrants may

[1] We thank Francesc Ortega for allowing us access and use of the data on labour inputs, capital, and productivity that are used in the empirical analysis of this chapter.

work in more capital-intensive sectors, or may use capital-complementary techniques, the composition of immigrants by skills may have an impact on capital intensity and on capital accumulation in the short and long run. Finally, immigrants may reduce productivity by increasing pressure on some fixed production factors (such as land) or by diluting average human capital in the economy; alternatively, they may increase productivity by adding to the varieties of ideas and products in the recipient country; depending on which effects prevail, this may result in higher or lower total factor productivity. In order to capture these different channels, we separately analyse the impact of immigrants on labour supply, capital supply, and productivity.

Since we are interested in the impact of highly skilled immigration, we extend the framework developed by Ortega and Peri (2009) and decompose the immigration effects into an effect due to the sheer scale of immigration, and into an effect due to the brain gain, measured as the share of immigrants with a tertiary education among total immigrants. In order to isolate supply-driven changes in immigration flows we use variations in the push-factors and the bilateral migration costs (both identified in gravity regressions similar to those estimated in Chapter 3) to predict the scale of migration and its composition by skills to each destination country, and we use these predicted flows as instruments for actual ones. Using the push-driven migration flows and their composition aggregated by receiving country as instruments in a 2SLS approach, we estimate the impact of these flows on employment, capital, total factor productivity, and income per capita in 14 OECD countries. This strategy is aimed at isolating the push-driven immigration flows. Hence we will refer to the estimated elasticities as 'effects' of immigration. Obviously there are several caveats in our identification strategy that the reader may want to keep in mind. For instance, shocks to countries of origin that also affect economic variables of the receiving countries via trade and capital flow linkages would produce a correlation between the instrument and the dependent variable invalidating the exclusion restriction. We will mention some of these issues in the remainder of the chapter.

To anticipate our main findings, we identify a robust and significant positive effect of the brain gain on employment and capital accumulation, on top of the effect produced by the total immigration rate. In line with Ortega and Peri (2009), we find that the total inflow of immigrants does not crowd out native employment while, to the contrary, it stimulates investment even in the short run. Moreover, the share of highly educated immigrants adds a positive employment and capital accumulation effect. This indicates, on the one hand, that highly educated immigrants may stimulate investment or induce specialization in capital-intensive sectors. On the other hand, the stimulus to job creation may be a sign that highly educated immigrants provide complementary production jobs to natives, attracting more of them into the labour force. We also find, plausibly, that the positive effects on employment and capital from the brain gain are stronger in the long run than in the short run. It may take some time for the productive structure to adjust to the optimal specialization structure and to take advantage of the skills of immigrants.

We also analyse whether the effects of migration differ in 'bad' economic times (when the output gap is below −1 per cent signalling a depressed level of aggregate demand) relative to 'good' times. Interestingly enough, we find that the employment and investment effects of immigration have a similar size in bad economic as in good economic times when the brain gain takes place. This suggests that brain gain can be an effective stabilizing measure that could be used to provide some stimulus in periods of slow demand.

Finally, we do not find significant effects of the immigration rates and of the brain gain on the aggregate total factor productivity (TFP) of the receiving country. This zero net effect may be due to positive productivity effects due to highly skilled immigrants' contribution to innovation and technological progress (e.g. Hunt and Gauthier-Loiselle, 2008 and Lincoln and Kerr, 2008) balanced by a negative effect of less skilled immigrants who dilute the human capital intensity of employment (such an effect will enter into the productivity effect in our framework). Combining all the effects we find that total immigration increases GDP per capita (for given GDP per worker) through a positive effect on employment rate. Moreover the brain gain substantially contributes to increase the average gains from immigration in the receiving country.

4.1 A production function framework

In order to evaluate the impact of immigration and brain gain on the receiving economy's employment, investments, and productivity we use an aggregate production function framework, akin to the one used in growth accounting and developed to study the effects of immigrants in Peri (forthcoming). Suppose that total GDP in each destination country, d, and year, t, denoted as Y_{dt}, is produced using a labour input represented by total hours worked by native and immigrants, L_{dt} (that in turn can be decomposed into 'employment$_{dt}$' times 'hours per worker$_{dt}$'), services of physical capital represented by K_{dt} and total factor productivity A_{dt}. Using the popular Cobb–Douglas production function yields

$$Y_{dt} = A_{dt} K_{dt}^{\alpha} L_{dt}^{1-\alpha}, \qquad [4.1]$$

where α is the capital income share and can be set for the destination countries in our sample at a value of 0.33 (see Gollin, 2002). If we intend to analyse how immigration flows affect income or wages (marginal productivity of labour) in such a framework, we need to identify first how immigration affects the supply of each input and total factor productivity. Then we can combine the effects of immigration using the implications of the model. Specifically, the percentage changes in total real GDP, Y_{dt}, is given by

$$\frac{\Delta Y_{dt}}{Y_{dt}} = \frac{\Delta A_{dt}}{A_{dt}} + \alpha \frac{\Delta K_{dt}}{K_{dt}} + (1 - \alpha) \frac{\Delta L_{dt}}{\Delta L_{dt}} \qquad [4.2]$$

The percentage change in real GDP per person in the receiving country is hence simply given by $\Delta Y_{dt}/Y_{dt} - \Delta Pop_{dt}/Pop_{dt}$. If we can identify the percentage changes in A_{dt}, K_{dt}, and L_{dt} in response to exogenous immigration and brain gain flows to the country, we will be able to evaluate the impact of immigration on total income, capital per worker, labour productivity, and also derive the effects on GDP per person.

Clearly, immigration flows directly affect labour input L_{dt} by adding potential workers. However, the increase in employment may be less than one-for-one if immigrants displace native workers, or larger than one if they stimulate employment in complementary jobs. There is still disagreement in the literature about the effect of immigrants on employment, but most studies (Card, 2001; Ottaviano and Peri, 2006) find no significant effect of immigration on native employment. More recently, models of research into the labour market show that immigrants, who have a lower reservation wage, may reduce the hiring costs for firms, induce more job creation, and reduce unemployment of natives as well (Chassaboulli and Palivos, 2010). In addition, there may also be additional effects stemming from the skill composition of immigrants. If the highly educated are likely to contribute to entrepreneurship and innovation and this increases labour demand, the brain gain may also further increase the employment opportunities of natives.

Regarding the capital input, standard neoclassical models with endogenous capital accumulation imply that immigration-induced increases in the labour force will generate investment opportunities and greater capital accumulation, up to the point that the marginal product of capital returns to its pre-shock value. Recent evidence confirms the idea that new immigrants attract flows of international capital (Lange and Gollin, 2007). However, the short-run response of the capital stock to an international immigration flow can be less than complete and it has yet to be quantified empirically. Moreover the inflow of the highly educated, if there are complementarities between high skills and investments (as in Acemoglu, 1998), may further stimulate investments, potentially increasing the capital–labour ratio of the receiving economy.

Concerning TFP, on the one hand immigrants and particularly highly educated ones may promote specialization/complementarities (Ottaviano and Peri 2008) which increase the set of productive skills (Peri and Sparber, 2009) and increase competition in the labour markets, generating efficiency gains that increase TFP. On the other hand, it is also possible that immigration induces crowding of some fixed factors (such as space and land) or the adoption of less 'productive', unskilled-intensive technologies (as in Lewis 2005), or the dilution of average human capital that would lead to reductions in the measured TFP (inclusive of human capital contribution).

Ultimately, it is an empirical question whether an immigration shock increases, decreases, or does not affect employment, capital intensity, and TFP. Let us denote by ($\Delta F_{dt}/Pop_{dt}$) the immigration rate in destination country d and year t, measured as the change in the foreign-born population F_{dt} over the year t (immigration flows to country d in year t) relative to the total population of country d at the beginning of year t (Pop_{dt}). Let us also denote with h_{Fdt} the share of tertiary educated individuals in the immigrant population of country d in year t. That is our measure of the 'brain gain' in country d, which is sometimes also referred to as the skill-intensity of immigrants.

Based on these definitions, we estimate the following regressions for identifying the effects of total immigration and the brain gain:

$$\frac{\Delta X_{dt}}{X_{dt}} = D_t + \gamma_X \frac{\Delta F_{dt}}{Pop_{dt}} + \beta_X h_{Fdt} + e_{dt}, \qquad [4.3]$$

where the variable X is a place-holder that will be, alternately, total hours worked (L_{dt}), employment, services of physical capital (K_{dt}), and total factor productivity (A_{dt}). We also analyse directly the effect of ($\Delta F_{dt}/Pop_{dt}$) and h_{Fdt} on capital per worker (that affects wages) and on output per person (that is affected by all terms in the decomposition plus population growth). The term D_t captures a set of year fixed effects that absorb common movements in productivity and inputs across countries in each year (worldwide business cycle).

In order to assure that the estimated coefficients γ_x and β_x identify the causal effect of immigration and brain gain on the domestic variables we adopt a 2SLS strategy. The instrument for the total immigration flows and the share of tertiary educated in the immigrant population are the sum of bilateral flows to that country as predicted by a gravity model similar to that presented in Chapter 3, but including only push-factors that vary by country of origin and time interacted with bilateral-cost variables, while omitting all receiving-country variables that may be correlated with employment, productivity, and capital accumulation.

Essentially we predict the flows of immigrants and intensity of tertiary educated workers in these flows for each bilateral relation using the components included in the gravity regression that vary by country of origin and time and those capturing bilateral migration costs. We omit, however, any country of destination variable. Then we sum those predicted flows for all countries of origin and the same destination country. Similarly we average (weighting by predicted total flows) the predicted shares of the tertiary educated from all countries of origin into the same destination country. The exact procedure to construct the instruments is described in Section 4.3.2 below.

4.2 Data on employment, capital intensity, and productivity

The data on income and factors of production are mostly from OECD data sets; GDP data are from the OECD productivity data set and employment and hours worked are from the OECD-STAN database. The data cover the whole period 1980–2005 for the 14 countries in our sample.[2] The capital services data are also from the OECD productivity data set, extended using measures of investment rates from the Penn World Tables (version 6.2) to cover the 25 years and 14 countries considered. The conceptually preferred measure of capital that we use is the services of the capital stock that contribute to current production.[3]

Equipped with a full panel for real GDP and labour and capital inputs, we compute total factor productivity as a Solow residual, imposing a labour share of 0.66 and using total hours worked and capital services as the inputs of production.[4] Annex Table A4.1 reports annualized growth rates of these variables for three sub-periods: the 1980s, the 1990s, and 2000–2005. Three features stand out. First, there is a noticeable slowdown in economic growth between 1980 and 2005 for our sample of OECD countries. In the three sub-periods real GDP grew annually by 2.72 per cent, 2.62 per cent, and 1.98 per cent, respectively. The slowdown is also noticeable in terms of lower employment growth (from 0.68 per cent to 0.34 per cent), lower capital growth (from 3.43 per cent to 3.11 per cent), and lower TFP growth (from 1.14 per cent to

---

[2] These data are the same as those used in Ortega and Peri (2009) and they are described there in greater detail.

[3] Those are calculated by constructing separately each type of capital (six or seven, depending on the country), accumulating past investments and adjusting older units so that they provide fewer services than newer ones (efficiency weighting) and accounting for the productive life of each type of capital (retirement pattern). We then aggregate across all types of capital using the relative productivity of each type to obtain the stock of productive capital. The capital services data reported by the OECD is a rate of utilization of the stock of productive capital and it is interpreted as the flow of capital services that went into production during that period. We need to do some further imputations and interpolations/extensions in order to cover all our countries for the full 1980–2005 period. These are described in detail in Ortega and Peri (2009).

[4] The OECD productivity data set features an analogous measure of TFP for some countries covering part of our period of interest. Our own measure is very strongly correlated with theirs. We run a regression of growth rates of the two measures and find that the estimated coefficient is 0.92 and the standard error is 0.018.

0.73 per cent). Note also the large cross-sectional dispersion. Second, average employment growth was substantially higher than average growth in total hours worked between 1980 and 2005. That is, hours per worker on average fell during the period. Finally, capital intensity on average increased substantially over the period. The average annual growth in capital services (in real terms) was roughly three times as large as the annual growth rate in employment.

4.3 The effects of immigration and brain gain

4.3.1 *OLS estimates*

Table 4.1 presents the estimates, using least squares methods, of the coefficients Y_x and $\hat{a}_X$ from equation [4.3]. The dependent variables are, in row order, the inputs of production (total hours worked L, employment, and capital K), capital per worker, total factor productivity (A), and GDP per person. Notice that not all the estimated coefficients are independent of each other due to the relationship between inputs and output provided by the production function.[5]

Since we regress the percentage change of the dependent variable on the inflow of immigrants as a percentage of the initial population and on the share of highly educated the quantitative interpretation of the coefficients is straightforward. The coefficient Y_x captures the elasticity of each variable to immigration as per cent of population. Hence, for instance, a value of one in the second row of Table 4.1 implies that a 1 per cent increase in population due to immigrants provides 1 per cent extra employment. This would mean that immigrants have an employment rate similar to natives and they do not crowd out natives in the labour market. A value of this coefficient smaller than 1 would imply displacement of native workers. Conversely, a value larger than 1 implies that immigrants attract some native workers into the labour force, and produce some job creation on the firm side. The coefficient β_X captures the extra effect of the tertiary educated for given total inflow of immigrants. An increase of the share of tertiary educated by 1 per cent would affect the change in the dependent variable X by β_X per cent.

The different columns in Table 4.1 correspond to different samples and specifications. The estimates of γx are reported in the columns denoted as 'immigration rates' while the estimates of β_X are reported under the columns denoted as 'share of tertiary educated'. Specification (1) is the basic one and it

---

[5] Hence, for instance, the estimated coefficients on (Δ capital per worker/capital per worker) in the fourth row should be equal to the difference between the coefficients on $\Delta K/K$ and the one on (ΔEmployment/Employment).

Table 4.1. Impact of yearly immigrant flows and share of highly educated immigrants: yearly changes, OLS estimates.

Explanatory variable:	(1) Basic OLS 1980–2005		(2) Without USA		(3) 1990–2005	
	Immigration rate	Share of tertiary educated	Immigration rate	Share of tertiary educated	Immigration rate	Share of tertiary educated
$\Delta L/L$	1.03**	0.03**	1.08**	0.03**	1.11**	0.02**
	(0.17)	(0.006)	(0.15)	(0.06)	(0.18)	(0.01)
ΔEmployment/Employment	1.07**	0.02**	1.10**	0.02**	1.18**	0.02**
	(0.24)	(0.006)	(0.17)	(0.005)	(0.25)	(0.01)
$\Delta K/K$	0.91**	0.04**	0.96**	0.03**	1.14**	0.03**
	(0.31)	(0.01)	(0.30)	(0.01)	(0.35)	(0.01)
Δ Capital per worker/ Capital per worker	-0.16	0.01	-0.14	0.01	-0.03	0.01
	(0.20)	(0.01)	(0.20)	(0.01)	(0.21)	(0.01)
$\Delta A/A$	-0.06	0.01	-0.06	0.01	-0.29	0.002
	(0.30)	(0.08)	(0.30)	(0.01)	(0.25)	(0.009)
ΔGDP per Person/GDP per person	0.59	0.01	0.62	0.003	0.43	0.002
	(0.41)	(0.01)	(0.40)	(0.01)	(0.31)	(0.007)
Observations	336		322		210	

Note: The dependent variable in each regression is described in the first cell of the row and the explanatory variables are the immigration rate and the share of the highly educated. The method of estimation is Least Squares. Each regression includes year fixed effects. Specification (1) uses all the country-year observations, specification (2) omits the US data, and specification (3) uses only observations from the 1990–2005 period. The standard errors in parentheses are heteroscedasticity robust and clustered by country. **, * imply significance at the 5, 10% level.

estimates equation [4.3] on 25 yearly changes (1980–2005) for 14 OECD countries.

The method of estimation is OLS with year fixed effects (since the variables are already in changes we do not include country-level effects). The standard errors in parentheses are heteroscedasticity robust and clustered by destination country to account for correlation of the residuals over time within one country. Specification (2) omits the USA, which is one of the most studied cases and by far the largest country of destination of immigrants. We intend to show that the rest of the sample does not behave too differently from the USA. Specification (3) includes only the more recent years (1990–2005) for which the most accurate migration data from the OECD are available.

While there is significant potential for endogeneity in these OLS specifications, as capital and productivity are determinants of wages and those are, in turn, a determinant of immigration rates, let us begin from these simple OLS estimates and comment on some robust and clear correlations that emerge from Table 4.1. We will deal with the issue of endogeneity in Section 4.4.2 below. First, the coefficients γ_X on total inputs ($\Delta L/L$, ΔEmployment/Employment and $\Delta K/K$) are all close to or larger than 1. At the same time the coefficients β_X on the share of highly educated immigrants for the same dependent variables are all significantly positive. This suggests that the receiving economy is able to employ all new arrivals (within the year of arrival) without crowding out native workers, and that capital accumulation is stimulated accordingly to maintain a constant capital–labour ratio. In fact, combining the larger than 1 response to immigrant flow and the positive response to share of immigrants, we can say that increasing the number of highly educated immigrants, keeping the other groups of immigrants constant, would increase employment by more than the direct contribution of those workers, implying the creation of new jobs.

At the same time this would stimulate the investment in physical capital by creating new investment opportunities for the natives and maintaining capital intensity constant or slightly increased. Investments (or capital inflows) adjust to the larger potential worker pool and to its higher skills (brain gain) in just one year, effectively leaving unchanged the capital–labour ratio. Second, capital per worker and total factor productivity are not significantly affected by total immigration or by the share of the highly educated. These estimates suggest that immigrants in general, and the highly educated in particular, stimulate the receiving economy in its employment rate and total investments without much altering productivity and capital per worker.

These effects, combined together, imply that a larger inflow of immigrants, or a selection of more highly educated immigrants for given total flows, are associated with larger employment, proportionally larger total capital, and unchanged or slightly higher capital intensity and unchanged TFP. These effects together would imply unchanged wages for native workers and higher employment rates of natives. This results, in fact, in a positive contribution (although not significant in the OLS specification) of immigration and brain gain to GDP per person in the receiving country. These correlations also hold when we consider the estimates in specification 2, without the USA, or when we restrict the analysis to the more recent period 1990–2005 (in specification 3). In fact the coefficients on all the variables are rather stable across specifications. Immigration and brain gain seem to have a positive 'extensive' effect increasing employment and capital stock of natives and no negative 'intensive' effect on productivity, capital per worker, and hence wages.

4.3.2 Instrumental variables and 2SLS estimates

The most significant limitation of the estimates presented in Table 4.1 is that immigration flows and brain gain are endogenous to the productivity and wages of the receiving country. In fact, we have shown in Chapter 3 that immigration flows respond vigorously to changes in the wage difference between origin and destination. Moreover the inflow of the highly educated responds to the increase in the skill premium in the receiving country. Employment, capital, and TFP are the determinants of those wages, hence we cannot consider immigration (or the share of highly educated immigrants) as exogenous to them. However, the framework developed in the last chapter, in which we analyse the migration flows and the brain flows across countries, provides a framework to separate sending- and receiving-country determinants of the international migration flows as well as the contribution of bilateral migration costs. Hence that framework also lends us a possible solution to the problem of endogeneity of migrant flows. In particular, consider the bilateral regression models used in the previous chapter. The basic model to analyse total immigration is as equation [3.1] in Chapter 3:

$$\ln n^{odt} = D^{ot} + D^d + \beta^1 W^{d,t-1} + X^{od} + \beta^3 Y^{dt} + e^{odt}, \qquad [4.4]$$

where the dependent variable is the logarithm of the total bilateral migration flows from country o to country d in year t, $W_{d,t-1}$ is the destination-country average wage in period $t-1$ and Y_{dt} captures the other receiving-country determinants of migration flows (mainly the immigration laws). The country-of-origin by year fixed effects, $D_{ot,}$ capture the economic, demographic, and cost determinant of migration out of country o which varies over time t. That set of dummies captures all the so called 'push-factors' of immigration that do not depend on specific destination countries but only on conditions in the countries of origin. As long as one country of origin does not have all (or most) of its emigrants going to the same country of destination we can consider these terms as exogenous to the economic conditions of each destination country. For most sending countries (with some exceptions) this is the case in our data set. The country-pairs fixed effects X_{od}, on the other hand, capture the fixed bilateral costs of migrating from o to d. They mostly reflect geographic factors and the existence of historical networks which provide information and ease the adjustment of immigrants to the destination country.

Hence we estimate the gravity equation without any destination specific variable, namely,

$$\ln n^{odt} = D^{ot} + X^{od} + e^{odt}, \qquad [4.5]$$

We then calculate the predicted flow of immigrants $\hat{n}_{odt} = \exp(\hat{D}_{ot} + \hat{X}_{od})$ from any country o into d and sum them over all countries o, to obtain the predicted flow into d.

Similarly for highly educated migrants, we estimate:

$$\ln n^{H}_{odt} = D^{H}_{ot} + X^{H}_{od} + e^{odt}, \qquad [4.6]$$

and calculate the predicted flow of highly educated immigrants as $\hat{n}_{odt}H = \exp(\hat{D}_{ot}H + \hat{X}_{od}H)$. We then divide this estimate by the total imputed flows to obtain the imputed shares and average across countries of origin. This in turn enables us to receive the predicted share of highly educated immigrants in d. These constructed flows constitute the imputed immigration rate and the imputed share of highly educated immigrants for each of the 14 destination countries in each year. They are what we use as instruments for the actual immigration rates.[6] While we use the same fixed effects in the bilateral equation for total and highly educated migrants, the estimates of bilateral costs and country of origin effects are very different. This is due to the fact that some countries have much larger overall migration than others, but also a much smaller share of the highly educated than others. Also the bilateral costs estimates are very different as geographic factors affect skilled and unskilled migration very differently. This is what allows us to identify different instruments (and effects) for total immigration and highly skilled immigration.[7]

Table 4.2 shows the statistics for the first stage regressions using the predicted immigration rates based on predicted flows from [4.5] and [4.6] to

---

[6] One further source of error in proxying the actual immigration rates and actual share of tertiary educated is that in the bilateral regression we only have 74 countries of origin (the most important ones) and add the predicted flows from those. The immigration rates, instead, measure the total immigration flows from these countries plus any other country in the world. This may introduce measurement error bias and produce an underestimate of coefficients in Table 4.3.

[7] Also as the instrumental variables are constructed we should bootstrap the standard error in the second stage. We did not do this yet, however, as the first stage is very strong and we do not think this would make a large difference.

Table 4.2. First stage of the 2SLS: power of the instruments.

	(1)		(2)		(3)	
	Basic OLS		Without USA		1990–2004	
Dependent variable	Immigration rate	Share of tertiary educated	Immigration rate	Share of tertiary educated	Immigration rate	Share of tertiary educated
Predicted Value from push-factor and fixed bilateral factors	0.66** (0.04)	1.03 (0.09)	0.66** (0.04)	1.01** (0.11)	0.62** (0.04)	1.07** (0.10)
F-Test	234	83	231	83.6	178	110
Partial R-Square	0.43	0.85	0.44	0.84	0.52	0.83
Observations	336		322		210	

Note: The dependent variable in all first stage regressions is the immigration rate measured as gross immigration flows relative to initial population. The explanatory variable (instrument) is the predicted immigration rate using the estimated values of D_{ot} and X_{od} from the empirical equations [4.5] and [4.6]. All regressions include year fixed effects. Specification (1) includes all countries and all years 1980–2004, specification (2) omits the USA, specification (3) considers only observations relative to the period 1990–2005. In parentheses below the coefficient estimates we report heteroscedasticity robust standard errors clustered by country. Below the F-statistics we report the probability of rejecting the inclusion of the instruments in the first stage. **,* imply significance at the 5, 10% level. The third row reports the partial R-square that measures the share of variance of the dependent variable accounted for by the instrument.

predict immigration rates and the shares of highly educated. We report some measures of the significance of the instruments (F-test and partial R-square) using the whole sample (specification 1) or using the sample that omits the USA (specification 2), or only including the more recent period, whose data are more reliable (specification 3).

In each case the coefficient on each of the two constructed instruments is positive and very significant. The partial R-squared of the instrument for immigration rates is around 0.41 while the partial R-squared for the imputed share of highly educated is 0.85. Each regression includes time fixed effects. The F-statistics of significance of the instrument are all above 80. Thus, the instruments are quite powerful. In particular they are powerful in predicting the share of the highly educated which implies that the sending-country characteristics and the fixed bilateral migration costs are very important in determining the selection of highly skilled migrants. Possibly highly educated migrants are even more sensitive than less educated ones to sending-country conditions. They may respond to crisis in the country of origin by leaving it to a greater extent than the less educated are able to.

An example of a push-factor that affects migration differently across skills and across receiving countries is the increase in income of the Chinese upper class during the 1990s. This generated a higher propensity of Chinese, mainly those highly educated, to migrate (large values of estimated D_{ot} and even larger of D^H_{ot} for o = China). This would likely imply larger immigration to Australia and the USA, both closer to China and with larger old-time Chinese immigrant communities (quantified in larger X_{od} and X^H_{od}) than, say, France or Switzerland. Also the differential effect on skilled immigration would be greater than on total immigration (hence the differentiation between the two). On the other hand shocks that affect migration out of the sending country but also affect the receiving-country economies through unobserved channels (such as an oil shock or a shock to productivity of the sending country that spills to other countries via trade, capital flows, or contagion) would produce a spurious correlation and bias the IV estimates.

Table 4.3 shows the 2SLS estimates of the effect of immigration on inputs, productivity and income per person. The specifications and the dependent variables in each row of Table 4.3 are exactly as in Table 4.1. Most of the estimates are also consistent qualitatively with (and not too different quantitatively from) those obtained using OLS estimation methods in Table 4.1. In particular, the effect of immigration on *total labour supply, employment, and capital services* are now always larger than 1 (and in some case significantly larger than 1 from a statistical point of view) and the extra-contribution of the highly educated is always significantly larger than 0.

This suggests again no crowding-out of natives from existing jobs, but rather some stimulating effect of immigrants on native employment, enhanced by the presence of the highly educated among them, so that the share of highly educated, for given flows, has a positive effect on the employment and capital accumulation of natives. The capital stock adjusts to immigrants and to the extra-employment effect on natives within one year, so that the change in the capital labour ratio (ΔCapital per worker/Capital per Worker) is never significantly different from zero and the point estimate of its effect is actually positive.

Again, there seems to be no significant effect of immigrants and of brain gain on the productivity changes ($\Delta A/A$) of the receiving country. Our estimates are robust to the choice of countries in the sample (specification 2 omits the USA) and to the choice of the period (specification 3 considers only 1990–2005).

The results of Table 4.3 confirm the correlations obtained by the OLS estimates in Table 4.1. Immigrant flows predicted using country-of-origin yearly effects and bilateral fixed factors increase the employment and labour supply in the receiving country more than one-for-one. On top of this average effect, a higher share of highly educated immigrants provides an extra-stimulus to total employment of natives. Also immigration and brain gain induce increases in the stock of capital (through capital inflows or domestic investment) that, even within one year, allow the capital–labour ratio (and therefore

Table 4.3. Impact of yearly immigrant flows and share of highly educated immigrants: yearly changes, 2SLS estimates.

	(1) Basic 2SLS		(2) Without USA		(3) 1990–2005	
Explanatory variable:	Immigration rate	Share of tertiary educated	Immigration rate	Share of tertiary educated	Immigration rate	Share of tertiary educated
Δ L/L	1.03**	0.03*	1.01**	0.03**	1.00**	0.02
	(0.11)	(0.01)	(0.12)	(0.01)	(0.10)	(0.012)
Δ Employment/Employment	1.23**	0.03**	1.25**	0.02**	1.27**	0.01
	(0.14)	(0.008)	(0.14)	(0.01)	(0.14)	(0.01)
Δ K/K	1.42**	0.04**	1.43**	0.04**	1.46**	0.04**
	(0.24)	(0.02)	(0.25)	(0.02)	(0.23)	(0017)
Δ Capital per worker/Capital per worker	0.15	0.02	0.18	0.02	0.19	0.024
	(0.16)	(0.016)	(0.16)	(0.02)	(0.16)	(0.018)
Δ A/A	-0.11	0.01	-0.09	0.01	-0.16	0.01
	(0.13)	(0.01)	(0.12)	(0.01)	(0.13)	(0.01)
Δ GDP per person/GDP per person	0.60**	0.01	0.60**	0.01	0.53**	0.01
	(0.16)	(0.01)	(0.16)	(0.01)	(0.14)	(0.01)
Observations	336		322		210	

Note: The dependent variable in each regression is described in the first cell of the row and the explanatory variables are the immigration rate and the share of the highly educated. The method of estimation is 2SLS using the predicted flow of immigrants and the predicted share of the tertiary educated from the gravity push-factors in the total immigration and selection equation as instruments. Each regression uses yearly differences by country and includes year fixed effects. Specification (1) uses all the country-year observations; specification (2) omits the US data, specification (3) uses only observations from the 1990–2005 period. The standard errors in parentheses are heteroscedasticity robust and clustered by country. **, * imply significance at the 5, 10% level.

Table 4.4. Five-year differences 2SLS estimates, instruments: gravity push-factors only.

	(1) Basic OLS		(2) 5- Without USA		(3) 1990–2005	
Explanatory variable:	Immigration rate	Share of tertiary educated	Immigration rate	Share of tertiary educated	Immigration rate	Share of tertiary educated
Δ L/L	0.99**	0.13**	0.99**	0.13**	1.01**	0.12**
	(0.11)	(0.04)	(0.12)	(0.04)	(0.12)	(0.04)
Δ Employment/Employment	1.14**	0.07**	1.14**	0.07	1.15**	0.08*
	(0.12)	(0.04)	(0.14)	(0.05)	(0.13)	(0.04)
Δ K/K	1.25**	0.17**	1.31**	0.17**	1.29**	0.18**
	(0.19)	(0.07)	(0.21)	(0.08)	(0.20)	(0.08)
Δ Capital per worker/Capital per worker	0.11	0.09	0.17	0.10	0.13	0.10
	(0.13)	(0.08)	(0.14)	(0.10)	(0.14)	(0.09)
A/A	–0.18	0.01	–0.19	–0.02	–0.20	0.02
	(0.11)	(0.04)	(0.11)	(0.04)	(0.11)	(0.04)
Δ GDP per person/GDP per person	0.49**	0.01	0.47**	0.04	0.47*	0.03
	(0.12)	(0.03)	(0.12)	(0.04)	(0.12)	(0.04)
Observations	70		65		42	

Note: Each cell shows the coefficient from a different regression with the dependent variable described in the first cell of the row and the explanatory variable equal to the total flow of immigrants as a share of the initial population of the receiving country. The method of estimation is 2SLS using the predicted flow of immigrants from the gravity push-factors as instruments. Each regression uses changes over five years between 1980 and 2005 and includes period fixed effects. The standard errors in parentheses are heteroscedasticity robust and clustered by country. **, *, imply significance at the 5, 10% level.

the wage and return to capital) to maintain its pre-immigration level. Thus, immigration and brain gain lead to an increase in the overall size of the economy (employment and capital increase more than proportionally and, if the share of highly educated is higher, the effect is even stronger) without significant changes in total factor productivity and constant (or mildly increasing) capital intensity and hence stable (or slightly increasing) wages. For given output per worker, the increase in employment rate implies an increase in output per person (last row).

As a further check that our short-run estimates are not driven by some bias arising from serial correlation in the data, and also to obtain the long-run response of the variables to immigration and brain gain, we have re-estimated the responses of hours worked, employment, capital, TFP, and income per person to immigration and brain gain over five-year changes (rather than yearly changes). Table 4.4 reports the estimated coefficients from the usual three specifications. The coefficients γx for labour adjustment ($\Delta L/L$) and capital adjustment ($\Delta K/K$) are still close to 1 and not significantly different from the short-run effects. However the extra effect of highly educated β_X on those variables is larger (two to three times) than in the short run. In the long run the employment-stimulating and capital-stimulating effect of highly skilled immigrants seems larger than in the short run. If such a positive effect derives from increased specialization and adjustment of the productive structure in order to take advantage of the skills of immigrants, it makes sense that it takes some time before the full effect is manifested. The effects on productivity ($\Delta A/A$) and on the capital–labour ratio are all still insignificant, hence average wages should not be affected by immigration in the long run either. Output per person, however, is positively affected by the increase of employment rates (last row of Table 4.4).

4.4 The effects of immigration and brain gain in bad economic times

The results of Table 4.3 show that, on average, push-driven immigration triggers a one-for-one increase in total labour supply (hours worked) and in the capital stock, leaving the capital–labour ratio unchanged even in the short run. At the same time skill intensity of this inflow adds an extra positive effect to total employment and capital accumulation, also leaving unchanged productivity and capital–employment ratios. These effects can be explained by thinking of a model with human capital externalities generated by capital-skill complementarities (as in Krusell et al., 2000) and labour markets with wage rigidity. In such a case a higher share of the highly educated triggers more physical capital accumulation. However as the marginal productivity of labour must remain constant, due to wage rigidities, this increase in skill intensity results in more hiring (higher employment) rather than higher output per worker (constant productivity). Native workers have, on average, a positive surplus from immigration but rather than manifesting itself in higher wages this shows up in the form of higher employment rates and hence higher income per person. In the presence of labour market rigidities that keep the wage inelastic a productivity effect of highly skilled immigrants is mainly translated into more employment opportunities and higher job creation.

But do the short-run effects of immigration and/or the extra effect of brain gain vary depending on the business cycle in the receiving country? In particular, what is the response of capital and labour to an immigration shock and to its skill intensity during 'bad economic times'? When the demand is weak, that is, does employment expand so as to employ all of the newly arrived workers, and does capital adjust in response to the skill intensity of immigrants or is there more displacement? While the timing of immigration is rarely discussed in the policy arena, it is well known that periods of economic recession trigger stronger anti-immigrant sentiments. If displacement and adjustment costs of immigration are indeed higher in economic recessions (due to weak demand) then receiving countries could establish some automatic mechanisms that affect immigration quotas along the business cycle, to maximize the long-run gains and minimize the short-run costs.

This section attempts to estimate the effects of immigration shocks, allowing for differences in the estimates of γ_X and β_X between 'bad economic times' and normal periods for the receiving country. Specifically, we shall say that a country in a given year is in 'bad economic times' if its output gap is below −1 per cent. The output gap, as defined by the OECD in the Economic Outlook, is the difference between actual Gross Domestic Product (GDP) and potential GDP as a percentage of potential GDP. Data on the output gap for the 14 countries over the period 1980–2005 are available from the OECD-STAN database. When actual output is below potential output, the output gap is negative. According to our definition, the OECD economies have been in 'bad economic times' during 36 per cent of the period between 1980 and 2005.[8] When an economy is not in bad times we shall say it is in 'normal times'.

We proceed to estimate a regression model analogous to [4.3] but allow the coefficients Y_x and β_X to take on different values in bad and in normal times. We do this by multiplying the explanatory variables (immigration rates and share of the highly educated) by a dummy that is equal to 1 when the country

---

[8] That is in 133 observations out of 336.

is in 'bad economic times' and with another dummy that is equal to 1 when the country is in normal economic times. This allows us to estimate separate responses using only data from years in one or the other 'states of the world'. Table 4.5 reports our findings for the basic specification using 2SLS as method of estimation and the same instruments as in Table 4.4, also interacted with dummies to specialize them to bad and normal times. The two columns on the left correspond to the IV estimates of Y_x and β_X, the effects of total immigration and of its skill intensity, during normal times. The two columns on the right correspond to the estimates of the same parameters, but during 'bad economic times'.

Three results emerge consistently from Table 4.5. First, the response to total immigration flows of total labour used in production (hours worked) is much lower in bad times (0.7) than in normal times (1.6) and also the response of the stock of capital is larger in normal times (1.55) than in bad economic times (1.20). In comparison, TFP is unaffected by total immigration, both in bad and in normal times.

Table 4.5. Impact of immigration in 'normal' and 'bad' economic times: period 1980–2005, 2SLS estimates, instruments: gravity push-factors only.

Specification:	Basic 2SLS			
	Normal times		Bad times	
	Output gap>−1 per cent		Output gap<−1 per cent	
Explanatory variable:	Immigration rate	Share of tertiary educated	Immigration rate	Share of tertiary educated
$\Delta L/L$	1.60**	0.04**	0.72	0.027**
	(0.23)	(0.01)	(0.14)	(0.012)
Δ Employment/	1.55**	0.03**	1.20**	0.01
Employment	(0.19)	(0.01)	(0.11)	(0.01)
$\Delta K/K$	1.55**	0.05**	1.42**	0.03**
	(0.32)	(0.02)	(0.20)	(0.01)
Δ Capital per worker/	−0.01	0.016	0.22	0.022*
Capital per worker	(0.22)	(0.017)	(0.17)	(0.12)
$\Delta A/A$	−0.11	0.007	−0.16	0.016
	(0.10)	(0.008)	(0.22)	(0.02)
Δ GDP per person/GDP per	1.02**	0.01	0.33**	0.002
person	(0.19)	(0.008)	(0.15)	(0.008)
Observations		336		

Note: The coefficients in each row are from the same regression. The explanatory variables are the immigration rates and the share of highly educated among immigrants interacted with a dummy equal to1, when output gap is larger than −1 per cent (normal times) or to 1 when the output gap is smaller than −1 per cent (bad times) The dependent variable is described in the first cell of the row. The estimated specification includes time fixed effects in each regression. The method of estimation is 2SLS using the predicted flow of immigrants and the share of the tertiary educated from the gravity push-factors as instruments, as described in the text. The standard errors in parentheses are heteroscedasticity robust and clustered by country. **,* imply significance at the 5, 10% level.

Second, the positive extra effect of skill-intensity of migrants on employment, hours worked, and capital is present and significantly positive both in bad and normal times and only a bit smaller in bad times. Interestingly enough, the incentive effect of highly educated immigrants on capital accumulation during bad times is large enough that they have a significantly positive effect on capital per worker in bad (but not in normal) times.

Third, the effects on total factor productivity are not significant while the effect of total immigration for given composition on output per person is much larger in good times (due to the large impact on employment and capital) than in bad times.

This suggests that either reducing total immigration or increasing its skill intensity in bad economic times could act as an automatic stabilizer. The measure, proposed during the great economic recession of 2007–08 in the USA, of automatically providing a green card to each foreign-born with a PhD, would have gone exactly in this direction.

We do not have a model that allows us to derive the welfare implication of our results and we have only focused on the productivity and labour market effects of immigrants (while there may also be some fiscal and redistribution effects). Nevertheless our results seem to point, consistently, to a positive employment and investment effect of immigration, enhanced by the presence of brain gain. These positive effects of brain gain on employment and capital accumulation seem particularly strong in the long run suggesting that a positive human capital externality may take some time to manifest itself. At the same time, in the short run, while total immigration seems to create some crowding-out of natives in periods of low aggregate demand (high output gap) brain gain seems to still have positive short-run effects even in bad economic times.

4.5 Conclusions

There is some anecdotal evidence that highly educated immigrants are beneficial to their destination country. As all highly skilled workers, they may have high average productivity, they may be selected among the highly motivated and productive, and they usually specialize in the areas of science and technology that are good for economic productivity. So far, however, nobody has produced any quantification of how large their effect is at the country level, whether it takes the form of increased TFP, larger employment opportunities for natives, or more capital investment opportunities. This chapter, building on the estimates of the determinants of immigration, provides a framework for identifying these effects. In particular, we have considered the effects of the 'brain gain', measured as the share of the highly skilled among the immigrants, in estimating these effects. This way we can distinguish general effects of immigration and the specific contribution of its skill intensity.

Four of our findings are important to highlight. First, total immigration is not associated with lower employment of native workers; rather it produces some positive effects on native employment. A larger share of skilled immigrants substantially strengthens the positive employment effect. This can be due to the fact that immigrants with high education provide services and jobs that complement those of natives. Alternatively immigration may increase the efficiency of specialization in production, thereby increasing the productivity which generates higher incentives for native workers to participate in the labour force.

Second, higher employment due to immigration is accompanied by a more than proportional increase in capital stock, already in the short run. Even this effect on capital accumulation is enhanced by the share of the highly skilled. Thus, more workers stimulate more firms and/or more investment, such that the capital per worker on average remains constant or increases slightly.

Third, immigrants and their skill-intensities do not much affect the total factor productivity of the receiving economy. Combining the null productivity effects, the null effect on capital–labour ratio, and the increase in employment more than proportional to population, immigration has a positive effect on GDP per person and no effect on GDP per worker. These facts can be explained by positive capital–skill complementarities which, because of rigid wages, generate job creation and higher employment and increase the welfare of the average person in the host country.

Finally, we find that immigration has a different impact in 'normal' or in 'bad' economic times. While total immigration triggers a more than proportional increase in hours worked and employment in normal times, working hours and employment increase less than the increase in labour supply triggered by immigration in bad economic times. In contrast, the impact of highly skilled new immigrants is positive in any phase of the business cycle, which suggests that admitting highly skilled immigrants, particularly during bad economic times, can stabilize demand and production.

Altogether, we can conclude that empirical evidence associates immigration with positive employment and investment effects for natives that are reinforced by the skill intensity of immigrants, and that there is no evidence of an effect on TFP.

Annex Table

Table A4.1. Annualized growth rates of inputs, productivity, and output.

Variable	Observations	Mean	Std. dev.	Min	Max
	1980–1990				
Real GDP	14	2.72	0.79	1.99	4.83
Total hours worked	14	0.68	0.84	−0.50	1.78
Employment	14	1.07	0.63	0.18	1.88
Capital services	14	3.43	1.04	2.25	5.59
Total factor Productivity	14	1.14	0.71	−0.25	2.50
	1990–2000				
Real GDP	14	2.62	1.02	1.06	4.91
Total hours worked	14	0.58	0.96	−0.92	2.77
Employment	14	0.92	0.97	−0.67	3.40
Capital services	14	3.75	1.05	2.06	6.12
Total factor Productivity	14	1.01	0.65	−0.56	2.38
	2000–2005				
Real GDP	14	1.98	0.86	0.60	3.65
Total hours worked	14	0.34	0.84	−0.93	1.96
Employment	14	0.73	0.97	−0.41	3.08
Capital Services	14	3.11	1.26	1.37	6.02
Total factor Productivity	14	0.73	0.54	0.17	1.79

Note: The data were constructed by the authors using the OECD-STAN data set and the PWT 6.2 data as sources.

5

The Political Economy of Skilled Immigration

As we saw in Chapter 4, skilled migrants are likely to increase the receiving country's income through higher output, investment, and employment.[1] Moreover, the contribution of immigrants to the fiscal balance of the welfare state improves with their skill level (e.g. Boeri, Hanson and McCormick, 2002; Bonin, Raffelhüschen, and Walliser, 2000). At the same time, as we documented in Chapter 1, only a few countries have devised policies aimed at selecting immigrants on the basis of their skills, and this is mirrored in the skill composition of the immigrant workforce (see Chapters 2 and 3). How can this puzzle be explained? In this chapter we will argue that political economy forces play a key role in shaping actual policies and, in particular, that pressure groups are likely to be key drivers of observed outcomes.

To carry out our analysis, we start by outlining the basic elements of a political economy model of immigration policy (Section 5.1). Public opinion represents one of the main elements of this framework. We next analyse the drivers of individual attitudes towards skilled immigration (Section 5.2), looking at the question from two different perspectives. First, we study how preferences towards overall immigration change, depending on the relative skill composition of the native vs. immigrant population (Section 5.2.1). Second, more directly, we turn to consider the drivers of attitudes towards skilled immigration (Section 5.2.2). In our empirical analysis we focus on two main economic channels through which immigration can affect natives, that is the labour market and the welfare state channels. Interestingly, we find

---

[1] The positive effects shown in Chapter 3 are aggregate. In that chapter, we have not analysed the distributional effects of immigration, which are instead at the centre of the analysis in this chapter. Some studies—for example, national labour market studies—show that, even if possibly small, there is a negative effect of immigration on the wages of the skill group that is relatively abundant among immigrants. In any case, even if the effect is very small (or even positive), what matters to politicians is how public opinion perceives these effects, hence in order to analyse policies it is important to understand opinions more than actual wage and employment effects.

that both play a statistically significant and economically relevant role. Our results are consistent with the factor proportions analysis model of the labour market and with a model of a redistributive welfare state in which taxes adjust following the arrival of migrants.

Our next step is to consider, from a theoretical point of view, how individual preferences can be aggregated into policy outcomes in a democratic society. In particular, we illustrate the working of a simple median voter model and of a framework in which policy outcomes are instead the result of lobbying efforts by organized groups (Section 5.3). Finally, we take the two models to the data to assess their ability to explain the actual policy outcomes. Our evidence suggests that a simple median voter model is not consistent with skilled migration policies in the main destination (European) countries. On the other hand, we provide evidence for the USA pointing out that interest-group dynamics may instead play a very important role.

5.1 The elements of a political economy model of immigration policy

A useful conceptual scheme to analyse the formation process of skilled migration policy is based on Rodrik (1995)[2] and is illustrated in Figure 5.1. The basic idea is that the formulation of migration policy involves at least four elements. First, policymaking necessarily needs to take into account voters' individual preferences, and how these preferences are shaped by the inflow of foreign workers. Both economic and non-economic factors are likely to play a role in shaping public opinion. The second step is to map these preferences onto an aggregate policy demand. Various channels have been suggested in the literature, ranging from majority voting, to pressure groups and grassroots movements. On the supply side of migration policies, we need to identify the policymakers' preferences and the details of the institutional setting in which policies are decided.

A substantial body of literature has studied the impact of both economic and non-economic factors on individual attitudes towards immigrants. The overall message from these studies is that, whereas non-economic drivers have an important and independent effect on individual preferences, economic characteristics of the respondents systematically shape attitudes towards international labour mobility.

---

[2] Rodrik (1995) uses the conceptual scheme in Figure 5.1 to analyse *trade* policy outcomes.

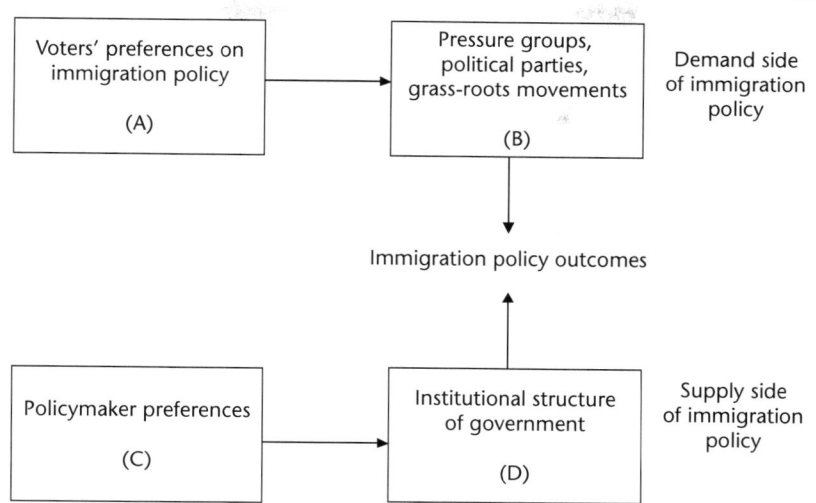

Figure 5.1. Determination of immigration policy.

The early contributions have mainly focused on individual countries like the USA (Citrin et al., 1997; Espenshade and Hempstead, 1996; Kessler, 2001; Scheve and Slaughter, 2001; Hainmueller and Hiscox, 2007) and the UK (Dustmann and Preston, 2001, 2004, 2007). More recently, cross-country studies have taken advantage of newly available social surveys which cover large samples of both advanced and developing countries (Chiswick and Hatton, 2003; Mayda, 2006; O'Rourke and Sinnott, 2005; Facchini and Mayda, 2008, 2009a, 2009b; Mayda, 2008).

Individual preferences are aggregated into political demands through the working of majority voting, grassroot movements, political parties, and/or interest groups (box B in Fig. 5.1). This process of aggregation is clearly affected by how severe the collective action problem is for certain groups, which in turn is a function of several factors, for example the geographic concentration of members of a group. On the supply side of migration policy, government preferences play an important role (box C). Do officials only care about aggregate welfare, that is do they just wish to maximize society's well-being? Or rather, do they only care about being re-elected? Are their choices driven by ideological considerations? Do they care more about the demands of specific groups within society—that is do they intend to use migration policy as a tool to transfer resources to a specific group?

Finally, the institutional structure of the government, that is whether for instance the electoral system is proportional, or more specifically which body is in charge of setting migration policy, plays an important role (box D).

The latter three dimensions of the policymaking process (boxes B, C, and D) are modelled together by the existing literature, and the level to which they are analysed varies substantially. While quite a bit of attention has been devoted to the process through which individual preferences are aggregated, the policymakers preferences are typically modelled in a very reduced-form fashion, and almost no attention is paid to the details of the institutional setting in which migration policy is set. This is an important shortcoming, as destination countries vary substantially in the features of their political institutions.

5.2 Understanding individual attitudes towards skilled migrants

Individual attitudes towards skilled migrants are affected by a number of factors, both economic and non-economic. We assume that voters are characterized by self-interest maximizing behaviour. This implies that, in forming their opinion, voters will consider the impact of skilled migration on their individual utility. Since the economic impact of skilled migration tends to be uneven across the population, the main economic drivers of individual attitudes are associated with the income-distribution effects of skilled migration. Finally, voters' perception of skilled migration from a non-economic point of view is related to political, cultural, and security issues.

The income-distribution effects of skilled migration can take place through three main channels, that is the labour market, the welfare state, and the price channels. Assume that skilled and unskilled labour are combined to produce one good according to a constant returns to scale production function (factor-proportions-analysis model). Theory predicts that, through the labour market channel, the income-distribution effects of migration depend on the skill composition of migrants relative to natives in the destination country. If immigrants are on average more skilled than natives, they will hurt skilled natives and benefit unskilled ones through the labour market channel, as their arrival will induce a decrease in the skilled wage and an increase in the unskilled wage. On the other hand, if immigrants are on average less skilled than natives, the income-distribution effects of migration through the labour market are reversed, that is skilled workers end up benefiting from migration, while unskilled workers are on the losing end. Thus, if we want to empirically test these predictions using data on public opinion towards *overall* migration, we need to assume that voters are aware of the skill level of migrants who arrive in their country. In that case, we expect to find the following patterns: if a country receives skilled immigrants, pro-migration attitudes should be negatively correlated with voters' individual skill while, if a country receives unskilled immigrants, pro-migration attitudes should be positively correlated with voters' individual skill. Using data on public opinion towards specifically *skilled* migrants, we expect to find, in every country, a negative relationship between voters' individual skill and attitudes in favour of skilled migration.

The main OECD destination countries of immigrant flows are characterized by large welfare states (Boeri, Hanson, and McCormick, 2002), in which the public sector redistributes a substantial fraction of national income across individuals. In these contexts, immigration has a non-negligible impact on public finances, since foreign workers both contribute to and benefit from the welfare state. The aggregate net effect of immigration on the welfare state is either positive or negative, depending on the socio-economic characteristics of immigrants relative to natives. Besides the aggregate effect, the arrival of immigrants also implies income-distribution effects through the welfare-state channel. These effects are crucial to understand public opinion on migration.

To understand the income-distribution effects, consider a simple redistributive system, in which all income is taxed at the same rate, and all individuals in the economy, that is both natives and immigrants, are entitled to receive an equal lump sum per capita benefit. By construction, this simple welfare system redistributes resources from high-income to low-income individuals. Assume that immigration can affect the working of this system in two extreme directions. On the one hand, migration can bring about changes in the tax rate, while per capita benefits are kept constant (*tax adjustment model*). On the other, the per capita benefits can adjust while tax rates are unchanged (*benefit adjustment model*).

If immigration is skilled, under both policy scenarios, all natives are likely to benefit from the presence of foreign workers, due to a positive welfare spillover. On the other hand, if migration is unskilled, all natives are negatively affected, through a welfare state leakage effect. However, the extent to which natives benefit (suffer) from skilled (unskilled) migration through the welfare state channel differs according to each voter's income level. That is, there will be income distribution effects. These income distribution effects will depend on the adjustment mechanism of the welfare state to migration.

Figure 5.2 illustrates what happens under the tax adjustment model. In the two panels, we plot the correlation between an individual's pre-tax income and pro-migration attitudes. Under the tax adjustment model, if immigration is skilled compared to the native population (left panel), all individuals benefit from the inflow of foreign workers (the line is in the positive hortant), since the government will be able to lower the tax rate (while keeping the level of per capita benefits unchanged). However, the reduction in the tax rate will benefit rich individuals to a greater extent than poor ones, since tax payments represent a larger fraction of rich voters' net income. If, on the other hand, immigration is unskilled, all individuals are worse off (the line is in the negative hortant in the right panel), since the tax rate needs to increase to

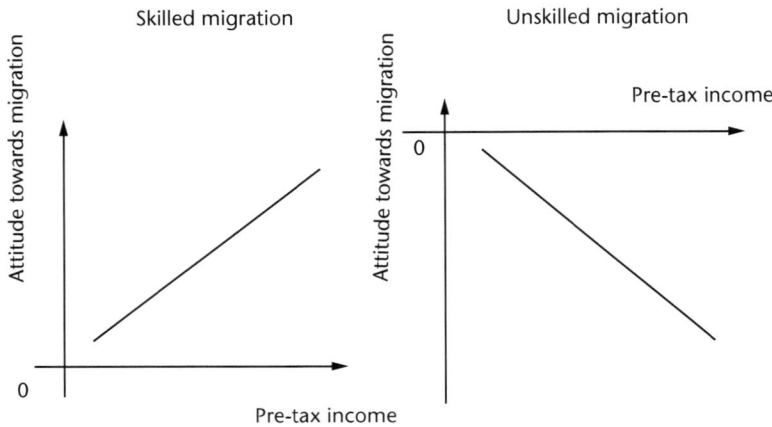

Figure 5.2. The tax adjustment model.

keep the level of per capita benefits unchanged. Richer individuals are those more negatively affected, since the burden of financing the welfare state falls disproportionately more on richer members of society. To summarize, under the tax adjustment model, any change in tax rates (either negative or positive, depending on the skill mix of migrants) will have a bigger impact on high-income individuals.

Figure 5.3 illustrates instead the working of the benefit adjustment model, under which the welfare state adjusts with changes in per capita benefits, while tax rates are kept constant. Also in this case, as can be seen from the left panel, an inflow of skilled immigrants benefits all individuals, while an inflow of unskilled immigrants worsens the position of all voters. Under the

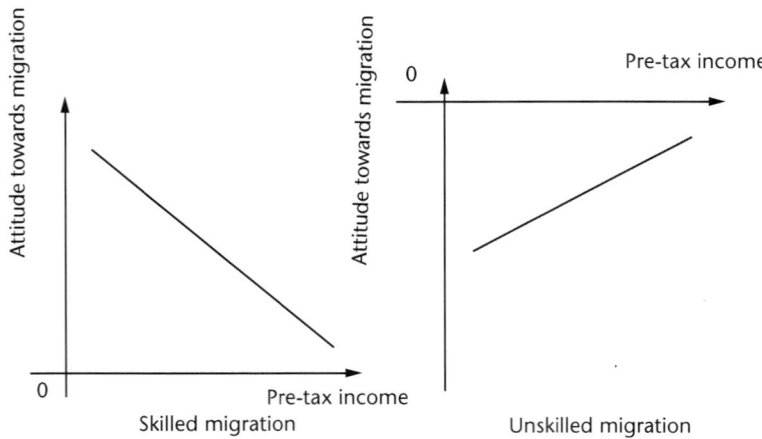

Figure 5.3. The benefit adjustment model.

benefit adjustment model, an inflow of immigrants will have a more pronounced effect (either positive or negative, depending on the skill mix of migrants) on those individuals that are at the receiving end of the welfare system, that is low-income individuals. The reason is that the per capita benefit represents a larger fraction of a poor individual's net income, thus changes in per capita benefits affect this income category more strongly. In particular, if a country receives skilled migrants, the per capita benefit will increase, therefore all natives will benefit, but poor ones more so than rich ones. On the other hand, a country receiving unskilled migrants will be forced to reduce per capita benefits, thus hurting everybody, but again low-income voters to a greater extent than high-income ones.

Let us turn now to the implications of the theoretical model for our empirical analysis, starting with the tax adjustment model. Using data on public opinion towards *overall* migration and assuming that voters are aware of the skill level of migrants to their country, we expect to find that, if migration is skilled, pro-migration attitudes are positively correlated with voters' individual income (left panel of Fig. 5.2). The opposite is true if immigration is unskilled, in which case pro-migration attitudes should be negatively correlated with voters' individual income (right panel of Fig. 5.2). Under the benefit adjustment model, we should find that if immigration is skilled, pro-migration attitudes are negatively correlated with individual income (left panel of Fig. 5.3). On the other hand, if immigration is unskilled, pro-migration attitudes are positively correlated with individual income (right panel of Fig. 5.3). Using instead a direct measure of individual attitudes towards skilled migration, we should find in every country a positive correlation between pro-skilled migration attitudes and individual income under the tax adjustment model and a negative correlation under the benefit adjustment model.

See Table 5.1 for a summary of the labour market and welfare state determinants of individual attitudes towards skilled (and unskilled) migration. The Technical Appendix develops a formal model of individual attitudes towards immigration.

The third economic channel through which attitudes towards skilled migrants are affected is price changes. This channel is absent if we assume that the destination country is a small open economy which produces only internationally traded goods, in which case all goods prices are fixed, thus immigration does not alter them (see for example the model in the Appendix). If, on the other hand, the country is a large open economy and/or produces a non-traded good or service, then the arrival of immigrants will affect prices. This price effect is going to be homogenous across the population if preferences are homothetic and identical across individuals. In this case, there will be no income distribution effects through the price channel. In a more general model, individuals belonging to different income groups might

Table 5.1. Correlations between pro-immigration attitudes and, respectively, individual skill and income through the labour market and the welfare state channels.

Relative skill composition	Skilled immigration			Unskilled immigration		
Channel	Labour market	Welfare state		Labour market	Welfare state	
		Tax adjustment model	Benefit adjustment model		Tax adjustment model	Benefit adjustment model
Correlation b/w Attitudes & *Skill*	Negative			Positive		
Correlation b/w Attitudes & *Income*		Positive	Negative		Negative	Positive

be characterized by different consumption baskets, in which case heterogeneous agents might have different preferences over immigration because of price effects. The empirical evidence on the price impact of migration is scarce and, for the most part, focuses on unskilled migration (see, for example, Cortes, 2008 and Frattini, 2008). To the best of our knowledge, there is no work in the literature focusing on the price effects of skilled migration. The latter, however, are likely to exist and be substantial. For example, skilled migrants (for example, university professors and doctors) have most likely had an effect on prices of services such as higher education and health in countries like the UK and the USA. To conclude, since there is no clear prediction on the income distribution effects of skilled immigration through the price channel, we will not consider this channel in our empirical analysis.

Finally, besides the labour market, welfare state, and price channels, there is a fourth economic determinant of individual attitudes, that is efficiency considerations. If the inflow of immigrants is non-marginal, there will be *aggregate* gains from skilled migration, as pointed out by Berry and Soligo (1969) and Borjas (1999) and as documented empirically in Chapter 4. This aggregate 'migration surplus' will relax the government budget constraint and increase the tax base. Thus all natives should be in favour of skilled immigration through the efficiency channel because they will end up paying a lower tax rate and/or receiving a higher per capita benefit. In the standard migration model, the migration surplus is related to labour market complementarity effects. However, we can broaden the interpretation of this aggregate effect by considering other types of gains—for example, the benefit of skilled migration through its impact on capital accumulation, employment, productivity (see Chapter 4), and innovation activity. In relation to the latter effect, Kerr and Lincoln (2008) evaluate the impact of high-skilled immigrants on US technology formation. The paper finds evidence of a positive effect of higher admission levels of highly skilled immigrants on total invention, primarily through the direct contributions of ethnic inventors. The effect of skilled migration on innovation activity is likely to be taken in great consideration by public opinion—especially in countries at the frontier of technological research, such as the USA—as evidenced by the media coverage of this topic (see, for instance, *Economist*, 7 March 2009).

To conclude, there are a number of economic channels through which public opinion on skilled migration is affected. All of them, except the labour market channel, will imply a favourable attitude towards skilled migrants, to a greater or lesser extent for different types of individuals. Through the labour market channel, skilled migration is likely to be opposed by native skilled workers. Whether the labour market channel has a substantial effect will depend on how vocal skilled native workers are in the immigration policy process.

From a non-economic point of view, public opinion on skilled migration is shaped by political, cultural, and security issues. Political considerations imply that skilled natives should favour skilled migrants—since their arrival will increase the likelihood that the median voter is skilled—while unskilled natives should oppose them (see Ortega, 2005).[3] From a cultural point of view, both skilled and unskilled natives should welcome inflows of educated migrants, who are likely to adjust to the destination country's culture, with few or no assimilation costs. Finally, from a security point of view, we do not expect public opinion to be concerned about skilled migration. Thus, our overall conclusion of this analysis is that attitudes towards skilled migration should be overwhelmingly favourable.

5.2.1 *Empirical evidence on individual attitudes towards migration (ISSP data sets)*[4]

In this section we use data on preferences towards overall immigration and draw implications regarding attitudes towards skilled migrants. We use the 1995 and 2003 National Identity modules of the International Social Survey Programme (ISSP) data set. Regressions (5.1)–(5.5), Table 5.2 presents the results based on the 1995 ISSP National Identity module, while regressions (5.1')–(5.5') show the results based on the 2003 ISSP National Identity module.

---

[3] The underlying assumption is that immigrants' children (or immigrants themselves) can become citizens and vote—this is true in *jus soli* countries—and skill levels are persistent across generations.

[4] The analysis in this section draws on Facchini and Mayda (2009a).

Table 5.2. Economic and non-economic determinants of attitudes.

Ordered probit with country dummies	1995					2003				
Dependent Variable → Pro Immig Opinion	1	2	3	4	5	1′	2′	3′	4′	5′
Age	-0.0037** (0.0010)	-0.0037** (0.0010)	-0.003** (0.0009)	-0.0032** (0.0010)	-0.0039** (0.0011)	-0.0008 (0.0011)	-0.0008 (0.0011)	-0.0009 (0.0013)	-0.0019 (0.0013)	-0.0018 (0.0011)
Male	-0.0217 (0.0257)	-0.0249 (0.0261)	-0.0372 (0.0279)	-0.0209 (0.0272)	-0.0534 (0.0329)	0.021 (0.0206)	0.0166 (0.0201)	0.0046 (0.0229)	0.0227 (0.0222)	0.0172 (0.0266)
Citizen	-0.3082** (0.0972)	-0.3051** (0.0958)	-0.2147* (0.0992)	-0.1555 (0.1042)	-0.3632** (0.1325)	-0.1908** (0.0646)	-0.1898** (0.0649)	-0.2114** (0.0800)	-0.207* (0.0967)	-0.2987* (0.1266)
Parents' foreign citizenship	0.2568** (0.0470)	0.2534** (0.0471)	0.2385** (0.0461)	0.1334** (0.0425)	0.229** (0.0619)	0.2542** (0.0196)	0.2552** (0.0201)	0.2532** (0.0241)	0.1297** (0.0247)	0.219** (0.0314)
Education (years of education)	0.0587** (0.0081)	-0.4627** (0.0824)	-0.5207** (0.1193)	-0.269* (0.1270)	-0.696** (0.1566)	0.0565** (0.0048)	-0.2225** (0.0581)	-0.6969** (0.2674)	-0.4899+ (0.2613)	-0.8082** (0.2874)
Education* gdp		0.0539** (0.0084)	0.0598** (0.0121)	0.0315** (0.0129)	0.0768** (0.0158)		0.0279** (0.0060)	0.074** (0.0262)	0.0511* (0.0255)	0.0843** (0.0282)
Log of real income	0.0339* (0.0158)	0.7311* (0.3679)	1.2235** (0.3939)	1.4351** (0.2780)	1.5677+ (0.8295)	0.0517** (0.0180)	-0.0841 (0.3292)	1.7827* (0.8200)	2.0632* (1.0329)	2.0485+ (1.1140)
Log of real income* gdp		-0.0715+ (0.0379)	-0.1212** (0.0405)	-0.1443** (0.0285)	-0.1557+ (0.0855)		0.0143 (0.0335)	-0.1665* (0.0804)	-0.1973* (0.1005)	-0.1922+ (0.1081)
Pro-imming crime				0.5855** (0.0568)					0.5739** (0.0355)	
Pro-imming culture				0.5811** (0.0545)					0.6369** (0.0435)	
Pro-imming economy				0.5747** (0.0575)					0.569** (0.0250)	
Upper social class					0.0546** (0.0180)					0.0324** (0.0105)
Trade union member					0.018 (0.0317)					-0.0516* (0.0236)
Political affiliation with the right					-0.1409** (0.0462)					-0.1911** (0.0329)
religious					0.0378** (0.0122)					0.029** (0.0057)
Observations	14659	14659	13045	13045	6043	23801	23801	17943	17943	10956
Pseudo R-squared	0.07	0.07	0.07	0.15	0.07	0.06	0.06	0.06	0.14	0.07

Data source: 1995 and 2003 ISSP National Identity Module. The table reports coefficient estimates for ordered probit regressions (the cut-off points are not shown). Robust standard errors, clustered by country, are presented under each coefficient. + significant at 10%; * significant at 5%; ** significant at 1%. All regressions control for country fixed effects. Regressions (3)–(5) and (3′)–(5′) are restricted to countries with well developed Western-style welfare states. gdp is the log of per capita GDP in 1995 and 2003 PPP (current international dollars).

We present the estimates of the coefficients of ordered probit models which control for country fixed effects—to account for unobserved, additive, country-specific effects—and have standard errors clustered by country—to account for heteroscedasticity and correlation of individual observations within a country. Finally, in both sets of regressions, the dependent variable is pro immig opinion which ranges between 1 and 5 and is higher the more pro-migration the individual is.[5] See Annex Tables A5.1 and A5.2 for summary statistics of pro immig opinion and other variables used in the empirical analysis.[6]

Our general finding in Table 5.2 is that a key driver of attitudes towards migration is the skill composition of migrants relative to natives. In particular, we find evidence that migrants' skill composition plays a key role in shaping the (perceived) income distribution effects of migration through the labour market and the welfare state channels. In what follows, we describe the results of Table 5.2 in more detail.

As pointed out by the theoretical model, the two key individual level variables for the income distribution effects are the level of education—which captures the impact of labour market effects on attitudes—and the level of income—which captures the effect of welfare state considerations on attitudes. The two variables are clearly correlated, since well-educated individuals tend to have higher incomes. This implies that it is problematic to analyse the two channels independently from each other since the exclusion of one of the two variables would produce an omitted variable bias in the estimation of the impact of the other variable. On the other hand, while education and income are positively and significantly correlated, they are far from being perfectly collinear,[7] which makes it possible to analyse them together. Thus, in the following regressions, we introduce education and log of real income together in the same specification. In regressions (5.1) and (5.1'), we constrain the coefficients on the two individual-level variables to be the same across

---

[5] In particular, to construct the variable Pro Immig Opinion, we use respondents' answers in the two rounds of the ISSP survey to the following question: 'There are different opinions about immigrants from other countries living in (respondent's country). By "immigrants" we mean people who come to settle in (respondent's country). Do you think the number of immigrants to (respondent's country) nowadays should be: (1) reduced a lot, (2) reduced a little, (3) remain the same as it is, (4) increased a little, or (5) increased a lot'? The survey format also allows for 'can't choose' and 'not available' responses which we treat as missing values and thus exclude from the sample in our specifications. To investigate whether omitting missing values results in a selection bias, we also estimate a Heckman selection model and confirm the robustness of the results in Table 5.2 (see Appendix A5.3 and A5.4).

[6] Notice that, in Table 5.2, gdp (which is the per capita GDP of the destination country) is a country- level variable while the other regressors are individual level variables.

[7] In the 1995 ISSP data set, the correlation is 0.25 (significant at the 1per cent level), while in the 2003 ISSP data set it is 0.38 (significant at the 1per cent level).

countries. We find that both variables have a positive and significant impact on pro-migration attitudes, both in 1995 and 2003.

Regressions (5.2)–(5.5) and (5.2')–(5.5') are more closely related to the theoretical model, which predicts that the impact of education and income should be country-specific. In particular, the theoretical model implies that the effect of individual skill and income should be a function of the relative skill composition of natives to immigrants. Thus, we build the empirical (ordered probit) specification around the following latent regression:

$$y_{ic}^* = \beta_1 age_i + \beta_2 male_i + \beta_3 educ_i + \beta_4 educ_i \times RSC^c + \beta_5 income_i + \beta_6 income_i \times RSC^c + \ldots + \epsilon_{ic} \qquad [5.1]$$

where RSC denotes the relative skill composition of natives to immigrants in the destination country c.[8] The probabilities of the five ordered categories in the ordered probit model are based on y_{ic}^*, which is unobserved. From theory we expect to find that the impact of education on pro-immigration preferences is negative in countries that receive skilled immigrants ($\beta_3 < 0$) and positive in countries that receive unskilled immigrants ($\beta_4 > 0$). Furthermore, if the tax adjustment model holds, the effect of individual income should be positive in countries that receive skilled immigrants ($\beta_5 > 0$) and negative in countries that receive unskilled immigrants ($\beta_6 < 0$). On the other hand, if the benefit adjustment model holds, the effect of individual income should be negative in countries that receive skilled immigrants ($\beta_5 < 0$) and positive in countries that receive unskilled immigrants ($\beta_6 > 0$).

Since the relative skill composition of natives to immigrants is not available for many countries in our samples, we use a proxy for it, namely the per capita GDP level in the same year. There are both theoretical and empirical reasons for using this proxy. In the standard international migration model with no productivity differences across countries, rich countries have a higher supply of skilled to unskilled labour than poor countries, therefore lower skilled wages and higher unskilled wages. This creates an incentive for unskilled migrants to move from low to high per capita GDP countries, while skilled migrants will tend to move in the opposite direction. Therefore, this simple model predicts that the relative skill composition of natives to immigrants is high in rich countries and low in poor countries. To take into account the fact that, in reality, there exist productivity differences across countries, we also provide empirical evidence that per capita GDP levels are positively

---

[8] The skill composition of immigrants is shaped by migration policy which, in turn, is likely to be a function of attitudes. However, in an individual-level analysis such as this one, reverse causality is not an issue, since each individual has an infinitesimal impact on the aggregate policy outcome. In addition, in the latter part of this chapter, we find no evidence of correlation between public opinion and policies on skilled migration.

associated with the relative skill mix of natives to immigrants for all countries for which data is available. Figure A5.1 and A5.2 illustrate this relationship for 1995 and 2003, respectively.

Once we account for cross-country heterogeneity in terms of the impact of individual-level variables, we find that individual skill affects migration preferences as predicted by the theoretical model (regressions (5.2) and (5.2')). Consistent with the labour-market channel, education has a negative impact on pro-migration attitudes in countries that receive skilled migrants on average, relative to natives (low per capita GDP countries) and a positive impact in countries that receive unskilled migrants on average, relative to natives (high per capita GDP countries). These results hold using both the 1995 and 2003 data sets.

In addition, these findings are consistent with the evidence in the existing literature. In an early influential study using the 1992 US National Election Study, Scheve and Slaughter (2001) find that, in the USA—where immigrants are on average less skilled than natives—unskilled workers are more likely to oppose immigrants, relative to skilled workers. Using the 1995 round of the ISSP data set and the 1995–1997 round of the World Value Survey, Mayda (2006) provides strong evidence that individual skill is positively correlated with pro-immigration attitudes in countries where immigrants are on average unskilled, while it is negatively correlated with pro-immigration attitudes in countries where migrants are on average skilled, relative to the native population.[9] O'Rourke and Sinnott (2005) find similar results.

We next analyse the role played by public finance considerations. Regressions (5.2) and (5.2') are based on the full sample of countries of each data set. Thus, it is not surprising that we do not find strong evidence for the welfare state channel. However, once we restrict the sample to countries with well developed Western-style welfare states (regressions (5.3)–(5.5) and (5.3')–(5.5')), we find estimates which are in line with the welfare-state predictions of the theoretical model, in particular in the case of the tax adjustment model. Individual income has a positive impact on pro-migration attitudes in countries that receive skilled migrants on average (low per capita GDP countries) and a negative impact on pro-migration attitudes in countries that receive unskilled migrants on average (high per capita GDP countries). These results are robust to controlling for the labour market channel and hold using both the 1995 and 2003 data sets. Thus, these estimates strongly confirm the findings of the existing literature. Using US data, Hanson, Scheve, and Slaughter (2007) and Hanson (2005) find that the negative relationship between education and anti-immigrant preferences—driven by the labour

---

[9] See also Facchini and Mayda (2009a).

market—becomes smaller in absolute value and sometimes positive in states with high exposure to immigrant fiscal pressure. Using the 1995 ISSP data set, Facchini and Mayda (2009a) find that, in countries where immigrants are unskilled relative to natives, individual income is negatively correlated with pro-immigration preferences, while the correlation changes sign in destinations characterized by skilled migration. See also Dustmann and Preston (2007) for the role played by welfare state drivers relative to other economic and non-economic drivers of attitudes.

Regressions (5.4) and (5.4′) show that these results are also robust to controlling for *pro-immig crime*, *pro-immig culture*, and *pro-immig economy*, which measure the perceived impact of migration (by the respondent) from respectively a crime, a cultural and a nationwide economic point of view (these three variables are higher the more positive the attitude of the individual towards migration along that particular dimension). Finally, in columns (5.5) and (5.5′), we control for additional socio-economic/ideological background variables—that is upper social class, trade union member, political affiliation with the right, and religious—and find very similar results. Thus, our findings on the labour market and welfare state channels are not qualitatively affected by the introduction of non-economic controls.

To conclude, and focusing specifically on skilled migration, the findings in Table 5.2 show that skilled migration produces pronounced income distribution effects. Interestingly, since the data are consistent with the tax adjustment model, the income distribution effects implied by the welfare state channel work in the opposite direction relative to the labour market. In particular, individual skill and income have opposite effects on individual attitudes towards immigrants. Since education and income tend to be positively associated, the labour market and welfare state channels partially offset each other. For example, the very same skilled and high-income professional in Ireland may feel ambivalent regarding the arrival of skilled immigrants since he might benefit with them from a welfare-state point of view—through reductions in his tax burden—but be hurt by them through labour market substitution effects.

5.2.2 *Empirical evidence on individual attitudes towards skilled migration (ESS)*[10]

In this section we analyse, more specifically, the determinants of individual attitudes towards *skilled* migration. We use the 2002–2003 round of the

---

[10] The analysis in this section draws on Facchini and Mayda (2009c).

European Social Survey (ESS), which covers a different sample of countries than the ISSP data set and was run in a different period of time.[11] The immigration question we examine in the ESS data set is more specific than the one contained in the ISSP survey, as it asks *directly* about skilled migration. To the best of our knowledge, this chapter is the first one to carry out an analysis of this question and, therefore, to provide *direct* evidence on the determinants of attitudes towards skilled migration in a large cross-section of countries.[12]

In particular, in the ESS data set, respondents are asked whether they think it is important for immigrants to have good educational qualifications. We construct the variable *pro-skilled-migration*, which ranges between 0 and 10 and is higher the more the individual favours skilled migration. Summary statistics of *pro-skilled-migration* and the other ESS variables included in the regressions are presented in Tables 5.3 and 5.4. The summary statistics provide information also on the per capita GDP of the destination country (in 2002, PPP adjusted), which come from the World Development Indicators data set, and on the relative skill ratio of natives to immigrants, which uses 2002–2003 data on native and immigrant populations by level of education (lower secondary education, upper secondary, tertiary) from Table I.12 in SOPEMI (2005).

The summary statistics show that public opinion on average supports skilled migration. In the overall sample, the average of the *pro-skilled-migration* variable is 6.23. There is variation across countries but this is not substantial. All countries have average values of *pro-skilled-migration* which range between 4.6 (corresponding to Sweden) and 7.7 (corresponding to Greece) and median values which range between 5 (corresponding to Sweden and Norway) and 8 (corresponding to Greece and Israel).

Table 5.3. Summary statistics of individual-level variables (ESS).

Variable	Obs	Mean	Std. dev.	Min	Max
Pro-skilled-migration	30975	6.2273	2.7452	0	10
Year of birth	30975	1955	17.5685	1893	1988
Male	30975	0.4831	0.4997	0	1
Citizen	30975	1.0382	0.1917	1	2
Education (highest level attained)	30975	2.9868	1.4918	0	6
Real income	30975	2.8151	1.7838	0.1111	12

[11] For more information on the construction of the survey, see Jovell et al. (2003). The data is made available by the Norwegian Social Science Data Services.

[12] The only other paper we could find which investigates the determinants of attitudes towards, specifically, skilled migrants is Hainmueller and Hiscox (2010), which uses survey data for the USA only. This chapter provides evidence which is not consistent with labour market and welfare state predictions.

Table 5.4. Summary statistics of individual-level variables by country and of country-level variables (ESS).

Country	Pro-skilled-migration (mean)	Pro-skilled-migration (median)	Education	Real income	Per capita gdp	Relative skill composition (2002–2003)
Austria	6.641365	7	3.348189	3.013095	29014.66	3.141503
Belgium	6.097203	7	3.055944	2.780771	27459.14	1.804188
Czech Republic	6.381974	7	3.111588	1.816185	16556.42	2.641453
Denmark	6.243116	7	3.287962	3.563468	28956.7	1.163756
Finland	6.335023	7	2.971847	3.211368	26018.38	1.244552
France	6.21119	7	3.039401	2.345164	26612.92	3.508463
Germany	6.721546	7	3.373154	3.216287	25545.68	5.656399
Greece	7.738864	8	2.199889	2.107014	18834.2	0.8265503
Hungary	6.823139	7	2.289609	1.068756	14159.44	0.6697858
Ireland	6.11385	7	2.806338	1.907975	35652.91	0.4042847
Israel	6.908894	8	3.502169	1.975383	22002.85	
Italy	5.841424	6	2.317152	2.274649	25554.43	
Luxembourg	6.485214	7	2.742607	3.338771	59976.5	2.054675
Netherlands	5.592118	6	3.042857	3.402215	29550.49	1.65946
Norway	5.150543	5	3.51164	3.769239	34750.03	1.422166
Portugal	5.975758	6	1.686869	2.042577	18398.29	0.3274704
Slovenia	6.306743	7	3.378289	1.525227	18017.7	
Spain	6.135576	7	2.097859	2.140123	22444.72	0.5475358
Sweden	4.618788	5	3.090661	3.293816	26468.27	1.415028
Switzerland	6.218572	7	3.334807	4.539899	31019.92	5.193212
United Kingdom	6.287578	7	3.055587	3.754944	27175.5	2.038001

Summary statistics in these tables are based on the same observations as in regression 3, Table 5.5. These summary statistics do not use design and population size weights. Pro-skilled-migration ranges between 0 and 10 and it is higher the more the individual thinks that it is important for immigrants to have good educational qualifications. Education (highest level attained) goes from 0 to 6 (not completed primary education; primary or first stage of basic; lower secondary or second stage of basic; upper secondary; post-secondary, non-tertiary; first stage of tertiary; second stage of tertiary). Real income is household's total net income (expressed on a scale from 1 to 12) divided by the number of household members. Per capita GDP in 2002 (PPP, constant 2000 international $) is from the World Bank. The relative skill composition (RSC) is the ratio of skilled to unskilled labour in the native relative to the immigrant populations. For both natives and immigrants, the ratio of skilled to unskilled labour is measured as the ratio of the number of individuals with upper secondary or tertiary education to the number of individuals with lower secondary education. The RSC uses data on the stock of immigrants and natives in 2002–2003 (OECD 2005).

Using *pro-skilled-migration* as the dependent variable, we estimate ordered probit models which include, as regressors, country dummy variables and have robust standard errors clustered by country.[13] We find evidence which is remarkably consistent with the predictions of the theoretical model and with our findings in the previous section. Table 5.5 presents the results of our estimation. First, the higher the education level attained by the respondent, the *lower* is the probability that he favours good educational qualifications of immigrants. In particular, based on regression (2), a one unit increase in the education level (for example, going from 'lower secondary or second stage of basic' to 'upper secondary') decreases the likelihood that an

---

[13] As recommended in the ESS website, our estimation uses both design and population size weights.

Table 5.5. Determinants of individual attitudes towards skilled migration (ESS).

Ordered probit with country dummies	1	2	3	4
Dependent variable	Pro-skilled-migration			
Year of birth	−0.0067	−0.0057	−0.0054	−0.0047
	0.0011**	0.0013**	0.0014**	0.0011**
Male	0.0396	0.0499	0.0294	0.0681
	0.0119**	0.0116**	0.0137*	0.0143**
Citizen	0.0376	0.0364	0.021	−0.0062
	0.0589	0.0657	0.0663	0.052
Education (highest level attained)		−0.0603	−0.0714	−0.0613
		0.0133**	0.0143**	0.0174**
Real income			0.0084	0.0145
			0.0037*	0.0069*
Trade union member				−0.0321
				0.0166 +
Rural (area of residence)				0.0096
				0.0162
Political affiliation with the right				0.0515
				0.0109**
Religious				−0.0037
				0.0031
Concerned about security				0.0991
				0.0091**
Importance of traditions and customs				0.0353
				0.0056**
Observations	39035	38785	30975	25378
Pseudo R-squared	0.01	0.01	0.01	0.02

The table reports coefficient estimates for ordered probit regressions (the cut-off values are not shown). Robust standard errors, clustered by country, are presented under each coefficient. As recommended in the ESS website, our estimation uses both design and population size weights. + significant at 10%; * significant at 5%; ** significant at 1%. All regressions in this table control for country fixed effects. Pro-skilled-migration ranges between 0 and 10 and it is higher the more the individual thinks that it is important for immigrants to have good educational qualifications. Education (highest level attained) goes from 0 to 6 (not completed primary education; primary or first stage of basic; lower secondary or second stage of basic; upper secondary; post secondary, non-tertiary; first stage of tertiary; second stage of tertiary). Real income is household's total net income (expressed on a scale from 1 to 12) divided by the number of household members.

individual favours skilled migration by 2 percentage points.[14] This result suggests that skilled natives feel threatened by the labour market competition of skilled migrants. At the same time, the higher the level of income of the respondent the *higher* is the probability that he supports skilled migration. In particular, based on regression (3), a one unit increase in the real income level increases the likelihood that an individual favours skilled migration by

---

[14] To facilitate the presentation of the marginal effects, we estimate a probit model. In particular, this marginal effect is based on the estimation of a probit model which uses as the dependent variable a dichotomous definition of pro-skilled migration attitudes—the dichotomous variable equals 1 if *pro-skilled-migration* is greater or equal to 6, and equals 0 if *pro-skilled-migration* is smaller or equal to 5—and the same regressors as in column (2), Table 5.5.

0.6 percentage points.[15] This result is consistent with the tax adjustment mechanism of the welfare state model. In particular, skilled migration is likely to represent a net contribution for the destination country's welfare state. The reduction in tax rates implied by the arrival of highly qualified foreign workers benefits both poor and rich respondents, but the rich to a greater extent than the poor.

We also find that older respondents (i.e. respondents with a less recent year of birth), males, and individuals affiliated with the political right are more likely to favour good educational qualifications for immigrants. On the other hand, surprisingly, trade union members are less likely to support skilled migration. In addition, consistent with the discussion on the non-economic determinants, individuals who are concerned about security and those who value traditions and customs, respectively, are in favour of skilled migration.

5.3 From individual preferences to immigration policy

In this section and the next we describe how individual attitudes translate into migration policy outcomes. To this end, we use first a median voter framework and, next, we analyse the interest groups model.[16]

5.3.1 *The median voter model*

What is the migration policy chosen by a pure democracy? The median voter approach—pioneered by Benhabib (1996)—considers the human capital requirements that are imposed on potential immigrants by an income maximizing community under majority voting.[17] In Box 5.1 we use a similar median voter framework and, focusing on the labour market channel, we develop a theoretical model, which gives predictions in terms of the *levels* of skilled and unskilled migration.[18] In our model, skilled and unskilled labour are combined to produce one single output good. As we show, if the median voter is unskilled, he will choose to admit an immigrant population which is skilled

---

[15] This marginal effect is based on the estimation of a probit model which uses as the dependent variable the dichotomous definition of pro-skilled-migration attitudes and the same regressors as in column (3), Table 5.5.

[16] Of course the model discussed in Section 5.2 is not directly comparable to the median voter/ interest groups model we are considering here, as the latter models do not consider at all the role of the welfare state.

[17] Ortega (2005) extends this model to a dynamic setting. For a survey of the literature on the political economy of migration policy, see Facchini (2004), while for a review of the literature that looks at the welfare state dimension, see Krieger (2005).

[18] Notice that the political economy model we are discussing here focuses only on the effects of immigration through the labour market channel, and does not explicitly consider the role of the welfare state.

compared to natives. On the other hand, if the median voter is skilled, he will choose to admit an immigrant population which is unskilled compared to natives. In general, the median voter model predicts that policies are driven by public opinion, a summary measure of which is the opinion of the median voter. This is the prediction we bring to the data.

5.3.2 The pressure group model

The median voter model is a useful framework to understand the process of aggregation of individual preferences into migration policy, and this is particularly true when it comes to major reforms, which are introduced rather infrequently. On the other hand, it can hardly be used to gain a perspective on the drivers of changes in more specific provisions, like the number of visas of a certain category to be issued in a given year or the specific requirements of a labour market test. To this end, and more broadly to better capture the complexity of the political process in modern democratic societies, the role played by interest groups should also be considered. As a matter of fact, there is substantial anecdotal evidence suggesting that lobbies—acting on behalf of specific subsets of society—have been actively involved in shaping policies towards skilled immigration.

Both anti-immigrant and pro-immigrant interest groups have been at work. In the USA, professional associations representing highly qualified native workers have played an important role in limiting the inflows of foreign skilled migrants. For example, recently the Institute of Electrical and Electronics Engineers (IEEE) has been active in demanding a reduction in both the number of H1B visas for highly skilled professionals, and L1 visas for highly skilled intra-company transferees.[19] Similarly, as documented in a recent study by Glied and Sarkar (2009), '...the profession of medicine exerts a significant influence on the rate of skilled migration of foreign physicians'.

At the same time, there is ample evidence for the efforts of pro-immigrant lobbies—representing the business sector—in shaping migration policy. For example, during the boom of the late 1990s, Silicon Valley entrepreneurs trooped in front of Congress asking for an increase in the number of H1B visas for highly skilled professionals, and warned of a looming Y2K disaster if the large number of foreign engineers and computer scientists they requested was not allowed to enter the country (Goldsborough, 2000). Interestingly, this pattern is common across many destination countries. For instance, in August 2006, at the peak of the debate in the UK on whether to put a cap on migration from Bulgaria and Romania once the two countries became members of the

---

[19] See www.ieee.org.

European Union, the Business for New Europe group (BNE) issued a statement saying that '...the UK should continue with its open door policy'. The heads of the supermarket chain Sainsburys and the head of the European division of the investment bank Merrill Lynch were among the signatories of the statement.

To formally study the role played by pressure groups in shaping policy towards international factor mobility, Facchini and Willmann (2005) developed a simple theoretical model, which is based upon the menu auction framework pioneered by Bernheim and Whinston (1986). In their setting, policy is determined as the result of the interaction between organized groups representing production factors, who maximize the net welfare of their members, and an elected politician who—in determining policy—trades off aggregate welfare vis-à-vis political contributions. Using a one-good multiple factors framework, Facchini and Willmann (2005) find that policies depend on both whether a production factor is represented or not by a lobby and on the degree of substitutability/complementarity between domestic and imported factors. In particular, the paper shows that a non-organized factor will not be able to influence the policy determination process. Second, an organized factor will instead be effective in reducing the inflows of a substitute factor and in increasing the inflows of a complement factor. Thus, this model is able to rationalize both the intense lobbying activities recently carried out by doctors and health-care providers in the USA—which resulted in the introduction of the new H1C visa category in 1999 for foreign nurses—and the fierce opposition of professional associations representing local nurses. The working of the median voter and interest groups models is summarized in Box 5.1.

Box 5.1 THE POLITICAL ECONOMY OF INTERNATIONAL FACTOR MOBILITY

We outline here two simple models that can be used to understand the political economy of international factor mobility. Consider a small open economy, where GDP is produced using two factors: skilled (L_S) and unskilled labour (L_U), according to a production technology $Y = F(L_S, L_U)$. Production factors can relocate to the country from the rest of the world, but their flows are controlled by policies implemented by the national government. To take into account potential crowding effects, we assume that the production function exhibits decreasing returns to scale in the mobile factors. As a result, profits (π) are strictly positive in equilibrium. The country is populated by a continuum of agents and the total size of the population is normalized to one. Each agent in the interval [0,1] is indexed by i, and the domestic supply of each (mobile) factor is inelastic and equal to (l_S, l_U). For simplicity, we choose GDP as the numeraire, normalize international factor prices by setting them equal to 1 and assume the profits generated in the economy to be a lump sum equally distributed among all citizens. Domestic factor prices are represented by $\omega = (\omega_S, \omega_U)$. We model restrictions to the relocation of production factors across countries as a quota, accompanied by a tax levied on the relocating factor. As a result, the relocating factor retains a share of the surplus associated with the relocation, while the remainder is captured by the host country's government in the form of additional tax revenues which are a lump sum rebated to the domestic population.

A median voter model

Let $\lambda_{i,j}$ be the fraction of factor $j \in (s, u)$ supplied by agent i, with $\int \lambda_{i,j} di = 1$, for all j. Furthermore, assume that each agent is endowed with an identical amount of time, that must be allocated to the supply of the two factors, that is $\lambda_{i,j} = 1 + (1 + \lambda_{i,j'})$ for all $i \in [0, 1], j \neq j'$. As a result, the total endowment of the two factors in the economy is the same.

Let m_j be the quantity of factor j imported (exported, if negative) by the country and let y_j be the share of the rent on factor j captured by the government and assume that the revenues from the policy are lump sum rebated to all citizens. The utility function of citizen i is then represented by

$$u_i(\omega) = \sum_j \lambda_{ij} l_j \omega_j + \sum_j \gamma_j T_j + \pi \qquad [5.11']$$

The first term captures factor income, the second represent the revenues of the policy ($T_j = (\omega_j - 1)m_j$) that are lump sum rebated to the agents and the third term captures the profits—which can also be interpreted as the return to an immobile factor. Assuming that the production function is separable in each input,[20] let $q_j = \phi_j(\omega_j)$ be the quota implemented by the government on the inflow of factor j, with $\phi_j'(\omega_j) < 0$. Given our assumptions, ϕ_j can be inverted, and we can express $\omega_j = \phi_j^{-1}(q_j)$. This means that a more restrictive quota leads to a higher domestic factor return. Let λ_{mj} be the share of the factor owned by the median voter. Assuming $u_i(\omega)$ to be strictly concave, we can derive the policy that maximizes the well-being of the median voter, which is given by:

$$\Phi^{-1}(q_j) - 1 = \frac{1}{\gamma_j m_{j'}} [L_j(1 - \gamma_j) - (\lambda_{mj} - \gamma_j)l_j] \qquad [5.12']$$

To gain some intuition for this result, let us focus on the case in which rent capturing by the host country's government is complete, that is $\gamma_j = 1$. Equation [5.12'] then simplifies to:

$$\phi^{-1}(q_j) - 1 = -\frac{1}{m_{j'}}(\lambda_{mj} - 1)l_j \qquad [5.13']$$

The left hand side of [5.13'] describes the amount of protection granted to the domestic factor in terms of the difference between the return prevailing on the domestic market and the return fetched by the factor on the international market. Obviously, the higher the quota, the smaller the amount of protection granted to the factor. Notice also that $-1/m_{j'}$ is positive, as the import demand is a decreasing function of the factor price. If the median voter owns more than the average share of the population of factor j, that is if $\lambda_{mj} - 1 > 0$, then factor j will be protected, that is the imports of the factor will be

---

[20] This is a technical assumption we need to address the multidimensionality of the voting problem. See Helpman (1997) and Facchini and Testa (2009) for a discussion.

limited by a quota that leads the domestic price to be higher than the price prevailing on international factor markets. At the same time, this implies that factor j' imports will be subsidized. In other words, if the median voter is more unskilled than average, he will be both in favour of admitting skilled migrants and of restricting entry of unskilled migrants, that is, he will be in favour of a migration inflow which is skilled compared to the native population. The protection received by the factor is increasing with the importance of the factor (l_j), while it is decreasing with the size of the distortion induced by protection, which is captured by the sensitivity of the import demand to price variations (m'_j).

A lobbying model

Consider now an alternative framework, which is a simplified version of the model developed in Facchini and Willmann (2005). Here the policy choice, rather than the result of direct democracy, is modelled as the outcome of the interaction between organized pressure groups and an elected politician. Assume that a subset $\wedge$ of the production factors is organized and lobbies an elected politician to shape policy towards factor movements. The game is modelled as a menu auction, where in the first stage organized groups offer the elected official contributions $C_i(\omega)$ that depend on the entire vector of domestic factor prices, while in the second stage the government chooses the policy to be implemented and receives the lobby's payments.

Each organized group maximizes the total income of its members, net of the contributions paid to the politician. Denoting by α_j the share of the population that owns factor j, the gross pay-off received by each factor, lobbying or not, is given by:

$$g_j(\omega) = \omega_j \ell_j + \alpha_j [\pi + \sum_j \gamma_j T_j], \qquad [5.14']$$

The government trades off aggregate welfare vis-à-vis political contribution and thus maximizes:

$$W(\omega) = a \sum_{j \in J} g_j(\omega) + \sum_{j \in \lambda} C_j(\omega), \qquad [5.15']$$

where a is the weight attached to aggregate welfare. Solving the game, we can show that the interaction between the organized groups and the government results in a policy towards factor mobility that takes the following form:

$$\phi_j^{-1}(q_j) - 1 = -\frac{1}{\gamma_j} \sum_{i \in I} F_{ji} \left[\frac{(I_i - \alpha_\wedge)l_i}{a + \alpha_\wedge} - (1 - \gamma_i)(L_i - l_i) \right] \qquad [5.16']$$

To gain more intuition, let us assume once again that rent capturing is complete, that is $\gamma_j = 1$ and that factors are neither complements nor substitute, that is that $F_{ji} = 0$. Equation [5.16'] then becomes:

$$\phi_j^{-1}(q_j) - 1 = \left(\frac{I_j - \alpha_\wedge}{a + \alpha_\wedge} \right) \cdot \frac{l_j/m_j}{\varepsilon_j} \qquad [5.17']$$

where I_j is an indicator that is equal to one if the factor is organized, and zero otherwise, α_Λ is the share of the population that is engaged in lobbying activities, and ε_j is the import demand elasticity. Factor j thus receives positive protection, that is there is a positive differential between the domestic factor return and the international price as long as it is actively represented by a lobby. As in the median voter setup, protection is a function of the relevance of the factor for the domestic economy. In particular, protection is positively correlated with the number of native workers if such workers are politically organized. The opposite is true if native workers are not politically organized. Finally, protection is decreasing with the distortion introduced by the policy. What happens if we consider the more general situation in which production factors can be complements or substitutes? If factor i and j are complements then $F_{ji} > 0$, while if they are substitutes then $F_{ji} < 0$. From the first term in equation [5.16'] we can then see that, if the two factors are complements, the lobbying efforts of factor i will have a detrimental effect on the protection granted to factor j (and the more so, the higher the number of native workers who own factor i), and the opposite is true if the two are substitutes.

5.4 Empirical assessment

In this section we first investigate whether voters' attitudes towards skilled migration are consistent with skill-selective migration policies, if preferences are aggregated through a simple majority-voting mechanism. We next turn to analysing the role played by interest-group dynamics.

5.4.1 From preferences to policies: does the median voter rule?

In this section, we analyse the variation across countries in skilled migration policies, as a function of the opinion of the median voter and, in general, public opinion towards skilled migration. In Figure 5.4, we correlate the policy on highly skilled workers in each country in 2007—from the United Nations data set—with the opinion on skilled immigration of the *median* voter in that country in 2002–2003 (we use the variable *pro-skilled-migration (median)* from the ESS data set, see Table 5.6). In Figure 5.5, we consider the impact on the 2007 skill-selective policy in each country of *average* attitudes towards skilled migration in that country in 2002–2003 (we use the variable *pro-skilled-migration (mean)* from the ESS data set, see Table 5.6). Both figures show no correlation between public opinion and policies.

It is interesting to compare Figures 5.4 and 5.5 to the evidence provided in Facchini and Mayda (2009b) in relation to *overall* migration policies. That paper constructs very similar figures using information on policies and public opinion towards overall migration. It shows that overall migration policies are positively correlated with the opinion of the median voter and, in general, public opinion towards overall migration across countries. Thus, the median voter model appears to work much better in explaining overall migration policies as compared to skill-selective migration policies.

Table 5.6. Does the median voter rule?

	Pro-skilled-migration (mean)	Pro-skilled-migration (median)	Policy on highly skilled workers
Sweden	4.6269	5	Maintain
Norway	5.1477	5	Raise
Netherlands	5.6520	6	Raise
Italy	5.7260	6	No intervention
Portugal	6.0586	6	Maintain
Spain	6.0938	7	Maintain
Ireland	6.1062	7	Raise
Belgium	6.1169	7	Maintain
Switzerland	6.2178	7	Raise
Denmark	6.2653	7	Raise
Luxembourg	6.2751	7	
France	6.2903	7	Raise
United Kingdom	6.3077	7	Raise
Finland	6.3266	7	Raise
Czech Republic	6.3285	7	Raise
Slovenia	6.3300	7	Maintain
Austria	6.6670	7	Maintain
Germany	6.7234	7	Raise
Israel	6.7531	8	Maintain
Hungary	6.8384	7	No intervention

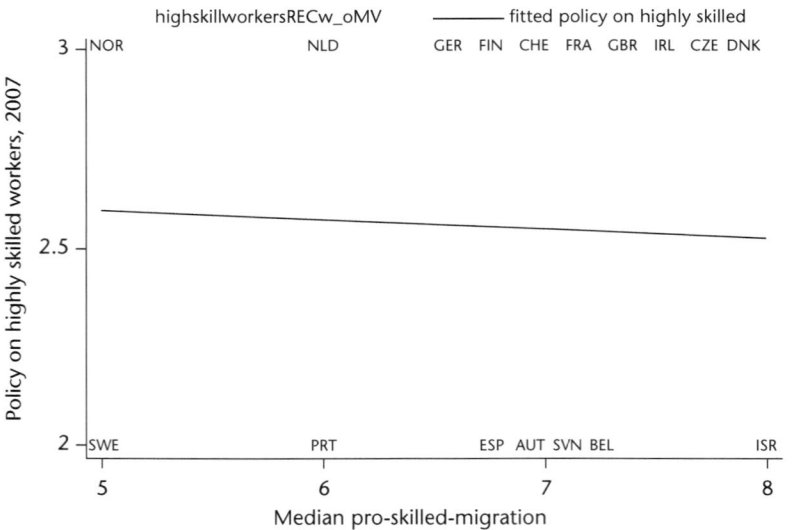

Figure 5.4. The impact of the median of individual attitudes towards skilled immigrants (2002–2003) on skilled migration policies (2007).

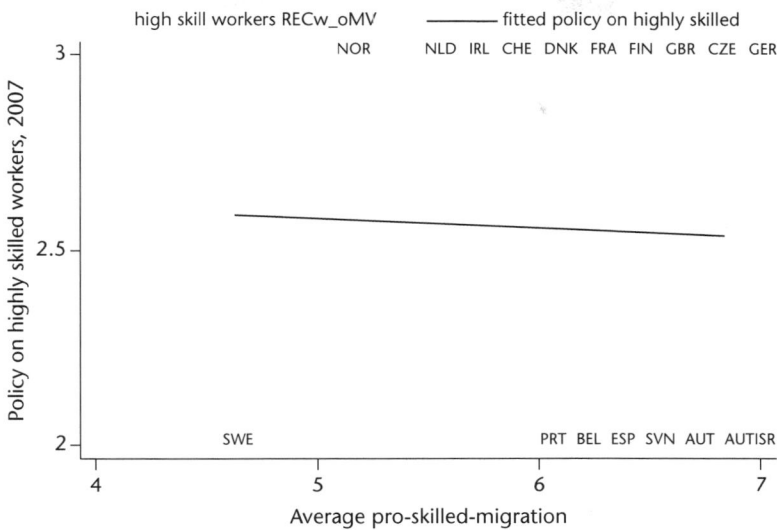

Figure 5.5. The impact of the mean of individual attitudes towards skilled immigrants (2002–2003) on skilled migration policies (2007).

Table 5.6 provides additional evidence on the importance of public opinion in shaping policies towards skilled migrants. To facilitate the interpretation of the statistics, we order countries by increasing values of *pro-skilled-migration (mean)*, which appears in the first column of the table. In the second and third columns, respectively, we show the median value of *pro-skilled-migration* and a summary measure of policy on highly skilled workers. Out of the top five countries where public opinion is most in favour of good educational qualifications of immigrants (Slovenia, Austria, Germany, Israel, and Hungary), not one has policies in place to raise the migration of highly skilled workers. Only Germany implemented some incremental policy changes in this direction. On the other hand, among the three countries whose voters are least concerned about the skill composition of migrants (Sweden, Norway, and the Netherlands), two of them (Norway and the Netherlands) have skill-selective policies in place (according to the United Nations data).

The evidence in Figures 5.4 and 5.5 and Table 5.6 is only anecdotal for a number of reasons: for example, it is based on a small number of countries, which are the only ones with data on both public opinion and policies; it does not take into account Canada, Australia ,and New Zealand, which have been actively engaged in skill-selective policies. However, this evidence provides very little support for a median voter explanation of policies towards skilled migration.

5.4.2 The pressure group model at work: evidence from the H1B visa programme

An interesting context to empirically assess the role played by lobbying groups—in the shaping of immigration policy towards highly skilled workers—is represented by the H1B visa programme in the USA. As we discussed in Chapter 1, the H1B visa programme in its current form was introduced in the Immigration Act of 1990. Under the original legislation, the number of visas to be issued was capped at 65,000 per year, but this has been subsequently increased to 115,000 in 1998 and again to 195,000 in 2000, reverting back to 90,000 in 2004. How are the visas allocated among different sectors of the economy?

Following the introduction of the Lobbying Disclosure Act of 1995, lobbying organizations have been required to provide a substantial amount of information on their activities. Starting from 1996, all lobbyists must file reports to the Secretary of the Senate's Office of Public Records (SOPR) and the Clerk of the House of Representatives which list the name of each client (firm or professional association/union) and the total income they have received from them to lobby on their behalf. At the same time, all firms with in-house lobbying departments are required to file similar reports stating the *total* dollar amount they have spent in lobbying. Importantly, legislation requires the disclosure not only of the dollar amounts actually received/spent, but also of the issues for which lobbying is carried out. Immigration (IMM) is one of the issues for which lobbying is carried out. The reports filed by two major US academic institutions, Harvard University and the University of California system, and by Microsoft Corporation are available from this site http://www.senate.gov/legislative/Public_Disclosure/LDA_reports.htm.[21]

Between January and March 2008, the UC system spent US $270,000 in lobbying, while Harvard's total spending amounted to US $235,000 for the period April–June of the same year. For both institutions, lobbying on immigration is an important issue: the UC system lists explicitly H1B visa issues as the specific item of interest, while Harvard refers more generally to 'student, scholar visa issues'. In its report, Microsoft lists immigration as a general issue and, among the specific issues, H1B visas and L1 visas.

Data on lobbying expenditures has been systematically collected by the Center for Responsive Politics in Washington DC, and has been used in a recent paper by Facchini, Mayda, and Mishra (2008) to analyse the effect of immigration lobbying on the allocation of work and related visas across sectors of the economy. Figures 5.6 and 5.7—taken from Facchini, Mayda, and Mishra (2008)—illustrate respectively the top ten sectors by spending on

---

[21] http://www.senate.gov/legislative/Public_Disclosure/LDA_reports.htm.

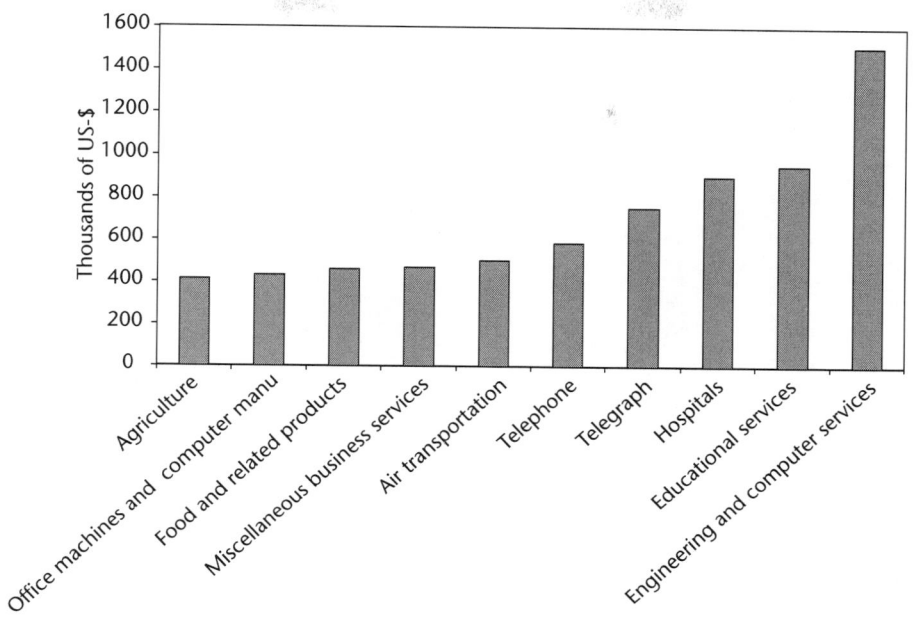

Figure 5.6. Top 10 spenders for immigration, 2001–2005.

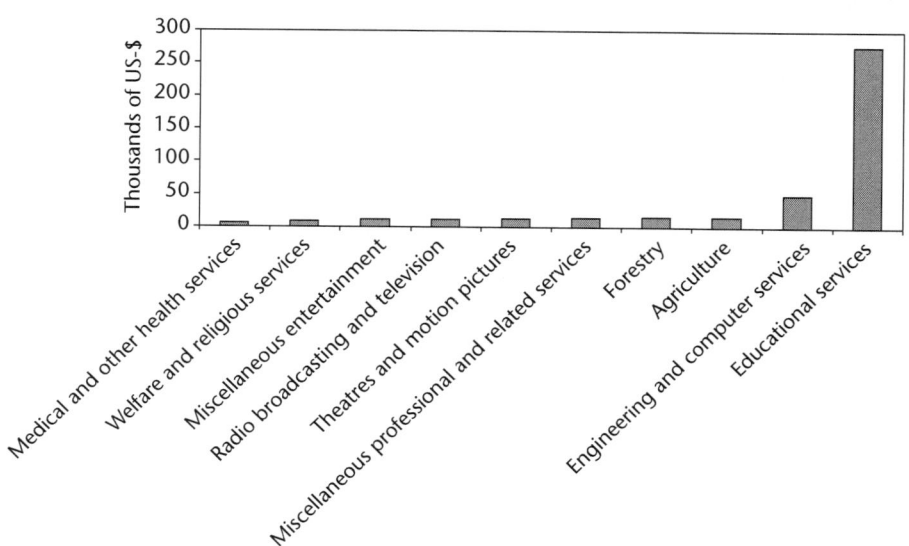

Figure 5.7. Top 10 sectors with the highest number of visas, 2001–2005.

immigration issues, and the top ten work visa receivers. Interestingly, human capital-intensive sectors, like 'educational services' and 'engineering and computer services' appear at the very top of both distributions.

Drawing from Facchini, Mayda, and Mishra (2008), in the next figures we focus on highly skilled workers—in particular, those admitted to the USA under the H1B visa programme—and investigate the role of business lobbying groups and professional associations/trade unions in shaping the allocation of H1B visas across sectors. We expect that—in a given industry—the former will lobby to increase the number of H1B visas, as skilled labour complements capital, while the latter will lobby in the opposite direction, as foreign qualified workers compete with members of professional associations and unions.

Figure 5.8 shows that sectors in which employers spend more on migration lobbying tend to have a higher number of H1B visas as a share of total employment. On the other hand, Figure 5.9 suggests that sectors in which labour unions and professional associations are more active—as measured by sectoral membership rates[22]—tend to see a lower number of highly skilled

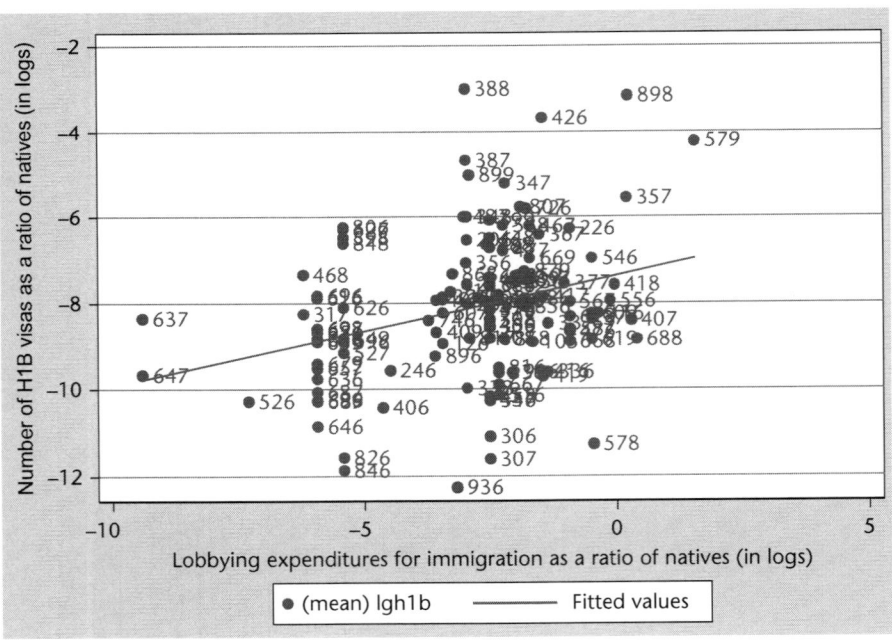

Figure 5.8. Scatterplot—lobbying expenditures for immigration and number of H1B visas.

---

[22] For details on the variable definitions etc., see Facchini, Mayda, and Mishra (2008).

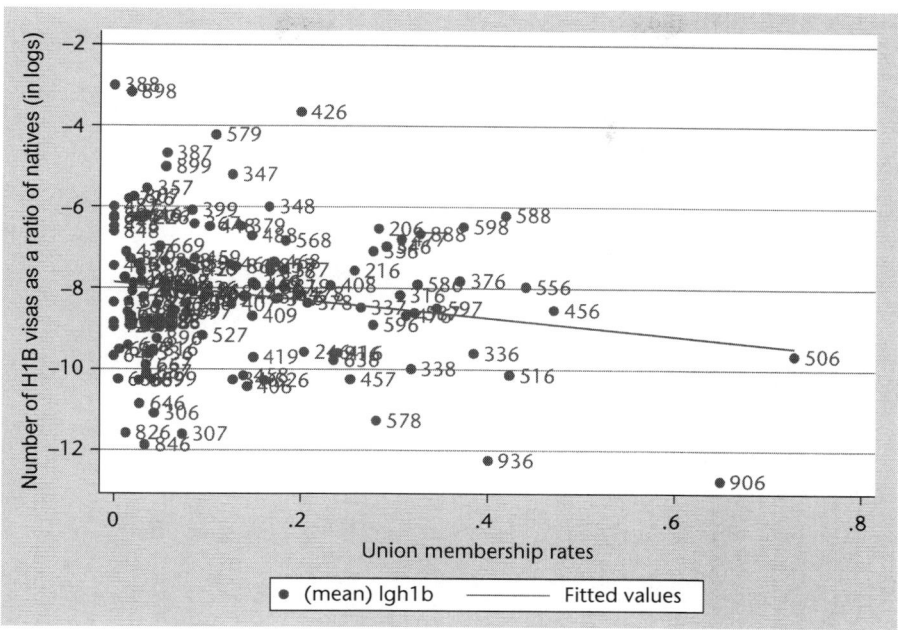

Figure 5.9. Scatterplot—membership rates in unions and employee professional associations and number of H1B visas.

foreign workers employed. The evidence highlighted in the figures finds further support in the regressions reported in Table 5.7, which control for a series of sector-specific drivers of immigration—both demand-side factors and supply-side factors.[23] Interestingly, the relationships between interest group activity and the number of H1B visas are not only statistically significant, but also quantitatively important. The estimated effects imply that an increase by 10 per cent in firms' lobbying on migration (per native worker) is associated with an increase by 1.8 per cent in the number of H1B visas (per native worker) allocated to that particular sector. Similarly, a one percentage point increase in union membership—for example, moving from 10 to 11 percentage points, which amounts to a 10 per cent increase in the union membership rate—reduces it by 3.6 per cent.

[23] Although in Table 5.7 we check the robustness of our findings for the introduction of a number of controls, we are still concerned that our estimates might be driven by endogeneity and reverse causality. In additional robustness checks, we check that our results are robust to performing a falsification exercise and, also, to using an instrumental variables strategy. See Facchini, Mayda, and Mishra (2008).

Table 5.7. The impact of interest groups on US H1B visas.

Dependent variable	Log (H1B visas/native workers)
Log (lobbying exp/native workers)	0.182***
	0.065
Union membership rate	−3.623***
	1.292
Lg (output)	−0.114
	0.181
Unemployment rate	1.661
	4.323
Log (price)	1.112
	2.165
Log (capital)	0.009
	0.151
Log (FDI)	0.107
	0.066
Shocks	−4.892**
	2.444
Log (lag US wages)	9.834***
	2.951
Log (number of native workers)	−0.169
	0.198
N	120
R-squared	0.34

Notes: All data are averaged over 2001–2005. Standard errors are corrected for heteroscedasticity and denoted in parentheses. ***, ** and * denote significance at 1, 5, and 10% respectively.

5.5 Conclusions

To conclude, we find that attitudes towards skilled migrants are consistent with the predictions of economic models. More educated natives are *less* likely to favour high educational qualifications of migrants across several countries—consistent with the labour market channel—while richer individuals are more likely to—consistent with the welfare state channel under the tax adjustment model. In addition, we do not find evidence consistent with the median voter model, which suggests that public opinion does not play a key role in shaping policies towards skilled migration. On the other hand, we show that interest groups are actively engaged and effective in affecting policies towards skilled migrants. Our results are not surprising. While public opinion has a perception of the effect of skilled migration which is 'correct'— that is consistent with what economic models predict—it appears to count less in shaping policies towards skilled migration than in affecting the overall number of migrants (see Facchini and Mayda, 2009b). Instead, interest groups representing specific segments of society (firms who benefit from and professional native workers who are hurt by the arrival of qualified foreign workers) appear to play a much more active role in this policy dimension.

Does our analysis explain the strong status quo bias discussed in Chapter 1—that is, the slow progress towards skill-selective immigration policies in several OECD destination countries? Our answer is yes, but only in part. On the one hand, we do find evidence of one important source of opposition to the arrival of foreign talents. Skilled native workers—organized in interest groups, that is professional associations/unions—are vocal and effective in reducing the number of visas for skilled migrants in one of the most important destinations of migration flows, the USA, according to our analysis. However, our results also show that pro-skilled migration interest groups—that is, groups that lobby on behalf of business owners—are powerful in shaping (increasing) the number of skilled immigrants in the USA. Therefore, how do we explain the status quo bias in skill-selective immigration policies?

One possibility is that, while the two groups—in favour of and against skilled migration—are both effective, the impact of pro-skilled migration interest groups on long-term reforms of the migration system might be hindered by lack of consensus on how best to proceed. For example, in the USA, the establishment of a point system has been slowed by the opposition of business groups who do not want to lose flexibility in hiring skilled migrants, which would happen given the bureaucracy of a point system.

Another explanation is that, although public opinion does not appear to have an important effect on the skill bias of migration policies, the opposite is true as regards policies that affect the *overall* number of migrants. In other words, policymakers do take public opinion into account as they formulate policies regarding the overall number of immigrants (see Facchini and Mayda, 2009b). Therefore, policymakers might be reluctant to encourage increases in the number of skilled migrants since, to the extent that a given number of unskilled migrants will come no matter what (for example, as illegals or through family reunification), this will imply increases in the total number of migrants, to which public opinion is opposed.

Alternatively, we can assume that policymakers are in control of the number of both skilled and unskilled migrants who arrive in their country. In that case, given that public opinion is willing to absorb only a limited total number of immigrants, there exists a trade-off between the number of skilled migrants and the number of unskilled migrants admitted by policymakers. In that case, what counts is the relative power of industries which favour skilled versus unskilled migration. Policymakers may not be willing to disappoint powerful sectors—such as agriculture, construction, textile, and apparel—which rely on large numbers of unskilled migrants.

What do we expect looking forward? Our guess is that more and more countries will try to implement skill-selective immigration policies. The reason is that, notwithstanding the opposition of some skilled native workers and the difficulty of reaching a consensus on the best way to set up a skill-selective immigration policy, the gains are too big to be forgone.

We know that, from the point of view of each destination country, there are large gains from setting up a skill-selective migration policy (see Chapter 4). In the next chapter, we ask whether there are also some unintended side-effects from these policy changes.

Appendix A: model of individual attitudes towards immigration

To study the effect of immigration on individual attitudes we use a simplified version of the model developed in Facchini and Mayda (2009a). This framework will allow us to identify three channels through which migration can have an impact on individual attitudes: the labour market channel, the welfare state channel, and the efficiency channel.

In a small open economy, two production factors, skilled (L_S)and unskilled labour (L_U) are combined using a constant returns to scale technology $F(L_S, L_U)$ to produce a single output Y. The economy is populated by a set N of natives (indexed by n) and a set M of immigrants (indexed by m). Each native is endowed with one unit of labour, either skilled or unskilled, and with an amount $e^n \in \{e^L, e^H\}$ of the output good, where $e^H > e^L$. Immigrants supply instead only one unit of skilled or unskilled labour. The total endowment of the numeraire good in the economy is thus equal to $\sum_n e^n = E$. The total supply of each skill is given instead by $L_j = \phi_j N + \varphi_j M$ with $j \in \{U, S\}$, where ϕ_j and φ_j are respectively the share of workers with skill profile j in the native and immigrant populations. The key variable to assess the effects of migration on individual attitudes is the migrants to native ratio $\pi = M/N$, which is assumed to be equal to zero in the initial equilibrium. Furthermore, we will hold the number of natives constant throughout the analysis. Setting the price of output equal to one, let w_S and w_U be, respectively, the unskilled and skilled wage, with $w_S > w_U$. Domestic equilibrium is characterized by the solution of the following system of equations:

$$1 = c(w_U, w_S) \tag{A5.1}$$

$$L_U = Y \frac{\partial c(w_U, w_S)}{\partial w_U} \tag{A5.2}$$

$$L_S = Y \frac{\partial c(w_U, w_S)}{\partial w_S} \tag{A5.3}$$

where $c(w_U, w_S)$ is the unit production cost and equation [A5.1'] is the zero profit condition, while equations [A5.2'] and [A5.3'] are the factor markets clearing conditions.

The presence of a redistributive welfare state in the host country is modelled by introducing an egalitarian income tax τ levied on all sources of income, the revenues of which are lump sum rebated to all residents through a per capita transfer b. The government budget constraint is thus given by:

$$\tau(w_U L_U + w_S L_S + E) = b(N + M) \qquad [A5.4]$$

Notice that individuals take as given the initial size of the welfare state (τ and b), that is we do not develop a political economy model of the extent of redistribution carried out within society. This implies that our analysis can be considered as a short-run view of the consequences of immigration. In the presence of a welfare state, the well-being of a native n of skill level j is a function of her income net of taxes/transfers, which is given by:

$$I_j^n = (1 - \tau)G_j^n + b \qquad [A5.5]$$

where $G_j^n = w_j + e^n$. The effect of migration on her net income can thus be measured by

$$\frac{\hat{I}_j^n}{d\pi} = \frac{(1 - \tau)w_j \frac{\hat{w}_j}{d\pi}}{I_j^n} - \frac{\tau G_j^n \frac{\hat{\tau}}{d\pi}}{I_j^n} + \frac{b \frac{\hat{b}}{d\pi}}{I_j^n} \qquad [A5.6]$$

where $\hat{I}_j^n = dI_j^n / I_j^n$ etc. Thus, immigration will have an effect on the net income of a native through three channels. The first term on the right hand side of equation [A5.6'] represents the *labour market* channel, while the second and third terms capture the *welfare state* channel. In particular, the second term represents the effect of migration through the adjustment of the tax level, and the third term captures instead the effect of immigration through adjustments in the government's transfer to residents.

How will different native individuals react to an inflow of foreign workers? First of all, domestic workers might face competition in the host country's labour market. It is easy to show that an unskilled native will see his wage decrease as a result of immigration ($\frac{\hat{w}_U}{d\pi} < 0$) if and only if immigrants are relatively less skilled than natives. The opposite is true for skilled immigration. Thus, through the labour market, we expect skilled (unskilled) natives to be in favour of (against) immigration in countries where immigrants are unskilled compared to the native population. Vice versa, in countries where immigrants are skilled compared to the natives, we expect unskilled (skilled) natives to be in favour of (against) immigration.

To gain some intuition for the importance of the type of welfare state response to immigration in shaping individual attitudes, we consider a simplified setting in which one of two possible adjustments occur. In the first, which we label the *tax adjustment model*, per capita benefits are held constant (thus the third term in equation [A5.6'] equals zero), while the tax rate reacts to maintain the government budget in equilibrium. In the second, which we label the *benefit adjustment model*, tax rates are held constant (thus the second term in equation [A5.6'] equals zero) and the benefit level instead adjusts to restore the government budget's equilibrium.

Totally differentiating equation [A5.4'], holding the benefit level constant (*tax adjustment model*), we obtain that $d\pi = \hat{\tau} + \sum_j \eta_j \hat{L}_j + \sum_j \eta_j \hat{w}_j$ and thus the effect of immigration on the tax level is given by:

$$\frac{\hat{\tau}}{d\pi} = \frac{(\phi_U - \eta_U)(\beta_U - 1)}{(1 - \phi_U)} + \frac{\eta_E(1 - \psi_U)}{1 - \phi_U} - \sum_j \eta_j \frac{\hat{w}_j}{d\pi} \qquad [A5.7]$$

where $(\phi_U - \eta_U) > 0$ is the difference between the share of the unskilled in the initial population (ϕ_U) and their share in the initial GDP (η_U), ψ_U is the share of unskilled in the immigrant population, $\beta_U = \psi_U / \phi_U$ and n_E is the share of the initial endowment in total domestic income. If $\eta_E = 0$, and ignoring for now the effects of immigration through the labour market channel, it is easy to see that if immigration is low (high) skilled, that is if $\beta_U > 1 (\beta_U < 1)$, immigration will lead to an increase (decrease) in the overall tax rates in order to keep the per capita benefit constant. To assess the effect of immigration on an individual characterized by a pre tax income level G, we need to substitute equation (A5.7) in equation (A5.6') and obtain

$$\frac{\hat{I}}{d\pi} = -\frac{G\tau}{b + G(1 - \tau)} \left[\frac{\hat{\tau}}{d\pi} \right] \qquad [A5.8]$$

From here we can easily see that under the *tax adjustment model, an inflow of skilled immigrants (implying that $\frac{\hat{\tau}}{d\pi} < 0$) is more desirable for an individual the higher is her pre-tax income.* To the contrary, *an inflow of unskilled immigrants (implying that $\frac{\hat{\tau}}{d\pi} > 0$) is more desirable for an individual the lower is her pre-tax income* (see Fig. 5.2). The intuition for this result is that, if the demogrant is held fixed, the cost of an inflow of unskilled immigrants (higher tax rate) will fall disproportionately more on higher-income natives. Analogously, in the presence of skilled immigration, the higher-income natives will be the largest beneficiaries, as they will enjoy a disproportionately larger decrease in their net tax burden due to the decrease in the tax rate.

If we turn now to the *benefit adjustment model*, totally differentiating equation [A5.4'] and holding the tax rate constant, we can show that the effect of an immigrant inflow on the per capita benefit is given by:

$$\frac{\hat{b}}{d\pi} = \frac{(\phi_U - \eta_U)(1 - \beta_U)}{(1 - \phi_U)} + \frac{\eta_E(1 - \psi_U)}{1 - \phi_U} - \sum_j \eta_j \frac{\hat{w}_j}{d\pi} \qquad [A5.9]$$

Once again, assuming $n_E = 0$, and ignoring the labour market channel, it is easy to see that an inflow of unskilled (skilled) immigrants will lead to a decrease (increase) in the per capita benefit level. To assess the effect of immigration on an individual of pre-tax income G under these hypotheses we need to substitute equation [A5.9'] in [A5.6'] and obtain

$$\frac{\hat{I}}{d\pi} = \frac{b\frac{\hat{b}}{d\pi}}{b + G(1 - \tau)} \qquad [A5.10]$$

From here it is easy to show that, under the *benefit adjustment model, an inflow of skilled immigrants is more desirable for an individual the lower is her pre-tax income*. To the contrary, *an inflow of unskilled immigrants is more desirable for an individual the higher is her pre-tax income* (see Fig. 5.3). To understand this result, notice that the reduction in the demogrant brought about by unskilled immigration will carry a larger impact on the individuals with a smaller income. If immigration is instead skilled, the resulting increase in the demogrant will disproportionately benefit lower-income individuals. The reason is that the transfer represents a larger fraction of a low-income person's net income.

Notice that under both welfare state scenarios, unless the skill composition of the migrant and native populations is identical, the effects of migration on the two dimensions of the welfare state are mediated by a third channel, the efficiency channel that affects the size of the tax base. At the margin, labour is paid to the value of its marginal product, so an infinitesimal inflow of immigrants will leave the total remuneration of the existing labour force unchanged ($\sum_j \eta_j \frac{\hat{w}_j}{d\pi} = 0)$) and have no effect on the redistribution carried out by the welfare state. On the other hand, if the inflow of immigrants is large, the total remuneration of existing workers will increase $\sum_j \eta_j \frac{\hat{w}_j}{d\pi} = 0)$, and relax the government budget constraint (these are the gains from migration pointed out first by Berry and Soligo (1969)).

Annex Tables and Figures

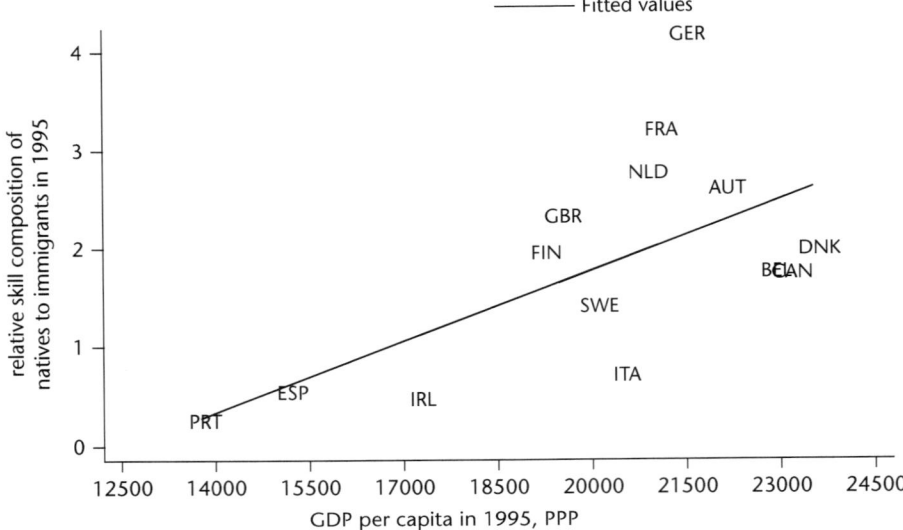

Figure A5.1. Per capita GDP and skill composition of natives relative to immigrants, 1995.

Data source: World Development Indicators, World Bank and SOPEMI, OECD.

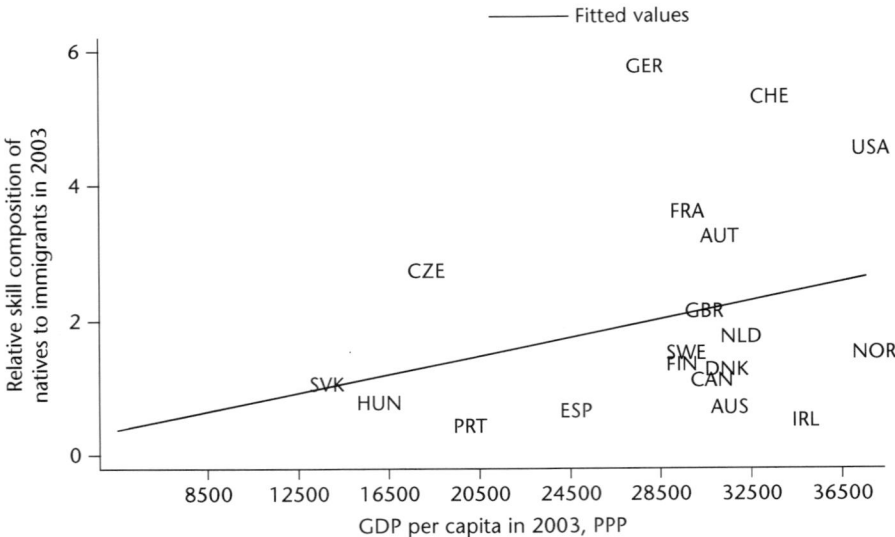

Figure A5.2. Per capita GDP and skill composition of natives relative to immigrants, 2003.

Data source: World Development Indicators, World Bank and SOPEMI, OECD.

Table A5.1. Summary statistics of individual attitudes towards immigration (ISSP 1995) and country-level variables.

Country	Pro Immig Opinion						average Pro Immig Opinion (7)	median Pro Immig Opinion (8)	average Pro-Immig Dummy (9)	average educ years (10)	median educ years (11)	per capita GDP (12)	relative skill mix (natives vs. imm) (13)	net migration 2000 (14)
	reduced a lot (1)	reduced a little (2)	remain the same as it is (3)	increased a little (4)	increased a lot (5)	missing values (6)								
Austria	28.36	24.72	37.74	2.93	0.81	5.45	2.19	2	3.95	10.36	9	22,090	2.53	0.0011
Bulgaria	32.58	17.19	9.77	2.17	1.54	36.74	1.78	1	5.87			5609		-0.0012
Canada	16.48	20.58	32.89	12.17	5.99	11.9	2.67	3	20.61	14.76	15	23,085	1.67	0.0048
Czech Republic	39.75	25.75	21.14	1.9	0.27	11.2	1.84	2	2.44	12.91	12	12,426		0.0010
Germany	48.07	22.37	17.37	1.74	0.54	9.9	1.72	2	2.54	10.92	10	21,479	4.09	0.0028
Great Britain	40.1	23.77	25.89	2.8	1.06	6.38	1.94	2	4.13	11.32	11	19,465	2.25	0.0019
Hungary	55.95	24.19	13.51	0.71	0.71	4.94	1.59	1	1.48	10.49	11	9315		0.0020
Ireland	6.63	13.56	55.35	15.6	2.24	6.62	2.93	3	19.10	12.25	12	17,264	0.40	0.0047
Italy	41.76	30.31	19.87	2.56	0.82	4.67	1.85	2	3.55	11.03	12	20,513	0.64	0.0021
Japan	13.38	21.82	35.03	10.11	2.95	16.72	2.61	3	15.68	11.87	12	23,212		0.0004
Latvia	49.74	20.05	17.19	0.26	0.13	12.63	1.64	1	0.45	11.61	11	4919		-0.0047
Netherlands	26.37	30.99	30.79	4.42	0.68	6.75	2.16	2	5.47	12.69	12	20,812	2.69	0.0020
New Zealand	26.79	31.65	24.06	8.59	2.22	6.68	2.23	2	11.59	14.31	14	17,706		0.0010
Norway	29.53	29.26	27.32	5.7	1.21	6.98	2.14	2	7.43	12.66	12	24,694		0.0030
Philippines	31.91	27.14	25.63	7.2	3.77	4.36	2.20	2	11.47	9.39	10	3519		-0.0024
Poland	25.92	17.53	19.91	4.13	1.82	30.68	2.11	2	8.58	10.29	10	6606		-0.0004
Russia	16.08	22.15	22.28	3.99	1.46	34.05	2.28	2	8.25	11.19	11	7093		0.0032
Slovak Republic	30.22	24.51	24.3	1.81	0.65	18.51	2.00	2	3.02	11.84	12	8487		0.0003
Slovenia	29.92	29.92	31.76	1.35	0.39	6.66	2.06	2	1.86	10.68	11	12,978		0.0008
Spain	8.77	26.64	45.49	6.39	1.07	11.64	2.60	3	8.44	10.13	9	15,163	0.47	0.0033
Sweden	35.66	29.25	21.88	4.13	2.11	6.97	2.01	2	6.71	11.41	11	20,031	1.34	0.0014
USA	29.69	25.19	21.83	4.58	2.14	16.57	2.09	2	8.05	13.43	13	27,395	1.79	0.0044
Overall	29.60	24.59	26.27	4.82	1.60	13.12	2.13	2	7.39	11.68	12	15,630	1.79	0.0014

Data source: 1995 ISSP National Identity Module. The survey sample excludes non-citizens. Pro Immig Opinion uses answers to the immigration question ('Do you think the number of immigrants to (R's country) nowadays should be . . .': reduced a lot, reduced a little, remain the same as it is, increased a little, increased a lot) and ranges from 1 (reduced a lot) to 5 (increased a lot). Pro-Immig Dummy equals one if Pro Immig Opinion is equal to 4 or 5, zero if Pro Immig Opinion is equal to 1, 2, or 3. Both variables exclude missing values. Net migration is equal to the net migration inflow, divided by the destination country's population, in 2000 (source: United Nations). All other variables are for the year 1995.

Table A5.2. Summary statistics of individual attitudes towards immigration (ISSP 2003) and country-level variables.

Country	Pro Immig Opinion						average Pro Immig Opinion (7)	median Pro Immig Opinion (8)	average Pro-Immig Dummy (9)	average educ years (10)	median educ years (11)	per capita GDP (12)	relative skill mix (natives vs. imm) (13)
	reduced a lot (1)	reduced a little (2)	remain the same as it is (3)	increased a little (4)	increased a lot (5)	missing values (6)							
Australia	16.79	19.65	34.71	15.81	5.72	7.32	2.72	3	23.23	13.06	13	31,268	0.60
Austria	32.72	26.75	29.94	5.25	1.03	4.31	2.11	2	6.56	11.08	10	30,851	3.14
Bulgaria	16.17	18.89	20.11	2.26	0.85	41.72	2.19	2	5.32	11.11	11	7620	
Canada	10.21	18.65	34.51	19.92	5.99	10.72	2.92	3	29.02	13.46	13	30,433	1.01
Chile	22.78	37.23	29.23	4.84	1.61	4.31	2.22	2	6.74	10.71	12	10,298	
Czech Republic	26.19	30.95	4.76	2.38	2.38	33.34	1.86	2	7.14	13.15	12	17,891	2.64
Denmark	25.87	21.63	35.93	7.87	1.21	7.49	2.32	2	9.81	13.18	13	31,074	1.16
Finland	15.83	15.61	36.97	18.70	3.02	9.87	2.75	3	24.10	11.98	12	29,215	1.24
France	35.37	21.38	22.30	4.09	2.20	14.66	2.02	2	7.37	13.68	13	29,500	3.51
Germany	44.29	23.66	19.39	2.79	0.90	8.97	1.82	2	4.06	10.68	11	27,612	5.66
Great Britain	50.88	22.68	14.81	3.41	1.76	6.46	1.74	1	5.53	11.78	11	30,171	2.04
Hungary	34.38	30.56	27.23	1.67	0.39	5.77	1.97	2	2.18	10.74	11	15,728	0.67
Ireland	27.65	28.81	30.73	7.32	1.06	4.43	2.22	2	8.77	12.92	13	34,742	0.40
Israel	26.68	16.49	26.68	12.10	13.92	4.13	2.69	3	27.14	13.41	12	23,062	
Japan	20.15	22.32	28.58	8.44	2.36	18.15	2.40	2	13.19	12.03	12	27,710	
Latvia	26.36	24.09	30.01	1.51	0.63	17.40	2.10	2	2.60	12.69	12	10,666	
Netherlands	37.84	26.95	23.86	2.47	0.95	7.93	1.93	2	3.72	13.59	13	31,728	1.66
New Zealand	26.81	27.62	25.28	10.70	3.06	6.53	2.31	2	14.72	13.28	13	23,528	
Norway	36.37	29.80	19.28	5.01	1.13	8.41	1.96	2	6.71	13.45	13	37,561	1.42
Philippines	17.92	19.58	37.67	11.50	5.58	7.75	2.64	3	18.52	9.66	10	4519	
Poland	19.42	20.67	28.97	3.52	1.72	25.70	2.29	2	7.06	10.82	10	12,277	
Portugal	19.09	35.01	39.10	2.38	0.59	3.83	2.28	2	3.09	8.12	6	19,879	0.33
Russia	39.01	25.14	10.26	1.64	1.68	22.27	1.74	1	4.27	11.59	12	8902	
Slovak Republic	26.37	15.58	25.15	7.14	2.09	23.67	2.25	2	12.09	13.51	13	13,550	0.95
Slovenia	16.71	32.05	43.34	2.48	0.37	5.05	2.34	2	3.00	11.20	11	19,448	
South Korea	9.13	33.35	34.52	17.57	5.32	10.11	2.85	3	25.47	12.30	12	19,317	
Spain	13.20	35.16	35.66	5.80	2.44	7.74	2.45	2	8.93	10.00	10	24,556	0.55
Sweden	25.55	27.30	26.95	8.05	2.27	9.88	2.27	2	11.46	12.10	12	29,341	1.42
Switzerland	16.91	27.02	45.64	5.11	0.32	5.00	2.42	3	5.71	11.36	10	33,080	5.19
Taiwan	34.34	31.76	18.01	3.33	1.09	11.47	1.93	2	4.99	11.30	12	20,701	
Uruguay	6.17	20.35	46.41	12.80	5.89	8.38	2.91	3	20.40	9.12	9	8276	
USA	23.70	28.74	28.66	5.47	3.34	10.09	2.29	2	9.80	13.88	14	37,545	4.44
Venezuela	20.04	28.38	42.18	3.95	2.81	2.64	2.40	3	6.95			5040	
Overall	23.88	23.78	27.32	6.63	2.48	15.91	2.29	2	10.84	11.89	12	22,336	2.00

Data source: 2003 ISSP National Identity Module. The survey sample excludes non-citizens. Pro Immig Opinion uses answers to the immigration question ('Do you think the number of immigrants to (R's country) should be '; 'reduced a lot', reduced a little', 'remain the same as it is', increased a little', increased a lot') and ranges from 1 (reduced a lot) to 5 (increased a lot). Pro-Immig Dummy equals one if

Table A5.3 Heckman selection model—ISSP 1995.

Linear regression with country FE	1	2	3	1'	2'	3'
Dependent variable	Pro Immig Opinion					
Method	OLS	OLS	OLS	Heckman	Heckman	Heckman
Age	-0.0029	-0.0029	-0.0024	-0.0029	-0.0029	-0.0024
	0.0005**	0.0005**	0.0005**	0.0005**	0.0005**	0.0005**
Male	-0.0188	-0.021	-0.0311	-0.0189	-0.0207	-0.0331
	0.0159	0.0158	0.0168 +	0.0166	0.0166	0.0180 +
Citizen	-0.2603	-0.2571	-0.1953	-0.2606	-0.256	-0.2004
	0.0588**	0.0587**	0.0683**	0.0625**	0.0625**	0.0700**
Parents' foreign citizenship	0.2242	0.2205	0.2099	0.2242	0.2204	0.2106
	0.0200**	0.0199**	0.0206**	0.0200**	0.0200**	0.0207**
Education (years of education)	0.0499	-0.4135	-0.4948	0.0499	-0.4128	-0.5014
	0.0025**	0.0493**	0.0816**	0.0026**	0.0512**	0.0841**
Education*gdp		0.0479	0.0562		0.0479	0.0569
		0.0051**	0.0083**		0.0053**	0.0086**
Log of real income	0.0272	0.59	0.9813	0.0272	0.5884	0.9929
	0.0128*	0.2415*	0.4256*	0.0132*	0.2436*	0.4269*
Log of real income*gdp		-0.0578	-0.0973		-0.0576	-0.0986
		0.0249*	0.0432*		0.0252*	0.0434*
Inverse Mills' ratio				-0.0015	0.0068	-0.0554
				0.1396	0.14	0.1736
Selection equation						
Probit with country FE						
Dependent variable				Immig Select	2'	3'
Age				0.0019	0.0019	0.0022
				0.0009*	0.0009*	0.0010*
Male				0.1043	0.1081	0.1263
				0.0285**	0.0286**	0.0323**
Citizen				0.4257	0.4257	0.2801
				0.0920**	0.0922**	0.1105*
Parents' foreign citizenship				-0.0341	-0.031	-0.044

continued

Table A5.3 Continued

Linear regression with country FE	1	2	3	1'	2'	3'
Dependent variable			Pro Immig Opinion			
Method	OLS	OLS	OLS	Heckman	Heckman	Heckman
Education (years of education)				0.0356	0.0357	0.0372
				-0.0108	0.3277	0.3742
				0.0045*	0.0754**	0.1422**
Education*gdp					-0.0354	-0.04
					0.0079**	0.0145**
Log of real income				0.0687	-0.8834	-0.6732
				0.0221**	0.3581*	0.7294
Log of real income*gdp					0.0992	0.078
					0.0373**	0.074
Trade select				0.7817	0.7776	0.712
				0.0535**	0.0536**	0.0603**
Observations	14,659	14,659	13,045	16,542	16,542	14,304
R-squared	0.17	0.18	0.18			

Standard errors in parentheses. Constants not shown. + sign at 10%; * sign at 5%; ** sign at 1%. Regressions (3) and (3') are restricted to countries with well developed Western-style welfare states.

Table A5.4. Heckman selection model—ISSP 2003.

Linear regression with country FE	1	2	3	1'	2'	3'
Dependent variable	Pro Immig Opinion					
Method	OLS	OLS	OLS	Heckman	Heckman	Heckman
Age	-0.0006	-0.0006	-0.0007	-0.0005	-0.0006	-0.0006
	0.0004	0.0004	0.0005	0.0004	0.0004	0.0005
Male	0.0233	0.0195	0.008	0.0246	0.0199	0.012
	0.0134 +	0.0134	0.0153	0.0142 +	0.0143	0.0167
Citizen	-0.1746	-0.1733	-0.1954	-0.1722	-0.1725	-0.1902
	0.0483**	0.0482**	0.0544**	0.0492**	0.0491**	0.0551**
Parents' foreign citizenship	0.2402	0.2405	0.2366	0.2395	0.2403	0.2344
	0.0141**	0.0141**	0.0156**	0.0143**	0.0143**	0.0160**
Education (years of education)	0.0519	-0.1989	-0.6183	0.0519	-0.1975	-0.6088
	0.0020**	0.0372**	0.0996**	0.0020**	0.0410**	0.1009**
Education*gdp		0.0251	0.0658		0.025	0.0648
		0.0037**	0.0097**		0.0041**	0.0099**
Log of real income	0.0471	-0.0633	1.5134	0.0476	-0.065	1.5028
	0.0090**	0.1512	0.4620**	0.0092**	0.1524	0.4624**
Log of real income*gdp		0.0116	-0.1411		0.0118	-0.1399
		0.0152	0.0450**		0.0153	0.0450**
Inverse Mills' ratio				0.0352	0.0122	0.1084
				0.143	0.1444	0.18
Selection equation						
Probit with country FE				1'	2'	3'
Dependent variable				Immig Select		
Age				0.0038	0.0038	0.0052
				0.0008**	0.0008**	0.0009**
Male				0.1214	0.1259	0.1431
				0.0238**	0.0239**	0.0289**
Citizen				0.2038	0.1959	0.1569
				0.0756**	0.0758**	0.0893 +
Parents' foreign citizenship				-0.0776	-0.0772	-0.0854

continued

Table A5.4. Continued

Linear regression with country FE	1	2	3	1'	2'	3'
Dependent variable			*Pro Immig Opinion*			
Method	OLS	OLS	OLS	Heckman	Heckman	Heckman
Education (years of education)				0.0252**	0.0252**	0.0280**
				-0.0089	0.4205	0.2843
Education*gdp				0.0036*	0.0615**	0.1821
					-0.0432	-0.0297
					0.0062**	0.0178 +
Log of real income				0.0486	-0.5007	-0.2821
				0.0160**	0.2575 +	0.8097
Log of real income*gdp					0.0548	0.0331
					0.0259*	0.0788
Trade select				0.6899	0.6746	0.6539
				0.0449**	0.0451**	0.0537**
Observations	23,801	23,801	17,943	26,382	26,382	19,487
R-squared	0.15	0.16	0.15			

Standard errors in parentheses. Constants not shown. + sign at 10%; * sign at 5%; ** sign at 1%. Regressions (3) and (3') are restricted to countries with well-developed Western-style welfare states.

6

Can the Battle for Brains Turn into a Tragedy of the Commons?

The Battle for Brains has just begun, as argued in the previous chapters. Traditional immigration countries such as Australia, Canada, New Zealand, and—to a lesser extent—the USA have in the past successfully pursued immigration policies aimed at attracting highly skilled immigrants, as Chapters 1 and 2 have shown. The resistance of organized interest groups—which was analysed in Chapter 5—against skilled immigration notwithstanding, there are several reasons why these policies will not remain uncontested in the future. Skill-biased technological change and the increasing specialization of developed countries in human capital-intensive activities will further increase the demand for highly skilled labour, while demographic change and ageing will reduce labour supply in developed countries. The positive effects of an increase in the supply of highly skilled labour through immigration can be substantial, as we have discussed in Chapter 4. As a consequence of all this, it is likely that countries which have so far played only a limited role in the Battle for Brains will shift toward the adoption of selective immigration policies, as these can effectively influence the scale and composition of migration flows, as shown in Chapters 2 and 3. Specifically 'countries that are non-selective and have relatively few highly skilled immigrants [. . .] may be most likely to demand increased levels of highly skilled migration in the future' (OECD, 2009, p. 97).

Several European countries, which have so far received a disproportionately large share of unskilled migrants, are currently attempting to reverse this pattern with moderate reforms of the legal framework which regulates immigrants' admission (e.g. the UK, the Czech Republic, and Germany). The Directive 2009/50/EC adopted by the Council of the European Union on the so-called 'blue card' in May 2009 is another—albeit timid—instance of a move toward more selective immigration policies. These initial policy changes have raised some concerns in other destination countries, such as the USA, that they may lose their leading, and so far uncontested, role in the competition to attract 'the best and the brightest'.[1] These concerns reflect the idea that lifting restrictions on the admission of talented workers may not suffice to attract them,[2] as the scale of skilled migration is not only determined by the demand expressed by a country of destination. There might be relevant constraints on the supply side at play, so that an increase in the demand by one destination country could reduce the number of talented migrants directed toward other destinations.

The previous chapters have discussed the benefits of highly skilled immigration, and which institutional, economic, and social characteristics of a country shape its capacity to attract talented immigrants. Here, we contribute to a better understanding of how this capacity is influenced by the immigration policies adopted by other destination countries, and by the policies toward public education policies at origin. We take a distinct and complementary approach to the one adopted in Chapter 5 which explored the process of policy formation in a single destination country, focusing on the strategic interactions among the contenders in the Battle for Brains. The analysis takes a forward-looking perspective, and it focuses on the possible consequences for the countries of origin and destination of a widespread shift toward selective immigration policies.

The policies adopted in the past by other destination countries certainly influence the current ability of latecomers in the global competition for talent, such as the European countries, to attract skilled migrants. Migration processes have a substantial inertial character, as new migrants tend to opt for the destinations where there is already a well-established community of co-nationals (Beine et al., 2011; Bertoli, 2010). This implies that latecomers in the Battle for Brains have to overcome the initial advantage that traditional immigration countries have because of the larger size of the networks of talented migrants. While this factor is certainly relevant in shaping the short-term outcomes of the competition among various destination countries, a deeper question relates to how the long-term outcome of this contest is influenced by the policies implemented by the other contenders. We need to understand whether a shift toward selective immigration policies can be matched by a systemic improvement in the skill mix of the immigrant population across destinations, and what are the welfare

---

[1] C. Barnett, A Talent Contest We're Losing, *The Washington Post*, 23 December 2007.

[2] This argument is reinforced by a significant change in the competition for talents: destination countries no longer rely exclusively on easing immigration restrictions, but actively provide incentives such as tax breaks to attract talented immigrants (Abella, 2006).

implications for the migrant-sending countries. Or, to rephrase the research question that represents the core of this chapter, is the upcoming Battle for Brains going to produce losers among its contenders? Is there a coincidence or divergence of interests between origin and destination countries?

As a first step, it is important to acknowledge that this contest is not a zero-sum game among destination countries, as the *reservoir* of talented would-be migrants that destination countries can draw from is large, and the adoption of selective immigration policies can actually increase the size of the pool of talented workers in migrant-sending countries, as the literature on the so-called beneficial brain drain has shown (Mountford, 1997; Stark et al., 1997; Beine et al., 2001; 2008).

Nevertheless, it is important to consider that migrant-sending countries might not act just as passive bystanders in the Battle for Brains, without reacting to an increased competition to attract their talents. This seems—to say the least—unlikely, as skilled migration can produce significant economic and social effects upon the countries of origin (Hanson, 2010), and even more so if the competition among the recipient countries becomes tougher. A global competition for talent could negatively influence the capacity or the incentives of the governments in migrant-sending countries to invest in public education, and this would, in turn, adversely affect the future size of the pool of talented would-be migrants. Consequently, the non-coordinated policy equilibrium may result in a shrinking pool of talents, along the lines of the Tragedy of the Commons (Hardin, 1968), as there are no shared rules that regulate the use of this *free access* resource (Ostrom, 1990).

The reaction of migrant-sending countries can have far-reaching consequences for the outcomes of the Battle for Brains for destination countries. From an analytical perspective, this drives a wedge between the focus of this part of the volume, which is represented by the countries of destination, and the scope of the analysis, which needs to include the countries of origin, which are the other relevant contenders in the upcoming Battle for Brains.

The remainder of the chapter is structured as follows: first, we discuss the relationship between selective immigration policies and education decisions at origin, which gives rise to a potential policy trade-off. Second, we present a simple game which depicts the Battle for Brains in a three-country setting. Third, we describe the outcomes of the model, and we discuss its implications for the countries of origin and of destination.

6.1 International mobility of labour and human capital formation at origin

The recent literature on the so-called *beneficial brain drain* highlights the fact that the option to migrate can induce additional human capital investment.[3] This literature identifies two main channels through which the opportunity to migrate to a high-income country can influence the education decisions taken by prospective migrants.

The first channel relates to the differences in the returns to human capital in destination and sending countries, as 'higher prospective returns to skills in a foreign country impinge on skill acquisition decisions at home' (Stark et al., 1997). More specifically, the prospect of migration increases the incentives to invest in education if the destination countries are characterized by a greater dispersion of wages—net of migration costs (Bertoli and Brücker, 2011a)—across skill groups (Beine et al., 2001). Selective immigration policies represent the second channel through which the prospect of migration can improve the incentives to invest in education in the migrant-sending country, as agents are induced to invest in education 'in order to be eligible for emigration' (Mountford, 1997). As Stark and Wang (2002) argue, in both cases the prospect of migration acts like a public subsidy which increases the level of education that is chosen by domestic agents. When a country decides to compete more actively to attract skilled migrants, this can be expected to produce an ambiguous effect on other destination countries: on the one hand, a possible negative effect resulting from a greater draw from the pool of talented would-be migrants, but on the other hand a possible positive effect emerges from the increase in the size of the pool itself.

Nevertheless, as we mentioned in the introduction to this chapter, selective immigration policies can influence the process of endogenous skill formation in the origin countries not only via the *lottery ticket* effect described by Mountford (1997).[4] Specifically, the emigration of skilled workers may erode the fiscal basis and the incentives for public investment in education.

The impact of highly skilled emigration on the fiscal balance in the sending countries has been already discussed in detail in the traditional brain drain literature; still, the empirical evidence is scarce, and it is often related to specific jobs or sectors. Connell et al. (2007) show that the training costs of the doctors who moved from Ghana to the UK amount to £35 million, while Mackintosh et al. (2006) have argued that the Ghanaian doctors that

---

[3] This literature is discussed in detail by Docquier and Rapoport in Part II of this volume.

[4] We abstract here from other possible relevant effects: for instance, the emigration of talented workers can hinder the education of the children left behind (Schapiro, 2009; Giannelli and Mangiavacchi, 2010), or the migration of a specific group of skilled workers, such as health-care workers, could hinder the ability to train the next generation of workers.

registered between 1998 and 2003 alone produced an estimated saving in training costs for the UK equal to £64.5 million, a 'perverse subsidy flowing from poor to rich'.[5] Based on conservative assumptions, Desai et al. (2009) argued that the fiscal cost—due to the loss of income taxes—of the emigration of skilled workers from India to the USA amounts to 2.5 per cent of the total fiscal revenues. The analysis by Desai et al. (2009) does not account for other relevant effects of skilled migration—such as increasing trade flows, incoming foreign direct investments, or technological transfers—that can have a positive impact on the fiscal balance. Thus, the net impact of skilled migration upon the fiscal revenues of the origin country probably does not jeopardize its ability to finance the education system, with the provision of public subsidies being motivated from the positive externalities that it generates. While externalities prevent the market from producing the level of private investment in education that maximizes social welfare, a government can step in with the introduction of an appropriately designed system of subsidies and taxes.

An increased international mobility of skilled workers could undermine not the capacity to subsidize education, but rather the government incentives to do so, as a country does not internalize the positive externalities that materialize outside its borders, and it finds it harder to recover a relevant part of the educational subsidies it has provided through taxation. The economic literature features several theoretical models which put forward this argument.

Justman and Thisse (1997) propose a two-country game where the level of public investment in education in equilibrium is decreasing with the size of labour mobility between the two countries, as mobility drives a wedge between the country where education is publicly funded and the country where it produces its positive externalities. Similarly, Poutvaara and Kannaiainen (2000) argue that the international mobility of labour can disrupt the social contract that underlies the subsidization of education for high-ability individuals. Demange et al. (2008) show that, in a model which also considers private investment in education, the share of tuition fees in the total funding of higher education increases with international labour mobility.[6]

These models rely on the assumption that the destination and sending countries are identical, so they are better suited to describe the effects of an increased mobility of labour within a homogenous region such as the EU. Still, the share of skilled migrants moving from low- to high-income countries has

---

[5] These income transfers from poor to rich countries are the rationale behind the proposal of Jagdish Bhagwati that the countries of origin should tax the income of skilled migrants and transfer back to the origin countries the revenues generated by such a tax (Bhagwati and Dellafar, 1973; Bhagwati, 1979).

[6] Poutvaara (2008) analyses the case where education can provide general or country-specific skills, showing that the international mobility of labour induces governments to favour the provision of skills that are not internationally transferable.

been growing over time, as Figure 2.2 showed, and this pattern would be reinforced by a widespread adoption of selective immigration policies. The effects of the international mobility of labour from low- to high-income countries have been analysed by Stark and Wang (2002) and Docquier et al. (2008) in models where the rationale for subsidizing human capital investment is represented by positive intra- or inter-generational externalities connected to education. Both papers predict that a government which maximizes the utility of the population left behind reduces the subsidies to higher education when destination countries lift the restrictions upon the admission of foreign workers. Better opportunities to migrate to a high-income country induce larger private investments in education, and the model by Stark and Wang (2002) predicts that the reduction in public subsidies is such to leave the equilibrium level of education unchanged, while Docquier et al. (2008) predict that the share of highly educated individuals in the population declines. A key analytical feature of these two theoretical models is that they consider the effects produced by *general immigration policies*, which give the same probability of migration to prospective migrants with different levels of education. For the analysis of migration on the optimal level of education subsidies by governments in sending countries see also Section 9.1 of Part II.

Does a higher international mobility of talented workers actually reduce public spending in education in the countries of origin? Johnstone (2004) argues that education systems are characterized by a 'worldwide trend toward greater cost-sharing', with a reduction in public spending and a larger share of the cost of education which is borne directly by the students, and Bray (2000) argued that 'present trends of cost-sharing will continue'. The observation of a recent progressive public disengagement in the financing of the education system is in line with the theoretical predictions described above, as a greater cost-sharing occurred at a time of rising flows of workers across borders. The Philippines, which represent the greatest nursery for migrants with a tertiary education (Docquier and Marfouk, 2006), have pursued, since the 1960s, 'the limitation of capacity in the low or tuition free public sector together with the encouragement (and frequently a public subsidisation) of a tuition-dependent private higher education sector' (Johnstone, 2004); in 1995, 794 out of 1,090 institutions providing higher education in the Philippines were privately run (Bray, 2000).

Docquier et al. (2008) represents, so far, the only empirical analysis which directly tested whether public subsidies in higher education decline with a higher level of international labour mobility. They found that a 10 per cent increase in the share of skilled emigrants in the population of the sending country leads to a statistically significant 2 per cent reduction in public spending in education. This evidence could represent a worrying signal for the destination countries which are currently engaging themselves in the

Battle for Brains, as it suggests that an increased competition to attract talent could actually adversely influence the size of the *reservoir* of talented would-be migrants. Nevertheless, we need to acknowledge that the adoption of more *selective* immigration policies, rather than a greater *openness* toward migration, would be a distinctive feature of the upcoming Battle for Brains. This is why further insights can be gained from a theoretical analysis that, differently from Stark and Wang (2002) and Docquier et al. (2008), explicitly allows for such a change in the legal frameworks that regulate immigrants' admission at destination.

6.2 A model of the Battle for Brains

The theoretical model that we present here contributes to obtaining a better understanding of the outcomes of the Battle for Brains by addressing the implications of selective immigration policies in a three-country framework, with two recipient and one sending country.[7] The destination countries are assumed to be identical, and characterized by a technological superiority with respect to the sending country, so that incomes for any level of education are higher in the two destinations than in the country of origin, while we do not introduce any assumption on the domestic and foreign private returns to schooling.[8]

Human capital formation is endogenous, with rational agents who invest in education depending on the private benefits and costs of such an investment. The action space of the governments of the two destination countries is represented by the choice of immigration policy, which is represented by a non-decreasing function which determines the probability of migration of a would-be migrant endowed with s years of schooling. The outcomes of the migration lotteries which regulate the access to the countries of destination are unknown when agents in the origin country take their educational decisions. The government of the sending country chooses the level of the education subsidies, and it finances them through lump-sum taxation.[9] The governments in the three countries maximize natives' welfare: specifically,

---

[7] The theoretical model presented in this chapter extends the analysis in Bertoli and Brücker (2011b).

[8] The empirical literature has not yet reached a shared consensus about the relationship between the level of income of a country and the private returns to schooling: Psacharopoulos and Patrinos (2004) suggest that 'the returns are lower in the high-income countries of the OECD', while Banerjee and Duflo (2005) argue that 'the returns to one more year of education are [...] no higher in poor countries' and Barro and Lee (2010) recently provided evidence that the private rate of return to schooling is higher in advanced countries.

[9] Education in the recipient countries is treated as given for the sake of analytical convenience, although it would be straightforward to consider education subsidies and private education decisions in the destination countries as well.

the government in the country of origin maximizes the *expected* utility of the representative domestic agent, given the immigration policies adopted at destination.

The demand for immigration stems from a positive intra-generational externality on the labour market. While a destination country benefits from attracting immigrants with a better education, it might also suffer from a cost connected to the scale of immigration.[10] The analysis of our three-country model is conducted without a full specification of the objective function of the governments in the two destination countries, which we assume to satisfy only the following basic property: for any given scale of immigration, destination countries prefer a higher level of education of the migrants.[11]

The three countries are populated by a continuum of identical, one-period lived, risk-neutral agents.[12] We assume perfect credit markets and no heterogeneity across agents as in Stark and Wang (2002) and Docquier et al. (2008). In contrast with these two models, which assume that destination countries adopt *general* immigration policies that do not out-select applicants according to their level of education, our model considers not only the effects of a greater *openness* but also the effects of a greater *selectivity*, which is likely to become an increasingly prominent feature of immigration policies.

6.2.1 Education decisions and the prospect of migration

An agent born in the country of origin and who is endowed with s years of schooling earns a log wage $\omega_0(s)$ equal to:

$$\omega_0(s) = \mu_0 + \delta_0 s \qquad [6.1]$$

if domestically employed. Education gives rise to a positive intra-generational externality, so that the baseline component μ_0 of wages in [6.1] is an increasing function of the average level of schooling in the origin country, denoted by s_0. We assume a linear relationship between μ_0 and s_0 :

[10] The existence of such a cost—which can be easily inferred from the widespread resistance to a greater openness toward talented immigrants—is assumed in our representative agent model, rather than endogenously determined as in models with heterogenous agents at destination (e.g. Facchini and Willmann, 2005); recent theoretical contributions assume the existence of such a cost, related to 'xenophobic preferences, feelings of insecurity, demographic congestion, and the costs of redistribution' (De la Croix and Docquier, 2010) or to 'direct cost of receiving the immigrants, administrative costs of processing their visa applications, social costs inherent to a possible conflict with local population, political cost associated with xenophobic sentiment' (Fernández-Huertas Moraga and Rapoport, 2011).

[11] This entails that we do not impose any assumption about the preferences of destination countries with respect the scale, so that we allow social welfare at destination to be non-monotonic in the scale of immigration as in Fernández-Huertas Moraga and Rapoport (2011).

[12] The assumption of risk-neutrality is standard in the literature, and it entails that it is immaterial to specify whether the government in the country of origin is able to levy taxes only on non-migrants, or it also imposes a Bhagwati-tax on migrants.

$$\mu_0 = \xi_0 s_0 \tag{6.2}$$

Agents optimally chose their level of education; the private cost $c(s)$ of acquiring s years of schooling is increasing and convex in s:

$$c(s) = \gamma_0 (1 - \sigma_0) s^2 \tag{6.3}$$

where γ_0 is a cost-shifter parameter, and σ_0 is a public subsidy which reduces the private cost of schooling below its actual level. The subsidy σ_0 is financed with a lump sum tax τ_0 which is levied on all natives, and whose amount is determined so to keep the fiscal budget balanced:

$$\tau_0 = \sigma_0 c(s_0^e) \tag{6.4}$$

where s_0^e represents the equilibrium level of schooling, which is correctly anticipated by the government. Agents can apply for migration to one of the two destination countries, where log wages $\omega_i(s)$, for $i = 1,2$, follow:

$$\omega_i(s) = \mu_i + \delta_i s \tag{6.5}$$

We assume that the baseline component at wages at destination is higher than at home, so that agents from the country of origin have an incentive to apply for migration. As discussed above, we do not introduce any assumption on the relationship between the private returns to schooling at destination and at origin, so that the model is consistent with alternative—and equally plausible—scenarios.

While agents can freely apply for migration their actual admission at destination is a probabilistic event, whose outcome is unknown when agents make their schooling choices. An agent with s years of schooling who applies for migration faces a probability $p(s)$ to be admitted in one of the two destinations, with $p(s)$ being non-decreasing in its argument, so that we allow destination countries to confer a better chance to migrate to applicants with a higher level of education. Individuals can apply for migration to both destinations, and—if accepted in both countries—they randomly chose where to actually move to. Let $p_1(s)$ and $p_2(s)$ be the functions that represent the immigration policies adopted in the two destination countries; the *openness* to migration of a destination country is given by the probability to migrate which is independent of the level of schooling s of the applicant, while its *selectivity* is given by the steepness of the function, which reflects the extent to which the probability to migrate increases with the level of schooling of the applicants. The probability $p(s)$ to migrate to either destination that prospective migrants face is equal to:

$$p(s) = p_1(s) + [1 - p_1(s)]p_2(s) \tag{6.6}$$

It is straightforward to verify that, for any $p_1(s)$ and $p_2(s)$, (i) $p(s)$ increases when either of the two destination countries opts for a greater *openness* to immigration, and (ii) $p(s)$ becomes steeper whenever there is a shift toward a greater *selectivity* at destination. For any function $p(s)$ determined by immigration policies at destination, agents chose the level of schooling that maximizes their expected utility $E[U(s)]$:

$$E[U(s)] = [1 - p(s)]\omega_0(s) + p(s)\omega_1(s) - c(s) - \tau_0 \qquad [6.7]$$

Given [6.1]–[6.6], and as agents regard the average level of schooling at home and at destination as independent from their own education choices, the optimal level of schooling is the value of s that satisfies:[13]

$$[1 - p(s)]\delta_0 + p(s)\delta_1 + p'(s)[\omega_1(s) - \omega_0(s)] = 2\gamma_0(1 - \sigma_0)s \qquad [6.8]$$

The left hand side of [6.8] represents the expected private return to schooling: it is equal to a weighted average of δ_0 and δ_1, plus a positive term that depends on the differential in wages between the countries of destination and the country of origin, and on the extent to which the probability of migration increases with schooling. This second component captures the *lottery-ticket effect* in Mountford (1997), which increases the expected rate of return over and above the average of the actual rates of return on the domestic and foreign labour markets. Such an effect is stronger (i) the higher the wage differential between sending and recipient countries, and (ii) the more immigration policies at destination are selective in education.

For analytical convenience, we consider a linearization of $p(s)$ around the equilibrium level of schooling:

$$p(s) = \varphi + \kappa s \qquad [6.9]$$

We can explicitly define the utility maximizing level of schooling s_o^a:

$$s_o^a = \frac{\delta_0 + \varphi(\delta_1 - \delta_0) + \kappa(\mu_1 - \mu_0)}{2[\gamma_0(1 - \sigma_0) - \kappa(\delta_1 - \delta_0)]} \qquad [6.10]$$

Combining [6.2] and [6.10], we can equate the utility maximizing to the average level of schooling, thus deriving the unique equilibrium level of schooling s_o^e:

$$s_o^e = \frac{\delta_0 + \varphi(\delta_1 - \delta_0) + \kappa\mu_1}{2\left[\gamma_0(1 - \sigma_0) - \kappa\left(\delta_1 - \delta_0 - \frac{\xi_0}{2}\right)\right]} \qquad [6.11]$$

For a given probability to migrate $p(s)$ determined by the immigration policies adopted at destination, the government in the country of origin determines

---

[13] Throughout the chapter, we assume that expected utility is concave in schooling s, so that the first order condition [6.8] uniquely identifies the optimal choice of s.

the level of the subsidy σ_0 in order to maximize social welfare, which we have assumed to coincide with the expected utility of natives. The maximization of [6.7], subject to the equilibrium condition of the fiscal balance, determines the welfare maximizing level of the subsidy, $\sigma_0^\star$:

$$\sigma_0^\star = \frac{\kappa}{2\gamma_0}\xi_0 + \frac{\xi_0(1-\varphi)\left[1 - \frac{\kappa}{\gamma_0}(\delta_1 - \delta_0 - \xi_0)\right]}{\delta_0 + \xi_0 + \varphi(\delta_1 - \delta_0 - \xi_0) + \kappa\mu_1} \qquad [6.12]$$

The adoption of $\sigma_0^\star$ induces the agents to opt for the level of schooling $s_0^\star$ which maximizes social welfare at origin:

$$s_0^\star = \frac{\xi_0 + \delta_0 + \varphi(\delta_1 - \xi_0 - \delta_0) + \kappa\mu_1}{2[\gamma_0 - \kappa(\delta_1 - \xi_0 - \delta_0)]} \qquad [6.13]$$

As we have ruled out any heterogeneity across agents, $s_0^\star$ represents both the level of education of the migrants and of the stayers.

6.2.2 Changes in immigration policies at destination

Changes in immigration policies at destination influence the shape of $p(s)$, which in turn determines both the private incentives of the agents in the country of origin to invest in education, and the optimal education subsidy which is set by the government. From [6.13], we can observe that the combined impact of these two distinct effects is given by:

$$\frac{\partial s_0^\star}{\partial\varphi} = \frac{\delta_1 - \xi_0 - \delta_0}{2[\gamma_0 - \kappa(\delta_1 - \xi_0 - \delta_0)]}, \qquad [6.14]$$

which has an ambiguous sign, and by:

$$\frac{\partial s_0^\star}{\partial\kappa} = \frac{\omega_1(s_0^\star) - \omega_0(s_0^\star)}{2[\gamma_0 - \kappa(\delta_1 - \xi_0 - \delta_0)]}, \qquad [6.15]$$

which is always positive. In words, a greater *openness* to migration in either of the two destinations raises φ, and a marginal increase in φ produces an impact on $s_0^\star$ which is ambiguous. The ambiguity would not be resolved by introducing assumptions on the *private* returns to schooling at origin and at destination; [6.14] is positive (respectively, negative) if the *private* return to schooling at destination is higher (lower) than the *social* return to schooling at origin, with this asymmetry following from the fact that the government does not internalize the impact of its education policies on the countries of destination of the migrants. When the social return to schooling at origin is larger than the private returns to schooling that migrants enjoy at destination,[14] then a

---

[14] This scenario becomes more likely if migrants experience a *brain waste* (Mattoo et al., 2008).

greater *openness* toward migration in one of the two countries of destination determines a reduction in the level of schooling of the migrants, in line with the prediction by Docquier et al. (2008).

The adoption of more *selective* immigration policies in one of the two destination countries also gives rise to an externality for the other destination, but this is unambiguously positive, as the level of migrants' education increases, as described by [6.15].

We can implicitly define a family of functions $f_s(\varphi)$, such that the probability to migrate $p(s)$ characterized by the pair of parameters $(\varphi, f_s(\varphi))$ determines an average level of education of the migrants equal to s. From [6.14]–[6.15], we can observe that:

$$f_s'(\varphi) = \frac{\delta_1 - \xi_0 - \delta_0}{\omega_1(s_o^\star) - \omega_0(s_o^\star)} \qquad [6.16]$$

with the sign of [6.16] the same as the sign of the effect of a greater *openness* to migration upon the equilibrium level of schooling $s_0^\star$. The family of functions $f_s(\varphi)$ identifies a map of—either upward or downward sloping—curves in the parameter space (φ, κ), where higher curves correspond to a higher level of migrants' education, as we know that—for a given *openness* to migration— policies that are more *selective* determine a higher level of education for the migrants.

A marginal variation in the pair (φ, κ) which identifies the function $p(s)$ also influences the aggregate scale of migration to the two destinations, which is proportional to $p(s_0^\star)$; along the same lines that we followed for $f_s(\varphi)$, we can implicitly define a family of functions $g_p(\varphi)$, such that the probability to migrate $p(s)$ characterized by the pair of parameters $(\varphi, g_p(\varphi))$ gives rise to an aggregate scale of migration which is proportional to $p(s_0^\star) = p$. The implicit function theorem implies that:

$$g_p'(\varphi) = \frac{1 + \kappa \frac{\partial s_o^\star}{\partial \varphi}}{s_0^\star + \kappa \frac{\partial s_o^\star}{\partial \kappa}} \qquad [6.17]$$

which is negative for any possible configuration of the parameters of the model. It is easy to prove, with some tedious but straightforward algebra, that the following relationship always holds:

$$g_p'(\varphi) < f_s'(\varphi) \qquad [6.18]$$

This relationship gives us the central theoretical prediction of our model: [6.18] entails that a marginal reduction in φ along the graph of the function $g_p(\varphi)$ improves migrants' education while leaving the scale of migration unchanged, as depicted in Figure 6.1, which is drawn under the assumption that the *private* return to schooling at destination is lower than the *social*

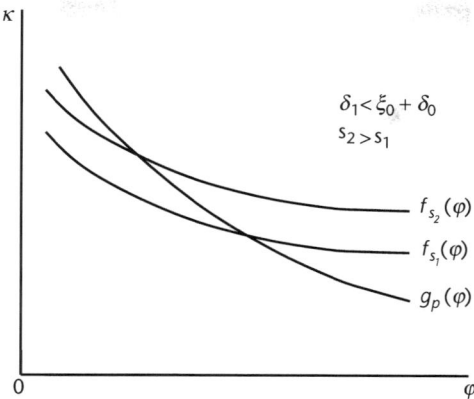

Figure 6.1. Aggregate scale of migration and migrants' education.

return to schooling at origin, so that the curves in the family $f_s(\varphi)$ are downward sloping. Differently from Docquier et al. (2008), Figure 6.1 also implies that destination countries can become more open to immigration while simultaneously increasing immigrants' average level of schooling: this occurs whenever we move from a point (φ, κ) toward a point that lies above both the $g_p(\varphi)$ and $f_s(\varphi)$ schedules that intersect in (φ, κ).

The analysis of our three-country model suggests that the Battle for Brains needs not produce losers among its contenders, at least on the side of the countries of destination. While the actual direction in which destination countries adjust their immigration policies—and hence the equilibrium of the game—depends on their preferences over the scale and quality of incoming migration flows (which we left unspecified), the model shows that there is scope for a shift in immigration policy which improves migrants' education while keeping the aggregate scale of migration unchanged. This appears to soften the—worrying—proposed analogy between the Battle for Brains and the Tragedy of the Commons (Hardin, 1968). Still, to evaluate the relevance of this parallel, we have to address the implications of a shift toward more selective immigration policies upon the countries of origin of the migrants. The argument that such a shift can lead to an increase in the level of education of the stayers does not suffice to conclude that this effect is welfare-improving, as the origin country is employing—both private and public—resources to finance the increase in schooling.

Hence, what is the impact upon social welfare at origin when the countries of destination increase the selectivity of their immigration policies? More formally, what happens with a marginal reduction in φ along the graph of the function $g_p(\varphi)$, so that the policy shift toward selectivity occurs with an invariant aggregate scale of migration? We can apply the envelope theorem to the social welfare function at origin to observe that

$$\left[\frac{\partial E[U(s_o^\star)]}{\partial \varphi} + g_p(\varphi)\frac{\partial E[U(s_o^\star)]}{\partial \kappa}\right]\partial \varphi = [\omega_1(s_o^\star) - \omega_0(s_o^\star)]\partial \varphi \qquad [6.19]$$

There are conflicting interests in the setting of immigration policies, as [6.19] reveals that a shift toward a greater selectivity at destination, that is a lower φ along the $g_p(\varphi)$ curve, is detrimental for social welfare at origin, notwithstanding the adjustment of the education subsidy in the face of a changing immigration policy. This result is noticeable, as social welfare is not defined only on the basis of the utility of the individuals left behind, but also accounts for migrants' utility, and it suggests that the Battle for Brains could indeed produce some losers among its contenders.

6.3 Conclusions

Australia, Canada, and New Zealand—the three countries which have so far succeeded in attracting talented migrants—have a total population that falls short of 100 million, while the EU, the most influential latecomer in this contest, has a population of approximately 500 million. As a result, the possible effects of an increased European demand for talented workers can hardly be inferred from what current data say, as the global competition for talent is undergoing a structural transformation which will reshape its salient traits and likely outcomes.

The countries that are engaging themselves in the global contest to attract talented workers should consider the consequences on the size of the pool of talented would-be migrants of the policy changes that they may induce. A recent paper by Razin et al. (2009), on the relationship between the welfare state and immigration, quotes a famous sentence by Milton Friedman, who used to say that 'it's just obvious that you can't have free immigration and a welfare state'. The countries of destination which are engaging in the Battle for Brains should probably be aware that a similar argument could relate migration and educational subsidies at origin. An attempt to draw on talented immigrants to satisfy the domestic demand for highly skilled labour could be short-sighted: lifting restrictions to immigration can determine a fall in the average level of education of the immigrants, as predicted by Docquier et al. (2008).

Still, the three-country model that we presented in this chapter predicts that the implications of the Battle for Brains for the level of education of the migrants depend crucially on how destination countries will revise the legal frameworks that regulate immigrants' admission. Destination countries can actually achieve their stated objective of attracting more talented immigrants through the adoption of more selective policies, which reward applicants with a higher level of education with better chances of being admitted at destination. While this implies that the Battle for Brains can produce positive outcomes among its contenders on the recipient side, the game that we analysed warns that origin countries may stand to lose from a widespread shift toward more selective immigration policies, unless legal restrictions on the mobility of lower-educated workers are eased. As this contest has just begun, there is only a limited understanding of its far-reaching effects: while the Battle for Brains need not resemble the Tragedy of the Commons, the way in which destination countries reform their immigration policies could have relevant distributional consequences across countries.

7

Conclusions

This study has analysed the phenomenon of highly skilled migration from a number of different angles, which all relate to the receiving countries' perspective. We first presented the descriptive evidence on the changes in immigration policies and, next, discussed the main trends in highly skilled immigration. We then analysed the determinants of highly skilled immigration and its impact on receiving countries' economies. Next, we investigated one of the most important drivers of skilled migration flows, namely immigration policies, from two different angles: first, we explained from a positive perspective why so many countries are still reluctant to open their borders to highly skilled immigrants. Second, in a forward-looking perspective, we analysed what might happen if—as seems likely—more and more developed countries enter a global competition for talent, that is if a Battle for Brains unfolds.

7.1 Incremental shifts toward more skill-selective immigration policies

Only a small number of countries with a limited population size have pursued consistent skill-selective immigration policies in the past, namely Australia, Canada, and New Zealand. These countries have point systems in place which select immigrants on the basis of their human capital characteristics. The main destination of migrants in the world, the USA, selects only a relatively small proportion of its immigrants based on their skills following an 'employer driven' approach. Most European countries have not yet adopted an immigration policy which aims to increase the number of skilled immigrants. Nevertheless, there is evidence that a Battle for Brains may unfold in the future. We currently observe incremental shifts toward more skill-selective immigration policies in many countries: the EU has recently adopted the 'blue card' proposal, which can be regarded as an important move towards an employer-driven approach which creates additional immigration options for highly skilled individuals. Some countries such as the UK and the Czech Republic have recently adopted point-based systems, and others, such as Germany, have undertaken incremental reforms towards a more skill-selective immigration policy. Moreover, many countries have facilitated the immigration opportunities for foreign students.

7.2 Skilled migration flows are concentrated in a few countries characterized by skill-selective immigration polices

Current trends in the migration of highly skilled workers reflect the trends in migration policies described above. About 20 million immigrants with a tertiary education degree reside in OECD member countries, a figure which corresponds to 11 per cent of the total population with a tertiary education residing in these countries. Half of these skilled migrants move within the OECD itself. Many OECD member countries are net senders of highly skilled individuals. The main winners are the USA, Canada, and Australia, that is English-speaking countries which either pursue consistent skill-selective immigration policies or have at least partially adopted these policies. The picture in Europe is heterogeneous. While most countries are net senders of skilled workers to other OECD countries, some small-sized high-income countries such as Luxembourg and Switzerland benefit from a net inflow of highly skilled labour.

The global pool of highly educated individuals has been increasing over time. The total number of individuals with tertiary education has increased by a factor of 3.5 over the last 25 years, while the world population has grown only by a factor of 1.5. At the same time, we observe that the share of middle- and low-income countries in the global pool of highly skilled labour, particularly the share of countries in Eastern and South Eastern Asia, has rapidly increased over the last 25 years. As a consequence, these countries have become a more and more important source for highly skilled migrants.

The share of immigrants at the top of the skill distribution, that is among those with a PhD degree, is even higher than the share of immigrants among all individuals with a tertiary education degree. This picture is confirmed by our analysis of the enrolment of foreign students. Enrolment rates of foreign students are particularly high in research-oriented education programmes. Moreover, we find that immigrants have meanwhile achieved high shares in top management and top professional occupations, although these shares are slightly below those of the foreigner shares among the highly skilled population. Finally, the available evidence from the literature suggests that immigrants at the top of the skill distribution receive lower wages than natives of the same skill level, controlling for the field of study.

7.3 The wage premium for education and skill-selective immigration policies is an important driver of skilled migration

International migration and the skill bias in the migrant population are driven by both economic incentives and immigration policies. Our detailed analysis of the determinants of overall immigration and of the brain gain finds, not surprisingly, that the average after-tax wage difference is a very important factor which determines the scale of overall migration, while the premium in post-tax wages for highly skilled labour is the main economic determinant for the selection of highly skilled individuals. Increasing the skill premium by US $10,000 increases the share of the highly skilled in the immigrant population between 20 and 40 per cent. Incremental changes in the immigration legislation in favour of highly skilled immigrants are also among the most important and robust determinants of the positive selection of immigrants. Moreover, we find that laws limiting the access of immigrants to welfare benefits and increasing the restrictions for residence permits or the requirements for political asylum discourage immigration, in particular of the less educated, producing a smaller total inflow of immigrants and a stronger selection bias of the immigrants towards the highly educated. Altogether, we can conclude that both economic incentives and skill-selective immigration policies can explain cross-country differences in the share of highly skilled immigrants.

7.4 Immigration and the brain gain are beneficial for receiving economies

Building on the analysis of the determinants of immigration and the brain gain, we have examined the impact of immigration on employment, capital accumulation, productivity, and output, thereby distinguishing the effect of total immigration from that of the brain gain measured as the share of highly skilled individuals in the immigrant population. While some issues of endogeneity and omitted variables remain, our findings suggest that total immigration is beneficial for aggregate employment and capital accumulation and it neither crowds out native employment nor reduces the capital output ratio in the short and the long run. The share of highly educated has an additional positive and significant effect on employment and physical capital accumulation, possibly because highly educated immigrants are complementary to natives and work in occupations that are capital intensive. We do not find a significant correlation between total immigration, brain gain, and total factor productivity in the receiving country.

Altogether, total immigration has two effects on the receiving economy: first, it stimulates employment of natives and total investment thereby broadening the productive base of the receiving country, and, second, it does not affect workers' productivity. Moreover the skill intensity of immigrants has an additional positive contribution to the first effect, while it leaves the second unchanged.

7.5 How do immigration and the brain gain affect economies in the downturn of the business cycle?

We have also analysed whether immigration has a different economic impact in 'good' and in 'bad' times. We find that the employment impact of total immigration is much larger in good economic times and falls short of its average impact in bad economic times. Thus, it is likely that new immigrants increase unemployment and reduce the participation in the labour force in receiving countries in an economic downturn. However, the coefficients for the skill-selectivity remain stable in bad economic times, such that we conclude that at a given immigration rate a higher share of highly skilled in the immigrant population can contribute to stabilize demand and output in a downturn of the business cycle.

7.6 Why do skill-selective immigration policies not find more support?

Altogether, we can conclude that the overall effects of immigration are positive and that the immigration of highly skilled individuals increases the beneficial effects of immigration. Nevertheless, most destination countries have opted for a restrictive immigration policy and do not yet pursue policies which select highly skilled immigrants (although we are currently observing some incremental moves in this direction). This study has proposed an explanation for this apparent puzzle, combining a theoretical framework with empirical evidence on voters' attitudes towards highly skilled immigration.

First, we examined the factors which affect the attitudes of individuals towards skilled immigration. We considered two main channels, that is the labour market and the welfare state. We found that more educated natives are *less* likely to favour high educational qualifications of migrants across several countries—consistent with the labour market channel—while richer individuals are more likely to—consistent with the welfare state channel.

In the second step we considered two alternative ways to map individual preferences into policy outcomes: the median voter and the organized pressure group approach. We find no correlation between the attitudes of the median voter and actual policy outcomes on a small sample of major destination countries. Out of the top five destinations where public opinion is most in favour of good educational qualifications of immigrants (Slovenia, Austria, Germany, Israel, and Hungary) no country actually has a policy in place to raise the fraction of highly skilled immigrant workers. Only Germany implemented some incremental policy reforms in this direction. On the other hand, among the three countries whose voters are least concerned about the skill composition of migrants (Sweden, Norway, and the Netherlands), two of them (Norway and the Netherlands) have skill-selective policies in place. In contrast, we find a strong correlation between the number of H1B visas in the USA, which are granted to highly skilled immigrants, and interest group activity. We thus conclude that immigration policies are only modestly affected by the preferences of the median voter. This can possibly be traced back to the fact that comprehensive reforms of immigration policies are difficult to implement, which in turn increases the room for manoeuvre of organized lobbying groups.

7.7 Will the policy equilibrium shift towards more skill-selective immigration policies?

What do we expect looking forward? The results from our analysis suggest that more and more countries will try to implement skill-selective immigration policies. The simple reason is that the gains from such policies are too big to be forgone and that they will further increase if technological change continues to be skill biased. We thus expect that the balance between interest groups which favour and reject highly skilled immigration will shift towards the former group. The incremental policy changes towards more skill-selective immigration policies which can be observed in many OECD countries support this view.

7.8 Can the upcoming skill contest produce losers among destination and sending countries?

At the present stage, the efforts of destination countries to attract the highly skilled from less developed sending countries are not large enough to affect other destinations seriously. However, if an intense competition for talented individuals eventually unfolds, strategic interactions would become more relevant. We have analysed the implications of a contest for talents in a three-country framework with endogenous human capital formation. The emigration of the highly skilled reduces the incentives for public investments in education in the sending country, which in turns reduces the investment of individual agents in education. Nevertheless, a widespread shift towards more selective immigration policies can be matched by a general improvement in the level of education of the immigrants. This entails that destination countries can actually reap large gains from the increased international mobility of talented labour, and that the Battle for Brains needs not produce losers among the destination countries. Still, welfare at origin might fall, unless the attempt to attract highly educated migrants is matched by a partial easing of the restrictions on the mobility of low-educated workers.

References

Abella, M. (2006), 'Global competition for skilled workers and consequences.' In: C. Kuptsch and P. E. Fong (eds), *Competing for Global Talent*, Geneva: International Labour Office (ILO), 11–32.

Acemoglu, D. (1998), 'Why Do New Technologies Complement Skills? Directed Technical Change and Wage Inequality.' *Quarterly Journal of Economics* 113, 1055–90.

Baltagi, B., Griffin, J. (1997), 'Pooled estimators vs. their heterogeneous counterpartsin the context of the dynamic demand for gasoline.' *Journal of Econometrics* 77, 303–27.

Baltagi, B.H., Griffin, J.M., Xiong, W. (2000), 'To pool or not to pool: homogeneous versus heterogeneous estimators applied to cigarette demand.' *Review of Economics and Statistics* 82(1), 117–26.

Banerjee, A. V., Duflo, E. (2005), 'Growth theory through the lens of development economics.' In P. Aghion, and S. N. Durlauf, (eds) *Handbook of Economic Growth*, Amsterdam: North Holland-Elsevier, Volume 1A.

Barro, R. J., Lee, J.-W. (1993), 'International comparisons of educational attainment.' *Journal of Monetary Economics* 32(3), 363–94.

Barro, R.J., Lee, J.-W. (2000), 'International Data on Educational Attainment: Updates and Implications.' Centre for International Development Working Paper No. 42, Harvard University.

Barro, R. J., Lee, J.-W. (2010), 'A New Data Set of Educational Attainment in the World, 1950–2010,' mimeo, Harvard University.

Beach C., Green, A.G., Worswick, C. (2006), 'Impacts of the point system and immigration policy levers on skill characteristics of Canadian immigrants.' Queen's Economics Department Working Paper No. 1115.

Becker, S., Ichino, A., Peri, G. (2004), 'How large is the Brain Drain from Italy?' *Giornali degli Economisti e Annali di Economia* 63(1), 1–32.

Beine, M., Docquier, F. Özden, C. (2011), 'Diasporas.' *Journal of Development Economics* 95(1), 30–41.

Beine, M., Docquier, F., Rapoport, H. (2001), 'Brain drain and economic growth: theory and evidence.' *Journal of Development Economics* 64(1), 275–89.

Beine, M., Docquier, F., Rapoport, H. (2007), 'Measuring international skilled migration: new estimates controlling for age of entry.' *World Bank Economic Review* 21(2), 249–54.

Beine, M., Docquier, F., Rapoport, H. (2008), 'Brain drain and human capital formation in developing countries: winners and losers.' *Economic Journal*, 118(528), 631–65.

Belot, M., Hatton, T. (2008), 'Immigrant Selection in the OECD.' CEPR Working Paper No. 6675.

Benhabib, J. (1996), 'On the political economy of immigration.' *Economic European Review* 40, 1737–43.

Bernheim, B.D., Whinston, M.D. (1986), 'Menu auctions, resource allocation, and economic influence.' *Quarterly Journal of Economics* 101, 1–31.

Berry, R.A., Soligo, R. (1969), 'Some welfare aspects of international migration.' *Journal of Political Economy* 77, 778–794.

Bertoli, S. (2010), 'Networks, sorting and self-selection of Ecuadorian migrants.' *Annales d'Economie et de Statistique* 97–98, 261–87.

Bertoli, S., Brücker, H. (2011a), 'Extending the case for a beneficial brain drain.' *Journal of Economics and Statistics* (Jahrbücher für Nationalökonomie und Statistik) 231(4) 466–78.

Bertoli, S., Brücker, H. (2011b), 'Selective Immigration Policies, Migrants' Education and Welfare at Origin.' *Economic Letters* 113(1), 19–22.

Bhagwati, J.N. (1979), 'International migration of the highly skilled: economics, ethics and taxes.' *Third World Quarterly* 1, 17–30.

Bhagwati, J.N. Dellafar, W. (1973), 'The brain drain and income taxation.' *World Development* 1, 94–100.

Bhagwati, J.N. Hanson, G. (eds) (2009), *Skilled Immigration Today: Problems, Prospects, and Policies*. Oxford: Oxford University Press.

Boeri, T. (2010), 'Immigration to the Land of Redistribution.' Economica, Vol. 77, Issue 4(308) pp. 651–687.

Boeri, T., Hanson, G., McCormick, B. (2002), *Immigration Policy and the Welfare State*. Oxford: Oxford University Press.

Bonin, H., Raffelhüschen, B., Walliser, J. (2000), 'Can immigration alleviate the demographic burden?' *FinanzArchiv* 57, 1–21.

Borjas, G.J. (1987), 'Self-selection and the earnings of immigrants.' *American Economic Review* 77(4), 531–53.

Borjas, G.J. (1999), *Heaven's Door: Immigration Policy and the American Economy*. Princeton N.J.: Princeton University Press.

Borjas, G.J. (2003), 'The wage curve is downward sloping: reexamining the impact of immigration on the labor market.' *Quarterly Journal of Economics* 118(4), 1335–74.

Bray, M. (2000), 'Financing Higher Education: Patterns, Trends and Options.' *Prospects* 30, 332–48.

Brekke, I., Mastekaasa, A. (2008), 'Highly educated immigrants in the Norwegian labour market: permanent disadvantage?' *Work, Employment and Society* 22(3), 507–26.

Brücker, H., Defoort, C. (2009), 'Inequality and the self-selection of migrants: theory and new evidence.' *International Journal of Manpower* 30(7), 742–64.

Brücker, H., Jahn, E. (2008), 'Migration and the Wage-Setting Curve: Reassessing the Labor Market Effects of Migration.' ASB Working Paper 08-04, Aarhus School of Business.

Brücker, H., Siliverstovs, B. (2006), 'On the estimation and forecasting of international migration: how relevant is heterogeneity across countries?' *Empirical Economics* 31(3), 735–54.

Bruquetas-Callejo, M., Garces-Mascarenas, B., Moren-Alegret, R., Penninx, R., Ruiz-Vieytez, E. (2008), 'Immigration and integration policy making in Spain.' IMISCOE Working Paper No. 21.

Card, D. (2001), 'Immigrant inflows, native outflows, and the local labor market impacts of higher immigration.' *Journal of Labor Economics*, XIX (2001), 22–64.

Carliner, G. (1980), 'Wages, earnings, and the hours of first, second and third generation American males.' *Economic Inquiry* 18, 18–102.

Carrington, W., Detragiache, E. (1998), 'How Big is the Brain Drain?' IMF Working Paper No. 98/102.

Chaloff, J., Lemaitre, G. (2009), 'Managing Highly Skilled Labour Migration: A Comparative Analysis of Migration Policies and Challenges in OECD Countries.' OECD Social, Employment and Migration Working Paper No. 79.

Chiswick, B.R. (1978), 'Are immigrants favorably self-selected? An economic analysis.' In C.D. Brettell, J.F. Hollifield, (eds), *Migration Theory: Talking Across the Disciplines*, New York: Routledge.

Chiswick, B.R., Cohen, Y., Zach, Z. (1997), 'The labor market status of immigrants: effects of the unemployment rate at arrival and duration of evidence.' *Industrial and Labor Relations Review* 50(2), 289–303.

Chiswick, B. R., Hatton, T.J. (2003), 'International migration and the integration of labour markets.' In *Globalization in Historical Perspective*, M. D. Bordo, A. M. Taylor, and J. G. Williamson (eds.), Chicago: University of Chicago Press, 65–119.

Chiswick, B.R., Miller, P.W. (2007), 'The International Transferability of Immigrant's Human Capital Skills.' IZA Discussion Paper No. 2670.

Citizenship and Immigration Canada (2008), 'Facts and figures: Immigration Overview.' Ottawa: CIC.

Citrin, J., Green, D., Muste, C., Wong, C. (1997), 'Public opinion toward immigration reform: the role of economic motivation.' *The Journal of Politics* 59, 858–81.

Clark, K., Drinkwater, S. (2008), 'The labour market performance of recent immigrants.' *Oxford Review of Economic Policy* 24(3), 495–516.

Clark, K., Lindley, J. (2009), 'Immigrant assimilation pre and post labour market entry: evidence from the UK Labour Force Survey.' *Journal of Population Economics* 22, 175–98.

Colussi, T., Duiella, M., Monti, P., Vecchiato, A. (2009), 'Indagine sugli studenti stranieri di dottorato in Italia.' Mimeo, Milan: Fondazione Rodolfo de Benedetti.

Congressional Research Service (2006), 'H1B visas: legislative history, trends over time and pathways to permanent residence.' Mimeo, Washington DC: US Congress.

Connell, J., Zurn, P., Stilwell, B., Awases, M., Braichet, J.-M. (2007), 'Sub-Saharan Africa: Beyond the health worker migration crisis?' *Social Science and Medicine* 64, 1876–91.

Constant, A., Massey, D.S. (2003), 'Self-selection, earnings, and out-migration: A longitudinal study of immigrants to Germany.' *Journal of Population Economics* 16 (4), 631–53.

Cortes, P. (2008), 'The effect of low-skilled immigration on U.S. Prices: evidence from CPI data.' *Journal of Political Economy* 116, 381–422.

D'Amuri, F., Ottaviano, G.I.P., Peri, G. (2010), 'The labor market impact of immigration in Western Germany in the 1990s.'*European Economic Review* 54(4), 550–70.

De la Croix, D., Docquier, F. (2010), 'An incentive mechanism to break the low-skill immigration dreadlock'., Paper presented at the Third Migration and Development Conference, World Bank and French Development Agency, Paris, September.

Defoort, C. (2008), 'Tendances de long terme des migrations internationales: Analyse partir des 6 principaux pays receveurs.' *Population* 63(2) 285–317.

Demange, G., Fenge, R., Uebelmesser, S. (2008), 'Financing Higher Education and Labor Mobility.' CESifo Working Paper No. 2363.

Desai, M.A., Kapur, D., McHale, J., Rogers, K. (2009), 'The fiscal impact of high-skilled emigration: Flows of Indians to the U.S.' *Journal of Development Economics* 88, 32–44.

Docquier, F., Faye, O., Pestieau, P. (2008), 'Is migration a good substitute for education subsidies?' *Journal of Development Economics* 86, 263–76.

Docquier, F., Lindsay Lowell, B., and Marfouk, A. (2009), A gendered assessment of highly skilled emigration. *Population and Development Review* 35 (2), 297–321.

Docquier, F., Marfouk, A. (2006), 'International migration by educational attainment, 1990–2000 (Release 1.1).' In: C. Özden and M. Schiff (eds), *International Migration, Remittances and Development*, New York: World Bank and McMillan and Palgrave, 151–201.

Docquier, F., Rapoport, H. (2009), 'Can we also gain from brain drain?.' Report for the Fondazione Rodolfo DeBenedetti (forthcoming).

Dolado, J.J. (2007), 'The Spanish approach to immigration.' VOX EU 29 June 2007.

Dumont, J.-D., Lemaitre, G. (2005), 'Counting immigrants and expatriates in OECD countries: a new perspective.' Directorate for Employment Labour and Social Affairs, OECD, Paris.

Dustmann, C., Preston, I. (2001), 'Attitudes to ethnic minorities, ethnic context, and location decisions.' *Economic Journal* 111(470), 353–73.

Dustmann, C., Preston, I. (2004), 'Is Immigration Good or Bad for the Economy? Analysis of Attitudinal Responses.' CReAM Discussion Paper No. 06/04. London: Centre for Research and Analysis of Migration, University College London.

Dustmann, C., Preston, I. (2007), 'Racial and economic factors in attitudes to immigration.' *The B.E. Journal of Economic Analysis & Policy* 7(1), (Advances), Article 62.

Elmeskov J., Martin, J.P., Scarpetta, S. (1998), 'Key lessons for labor market reforms: Evidence from OECD countries experiences.' *Swedish Economic Policy Review* 5(2), Autumn 1998, 205–52.

Epstein, G.S., Gang, I. (2009), 'Ethnicity, assimilation & harassment in the labor market.' *Research in Labor Economics* 29, 67–88.

Espenshade, T.J., Hempstead, K. (1996), 'Contemporary American Attitudes toward U.S. Immigration.' *International Migration Review* 30, 535–70.

European Commission (2004), Green Paper on an EU approach to managing economic migration, EC COM 2004/0811, Brussels.

European Commission (2005), Communication from the Commission—Policy Plan on Legal Migration, COM 2005, 0669, Brussels.

European Council (2004), Council Directive 2004/114/EC of 13 December 2004 on the conditions of admission of third-country nationals for the purposes of studies, pupil exchange, unremunerated training or voluntary service, Brussels.

European Council (2005), Council Directive 2005/71/EC of 12 October 2005 on a specific procedure for admitting third-country nationals for the purposes of scientific research, Brussels.

European Council (2009a), Council Directive on the conditions of entry and residence of third-country nationals for the purposes of highly qualified employment, 17426/08, Brussels.

European Council (2009b), Adoption for a proposal for a Council Directive on the conditions of entry and residence of third-country nationals for the purposes of highly qualified employment, 9057/09, Brussels.

Facchini, G. (2004), 'The political economy of international trade and factor mobility: a survey.' *Journal of Economic Surveys* 18, 1–31.

Facchini, G., Mayda, A.M. (2008), 'From individual attitudes towards migrants to migration policy outcomes: Theory and evidence.' *Economic Policy* 56, 651–713.

Facchini, G., Mayda, A.M. (2009a), 'Does the welfare state affect individual attitudes towards immigrants? Evidence across countries.' *Review of Economics and Statistics* 91, 291–314.

Facchini, G., Mayda, A.M. (2009b), 'The Political Economy of Immigration Policy,' Background paper for the 2009 United Nations Human Development Report.

Facchini, G., Mayda, A.M. (2009c), 'Individual attitudes towards skilled migration: an empirical analysis across countries,' Mimeo.

Facchini, G., Mayda, A.M., Mishra, P. (2008), 'Do Interest Groups Affect US Immigration Policy?' CEPR Working Paper No. 6898.

Facchini, G., Testa, C. (2009), 'Who is against a common market?' *Journal of the European Economic Association* 7, 1068–100.

Facchini, G., Willmann, G. (2005), 'The political economy of international factor mobility.' *Journal of International Economics* 67, 201–19.

Fernández-Huertas Moraga, J., Rapoport, H. (2011), 'Tradable Immigration Quotas,' FEDEA Working Papers 2011–10.

Fondazione Rodolfo DeBenedetti (2007), 'Social reform database' http://www.frdb.org/documentazione/scheda.php [accessed 10 Feb 2012].

Frattini, T. (2008), 'Immigration and prices in the UK.' Mimeo, London: University College London.

Freeman, R. (2006), 'People flows in globalization.' *Journal of Economic Perspectives* 20, 145–70.

Friedberg, R. (1996), 'You Can't Take it With You? Immigrant Assimilation and the Portability of Human Capital.' NBER Working Paper No. 5837.

Giannelli, G.C., Mangiavacchi, L. (2010), 'Children's schooling and parental migration: empirical evidence on the 'left-behind' generation in Albania.' *Labour* 24 (Special Issue), 76–92.

Glick, R., Rose, A. (2002), 'Does a currency union affect trade? The time-series evidence.' *European Economic Review* 46(6), 1125–51.

Glied, S., Sarkar, D. (2009), 'The role of professional societies in regulating entry of skilled immigrants: The American Medical Association.' In *Skilled Migration: Problems, Prospects, and Policies*, J. Bhagwati and G. H. Hanson (eds), Oxford and New York: Oxford University Press.

Goldsborough, J. (2000), 'Out-of-control immigration.' *Foreign Affairs* 79, 89–101.

Gollin, D. (2002), 'Getting income shares right.' *Journal of Political Economy* 100, 2, 458–74.

Green, A.G., Green, D.A. (1999), 'The economic goals of Canada's immigration policy, past and present.' *Canadian Public Policy* 25, 425–51.

Green, D.A. (1999), 'Immigrant occupational attainment: assimilation and mobility over time.' *Journal of Labour Economics* 17(1), 49–79.

Grogger, J., Hanson, G.H. (2008), 'Income Maximization and the Selection and Sorting of International Migrants', NBER Working Paper No. 13821.

Hainmueller, J., Hiscox, M.J. (2007), 'Educated preferences: explaining individual attitudes toward immigration in Europe.' *International Organization* 61, 399–442.

Hainmueller, J., Hiscox, M.J. (2010), 'Attitudes towards highly skilled and low skilled immigration: evidence from a survey experiment.' *American Political Science Review* 104, 61–84.

Hanson, G., Scheve, K., Slaughter, M. (2007), 'Public finance and individual preferences over globalization strategies.' *Economics and Politics* 19, 1–33.

Hanson, G. H. (2005), *Why Does Immigration Divide America? Public Finance and Political Opposition to Open Borders*. Washington, DC: Institute for International Economics.

Hanson, G.H. (2010), 'International migration and the developing world.' In: D. Rodrik, and M. Rosenzweig, (eds), *Handbook of Development Economics*, Amsterdam: Elsevier-North-Holland,Volume 5, pp. 4363–414.

Hardin, G. (1968), 'The Tragedy of the Commons.' *Science* 162, 1243–8.

Hatton, T.J. (1995), 'A model of U.K. emigration, 1870-1913.' *The Review of Economics and Statistics* 77(3), 407–15.

Hausman, J., McFadden, D. (1984), 'Specification tests for the multinomial logit model.' *Econometrica, Econometric Society* 52(5), 1219–40.

Head, K., Ries, J. (1998), 'Immigration and trade creation: econometric evidence from Canada,' *Canadian Journal of Economics* 31, 47–62.

Helpman, E. (1997) 'Politics and trade policy.' In D. M. Kreps and K. F. Wallis (eds) *Advances in Economics and Econometrics: Theory and Applications*, Cambridge: Cambridge University Press, Volume 1, pp. 19–45.

Holzmann, R., Koettl J., Chernetsky T. (2005), 'Portability regimes of pensions and health care benefits for international migrants: An analysis of issues and good practices' mimeo, The Global Commission on International Migration.

Home Office (2006), 'A Point Based System: Making Migration Work for Britain.' London: HMSO.

Hunt, J. (2011), 'Which immigrants are most innovative and entrepreneurial? Distinctions by entry visa.' *Journal of Labor Economics* 29(3), 417–57.

Hunt, J., Gauthier-Loiselle, M. (2008), 'How Much Does Immigration Boost Innovation?' NBER Working Paper No. 14312.

Hunt, J., Gauthier-Loiselle, M. (2010): 'How much does immigration boost innovation?' *American Economic Journal: Macroeconomics*, American Economic Association, 2(2), 31–56.

Jasso, G., Rosenzweig, M.R. (1985), 'How Well Do Immigrants Do? Vintage Effects, Emigration Selectivity, and Occupational Mobility of Immigrants.' Mimeo, University of Minnesota.

Jasso, G., Rosenzweig, M.R. (1990), 'Self-selection and the earnings of immigrants: comment.' *American Economic Review* 80(1), 298–304.

Johnstone, D. B. (2004), 'The economics and politics of cost sharing in higher education: comparative perspectives.' *Economics of Education Review* 23, 403–10.

Jovell, R., et al. (2003), 'European Social Survey 2003: Technical Report.' City University of London, Centre for Comparative Social Studies mimeograph.

Justman, M., Thisse, J.-F. (1997), 'Implications of the mobility of skilled labor force for local public funding of higher education.' *Economics Letters* 55, 409–12.

Kerr, W., Lincoln, W.F. (2010), 'The Supply-Side of Innovation: H1B Visa reform and US Ethnic Invention.' *Journal of Labor Economics* 28(3), 473–508.

Kessler, A. (2001), 'Immigration, Economic Insecurity, and the "Ambivalent" American Public.' CCIS Working Paper No. 41. San Diego: The Center for Comparative Immigration Studies, University of California.

Kler, P. (2006), 'Graduate Overeducation and its effects among recently arrived immigrants to australia: a longitudinal survey.' *International Migration* 44(5), 93–127.

Krieger T. (2005), *Public Pensions and Immigration: A Public Choice Approach*. Cheltenham UK: Edward Elgar Publishing.

Kuptsch, C. (2006), 'Students and talent flow—the case of Europe: From Castle to harbour?' In Kuptsch, C., and E.F. Peng (eds), *Competing for Global Talent*, Geneva: International Labour Office (ILO), 33–55.

Kuptsch, C., Peng, F.E. (2006), *Competing for Global Talent*. Geneva: International Labour Office (ILO).

Krusell, P.L., Ohanian, V., Rios-Rull, V.G. (2000), 'Capital-skill complementarity and inequality: a macroeconomic analysis.' *Econometrica* 68, 1029–53.

Lange, F., Gollin, D. (2007), 'Equipping Immigrants: Migration Flows and Capital Movements,' IZA Discussion Papers 2745, Institute for the Study of Labor (IZA).

Lewis, E. (2005), 'Immigration, Skill Mix, and the Choice of Technique', Federal Reserve Bank of Philadelphia Working Paper No. 05-08, Philadelphia, PA.

Linacre, S. (2007), 'Migration: Permanent Additions to Australia's Population.' Canberra: Australian Bureau of Statistics.

Mackintosh, M., Mensah, K., Henry, L., Rowson, M. (2006), 'Aid, restitution and international fiscal redistribution in health care: implications of health professionals' migration.' *Journal of International Development* 18, 757–70.

Mattoo, A., Neagu, I.C., Özden, C. (2008), 'Brain waste? Educated immigrants in the US labor market.' *Journal of Development Economics* 87, 255–69.

Mayda, A.M. (2006), 'Who is against immigration? A cross country investigation of individual attitudes towards immigrants.' *Review of Economics and Statistics* 88, 510–30.

Mayda, A.M. (2007), 'International Migration Flows: An Analysis of the forces and Constraints at Work.' Mimeo, Washington DC: Georgetown University.

Mayda, A.M. (2008), 'Why are people more pro-trade than pro-migration?' *Economics Letters* 101, 160–3.

Mayda, A.M. (2010), 'International migration: a panel data analysis of the determinants of bilateral flows.' *Journal of Population Economics* 23(4), 1249–74.

Mayda, A.M., Patel, K. (2004), 'OECD Countries Migration Policy Changes.' Available at http://www9.georgetown.edu/faculty/amm223/papers.htm [accessed 12 Feb 2012].

Mayda, A.M., Rodrik, D. (2005), 'Why are some people (and countries) more protectionist than others?' *European Economic Review* 49, 1393–691.

McFadden, D. (1974), 'Conditional logit analysis of qualitative choice behaviour.' In: P. Zarembka (ed.), *Frontiers in Econometrics*, New York: New York Academic Press, pp. 105–42.

McHale, J., Rogers, K. (2009) 'Selecting economic immigrants: A statistical approach' WP 0145, National University of Ireland.

Mountford, A. (1997), 'Can a brain drain be good for growth in the source economy?' *Journal of Development Economics* 53, 287–303.

O'Rourke, K.H., Sinnott, R. (2005), 'The determinants of individual attitudes towards immigration.' *European Journal of Political Economy* 22, 838–61.

OECD (2003a), *Spain: Economic Survey*. Paris: OECD.

OECD (2003b), *New Zealand: Economic Survey*. Paris: OECD.

OECD (2005), *Italy: Economic Survey*. Paris: OECD.

OECD (2006), *International Migration Outlook 2006*, Paris: OECD.

OECD (2009), *The Future of International Migration to OECD Countries*, Paris: OECD.

OECD Tax Database (2008), available at http://www.oecd.org/document [accessed 12 Feb 2012].

Ortega, F. (2005), 'Immigration quotas and skill upgrading.' *Journal of Public Economics* 89, 1841–63.

Ortega, F., Peri, G. (2009), 'The Causes and Effects of International Migrations: Evidence from OECD Countries 1980–2005.' NBER Working Paper No. 14833.

Ostrom, E. (1990), *Governing the Commons: The Evolution of Institutions for Collective Action*, Cambridge MA: Cambridge University Press.

Ottaviano, G.I.P., Peri, G. (2006), 'The economic value of cultural diversity: Evidence from U.S. cities', *Journal of Economic Geography* 6, 1, 9–44.

————— (2008), 'Immigration and National Wages: Clarifying the Theory and the Empirics' NBER Working Paper No. 14188.

Pedersen, P. J., Pytlikova, M., Smith, N. (2006), 'Migration into OECD countries 1990-2000.' In C.A. Parson, and T.M. Smeeding, (eds), *Immigration and the Transformation of Europe*. Cambridge, Ma: Cambridge University Press.

Peri, G. (2007), 'Higher education, innovation and growth', in G. Brunello, P. Garibaldi, E. Wasmer (eds), *Education and Training in Europe*, Oxford: Oxford University Press.

——(2009), 'The effect of immigration on productivity: evidence from US states.' NBER Working Papers 15507, National Bureau of Economic Research, Inc. Cambridge, MA.

197

Peri, G., Sparber, C. (2009), 'Task specialization, immigration and wages.'*American Economic Journal: Applied Economics*, American Economic Association, 1(3), 135–69, July.

Pesaran, H.M., Smith, R. (1995), 'Estimating the long-run relationships from dynamic heterogeneous panels.' *Journal of Econometrics* 68, 79–113.

Poutvaara, P., Kanniainen, V. (2000), 'Why invest in your neighbor? Social contract on educational investment', *International Tax and Public Finance* 7 (4/5), 547–62.

Poutvaara, P. (2008), Public and private education in an integrated Europe: studying to migrate and teaching to stay?', *Scandinavian Journal of Economics* 110 (3), 591–608.

Pritchett, L. (2006), 'Let Their People Come: Breaking the Gridlock on Global Labor Mobility.' Centre for Global Development, Washington DC.

Psacharopoulos, G., Patrinos, H.A. (2004), 'Returns to investment in education: a further update.' *Education Economics* 12(2), 111–34.

Rauch, J.R., Trinidade, V. (2002), 'Ethnic chinese networks in international trade,' *The Review of Economics and Statistics* 84, 116–30.

Razin, A., Sadka, E., Suwankiri, B. (2009), 'Migration and the Welfare State: Dynamic Political-Economy Theory.' NBER Working Paper No. 14784.

Rodrik, D. (1995), 'Political economy of trade policy.' In: G. Grossman and K. Rogoff (eds), *The Handbook of International Economics*, Vol. 3, Amsterdam: North-Holland, 1457–94.

Rosenzweig, M.R. (2005), 'Consequences of Migration for Developing Countries.' Paper prepared for the United Nations Expert Group Meeting on International Migration and Development, Population Division, July 6–8, New York.

Saint-Paul, G. (2004), 'The Brain Drain: Some Evidence from European Expatriates in the US.' CEPR Discussion Paper No. 4680.

Schapiro, K.A. (2009), 'Migration and Educational Outcomes of Children.' Human Development Research Paper No. 2009/57, Geneva: UNDP.

Scheve, K., Slaughter, M. (2001), 'Labour market competition and individual preferences over immigration policy.' *Review of Economics and Statistics* 83, 133–45.

SOPEMI (2005) *Trends in International Migration.* OECD, Paris.

Stark, O., Helmenstein, C., Prskawetz, A. (1997), 'A brain gain with a brain drain.' *Economics Letters* 55, 227–34.

Stark, O., Wang, Y. (2002), 'Inducing human capital formation: migration as a substitute for subsidies.' *Journal of Public Economics* 86, 29–46.

UNESCO (1997), ISCED 1997, Standard Classification of Education, Paris: UNESCO.

United Nations, World Population Policies, New York: United Nations, New York, various issues.

Venturini, A., Villosio, C. (2008), 'Labour-market assimilation of foreign workers in Italy.' *Oxford Review of Economic Policy* 2(3), 517–41.

Wadensjö, E. (2009), 'Migration to Sweden from the New EU Member States', IZA DP 3190.

World Bank (2008), *World Development Indicators.* World Bank: Washington DC.

Zimmermann, K.F. (1995), 'Tackling the European migration problem.' *Journal of Economic Perspectives* 9, 45–62.

Comments

by Franco Peracchi

The paper tries to gain as much mileage as possible using a very stylized theoretical model and, to my knowledge, the best longitudinal data currently available on international migration flows.

The theoretical model is from Grogger and Hanson (2008). It assumes that there are O countries of origin, indexed by $o = 1, \ldots, O$, and D countries of destination, indexed by $d = 1, \ldots, D$. The utility of migrating from country o to country d for individual i is

$$U_{odi} = \delta_{od} - \nu_{odi},\tag{1}$$

where δ_{od} depends on observable variables and ν_{odi} is an unobservable utility component, treated as a random variable distributed independently of δ_{od}. Individual i decides to migrate if and only if moving to some other country offers higher utility than staying in the country of origin. Thus, individual i migrates from country o to country d if and only if

$$U_{odi} - U_{ori} = (\delta_{od} - \delta_{or}) - (\nu_{odi} - \nu_{ori}) \geq 0, \text{for all } r \neq d.$$

It is further assumed that δ_{od} depends linearly on a vector Z_{od} of variables specific to the country pair (o,d), that is, $\delta_{od} = \beta Z_{od}$, where β is a vector of unknown parameters to be estimated. The variables in Z_{od} include expected life-cycle earnings from migrating W_d, a set ϑ_d of destination-country factors, and a set X_{od} of bilateral country factors. Thus, $\delta_{od} = f_1 W_d - g_1 \vartheta_d - g_2 X_{od}$, where f_1, g_1 and g_2 are the parameters of interest.

Under the additional assumption that the ν_{odi} are a set of independently and identically distributed (i.i.d.) random variables with a common Type I extreme value (Gumbel) distribution, the model delivers strong implications. First, the total migration flow from country o to country d obeys

$$\ln n_{od} = \ln n_{oo} + f_1 w_d - g_1 \vartheta_d - g_2 X_{od}. \tag{2}$$

Second, for any pair of destination countries d and r,

$$\ln \frac{n_{od}}{n_{or}} = f_1(w_d - w_r) - g_1(\vartheta_d - \vartheta_r) - g_2(X_{od} - X_{or}).$$

In particular, all else being equal, the ratio between the two flows depends only on the difference $W_d - W_r$ between expected life-cycle earnings in the two countries, and not on life-cycle earnings in other countries of possible destination. This very strong implication of the model, known as Independence of Irrelevant Alternatives (IIA), follows directly from the assumption that the v_{odi} are i.i.d.

Further suppose that the systematic part of (1) differs between highly skilled (H) and low-skilled (L) people. Specifically assume that

$$\delta_{od}^s = f_1 W_d - g_1^s \vartheta_d - g_2^s X_{od}, \quad s = H, L,$$

where f_1 is assumed to be the same for both skill groups. Then, a third implication of the model is the selection (or share) equation

$$\ln \frac{n_{od}^H}{n_{od}^L} = f_1(W_d^H - W_d^L) - \gamma_1 \vartheta_d - \gamma_2 X_{od}, \tag{3}$$

where $\gamma_j = g_j^H - g_j^L$, $j = 1,2$. Again notice that the ratio between the two flows depends only on the educational wage premium $W_d^H - W_d^L$ in country d, and not on the structure of wages in other countries of possible destination.

The total migration equation (2) may be estimated by an OLS regression of the log of total migration flow from country o to country d on average wage W_d in country d and a set of controls, while the share equation (3) may be estimated by an OLS regression of the log difference between migration flows of high- and low-skilled individuals from country o to country d on the educational wage premium $W_d^H - W_d^L$ in country d and a set of controls. If the model is correctly specified, both regressions should give similar estimates of f_1, which is one of the parameters of primary interest. An important advantage of using longitudinal data instead of a simple cross-section, and one of the novelties of the approach proposed in this book, is the possibility of controlling for time-invariant country effects and for macro shocks common to all countries through full country and year dummies.

The main findings may be summarized as follows. First, the average wage in the destination country always has a strong positive effect on total migration flows. The effect is stronger for after-tax wages. Second, the educational wage premium has a strong positive effect on the ratio of skilled to unskilled migration, except for the specifications that control for immigration laws and either labour market legislation or R&D spending. Third, tightness in asylum requirements and access to benefits negatively affect total migration flows. Fourth, pro-skilled immigration laws and restrictions from benefit positively affect the share of highly skilled migrants. Fifth, the effects of all other variables (the welfare system, labour market legislation, and R&D spending) tend to be weak and not very robust.

These results have unpleasant implications for Italy. First, given its after-tax wages and educational wage premia, Italy has already lost the Battle for Brains. Second, things are only made worse by the current Italian immigration laws favouring the unskilled. Since these conclusions are quite pessimistic, in order to retain some hope for the future of my country I must ask whether they can be trusted. Perhaps problems with the data or with the model are responsible for these results.

Let me start with the problems with the data. First, Part I uses total migration flows between 74 countries of origin and 14 destination countries for the period 1980-2005. These data are likely to be reliable only for legal immigrants, where the fraction of the highly skilled should be higher. Second, migration flows by educational level are imputed using the cross-sectional distribution of the stock of immigrants. Third, expected life-cycle earnings are proxied by current per capita GDP. This is a very crude measure. Somehow, we would like to have a measure that takes into account future earnings growth. Fourth, educational wage premia are not directly measured but are also imputed using per capita GDP, the Gini coefficient, and the strong assumption of log-normal earnings. Finally, the adjustment for after-tax wages is also very crude.

As for the model, the first issue is which variables are included in the systematic part of the random utility (1). The chapters assume that δ_{od} is linear in expected lifetime earnings W_d. This is equivalent to the strong and unrealistic assumption that agents are risk neutral. I recommend the authors to allow for risk aversion, for example by adding a measure of income variability (which, under the assumption of log-normal incomes may be derived from the available Gini coefficients).

Second, because of the IIA property, only educational premia in the destination country matter. This assumption could be relaxed by considering alternative specifications of the random part of the model, such as nested logit (which would require assuming a tree-structure for migration decisions) or mixed logit (which would also partly address issues of parameter heterogeneity).

Third, education decisions in the country of origin are not modelled. The model treats schooling choices as exogenous, and only asks how people with different skill levels choose their migration patterns. In fact, the decision to acquire high skills may be made jointly with the decision to migrate or even to migrate to a specific country.

Finally, the model imposes the strong homogeneity assumptions of no individual heterogeneity (except for random errors) and constancy of coefficients both across countries and across skills. Failure of these assumptions may have consequences for the crucial assumption that the random components v_{odi} are i.i.d. and independent of the systematic components δ_{od}. To see why identical distribution may fail, let $U_{odi} = \mu_{odi} - \eta_{odi}$, where the systematic component μ_{odi} is now individual-specific and depends on a vector of potentially observable individual characteristics Z_{odi}, say $\mu_{odi} = \beta Z_{odi}$. If Z_{od} is the mean of Z_{odi}, then the mean of μ_{odi} is $\delta_{od} = E(\beta Z_{odi}) = \beta Z_{od}$ (where E denotes the expectation operator) and we obtain the random utility model (1) after putting $v_{odi} = \eta_{odi} - (\mu_{odi} - \delta_{od})$. Even when the η_{odi} are i.i.d., there is no reason to think that the v_{odi} are i.i.d. The reason is that the random deviations of the μ_{odi} from their mean δ_{od} are unlikely to all have the same variance. If they are heteroscedastic, then the v_{odi} are better treated as a collection of independently but not identically distributed random variables.

To see why independence between the δ_{od} and the v_{odi} may fail, suppose that the β parameter is not constant but varies across countries. Specifically, suppose that β varies depending on the country pair considered. Now, $\delta_{od} = E(\mu_{odi}) = \beta_{od} Z_{od}$ and we have the random utility model (1) after putting

$$v_{odi} = \eta_{odi} - (\mu_{odi} - \delta_{od}) - (\beta_{od} - \beta)Z_{od},$$

where $\beta = E(\beta_{od})$ and $E[(\beta_{od} - \beta)Z_{od}] = C_{ov}(\beta_{od}, Z_{od})$. In this case, independence between the δ_{od} and the v_{odi} may fail if the covariance between the β_{od} and the Z_{od} is nonzero, that is, if there is a systematic association between the Z_{od} and the parameters β_{od}.

In the end, there is clearly a chicken-and-egg problem here. Is the model simple because the data are so crude or, instead, because the model is so simple, only crude data are needed?

Let me also briefly comment on the way results are presented. Part I focuses on f_1, g_1 and g_2, and treats the country fixed-effects as nuisance parameters. In fact, these effects are interesting because they capture time-invariant or very slowly changing country-specific characteristics that affect migration flows. Further, with 25 years of data, they are estimated precisely enough. I suggest estimating these fixed effects and then regressing them on a set of time-invariant country characteristics.

To conclude, the study by Brücker et al. tries to squeeze as much as possible out of the available data. It delivers some strong policy implications, but at the cost of strong assumptions. It is nevertheless very useful because it helps identify the limits of the models that are currently used and the data that are currently available. However, lots of work remains to be done with both the theory and the data before policy conclusions can be fully trusted.

Comments

by Sascha Becker

This is a very timely and impressive study. It gives an overview of the state of the art in migration research, with a particular view to the effect of migration on the receiving countries and on the specific features of skilled migration. My discussion will focus on the second half of the report because the first has been discussed by Franco Peracchi .

I only have two remarks on the first part, that is on the determinants of migration. First, the econometric model concentrates on classical economic variables like GDP differences to explain migration flows. These variables are certainly very important and enter the model as time-varying variables. Of course, time-constant factors measure those elements of the attractiveness of a country that do not vary over time. One might think of factors like climate: fewer people migrate to freezing Greenland than to warmer places. 'Cultural factors' like Italian cuisine would fall in this category. I am wondering about the importance of other time-varying variables like freedom or happiness. Clearly, changes in political freedom and/or corruption (see Becker, Egger, and Seidel, 2009 for a discussion of Heritage Foundation's Index of Economic Freedom) might be important drivers of migration, especially for the highly skilled.

Another, more technical, issue relates to the role of third-country effects in the estimation of gravity models as in Bertoli and Fernández-Huerta Moraga (2011). The trade literature recently emphasizes the importance of controlling for third-country effects in bilateral trade studies (see e.g. Baltagi, Egger, and Pfaffermayr, 2007). The same is likely to apply to migration flows. Migration flows between Italy and the USA are also influenced by the attractiveness of France and the UK and one might need to add suitable controls to the regression equations in order to capture these effects.

The effects of migration

Chapter 4 of the book presents a novel approach to the estimation of the effects of immigration on host countries. It employs an instrumental-variables (IV) strategy in which the push-factors, that is factors that drive migrants out of their home countries, are used as instruments for the total immigration level. As with every instrumental-variables strategy, two important conditions have to hold for an instrument to be valid. An instrument should be relevant and it should fulfil the exclusion restriction. The first condition can be easily checked by looking at the effect of the instruments (the push factors) on immigration levels. The instrument is doing well on that account, as shown by the F-statistic of first stage instruments. I am, however, missing a discussion of the exclusion restriction. Note that the exclusion restriction cannot be formally tested, so we are looking for plausible arguments for its credibility. One might think of and discuss possible threats to the exclusion restriction: China and India being big sending countries, their policies (broadly speaking) are likely not only to push migrants, but also to have other direct effects on destination countries. These direct effects (that pose a threat to the exclusion restriction) might be negligible in practice, but that should be given some thought.

Although the main focus of the report is on highly skilled immigration, some of the key references on (general) immigration should be cited, for example Card's (1990) Marial Boatlift study. Studies like his show that—even for the low skilled—negative effects of immigration are not straightforward. The presumption that immigrants and natives are substitutes is thus not obvious.

The book concentrates on migration flows and largely disregards other factor flows that are likely to interact with migration. Flows of people are closely related to flows of goods and foreign direct investments (see e.g. Checchi, De Simone, and Faini, 2007). The latter are likely to be co-determinants of migration. Trends in trade and FDI are likely to have an important predictive power for migration flows.

The political economy of skilled immigration

Chapter 5 takes a very interesting political economy perspective on skilled immigration. Clearly, future immigration policies will be shaped by the willingness of native residents to allow migrants into their country. The chapter mainly argues in terms of the impact of immigration on taxes and on the social security system. This is a clearly important first-order effect of immigration. Skilled migrants are likely to be net contributors to the tax system and the unskilled will welcome increases in the tax base. The chapter seems, however, to neglect another important source by which skilled migration might impact on both skilled and unskilled natives. In an intriguing study, Moretti (2004a, b) looks into the social returns to higher education in US cities. A 1 per cent increase in the share of university graduates in a city increases wages of incumbent workers on average by 1 per cent. This points to the existence of external effects, but—interestingly—the effect is largest on the low skilled, that is high school dropouts, whose wages increase by 2 per cent, whereas wages of high school graduates increase by 1.6 per cent and those of university graduates by only 0.4 per cent. Moretti's study thus finds external effects of skilled migration on all skill groups, which clearly go beyond mere demand and supply effects, and constitute effects beyond the tax and social security systems.

The chapter presents a series of interesting models to understand the political economy of skilled immigration. Section 5.2 presents an 'attitudes towards migration' model in which the attitudes towards migration depend on which of two alternative adjustments to the social security system skilled immigration brings about: tax adjustments (holding benefits constant) and benefit adjustment (holding taxes constant) bring about effects operating in opposite directions. Section 5.3, in contrast, presents a median voter model and compares it to a pressure group model. The latter two models seem to be disconnected from the 'attitudes towards migration' model because the median voter model makes an *unconditional* statement that 'if the median voter is more unskilled than average, he will be both in favour of admitting skilled migrants'. It would be useful to either integrate the model assumptions between Section 5.2. and 5.3 or state more explicitly that they are disconnected.

A technical point relates to the estimation of the ordered probit model. An assumption underlying ordered logit (and probit) models is that the effect of a covariate x is the same at each transition between outcome categories. This assumption is often too restrictive. An alternative is the generalized ordered logit model. This model is equally easy to estimate.[1] Furthermore, it would be very useful to show marginal effects instead of only the coefficients.

In some of the less analytical parts, Chapter 5 shows cross-plots of variables that are related to immigration. For instance, Figure 5.9 displays a negative relationship between membership rates in unions and employee professional associations and the number of H1B visas, the US visa category for highly skilled immigrants. The authors interpret the relation as one going from union membership on the number of H1B visas, that is higher unionization rates lower the demand for visas. One could think of the causality going the other way around. Sectors with lots of highly skilled immigrants are less likely to unionize.

---

[1] It is implemented in Stata as the command gologit2.

Is the 'Battle for Brains' a zero-sum game?

The final chapter gives an interesting outlook on the future development of high-skilled migration. It elaborates on the likely consequences of the Battle for Brains. Chapter 6 mainly concentrates on one battle front: the battle between high-income countries in the fight for attracting and/or keeping brains. It leaves a discussion of a second battle front, the fight between sending and receiving countries, to Part II of this volume by Docquier and Rapoport (2009) who study the impact of the brain drain on sending countries. A third battle front, however, is largely disregarded: the battle between different factors of production.

One of the key predictions of the report is that the Battle for Brains has just begun and that migration flows will consequently increase in the future. I see quite some evidence for the first part of the statement, that is the Battle for Brains—or the war for talent, as Marin (2009) puts it—is likely to become fiercer. However, whether that leads to larger migration flows is by no means obvious. Integration of labour markets does not necessarily lead to migration flows from poor to rich regions. In fact, despite labour market integration between West and East Germany or between Northern and Southern Italy, we observe high unemployment in one area but not in the other. Spilimbergo (1999) presents a theoretical model in which he rationalizes this empirical observation. Similarly, at the international level, rich countries may prefer to give aid to developing countries instead of permitting immigration.

Another argument relates to international trade and foreign direct investment. Marin (2004) presents evidence that Austrian and German multinationals offshored high-skill jobs to Eastern Europe after the fall of the Iron Curtain to take advantage of high skill levels in that area. Similarly, Becker, Ekholm, Jäckle, and Muendler (2005) show that German multinationals are skill-seeking. Several authors have argued that current offshoring in fact involves many tasks carried out by highly skilled workers and may perhaps even affect high-skilled workers more than low-skilled workers (see e.g. Markusen, 2006; Blinder, 2006). This may be particularly prevalent in the services sector. A prime example is that a low-skilled job like a janitor cannot be offshored. Medical diagnostics of computer-tomography images or X-rays, for instance, typically require education at the upper-secondary level, but can easily move offshore. India promotes itself as a location for the IT industry where firms can take advantage of the low wages of high-skilled workers.

Furthermore, to the extent that the seed for migration flows of highly skilled workers lies in international student mobility, it is interesting to note recent developments in the education industry. An increasing number of Western hemisphere universities provide both executive education and undergraduate and graduate education in other countries. For instance, the London School of Economics has an executive programme in Beijing. The University of

Nottingham has recently opened campuses in China and Malaysia. Missouri State University has an affiliate in China.

Another factor is that higher growth rates in developing countries contribute to a convergence of income levels between rich and poor countries. Finally, decreases in fertility levels—think of China's one-child policy—are likely to stop the pool of potential migrants from growing ever further.

All these aspects are likely to alleviate the pressure for further increases in migration. We will therefore not necessarily see large increases in the number of skilled migrants.

Still, the Battle for Brains is a reality, but it may well take the form of an increasing brain exchange by which the very highly skilled (top managers; the best-publishing university professors) will increasingly move between countries. It would be interesting to further understand the mobility patterns of these groups. Whereas in the past, professors moving to the USA were not very likely to return to their home countries, many countries now make an explicit effort to bring some of them home. For instance, the previous German Minister of Education and Research, Edelgard Bulmahn, travelled to the USA to meet with German researchers at top universities and to promote Germany as an attractive location for research and teaching. Similarly, in Genova, the Italian Institute of Technology was founded outside the constraints of the Italian state university system to allow for attracting foreign professors and to lure Italian researchers abroad to return home. The absolute number of superstars moving countries is likely to relatively small, but they might be lighthouses that affect other groups.

Data issues

The report concentrates on the use of macro-data. That is a conscious choice of the authors because macro-data are most comparable across countries. The only alternative data source discussed is household/worker-level data. How about firm-level data? Personnel records of (large) firms might constitute a valuable resource on hiring policies, ports of entry and so on for native and immigrant workers. Multinational Enterprise (MNE) data might be a particularly valuable data source to be exploited in the future because it will allow us to study flows of workers, trade, and investment in a unified framework.

Overall appraisal

The study by Brücker, Bertoli, Facchini, Mayda, and Peri is an impressive piece of work. Together with Part II of the volume on the brain drain from developing countries, it will be a major reference on migration issues for years to come!

References

Baltagi, Badi H., Egger, P., Pfaffermayr, M. (2007), 'Estimating Models of Complex FDI: Are There Third-Country Effects?' *Journal of Econometrics*, 140 (1), 260–281.

Becker, Sascha O., Egger, P. H., Seidel, T. (2009), 'Common political culture: Evidence on regional corruption contagion.' *European Journal of Political Economy*, 24(3), 300–10.

Becker, Sascha O., Karolina Ekholm, Robert Jäckle, and Marc-Andreas Muendler (2005), 'Location Choice and Employment Decisions: A Comparison of German and Swedish Multinationals,' *Review of World Economics*, 141 (4), 693–731.

Bertoli, S., Fernández-Huerta Moraga, J. (2011), 'Multilateral Resistance to Migration', IZA Discussion Paper No. 5958, September 2011, Bonn.

Blinder, Alan S. (2006), 'Offshoring: The Next Industrial Revolution?,' *Foreign Affairs*, 85 (2), 113–128.

Card, David (1990), 'The Impact of the Mariel Boatlift on the Miami Labor Market,' *Industrial and Labor Relations Review*, 43 (2), 245–257.

Checchi, Daniele, De Simone, Gianfranco and Riccardo, Faini (2007), 'Skilled Migration, FDI and Human Capital Investment,' IZA Discussion Paper No. 2795, May 2007.

Marin, Dalia (2004), 'A Nation of Poets and Thinkers—Less So with Eastern Enlargement? Austria and Germany', CEPR Discussion Paper 4358.

Marin, Dalia (2009), 'The Battle for Talent: Globalisation and the Rise of Executive Pay', Bruegel Working Paper 2009/01.

Markusen, James R. (2006), 'Modeling the Offshoring of White-Collar Services: From Comparative Advantage to the New Theories of Trade and FDI,' in S. Lael Brainard and Susan Collins, eds, *Brookings Trade Forum 2005: Offshoring White-Collar Work*, Washington: The Brooking Institution, pp. 1–34.

Moretti, Enrico (2004a), 'Estimating the Social Return to Higher Education: Evidence From Longitudinal and Repeated Cross-Sectional Data,' *Journal of Econometrics*, 121 (1–2): 175–212.

Moretti, Enrico (2004b), 'Human Capital Externalities in Cities', *Handbook of Regional and Urban Economics*, North Holland-Elsevier.

Spilimbergo, Antonio (1999), 'Labor Market Integration, Unemployment and Transfers', *Review of International Economics*, 7 (4): 641–650.

Part II

Quantifying the Impact of Highly Skilled Emigration on Developing Countries

By
Frédéric Docquier
and
Hillel Rapoport

Introduction

The global stock of international migrants (i.e. people living in a country different from their country of birth) more than doubled between 1960 and 2000, from 76 to 159 million (Ozden et al., 2011). In terms of percentage of the world population, this represents near stagnation at around 2.5 per cent, especially once the artificial rise in international migration due to the dislocation of the former Soviet Union is netted out. In other words, the rate of growth of international migration over the last four decades has been more or less equal to the world demographic growth rate. During that period, other globalization indicators (e.g. for trade, FDI, financial flows) have exploded and it would therefore seem that globalization is about everything that can cross borders, except people. While this impression is roughly correct, it must be nuanced as different components of international migration have evolved differently. Applying a double skilled/unskilled and North/South divide, it is clear that the most rapidly growing segment is the migration of skilled workers from developing to industrialized countries. Overall, the proportion of immigrants living in the OECD high-income countries has tripled since 1960, following the same growth pattern as the trade/GDP ratio. In addition, this migration is increasingly skilled and increasingly originating from developing countries; as a result of these two combined trends, the number of highly skilled immigrants living in the OECD and born in a developing country more than doubled between 1990 and 2000 (Docquier, Lowell, and Marfouk, 2009).

What are the causes of the brain drain at the international level, and what are the consequences for sending countries? To address these issues, Part II first provides (in Chapter 8) a quantitative assessment of the evolution and spatial distribution of the brain drain using updated data on emigration rates to the OECD by educational attainment. We expand the coverage of the database by introducing non-OECD host countries, study the age of entry structure of skilled emigration, and document the brain drain of scientists and of health-care professionals. In Chapter 9 we review the channels through which skilled emigration can affect the source countries. In particular, recent literature suggests that remittances, return migration, diaspora externalities, and network effects favouring international transactions and technology diffusion, as well as brain gain channels, may compensate the sending countries for their loss of human capital. We divide these channels into 'human capital', 'screening-selection', 'productivity', and 'institutional' channels, and also analyse the links between brain drain and remittances. The development of a simple partial equilibrium model allows us to combine these various channels in an integrated setting. Using numerical experiments and parameters taken from existing empirical studies, we then quantify the costs and gains of the brain drain for developing countries and analyse how these balance out. In most cases, our simulations suggest that at a macroeconomic level, the brain drain may generate short-run and long-run positive net gains for many developing countries, while adverse overall impacts are found only in a small number of countries exhibiting very high highly skilled emigration rates.

8

The Size of the Brain Drain

Due to the lack of harmonized data, the literature on the consequences of high-skill emigration has long remained essentially theoretical. Recently, new data sets have been developed to assess the magnitude of the phenomenon. This chapter describes these new data sets and expands their coverage to feature the multiple dimensions of the brain drain. It is divided into five sections providing an original set of indicators of highly skilled migration.

In Section 8.1, we start by describing the updated version of the data set of Docquier, Lowell, and Marfouk (2009) on emigration rates by educational attainment. Then Section 8.2 expands the coverage of this database, introducing non-OECD host countries (such as Eastern European, Latin American, Persian Gulf countries, South Africa, Singapore, etc.). However, the figures presented are for very large levels of aggregation, with just three education levels, with the highest (tertiary) education level serving as our measure of brain drain. This is questionable on several grounds. First, measuring the number of 'brains' (a term which has a distinct, elitist connotation) by the number of people with academic or professional training (college graduates) may seem too inclusive. To address this issue, let us first note that while it would certainly be excessive to consider 'college graduates' as the upper class of the labour force in the industrialized nations (where they typically represent more than a third of the workforce), this seems legitimate in the case of developing countries, which are the focus of this Part. Indeed, workers with tertiary education often represent just a fraction (typically less than 5 per cent) of the domestic workforce of developing countries and therefore deserve the qualification of 'best and brightest'. And second, one may want to distinguish not just across educational levels within the tertiary category but also to focus on specific professions or fields of strategic importance. To address this second issue, Section 8.3 produces adjusted skilled emigration rates by country of training whereas Section 8.4 presents original measures of the brain drain of PhD holders, scientists, and health-care professionals.

8.1 Extensive measures of the brain drain

The first serious effort to put together a harmonized international data set on migration rates by education level was by Carrington and Detragiache (1998, 1999). They used US 1990 Census data and other OECD statistics on international migration to construct estimates of emigration rates at three education levels for 61 developing countries (including 24 African countries). Adams (2003) used the same technique to build estimates for 24 countries in 2000. Although Carrington and Detragiache's study initiated new debates on skilled migration, their estimates suffer from a number of limitations. The two most important ones were: i) they transposed the education structure of the US immigration to the immigration to the other OECD countries (transposition problem); ii) immigration to EU countries was estimated based on OECD statistics reporting the number of immigrants for the major emigration countries only, which led to underestimation of immigration from small countries (under-reporting problem).

Docquier and Marfouk (2006) generalized this work and provided a comprehensive data set on international migration to the OECD by educational attainment. The construction of the database relies on three steps: i) collection of census and register information on the structure of immigration in all OECD countries (this solves the transposition and under-reporting problems noted for Carrington Detragiache); ii) summing up over source countries allows for evaluating the stock of immigrants from any given sending country to the OECD area by education level; and iii) comparing the educational structure of emigration to that of the population remaining at home, which allows for computing emigration rates by educational attainment in 1990 and 2000. Defoort (2008) computed highly skilled emigration stocks and rates from 1975 to 2000 (one observation every five years). She used the same methodology as in DM06 but only focused on the six major destination countries (the USA, Canada, Australia, Germany, the UK, and France). Her study shows that, at the world level or at the level of developing countries, the average emigration rate of highly skilled workers has been extremely stable over the period, except in sub-Saharan Africa and Central America where significant increases were observed. This suggests that the heterogeneity in highly skilled migration is mostly driven by the cross-section dimension.

More recently, Docquier, Lowell, and Marfouk (2009) updated the data using new sources, homogenizing 1990 and 2000 concepts, and introducing the gender breakdown. They provide new stocks and rates of emigration by level of schooling and gender. The methodology consists in aggregating homogenized immigration data collected in receiving countries, where information about the birth country, gender, and education of natives and immigrants is available from national population censuses and registers (or samples of them). Data collection conforms with the following principles:

- The researchers distinguish 195 source countries whereas the set of receiving countries is restricted to OECD nations.

- The database only considers the adult population aged 25 and over. This excludes students who temporarily emigrate to complete their education. In addition, this allows comparison of the numbers of migrants with data on educational attainment in source countries.

- Migration is generally defined on the basis of the country of birth rather than citizenship. Whilst citizenship characterizes the foreign population, the 'foreign-born' concept better captures the decision to emigrate and is time invariant. Due to the lack of data, migrants are defined on the basis of their citizenship in five receiving countries (Italy, Germany, Japan, Korea, Hungary).

- Three levels of education are distinguished ($s = l, m, h$). Medium-skilled migrants (indexed m) are those with upper-secondary education completed. Low-skilled migrants (indexed l) are those with less than upper-secondary education, including those with lower-secondary and primary education or those who did not go to school. Highly skilled migrants (indexed h) are those with post-secondary education.[1] This extensive definition is probably too broad to feature the brain drain of research-based economies; it is however pertinent if one aims at capturing the loss of professionals used in the adoption sector in developing countries.

Let $M_{t,g,s}^{i,j}$ denote the stock of adults 25+ born in i, of gender g, skill s, living in country j at time t. Aggregating these numbers over destination countries j gives the stock of emigrants from country i: $M_{t,g,s}^{i} = \sum_j M_{t,g,s}^{i,j}$.

Obviously, such extensive measures of the brain drain do not inform us about the occupational placement of emigrants at destination. Due to imperfection in transferability of human capital and heterogeneity in degrees, many educated emigrants may end up in low-skill jobs, a phenomenon defined as brain waste in Mattoo et al. (2008). Bearing in mind this limit, we use this data set to characterize the absolute and relative losses of talents in developing countries.

Unsurprisingly, the largest stocks of skilled emigration are obtained for the largest countries of the world or for large countries populated by a majority of educated people. Nine countries have more than 0.5 million skilled natives living abroad: United Kingdom (1,478,477), Philippines (1,111,075), India

---

[1] For example, this includes those with one year of college in the USA.

(1,034,373), Mexico (949,334), Germany (936,523), China (783,369), Korea (612,939), Canada (523,463), and Vietnam (505,503). Nevertheless, to allow comparison across countries and periods, it is more appropriate to use a relative measure of the brain drain. A more meaningful measure can then be obtained by dividing the emigration stocks by the total number of people born in the source country and belonging to the same educational (and/or gender) category. High-skill emigration rate can be defined as the proportion of the total educated population born in the source country and living abroad. Denoting by $N_{t,g,s}^i$ the stock of individuals aged 25+, of skill s, gender g, living in source country i, at time t, the emigration rate can be defined as $m_{t,g,s}^i = M_{t,g,s}^i / (N_{t,g,s}^i + M_{t,g,s}^i)$. In particular, $m_{t,g,h}^i$ is a gendered relative measure of high-skill emigration from the source country i. This step requires using data on the size, skill, and gender structures of the adult population in the source countries. Human capital indicators are taken from De La Fuente and Domenech (2006) for OECD countries and from Barro and Lee (2001) for non-OECD countries. For countries where Barro and Lee measures are missing, they can be predicted using alternative sources or indicators (Cohen and Soto, 2007, or enrolment rates in secondary/tertiary education).[2]

Figures 8.1 to 8.3 describe the geographic distribution of the brain drain. Figure 8.1 focuses on highly skilled emigration rates observed in 2000. The most affected countries are small islands of the Pacific and Caribbean which are hardly perceptible on the world map. The rate exceeds 75 per cent in Guyana (0.892), Jamaica (0.847), Saint Vincent and the Grenadines (0.846), Grenada (0.843), Haiti (0.834), Cape Verde (0.824), Palau (0.809), Trinidad and Tobago (0.789), Saint Kitts and Nevis (0.785), Seychelles (0.772), and Tonga (0.756). Excepting Haiti, all these countries have a very low population size. If one excludes small islands and considers countries with a population above 4 million, the most affected countries belong to Central America and Africa. In the first region, the main cause of the brain drain is the geographical proximity to the USA. For the second region, poverty acts as a push-factor.

The worldwide average brain drain rate increased from 5.0 to 5.4 per cent between 1990 and 2000. In low-income countries, it increased from 5.5 to 7.5 per cent. Figure 8.2 shows the geographic distribution of the rise in skilled emigration rate (measured by the 2000-to-1990 ratio). The rate of emigration has more than doubled in ten countries, including eight ex-Soviet members, Guinea-Bissau, and Rwanda. The ratio is above 1.5 in fourteen other countries, including large nations (India, Pakistan, Brazil) and seven sub-Saharan African countries.

---

[2] See Docquier, Lowell, and Marfouk (2009) for more details.

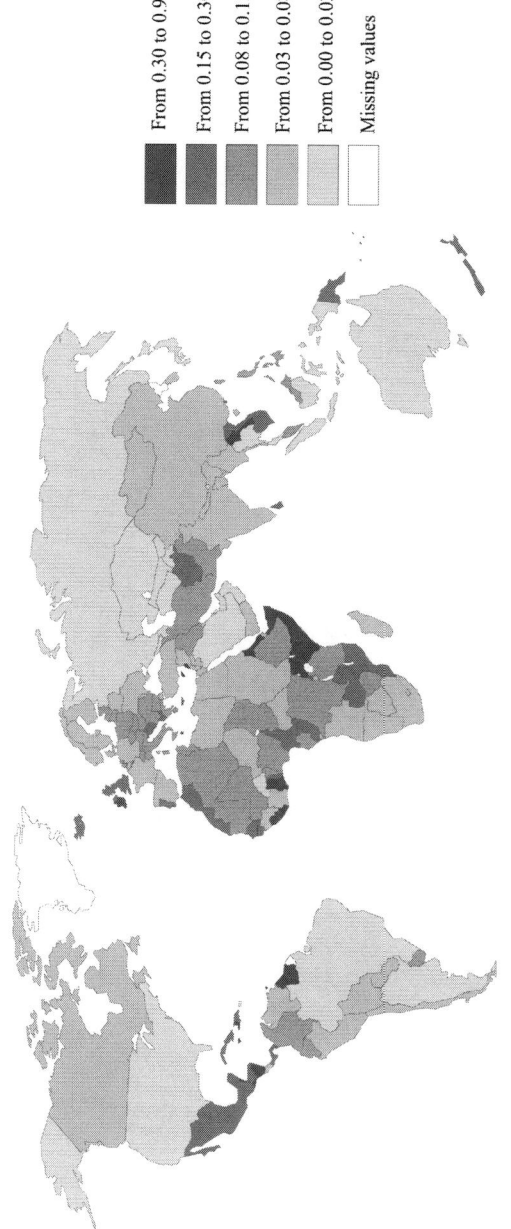

Figure 8.1. Highly skilled emigration rates in 2000.

From 0.30 to 0.9
From 0.15 to 0.30
From 0.08 to 0.15
From 0.03 to 0.08
From 0.00 to 0.03
Missing values

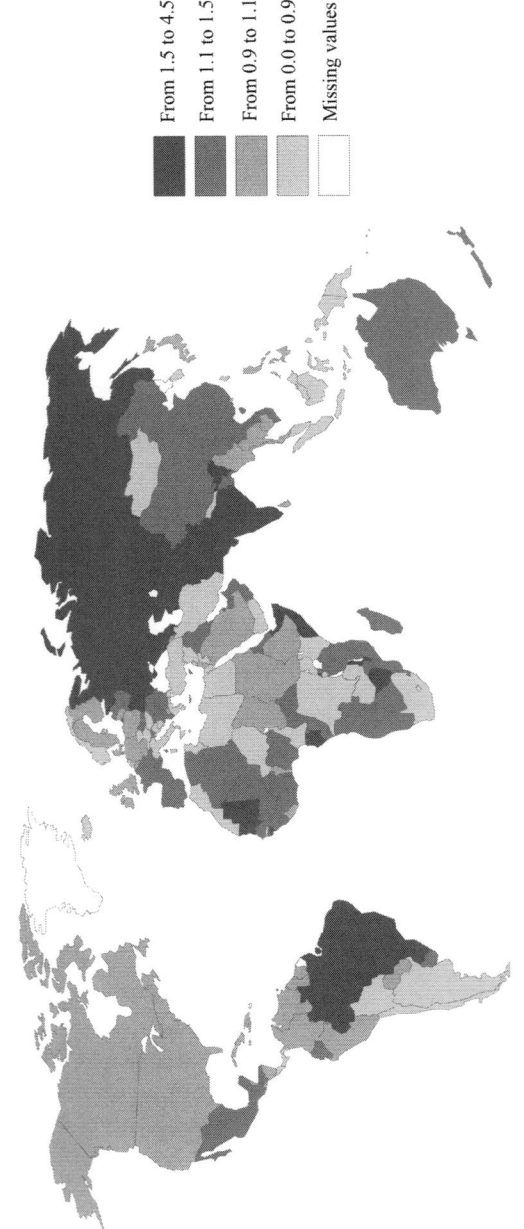

From 1.5 to 4.5
From 1.1 to 1.5
From 0.9 to 1.1
From 0.0 to 0.9
Missing values

Figure 8.2. Change in highly skilled emigration rates (1990-to-2000 ratio).

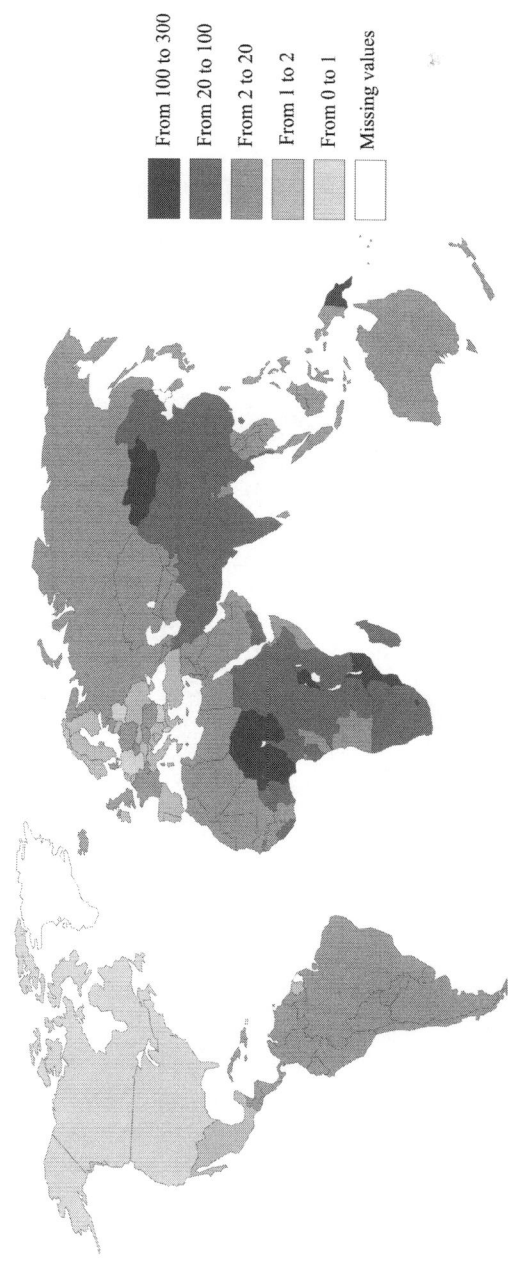

Figure 8.3. Skill ratio of emigration rates in 2000 (high-to-low ratio).

From 100 to 300
From 20 to 100
From 2 to 20
From 1 to 2
From 0 to 1
Missing values

Finally, Figure 8.3 shows the geographical distribution of the ratio of emigration rates of high-skill to low-skill adults. This indicator of quality selection in emigration clearly depends on the level of development of origin countries. Except in five cases (Belarus, Albania, Canada, Germany, and the USA), the ratio is above unity. It is usually low in high-income countries. Conversely, in poor countries with low levels of human capital, the emigration rate of the highly skilled is much above that of the low skilled. A ratio above 100 is obtained in eleven cases where low-skill emigration rates to OECD countries are extremely low (Mozambique, Rwanda, Chad, Malawi, Niger, Papua New Guinea, Lesotho, Mongolia, Uganda, Solomon Islands, and Nigeria). Migrants from sub-Saharan African and South Asian countries are particularly positively selected.

8.2 Magnitude of 'South–South' migration

The Docquier–Lowell–Marfouk's data set describes the structure of South–North and North–North migrations. Generally speaking, the skill level of immigrants in non-OECD countries is expected to be very low, except in a few countries such as South Africa (1.3 million immigrants in 2000), the six member states of the Gulf Cooperation Council (9.6 million immigrants in Saudi Arabia, United Arab Emirates, Kuwait, Bahrain, Oman, and Qatar), and some Eastern Asian countries (4 million immigrants in Hong Kong and Singapore only). Focusing on OECD countries, the database should capture a large fraction of the worldwide educated migration (a portion between 80 and 90 per cent). Nevertheless, by disregarding non-OECD immigration countries, it is likely to underestimate the number of high-skill emigrants from several developing countries (such as Egypt, Sudan, Jordan, Yemen, Pakistan, or Bangladesh in the neighbourhood of the Gulf states, Botswana, Lesotho, Namibia, Swaziland, and Zimbabwe, etc.).

To tackle this issue, we have collected immigration data from 29 additional non-OECD host countries, 9 EU members or candidates (Bulgaria, Croatia, Cyprus, Estonia, Latvia, Lithuania, Macedonia, Romania, Slovenia), 5 Latin American countries (Argentina, Brazil, Chile, Colombia, Costa Rica), 10 Asian countries including GCC members (Singapore, Saudi Arabia, Bahrain, Kuwait, Oman, Qatar, United Arab Emirates, Israel, Belarus, Philippines), and 5 African countries (Kenya, Rwanda, Uganda, Ivory Coast, South Africa).

In 2000, the OECD data set shows 58.2 million emigrants, including 20.4 million highly skilled. Adding these 29 non-OECD countries, the stock of emigrants increases to 75.6 million, including 23.2 highly skilled.

Adding non-OECD destinations thus increases the total and highly skilled stock of emigrants by 30.0 and 13.7 per cent, respectively. Extended measures are only available for the year 2000. Hence, the database does not allow us to quantify the relative evolution of South–North and North–North emigrations. However, it is very likely that new guest-worker policies in the Gulf countries have contributed to increase the brain drain of neighbouring countries. Between 1960 and 2005, the stock of immigrants has been multiplied by 100 in Saudi Arabia and by 1,464 in the United Arab Emirates. Over the same period, the immigration stock has been multiplied by 3.6 in high-income countries (by 20 in Spain, a new immigration country), and by 1.7 in developing countries.

Figure 8.4 shows the distribution of the ratio of emigration rates obtained in the extended and restricted OECD databases, from the highest to the lowest ratio. The maximal ratio amounts to 8.8 (Namibia) and thirteen countries exhibit a ratio above 2. On the contrary, the ratio is below 1.1 in 124 cases. Figure 8.5 compares the extended and restricted emigration rates in the 25 countries with brain drain above 5 per cent for which adding non-OECD countries increases the rate by more than one half. Southern African and Middle East countries are particularly affected. In Figure 8.6, it appears that the extended database also drastically modifies the emigration rates of the low skilled.

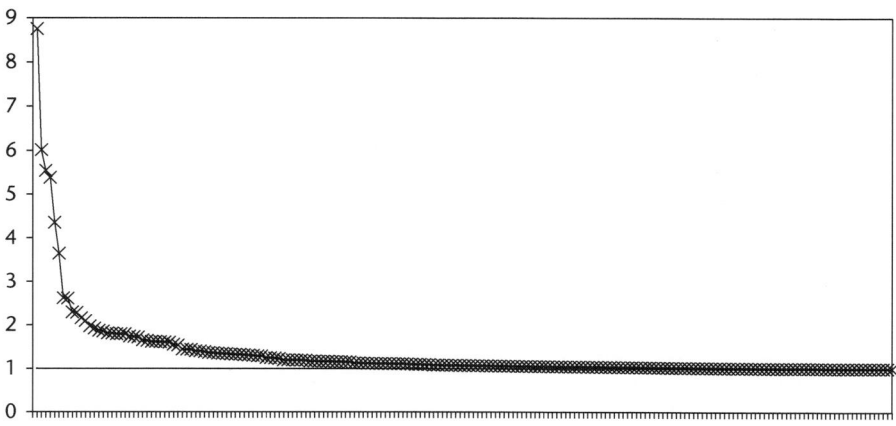

Origin countries (ranked by decreasing order)

Figure 8.4. Ratio of extended-to-OECD highly skilled emigration rates in 2000.

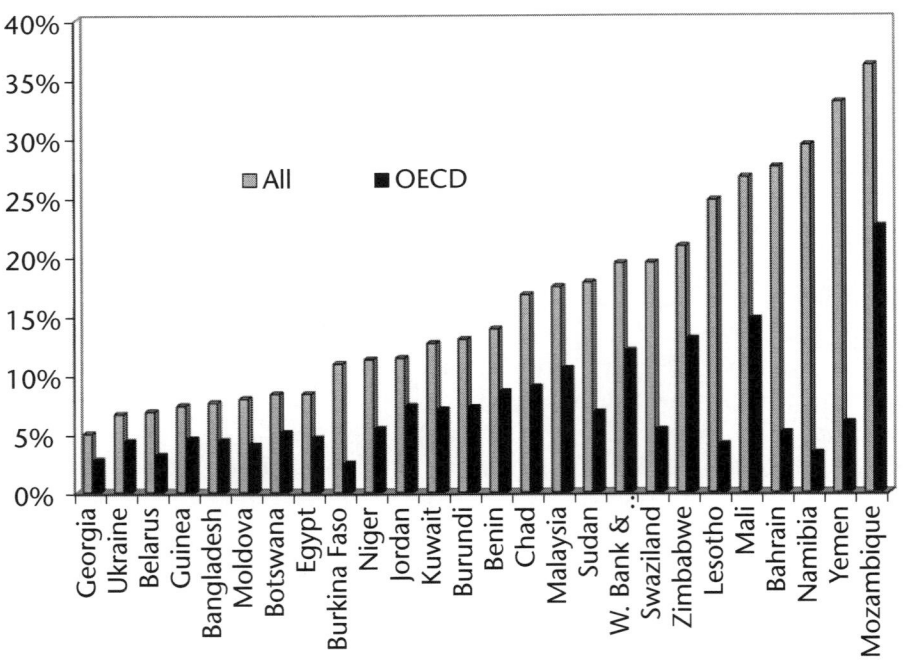

Figure 8.5. Impact of non-OECD destinations on highly skilled emigration rates in 2000.

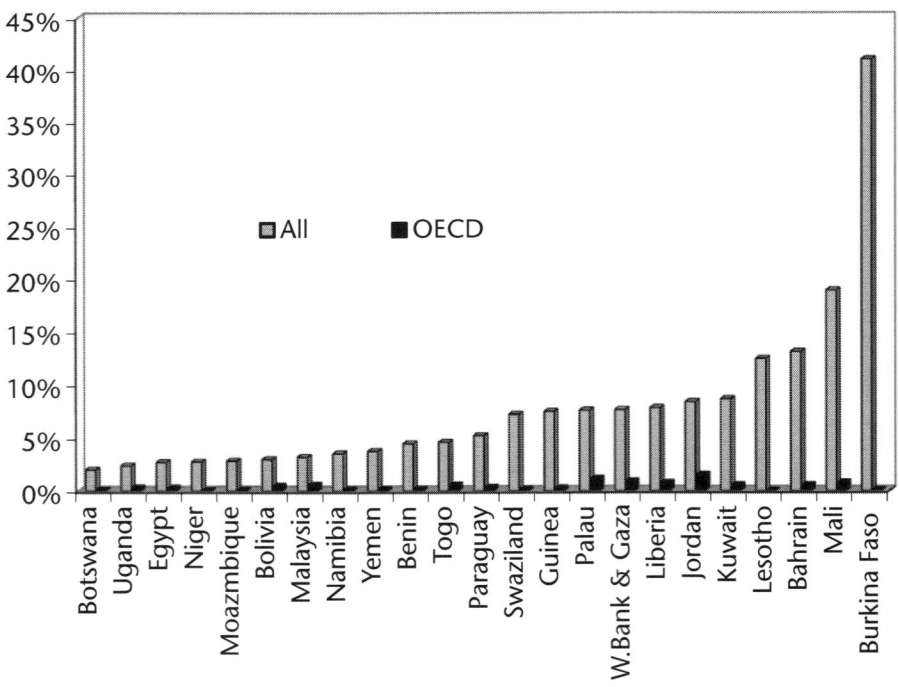

Figure 8.6. Impact of non-OECD destinations on low-skilled emigration rates in 2000.

8.3 Accounting for country of training

Counting all foreign born individuals as immigrants independently of their age at arrival, the previous data sets do not account for whether education has been acquired in the home or in the host country. Controlling for the country of training can be important when dealing with specific issues such as the fiscal cost of skilled emigration. Beine, Docquier, and Rapoport (2007) use immigrants' age of entry as a proxy for where education has been acquired and propose alternative measures by defining emigrants as those who left their home country after age 22, 18, or 12. Figure 8.7 shows the distribution of the ratios between corrected and uncorrected emigration rates. Countries are ranked on the basis of the ratio of 22+ to uncorrected rate. Also the correlations between these measures is high, the figure clearly indicates that eliminating individuals who emigrated before age 22 reduces the brain drain by about 50 per cent in some cases. Controlling for age of entry appears to have a strong influence on brain drain measures in the case of Central American and other countries such as Portugal, Cape Verde, Laos, Germany, or Italy (where the share of 'familial' migration exceeds 40 per cent). At the 22 threshold, the correction exceeds 40 per cent (i.e. the corrected brain drain is less than 60 per cent of the uncorrected rate) in 23 cases: East Timor (51.1 per cent), Mexico (51.4), Cambodia (53.0), Panama (53.3), Kuwait (54.7), Liechtenstein (55.6), Costa Rica (55.8), Gabon (56.7), Comoros

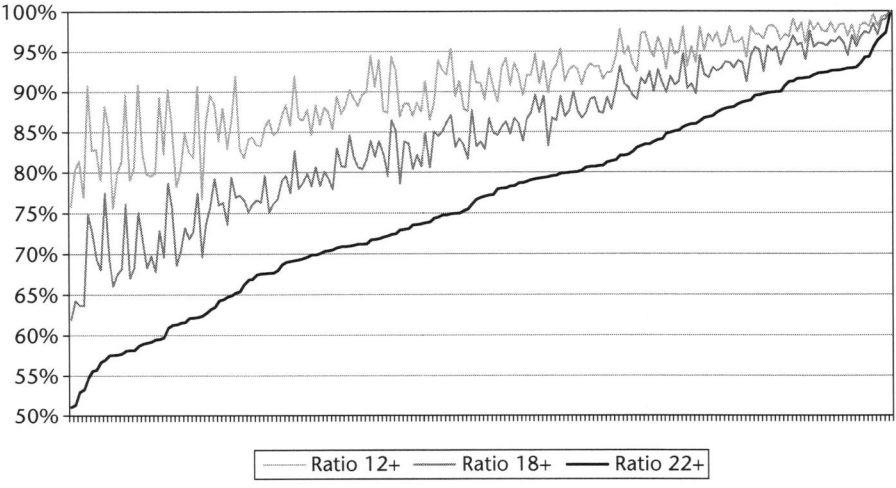

Figure 8.7. Ratio of corrected-to-general brain drain rates in 2000.

(57.0), Vietnam (57.5), Canada (57.6), Papua New Guinea (57.6), the Bahamas (57.7), Guatemala (58.1), Central African Republic (58.2), Laos (58.2), El Salvador (58.7), Vanuatu (59.0), Madagascar (59.1), Israel (59.2), Cuba (59.5), Dominican Republic (59.5), and Solomon Islands (59.8). Conversely, the correction is very small for many ex-Soviet and African countries. Figure 8.8 shows corrected and uncorrected brain drain rates for selected countries.

Obviously, an approach based on census data is not perfect. As Rosenzweig (2005, p. 9) explains, 'information on entry year is based on answers to an ambiguous question—in the US Census the question is "When did you first come to stay?" Immigrants might answer this question by providing the date when they received a permanent immigrant status instead of the date when they first came to the US, at which time they might not have intended to or been able to stay.' Only surveys based on comprehensive migration histories can provide precise information about the location in which schooling was acquired. Still, the census is the only harmonized data source available. Survey data are not available for many countries, and when they are (for example, in the EU Labour Force Survey and in the European Community Household Panel), they do not provide representative pictures of immigrants' characteristics. Their coverage can be very small for countries with few emigrants. An exception is the US New Immigrant Survey (NIS), a nationally representative multi-cohort longitudinal study of new legal immigrants and their

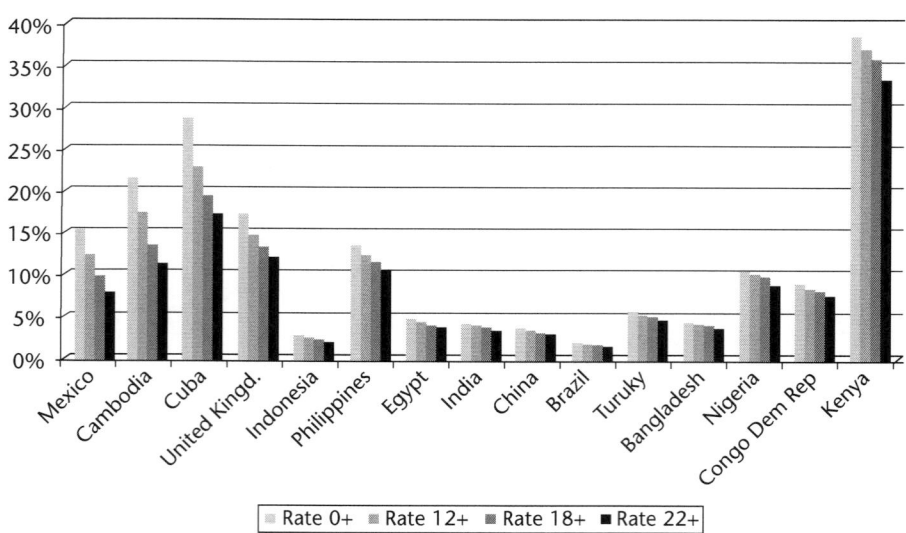

Figure 8.8. Corrected and general brain drain rates for selected countries in 2000.

children to the USA. Comparing proportions of skilled immigrants with US tertiary schooling obtained from the US census and NIS in 2000, we obtain a correlation of 26.4 per cent only. Out of 140 countries, the NIS reports 24 zeros and 14 proportions are equal to 100 per cent. Eliminating these observations computed for small diasporas, the correlation increases to 37.4 per cent, and even 47.7 per cent for countries sending more than 100,000 migrants to the USA. These comparisons indicate that, although NIS results are derived from answers to much more precise questions, there is a risk of bias for countries sending a small number of migrants to the USA.

8.4 The brain drain of scientists and health professionals

General emigration rates may hide important occupational shortages (e.g. among engineers, teachers, physicians, nurses, IT specialists, etc). A well-known channel through which a brain drain can be detrimental to source countries is when it strongly affects professionals which are key inputs for the human capital sector (e.g. teachers, physicians, nurses) or are essential for technology adoption (e.g. engineers, scientists in general). In this section, therefore, we focus on the upper tail of the skill distribution, looking specifically at PhD holders, researchers in science and technology (S&T), and health workers.

8.4.1 Scientists

Scientists are important for R&D and innovation, which are determinants of productivity growth when the distance to the technological frontier is not too large (Vandenbussche, Aghion, and Meghir, 2006). This is not the case in most developing countries. However, at lower levels of occupation, these researchers can play an important role in the adoption of foreign technologies.

Table 8.1 focuses on the emigration of PhD graduates. For 82 origin countries, we provide i) the numbers of PhD graduates working in the USA, ii) the shares of these PhDs among US post-secondary educated immigrants by country of origin, and/or iii) the ratio of PhD holders living in the USA to the estimated number of PhD holders trained in their country (an estimate of the emigration rate to the USA of PhD holders by country of origin). To compute i) and ii), we use the SESTAT database of the National Science Foundation. To calculate iii), we use UNESCO data on the flow of PhD graduates trained at origin (average 2002–2004) and assume that the flows of new PhD graduates represent 4 per cent in developed countries and 5 per cent

Table 8.1. Top-30 suppliers PhDs to the USA.

PhD graduates in the USA		Share in graduates in the USA		Estimated mig. rate to the USA	
China	63,153	Slovenia	71.4%	Panama	93.2%
United Kingdom	24,482	Cameroon	51.7%	Ethiopia	91.3%
Canada	19,122	Georgia	46.1%	Colombia	84.4%
Germany	17,840	Tunisia	31.8%	Honduras	78.5%
Russia	12,835	Saudi Arabia	26.8%	Iceland	72.9%
South Korea	12,172	Iceland	21.5%	Uruguay	71.8%
Iran	8996	China	21.3%	Tanzania	65.8%
France	7277	Estonia	19.6%	Cyprus	49.2%
Poland	6488	Uzbekistan	19.6%	Macao	49.1%
Japan	6478	Azerbaijan	19.6%	Trinidad and Tobago	47.2%
Mexico	5693	Switzerland	18.1%	Argentina	37.0%
Nigeria	4862	Croatia	18.1%	Cuba	30.7%
Egypt	4725	Finland	17.8%	Cameroon	23.7%
Israel	4694	Czech Republic	17.6%	China	22.8%
Argentina	4405	Slovakia	17.6%	Cambodia	22.7%
Romania	4122	Austria	17.4%	Bangladesh	21.7%
Italy	3997	Israel	16.5%	Ghana	16.6%
Brazil	3952	Hungary	16.3%	Ireland	16.0%
Turkey	3798	Ghana	15.9%	Israel	15.9%
Colombia	3787	Romania	15.8%	Canada	15.7%
Cameroon	3714	Turkey	15.4%	Iran	15.1%
Ukraine	3701	Russia	15.2%	Croatia	14.4%
Philippines	3658	Ethiopia	12.5%	Jordan	14.4%
Spain	3435	Spain	12.0%	Mexico	13.4%
Ireland	3294	Argentina	12.0%	Armenia	12.8%
Cuba	3246	Armenia	11.9%	Hungary	12.5%
Greece	2948	France	11.6%	Bulgaria	11.7%
Ghana	2909	Brazil	11.4%	Estonia	11.2%
Hungary	2877	United Kingdom	11.3%	Lebanon	10.7%
Australia	2477	Sweden	11.2%	Philippines	10.2%

Sources: SESTAT-NSF and UNESCO.

of the stock in developing countries: the size of the latter cohort of graduates amounts to 1/20 of the total number of PhD holders. Although it looks rather arbitrary, we believe this assumption is highly reasonable for different reasons. First, the average flow-to-stock ratio of PhD graduates is equal to 1/25 in rich countries. Second, using 1/20 in developing countries is compatible with mortality and population growth differentials with rich countries. Third, it delivers emigration rates of PhD holders which are strongly correlated with those obtained for researchers employed in science and technology (see below). The estimated emigration rate is obtained by dividing the stock living in the USA by the estimated stock domestically trained.

The highest numbers of foreign PhD holders are obtained for developed countries and large developing countries such as China, Russia, Iran, Nigeria, and Egypt. As a proportion of tertiary graduates living in the USA, the proportion of PhDs is extremely high in the cases of Slovenia, Cameroon, Georgia, and Tunisia. The last columns indicate that the estimated emigration rate of PhD holders is high for Latin American countries and some African countries.

Regarding the capacity to innovate, it is also interesting to focus on researchers employed in S&T. This includes many PhD holders but also many other college graduates employed in this sector. Table 8.2 compares migration of researchers employed in the US R&D sector (using the SESTAT database) to UNESCO data on researchers nationally employed in S&T. We provide researchers' emigration numbers and rates to the USA for 70 countries, including 39 developing states. The average emigration rates of developing countries (45.6 per cent) exceeds that of developed countries (21.4 per cent). The rate is particularly high (above 80 per cent) in the cases of Cambodia, Cameroon, Colombia, Costa Rica, Ecuador, Panama, and Vietnam.

8.4.2 Health professionals

In poor countries shortages are particularly severe in the medical sector where the number of physicians per 1,000 inhabitants is extremely low, as shown in Figure 8.9. As stated in the theoretical section, the collapse of a strategic sector is likely to negatively impact human capital accumulation and long-run economic performances.

Clemens and Pettersson (2006), and Docquier and Bhargava (2006) provide data on the emigration of health-care workers. The first paper is based on data on African physicians collected in nine important destination countries in 2000; emigrants are defined according to their country of birth. The second uses panel annual data from 16 receiving countries and defines foreign migrants according to their country of training. Both evaluate the medical brain drain in relative terms, dividing the number of physicians abroad by the total number of physicians born or trained in each origin country. The difference in the definition of a migrant is crucial since, due to the absence of medical school, 11 African countries have no domestically trained physician emigrants abroad while they exhibit medical brain drain rates of between 5 and 15 per cent if one uses the country of birth criterion. Here, we use the Docquier–Bhargava data set, add South Africa in the set of destinations, and use the concept of country of training for all host countries (the original data set relies on various definitions).

Figure 8.10 shows the geographical distribution of the medical brain drain computed in Docquier and Bhargava (2006). The average medical brain drain is particularly severe in sub-Saharan Africa, South Asia, East Asia, and Latin America. The most affected countries exhibiting emigration rates above 40 per cent are Grenada, Dominica, Saint Lucia, Ireland, Liberia, Jamaica, and Fiji. Figure 8.11 reveals that the medical brain drain rates have drastically increased in many African countries but also in Lebanon, Cuba, Cyprus, and the Philippines.

Table 8.2. Researchers employed in science and technology in the USA in 2003.

	Developing countries				High-income countries		
Birth country	S&T researchers in the USA	S&T researchers at home	Brain drain to USA	Birth country	S&T researchers in the USA	S&T researchers at home	Brain drain to USA
Algeria	1242	5678	17.9%	Australia	4889	79,919	5.8%
Bolivia	2214	1140	66.0%	Austria	3815	26,563	12.6%
Brazil	10,980	79,600	12.1%	Belgium	4767	32,229	12.9%
Bulgaria	4497	9400	32.4%	Canada	72,584	122,809	37.1%
Myanmar	1727	732	70.2%	Hong Kong	26,602	12,410	68.2%
Cambodia	3030	239	92.7%	Cyprus	591	532	52.6%
Cameroon	3643	472	88.5%	Czech Republic	2455	17,232	12.5%
Chile	5496	10,120	35.2%	Denmark	2561	25,035	9.3%
China	158,524	907,743	14.9%	Estonia	813	3063	21.0%
Colombia	19,362	4487	81.2%	Finland	791	39,897	1.9%
Costa Rica	4659	529	89.8%	France	16,072	195,638	7.6%
Cote d'Ivoire	288	1292	18.2%	Germany	59,213	269,703	18.0%
Croatia	1666	6722	19.9%	Greece	6554	16,546	28.4%
Ecuador	7012	595	92.2%	Hungary	4986	15,001	24.9%
Ethiopia	2549	1649	60.7%	Iceland	1002	2034	33.0%
Guatemala	1415	398	78.1%	Ireland	9270	10,741	46.3%
Indonesia	5163	45,567	10.2%	Italy	15,022	73,181	17.0%
Kazakhstan	1108	10,339	9.7%	Japan	34,757	677,723	4.9%
Latvia	2728	3291	45.3%	Kuwait	1118	202	84.7%
Lithuania	2285	7105	24.3%	Luxembourg	100	2108	4.5%
Macedonia	80	1147	6.5%	Netherlands	7616	41,082	15.6%
Madagascar	166	887	15.8%	New Zealand	3217	15,911	16.8%
Malaysia	7955	10,419	43.3%	Norway	3291	21,339	13.4%
Malta	452	359	55.7%	Portugal	2581	20,067	11.4%
Mexico	46,356	42,953	51.9%	Singapore	3397	21,821	13.5%
Nepal	1739	1627	51.7%	Slovakia	1227	10,008	10.9%
Pakistan	14,682	12,919	53.2%	Slovenia	202	4455	4.3%

Country			
Panama	7498	307	96.1%
Paraguay	335	489	40.6%
Romania	10,900	20,761	34.4%
Russia	35,588	478,090	6.9%
South Africa	5906	16,248	26.7%
Sri Lanka	4652	2703	63.3%
Thailand	7781	18,430	29.7%
Tunisia	2003	11,805	14.5%
Turkey	8878	31,587	21.9%
Uruguay	1625	1244	56.6%
Venezuela	8058	3537	69.5%
Vietnam		9863	81.8%
Average	44,236		*45.6%*

Country			
South Korea	50,605	154,884	24.6%
Sweden	3585	50,091	6.7%
Switzerland	3768	25,616	12.8%
United Kingdom	72,396	177,625	29.0%
Average			*21.4%*

Sources: SESTAT-NSF and UNESCO.

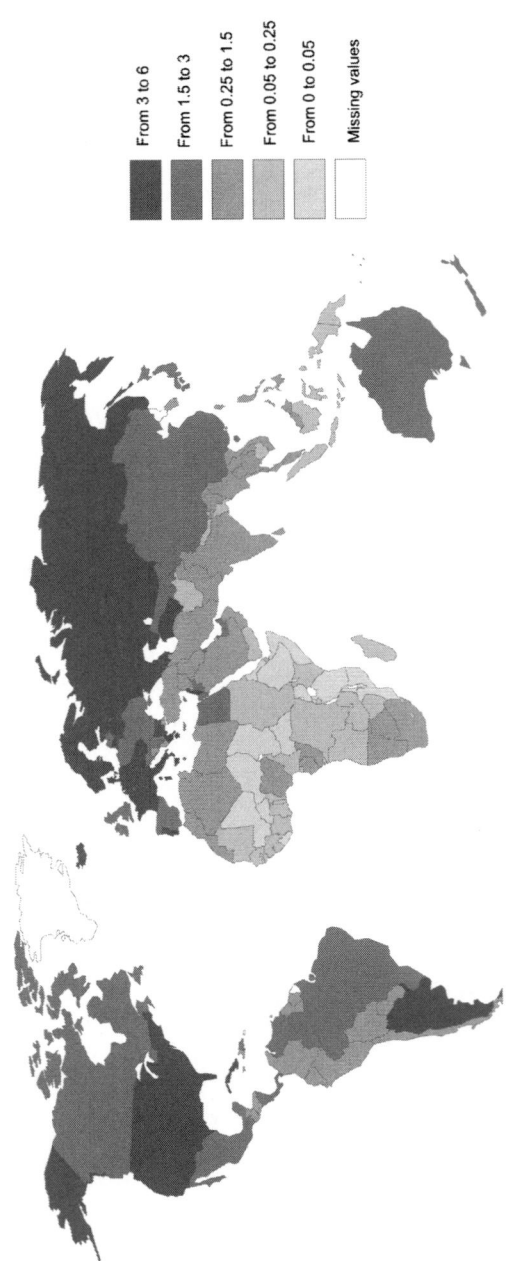

Figure 8.9. Physicians per 1,000 people, year 2004.

From 3 to 6

From 1.5 to 3

From 0.25 to 1.5

From 0.05 to 0.25

From 0 to 0.05

Missing values

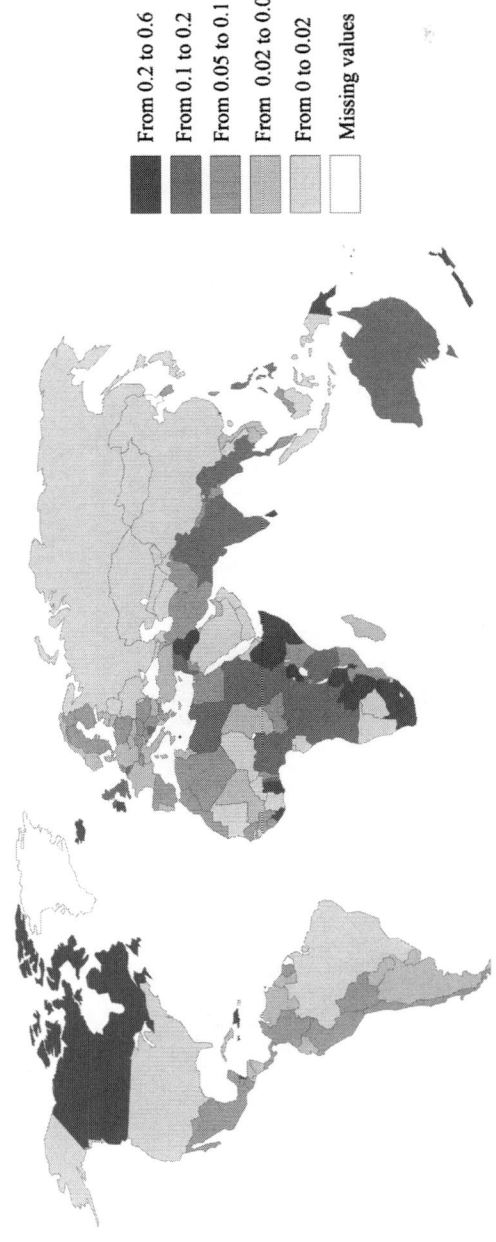

From 0.2 to 0.6
From 0.1 to 0.2
From 0.05 to 0.1
From 0.02 to 0.05
From 0 to 0.02
Missing values

Figure 8.10. Medical brain drain, year 2004.

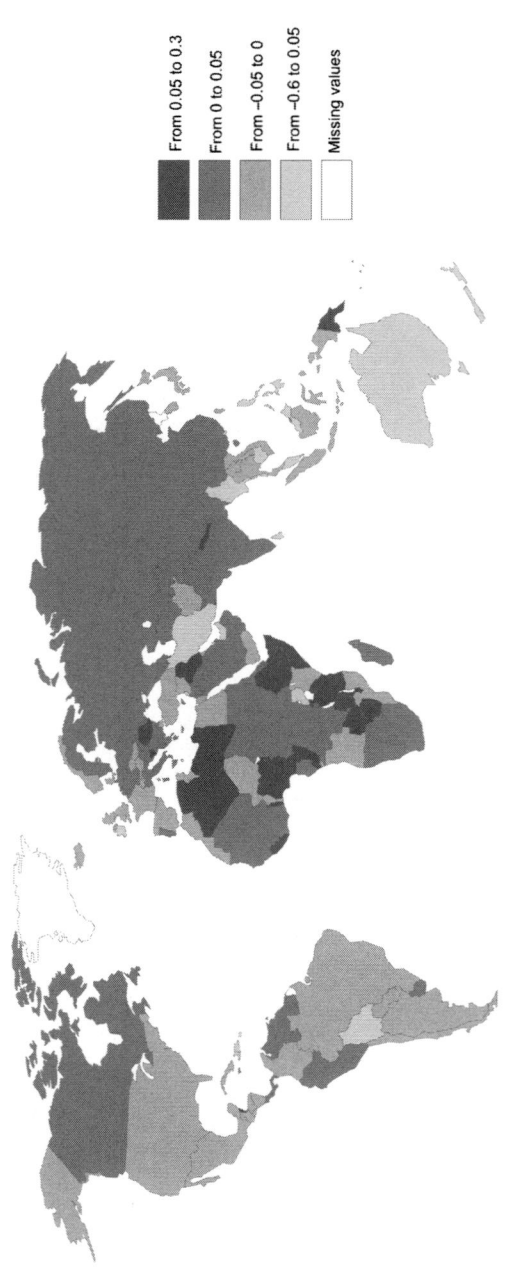

From 0.05 to 0.3

From 0 to 0.05

From −0.05 to 0

From −0.6 to 0.05

Missing values

Figure 8.11. Change in medical brain drain, 1991–2004.

9

Theory, Evidence, and Implications

The brain drain is usually considered a detrimental phenomenon for origin countries, especially for developing ones. While such human capital flight has long been perceived as a kind of spoliation, the new brain drain literature has emphasized many indirect and feedback channels through which the brain drain may positively affect sending countries. However, to the best of our knowledge, the positive and negative effects of the brain drain have never been *quantified* so as to make them comparable. This is the goal of this chapter, which builds on a partial equilibrium setting of endogenous economic performances. In the next sections:

- We survey the channels discussed in the new brain drain literature and integrate them in a unified theoretical framework. Given data availability, existing empirical studies are all based on the extensive measure of the brain drain described in Section 1.1. Hence, our partial equilibrium model will imperfectly account for the brain drain of elite workers and scientists. In Section 9.3, we will use rather arbitrary parameters to deal with positive selection in the location choice of skilled workers.

- We extend existing cross-country studies on some of these channels (brain gain and various diaspora externalities) and analyse their robustness using alternative brain drain measures or specification. The results are then used to help us calibrate the parameters of our partial equilibrium model.

- Finally, we provide comparable country-specific numerical experiments for each channel. We follow a 'What if?' strategy and compute the hypothetical level of GDP per capita obtained when the rate of highly skilled migration is set at value of the low-skilled migration rate.
  In countries where the low-skilled emigration rate is extremely low, we divide the highly skilled emigration rate by ten. Since emigration rates are based on stock values, our experiment consists in instantaneously and permanently repatriating many skilled emigrants. We consider the

difference between the simulated and observed levels of GDP per capita as a measure of the overall macroeconomic impact of the brain drain on economic performances.

Beine, Docquier, and Rapoport (2008) used identical counterfactual simulations to estimate the short-run net effect of the brain drain on human capital accumulation for each origin country and region. We generalize this experiment to other channels. We use the same shock, simulate the intensity of the major mechanisms depicted in the literature, and quantify the gains and costs of the brain drain for each developing country. We characterize the magnitude of the net impact of the brain drain on GDP and income per capita for 148 developing countries, distinguishing between the short-term (10 years) and the long-term impact.

In the remainder of this chapter, we first describe the general framework used to endogenize economic performances. We then review and quantify the effects conveyed through the 'human capital', 'screening-selection', 'productivity', and 'institutional' channels. These effects are combined in the general framework in Section 9.6. Finally, we discuss the 'transfer' channel and show it has a moderate impact. Note that among the various channels reviewed we did not include temporary/return migration. This is not to deny the importance of temporary/return migration both quantitatively (indeed, there is a lot of temporary and return migration taking place) and theoretically (for example, return migration is certainly an important diffusion channel for technology diffusion or the transmission of institutional norms). However, the current state of immigration data prevents us from looking at temporary migration specifically. As the previous section explains, current international migration data sets provide snapshots of immigration stocks at different moments in time but do not allow for tracking whether changes in these stocks over time are due to new flows of entry or to attrition through death, return migration, or emigration to a third country. Hence, the above analysis provides estimates of the overall effect of migration, be it permanent or temporary.

9.1 Endogenizing economic performances

Economic performances are reasonably gauged by the national level of GDP per capita. Quantifying the effect of highly skilled emigration on GDP per capita requires analysing how the brain drain affects the determinants of GDP. Box 9.1 describes the supply-side model used to predict the GDP level. Its basic ingredients are the following. We start with a standard production function which determines the amount produced as a function of two factors, physical capital and labour in efficiency units. We further assume that labour in efficiency units is itself a nested combination of high- and low-skill labour with constant elasticity of substitution between these two types of labour. Practically, the high-skilled labour force is proxied by the population aged 25 with college (tertiary) education.[1] The low-skilled labour force is measured by the population in the same age group with secondary education or less.

Education, obviously, affects the productivity of workers. By changing the proportion of college graduates in the labour force, the brain drain affects the average productivity of remaining workers through this 'human capital' channel. In addition, the productivity of domestic educated workers depends on the quality of education and on the distribution of innate abilities. If highly skilled emigrants have higher abilities than those left behind, the brain drain affects productivity through a second channel, the 'screening-selection' channel.

The model assumes that each developing country is too small to significantly affect the international return to physical capital (small open economy hypothesis). In other words, international movements of capital are such that the returns to capital (net of risk premium and transaction costs) are equalized across nations. From the perspective of potential investors, each developing country is characterized by a given risk premium (reflecting the quality of institutions and the extent of transaction costs). The domestic return to capital is equal to the international interest rate supplemented by a domestic risk premium.

Combining this arbitrage condition with the production function gives a simple expression for the GDP per capita, which becomes proportional to the average level of human capital of the labour force, and for the within-country wage differential between college graduates and less educated workers. The parameters of the model can then be calibrated so as to match data on wage differentials observed in developed and developing countries. Once properly parametrized, the model gives a simple and general expression for the GDP per capita of each country, expressed in proportion of the level observed in the leading countries. The log-ratio of GDP per capita is explained by differences in total factor productivity (TFP), in human capital (including educational and average ability of remaining high-skilled workers), and in institutions. We will refer to the following equation as the GDP equation:

> Log of GDP ratio
> = 1.5 × Log of TFP ratio
> + 1.0 × Log of ratio of average level of human capital in the labour force
> + 0.5 × Log of risk factor (one plus the risk premium associated to institutional quality)

---

[1] Following Barro and Lee (2001), Docquier, Lowell, and Marfouk (2009) consider that workers with one year of college in the USA have post-secondary education. The US proportion of post-secondary educated in the labour force was equal to 51.3 per cent in 2000.

The recent literature shows that each of these determinants of economic performances is likely to be affected by the brain drain. In addition, remittances can be factored if one aims at capturing the impact of the brain drain on GNI per capita. In the next sections, we will discuss the five channels through which the brain drain impacts the GDP ratio with leading countries, and use empirical elasticities of the recent literature to quantify them. On the one hand, disregarding these channels can generate strong biases in the assessment of the impact of the brain drain. On the other hand, it is worth noticing that the new empirical literature is still young and subject to identification problems. For example, the use of cross-section methods makes it very difficult to identify causation and deal with unobserved heterogeneity. For this reason, it is desirable to compare extreme scenarios and, for the sake of comparison, quantify the cost of the brain drain under the pessimistic and traditional view.

In the most pessimistic scenario, we assume that human capital formation is unaffected by migration prospects (we will relax this assumption in Section 9.2). Then we simulate the hypothetical level of the GDP per capita obtained when the highly skilled emigration rate is set at the level of the low-skill one. In the case of poor countries, where highly skilled people have emigration propensities that are ten to twenty times higher than for the low skill, this shock implies repatriating most skilled expatriates. This dramatically increases the proportion of educated in the labour force and labour in efficiency units. This shock can easily be calibrated using the data on migration stocks and labour force by education levels presented in Chapter 8.

We also assume that TFP is an increasing function of human capital as in Lucas (1988). Looking at the data, a reasonable value for the elasticity of total factor productivity to human capital is 0.4.[2] We use the above GDP equation to simulate the costs of the brain drain for each country. Figure 9.1 depicts the simulated change in GDP per capita (as a percentage of the observed level) that would follow such a shock as a function of the skilled emigration rate in 2000. The cost of the brain drain increases exponentially with the skilled emigration rate and, therefore, in a traditional view, reducing it should strongly increase GDP per capita in the most open countries: by 196 per cent in Guyana, by more than 150 per cent in Jamaica, Haiti, or Trinidad and Tobago. In PPP values, the GDP per capita in Guyana, Jamaica, and other small islands would become similar to that of Greece or Spain or Portugal. The effect would also be strong in African countries such as Gambia (+78 per cent), Cape Verde (+77 per cent), and Mauritius (+61 per cent), and Sierra Leone, Liberia, Ghana, and Kenya would experience a more than 40 per cent increase.

---

[2] A simple OLS regression gives ln(TFP) = 6.6 + 0.4ln(human capital). TFP data are taken from Lodigiani (2008).

Box 9.1 PREDICTING GDP PER CAPITA

Our partial equilibrium model is based on a Cobb–Douglas production function with two factors, physical capital (K_t), and labour in efficiency units (E_t). Labour in efficiency unit is itself a nested function of highly skilled labour (H_t), and low-skill labour (L_t), with constant elasticity of substitution (CES). The average productivity of educated workers employed domestically (q_t) depends on the quality of education and on the distribution of innate abilities. The national GDP is given by the following expression:

$$Y_t = A_t K_t^{1-\alpha} E_t^{\alpha} = A_t K_t^{1-\alpha} [q_t \theta H_t^{\rho} + (1-\theta) L_t^{\rho}]^{1/\rho}, \tag{9.1}$$

where A_t is a time-varying scale factor (total factor productivity), α is the share of labour in national income, θ is the weight of highly skilled labour in total labour, and ρ is a parameter determining the elasticity of substitution between highly skilled and low-skilled workers: the elasticity of substitution is given by $1/(1-\rho)$.

The domestic return to capital (i.e. the marginal productivity of capital) is equal to the international interest rate supplemented by a domestic risk premium. Hence, the following arbitrage condition implicitly defines the equilibrium amount of capital per worker in the economy:

$$R^*(1+\phi_t) = (1-\alpha) A_t K_t^{-\alpha} E_t^{\alpha}, \tag{9.2}$$

where R^* is the risk-free international interest factor (one plus the interest rate), defined as the interest factor in the most advanced countries and ϕ_t captures the risk premium associated to institutional quality (including the extent of international transaction costs).

Substituting (9.2) in (9.1) and dividing by the total population size ($H_t + L_t$) gives the following expression for the GDP per capita:

$$y_t = \left[\frac{1-\alpha}{R^*(1+\phi_t)}\right]^{\frac{1-\alpha}{\alpha}} A_t^{\frac{1}{\alpha}} e_t \tag{9.3}$$

where $e_t \equiv E_t/(H_t + L_t) = [q_t \theta h_t^{\rho} + (1-\theta)(1-h_t)^{\rho}]^{1/\rho}$ measures the average number of efficiency units of workers and $h_t \equiv H_t / (H_t + L_t)$ is the proportion of the highly skilled (with tertiary education) in the resident population.

The domestic wage ratio between highly skilled and low-skilled workers amounts to

$$\frac{w_{H,t}}{w_{L,t}} = \frac{\theta q_t}{1-\theta}\left(\frac{1-h_t}{h_t}\right)^{1-\rho} \tag{9.4}$$

Equation (9.4) allows us to calibrate the structural parameters of the technological function. In a rich country such as the USA, we have $1 - h_t \approx h_t$ and q_t can be normalized to unity. Since a tertiary educated worker earns a wage which is on average twice as high as the wage of another worker (with secondary or primary education), we choose $\theta = 2/3$. At the lowest tail of the distribution, the share of educated workers in the labour force of poorest countries is below one per cent. For example, we observe 0.2 per cent of educated in Mauritania whereas the skill premium is around 10 (see Epifani and Gancia, 2008). By choosing $\rho = 0.6$ (an elasticity of substitution of 2.5), we obtain a reasonable skill premium for developing countries. Many studies advocate using an elasticity greater than one (see Acemoglu, 2002). In their study on immigration and inequality, Otaviano and Peri (2008) use a range of estimates between 1.5 and 3. Angrist (1995) recommends a value around 2 to explain the trends in the college premium on the Palestinian labour market. Our value of 2.5 seems very plausible. Finally, a reasonable value for α, the share of labour in total income, is 2/3.

We focus on macro-economic performances and levels of development. Since productivity is time-varying, the level of GDP per capita is not a stationary variable. Using (9.3) and taking logs, we can express the GDP per capita in proportion of the level observed in the rich world (y_t^*) as

$$\ln\left(\frac{y_t}{y_t^*}\right) = \frac{1}{\alpha}\ln\left(\frac{A_t}{A_t^*}\right) + \ln\left(\frac{e_t}{e_t^*}\right) - \frac{1-\alpha}{\alpha}\ln(1+\phi_t) \qquad (9.5)$$

$$with\,\frac{1}{\alpha} = 1.5\,and\,\frac{1-\alpha}{\alpha} = 0.5.$$

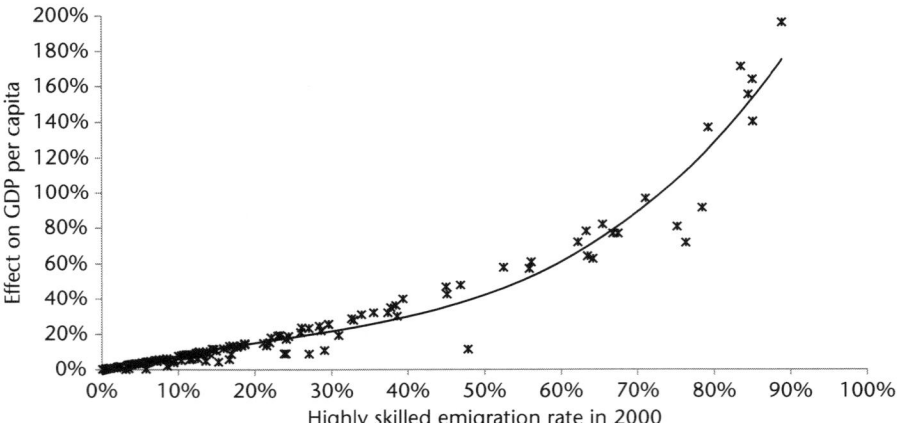

Figure 9.1. Costs of the brain drain under the traditional view (as a percentage of the observed GDP per capita) as a function of the highly skilled emigration rate.

Note: Percentage deviation in GDP per capita when the emigration rate of college graduates is set at the value of the low-skilled emigration rate.

Such figures are of course spectacular and questionable. In the next section, we list a series of arguments moderating the conclusion of traditional view.

9.2 The human capital channel

As stated above, the most obvious and measurable effect of the brain drain is the relocation of talented people from developing to developed countries. The question is: does the brain drain reduce human capital accumulation? In this section, we show that, when human capital formation is endogenous and depends on migration prospects, the human capital response to a restricted brain drain becomes ambiguous.

9.2.1 *Theory of brain drain and human capital formation*

Brain drain has a direct negative impact on human capital accumulation as a fraction of national college graduates leaves the country. However, the domestic enrolment rate or the proportion of educated within the new cohort of workers can be positively affected by emigration prospects. On the aggregate, the brain drain can thus stimulate human capital accumulation if the latter incentive effect dominates the direct negative effect. Box 9.2 provides a simple analytical description of this mechanism, which is sketched in the following paragraphs.

Considering educational investments as exogenous, the early literature of the 1970s viewed the brain drain as contributing to increased inequality at the international level, with rich countries becoming richer at the expense of poor countries. This effect clearly deteriorates average economic performances at origin.[3] Bhagwati and Hamada (1974) supported this view: although they already recognized the endogeneity of school enrolment rates, they did not consider it as a major mechanism.

A new generation of brain drain research has emerged since the mid-1990s around the idea that migration prospects can foster domestic enrolment in education in developing countries, raising the possibility of brain drain being beneficial to the source country. These studies look at how the country's stock of human capital is built up and how migration modifies the incentive structure faced by developing countries' residents when making their education decisions.

In line with this literature, we consider that the investment in education is endogenous and depends on two sets of variables:

- *The proportion of highly skilled in the labour force.* Its effect is theoretically ambiguous. Indeed, the fact that educated parents tend to invest more in the human capital of their children than the less educated implies a positive relationship between school enrolment and the countrywide average level of human capital. On the contrary, abundance of human capital negatively affects the domestic return to schooling, then discouraging people to invest. Cross-country comparisons suggest that the first effect dominates. In addition,

---

[3] If origin countries are large enough, this effect can be reinforced by the fact that rich countries benefit from the entry of talented workers. If the origin country is too small to significantly impact growth in leading countries (an assumption compatible with the small open economy hypothesis on the capital market), this effect vanishes.

Box 9.2 BRAIN DRAIN AND HUMAN CAPITAL ACCUMULATION

In the spirit of Barro, Mankiw, and Sala-I-Martin (1995), we disregard micro-foundations and consider that the dynamics of human capital is governed by the following process:

$$h_{t+1} = h_t(1 - \delta) + n(h_t)\,\Theta_t\,(1 - m_t) \tag{9.6}$$

where δ is a rate of depreciation of human capital capturing the level and differential in mortality or retirement of existing cohorts. The variable $n(h_t)$ captures the growth rate of the labour force or the replacement of old by young workers; it is reasonably decreasing in h_t since more educated parents tend to have fewer children. The variable Θ_t reflects enrolment rates in tertiary education and captures the proportion of educated within the new cohort of workers; it will be endogenized later. Finally, m_t is the emigration rate of these young educated adults. Introducing a probability of migration for the low skilled would not modify the nature of our results.

Clearly, if it exists, a steady state (denoted by subscript ss) of this economy implies $h_{ss} = n$ $(h_{ss}).\Theta_{ss}.(1 - m_{ss})/\delta$. Hence, for given enrolment rates Θ_t, the skilled emigration rate reduces h_{t+1} and h_{ss} other things equal.

In line with the recent literature on brain drain and human capital formation, let us now endogenize Θ_t, considering that the investment in education Θ_t is endogenous and depends on two sets of variables: the proportion of highly skilled, h_t, or the proportion h_t of educated workers employed in the production of human capital (such as teachers and health professionals or women), and migration prospects to developed countries (to capture the incentive effect). Among others, the magnitude of this incentive effect depends on the wage gap between origin and developed countries, $(1 - w_{H,t}/w_{H,t}^*)$. Therefore, we have:

$$\Theta_t = \Theta\left[h_t, \hat{h}_t, m_t\left(1 - \frac{w_{H,t}}{w_{H,t}^*}\right)\right] \tag{9.7}$$

with positive partial derivatives, $\Theta_1', \Theta_2', \Theta_3' > 0$.

Plugging (9.7) into (9.6) and deriving h_{t+1} with respect to m_t, a marginal increase in m_t stimulates human capital accumulation if and only if

$$\Theta_3'(1 - m_t)\left(1 - \frac{w_{H,t}}{w_{H,t}^*}\right) > \Theta_t \tag{9.8}$$

This condition holds if educational choices respond to incentives (Θ_3' is large), if the skilled emigration rate m_t is not to high, if the distance to the frontier is large enough (i.e. $w_{H,t}/w_{H,t}^*$ is small) and if domestic enrolment in education is not too high. When $\Theta_3'\left(1 - \frac{w_{H,t}}{w_{H,t}^*}\right) > \Theta_t(h_t, \hat{h}_t, 0)$, the human-capital maximizing emigration rate is positive. Under this condition, a limited positive skilled emigration rate increases the proportion of the educated among remaining residents.

---

human capital investments may depend on *the proportion of educated workers employed in the production of human capital,* such as teachers, health professionals, or educated women. A sector-specific or gender-specific brain drain can therefore be damaging for origin countries.

- *Migration prospects to developed countries*. If education increases the probability of migration to a high-wage destination, then migration prospects increase that expected return to schooling, reduce uncertainty on this return, reduce the cost of acquiring education (in case of students' migration), or allow minorities to escape discrimination. This could lead to higher investment in education. Among other things, the magnitude of this incentive effect depends on the wage differential between origin and leading countries.

A first consequence is that the brain drain is more likely to reduce human capital accumulation if it is concentrated in particularly strategic occupations. The sectoral dimension of the brain drain therefore matters. As stated above, a second implication is that if skilled migration prospects impact on educational choices, the net effect of skilled emigration becomes ambiguous. The idea that a country's pre-migration stock of human capital is endogenous to the prospect of migration is relatively old. As stated above, Bhagwati and Hamada (1974) or McCulloch and Yellen (1977) recognized that migration prospects increase the expected wage for high-skilled workers and stimulate human capital investments. More recent theoretical contributions (Mountford, 1997; Stark et al., 1998; Vidal, 1998; Beine et al., 2001; Stark and Wang, 2002) have explored the possibility for skilled migration to create more human capital ex-ante than the ex-post loss. The theory shows that an increase in high-skilled emigration is more likely to stimulate human capital accumulation if educational choices can respond to incentives (absence of liquidity constraints), if the skilled emigration rate is not too high, if the wage differential with destination countries is large, and if the effectiveness of domestic education policy is low. When these conditions hold, the human-capital maximizing emigration rate is positive, that is a limited positive skilled emigration rate increases the proportion of educated among remaining residents.

9.2.2 *Empirical evidence*

Recent theoretical developments suggest a positive effect of migration prospects on human capital investments for the reasons explained above. What is the empirical evidence for this incentive mechanism?

First, evidence of a brain gain effect has been found at a *micro-level*:

- Observing the very high rates of enrolment in higher education in the Philippines in spite of the low domestic returns to human capital, Lucas (2004) writes: 'It is difficult to believe that these high, privately financed enrolment rates are not induced by the possibility of emigration. There are signs that the choice of major field of study . . . responds to shifts in international demands. Higher education is almost certainly induced to a significant extent by the potential for emigration.'

- More recently, Batista et al. (2011) estimated that in the case of Cape Verde, the brain drain not only has a net positive effect, it is also responsible for the bulk of human capital formation in the country.

- Similarly, in their survey on Tonga's 'best and brightest', Gibson and McKenzie (2011) show that nearly all of Tonga's very top high school students (85 per cent) contemplated emigration while still in high school, which led them to take additional classes (e.g. holiday classes, English classes) and make changes in their course choices (e.g. favouring general disciplines such as sciences or commerce). According to Gibson and McKenzie, these substantial brain gain effects combined with high return rates explains the overall largely positive effects of migration for Tonga in terms of human capital formation.

- Another micro-example from the Pacific region is provided by Chand and Clemens (2008) who compare educational investments of ethnic Fijians v. Fijians of Indian ancestry in the aftermath of the 1987 military coup, which resulted in physical violence and then discriminative policies against the Indian minority. The coup sparked massive emigration among skilled Indo-Fijians, and led them to invest heavily in higher education in order to 'clear the bar' raised by the Australian (and New Zealand's) point system. While the political situation has stabilized since the mid-1990s, the Indian minority is now significantly more migratory and, for those who remain in Fiji, more educated than comparable ethnic Fijians. Since this was not the case prior to the military coup, the authors interpret this as quasi-experimental evidence of the brain gain channel.

- Conversely, the case of Mexico also offers interesting insights on the prospect channel, in a negative way. For example, McKenzie and Rapoport (2011) report that living in a migrant household has a substantial negative effect on children's educational attainment in rural Mexico. While migration may have positive effects on younger children, especially girls from very poor households thanks to remittances, migration actually depresses schooling for older children. This is consistent with the brain gain hypothesis as in the case of Mexico–USA migration, migration is massively illegal and illegal migrants are generally confined to low-skill jobs for a long period of time. Indeed, most first-time migrants from Mexico travel to the USA without documentation. Kossoudji and Cobb-Clark (2002) argue that there is no return on schooling in the first job for unauthorized workers, and find that finishing high school only pays off in terms of wages about four years after legalization. As a result, the prospect of future migration may actually lower incentives to invest in education. This is confirmed by Boucher et al. (2008) who compared internal and international migration from rural Mexico. Since there is no restriction on internal migration in Mexico and Mexico–USA migration is massively illegal, in their paper heterogeneity in migration probabilities is due to variation in pre-existing migration networks: people with higher internal/international networks will have a higher propensity to migrate and this will drive education investment up or down depending on whether migration raises or decreases the expected return to education.

These micro-studies strongly suggest that the prospect of highly skilled emigration exerts a causal impact on human capital decisions, although the direction of this impact might be country-specific. To calibrate our partial equilibrium model and capture the average impact of migration prospects on human capital accumulation, macro-studies are needed. The rest of this section reviews the empirical literature to date and evaluates the robustness of the results to specification choices and brain drain measures.

Beine, Docquier, and Rapoport (2008) used the Docquier and Marfouk (2006) estimates of emigration rates for the highest (tertiary) education as their measure of brain drain and found evidence of a positive effect of skilled migration prospects on gross (pre-migration) human capital levels in a cross-section of 127 developing countries. They obtain a short-run elasticity of human capital growth (log-change in the proportion of tertiary educated among natives) to skilled emigration prospects in the neighbourhood of 5 per cent. This is not negligible for countries where the average proportion of educated typically lies between 2 to 8 per cent. Although panel data would be better to refine the estimate of the convergence speed, the long-run elasticity amounts to 22.5 per cent. These elasticities are very stable across specifications and estimation methods (OLS and IV). Easterly and Nyarko (2009) use other sets of instruments (former colonial links, population size, and distance to the main destinations) for a sample of developing countries; using a growth accounting framework, they find that the brain drain causes (gross) skill creation, and no evidence it causes (net) skill depletion.[4]

Tables 9.1 and 9.2 give a general overview of empirical results obtained in cross-country regressions. In Table 9.1, we use the beta-convergence specification of Beine, Docquier, and Rapoport (2008). The dependent variable is the 1990–2000 log-change in the proportion of tertiary educated among individuals born in the home country. We regress it on the 1990 proportion of tertiary educated (to capture convergence), on the 1990 skilled emigration rate

---

[4] They also discuss feedback effects in the spirit of the next sections, with a focus on Africa, and conclude that once these feedback effects are taken into account, the brain drain is 'good for Africa'.

Table 9.1. Empirical analysis of the incentive mechanism.

	(1)	(2)	(3)	(4)	(5)	(6)
Constant	−0.013	−0.015	−0.242	−0.237	−0.123	−0.321
	(0.14)	(0.14)	(2.33)**	(2.31)**	(1.64)	(3.15)***
Log of skilled mig rate in 1990	0.054	0.054	–	–	0.046	
	(2.03)**	(2.15)**			(2.02)**	
Log of (1 + Skilled mig rate in 1990)			0.434	–		0.388
			(2.77)***			(2.80)***
Skilled mig rate in 1990			–	0.307		
				(2.67)***		
Log of human capital in 1990	−0.239	−0.239	−0.247	−0.248	−0.257	−0.263
	(6.52)***	(6.70)***	(6.56)***	(6.51)***	(6.34)***	(6.40)***
Sub-Saharan African dummy	−0.450	−0.450	−0.440	−0.440	−0.440	−0.435
	(4.29)***	(4.49)***	(4.35)***	(4.31)***	(4.44)***	(4.43)***
Latin American dummy	−0.091	−0.090	−0.086	−0.081	−0.080	−0.079
	(1.46)	(1.48)	(1.33)	(1.26)	(1.32)	(1.30)
Population density	−0.000	−0.000	−0.000	−0.000	−0.000	−0.000
	(1.36)	(1.39)	(1.60)	(1.58)	(1.31)	(1.40)
Remittances per capita in 1990	−0.798	−0.798	−0.659	−0.659	−0.730	−0.639
	(2.06)**	(2.13)**	(1.82)*	(1.82)*	(1.89)*	(1.70)*
Method	OLS	IV	OLS	OLS	OLS	OLS
F-stat first stage	–	124.41				
Hausman		0.967				
Observations	103	103	103	103	104	104
R-squared	0.46	0.46	0.47	0.47	0.45	0.46

Robust t statistics in parentheses
* significant at 10%; ** significant at 5%; *** significant at 1%

and the set of explanatory variables used in Beine, Docquier, and Rapoport (2010). To complement the latter study, we test several functional forms for the incentive mechanism and we use an adjusted measure of the brain drain to account for country of training. The following results emerge:

- Column (1) is the standard OLS regression based on Docquier and Marfouk's skilled emigration rates observed in 1990 for 103 countries. The incentive mechanism is modelled by introducing the log of the skilled emigration rate in 1990. We confirm the results commented above and obtain a short-run elasticity of 5.4 per cent and a long-run elasticity of 22.6 per cent (i.e. 0.054/0.239). The sub-Saharan dummy is negative and significant. The other controls are not.

- A potentially important problem with OLS regressions concerns the exogeneity of the migration rate. When trying to determine the impact of migration on education, one has to control for the reverse effect or for the joint impact of unobserved variables. To address this issue, we provide IV estimates in column (2). The skilled emigration rate is instrumented by the log of population size and the log of the total diaspora abroad. We obtain identical results and a similar elasticity for the incentive effect. The F-stat amounts to 124.41 in the first stage. The Hausman test rejects endogeneity, indicating that the skilled emigration rate can be treated as exogenous; we therefore proceed with reference to the OLS results only.[5]

- In columns (3) and (4), we use two alternative specifications for the incentive mechanism, one based on the log of one plus the skilled emigration rate and one based on the skilled emigration rate. In both cases, the incentive mechanism is always positive and highly significant.

- In columns (5) and (6), we replicate the analysis of columns (1) and (3) when using an alternative measure of the brain drain. We use the data set on emigration rates by age of entry developed in Beine et al. (2007) and exclude skilled emigrants who left their country before age 22. Our skilled emigration rate is thus very likely to concern individuals trained in their home country. Again, the incentive mechanism operates and is highly significant. In column (5), the short-run elasticity is equal to 4.6 per cent and the long-run elasticity becomes 17.9 per cent (i.e. 0.046/0.257). It is robust to the specification. It is worth noticing that similar results would be obtained by excluding individuals who left their country before age 12 or 18.

- In unreported regressions we also tested for non-linearities in the migration–human capital relationship using interactions between skilled emigration rates and origin-country dummies capturing their development levels. The interaction term was never significant, suggesting that the incentive effect operates with about the same magnitude in low-income and medium-income countries. The results are also robust to the use of a difference between (or a ratio of) high- to low-skilled emigration rates as a measure of skilled migration prospects.

In contrast, Faini (2003) found a depressing but not significant effect of tertiary emigration on domestic enrollment in higher education, a finding he attributed to the choice of would-be migrants to pursue their studies abroad.[6] Table 9.2 therefore uses alternative indicators of human capital investments. The regression method is OLS. Indeed, beta convergence models reveal that endogeneity issues are potentially minor, which seems reasonable

---

[5] Same conclusion as in Beine, Docquier, and Rapoport (2010) or Docquier, Faye, and Pestieau (2008) using different sets of instruments.

[6] As he himself acknowledged, however, his results must be taken with caution as they are based on enrolment data known to raise measurement problems.

Table 9.2. Robustness analysis of the incentive mechanism.

	(1)	(2)	(3)	(4)	(5)	(6)	(7)	(8)
	School enrollment rates in 1995 in logs						Literacy rates in 1990	
	Tertiary educ		Secondary educ		Primary educ			
Constant	-1.771 (3.34)***	-1.695 (3.03)***	-0.688 (1.34)	-0.802 (1.60)	4.525 (34.93)***	4.515 (35.63)***	4.414 (31.83)***	4.266 (29.92)***
Log of skilled mig. rate in 1990	-0.078 (1.27)		0.033 (1.19)		-0.001 (0.07)		0.043 (2.11)**	
Log of (1 + Skilled mig. rate)		-1.261 (3.02)***		0.563 (2.71)***		0.101 (1.03)		0.283 (2.14)**
Log of secondary enrolment in 1990	1.056 (10.1)***	1.092 (11.0)***						
Log of primary enrolment in 1990			0.897 (8.62)***	0.883 (8.63)***				
Log of public expend. per student	-0.029 (0.28)	0.007 (0.07)	0.177 (3.23)***	0.176 (3.36)***	0.024 (0.73)	0.022 (0.66)	0.054 (1.56)	0.053 (1.51)
Sub-Saharan African dummy	-0.635 (3.23)***	-0.668 (3.58)***	-0.639 (6.83)***	-0.619 (6.80)***	-0.294 (3.64)***	-0.290 (3.61)***	-0.370 (5.33)***	-0.358 (5.19)***
Remittances per capita in 1990							-0.956 (2.55)**	-0.890 (2.37)**
Method	OLS	OLS	OLS	OLS	OLS	OLS	OLS	OLS
Observations	118	118	123	123	123	123	88	88
R-squared	0.66	0.68	0.68	0.69	0.18	0.18	0.35	0.35

Robust t statistics in parentheses * significant at 10%; ** significant at 5%; *** significant at 1%

since the dependent variable is a flow measured on the recent period whereas migration rates are based on existing stocks of migrants.

- In columns (1) to (6), we follow Faini's specification and use enrolment rates in primary, secondary, and tertiary education.

- In columns (7) and (8), we use the youth literacy rate. In each case, the incentive mechanism transits through the log of the skilled emigration rate or the log of one plus the skilled emigration rate.

- Columns (1) to (6) reveal that the incentive mechanism is never significant at the primary level but becomes significant at the secondary and tertiary levels under the $log(1 + m)$ specification. However, it is not significant in the $log(m)$ model. The $log(1 + m)$ specification shows a significant and positive effect on secondary enrolment rates, but a negative effect at the tertiary level. This is consistent with a story where skilled migration prospects lead more students to invest in secondary schooling at home to buy and then exercise the option of studying abroad at the upper level (see also Rosenzweig, 2008), an interpretation we do not want to push too far given the lack of robustness of the results.[7] Enrolment rates are obviously linked to lagged enrolment rates at the lower level. The sub-Saharan African dummy is always significant.

- Regressions in columns (7) and (8) show that skilled emigration prospects positively and significantly impact the youth literacy rate whatever the specification.

Obviously, causality is hard to establish in cross-sectional regressions and the 'brain gain' concept deserves further empirical investigations accounting for bilateral variables (i.e. income differentials between origin and destination countries), better dealing with endogeneity issues, and based on richer data or more elitist measures of the brain drain, and so on. It is worth noticing that the incentive mechanism resists a panel evaluation. Beine, Defoort, and Docquier (2011) recently used a panel setting allowing them to control for unobserved heterogeneity and for the endogeneity of the emigration rate. They also found a significant incentive effect in developing countries and contrary to cross-country studies, evidence that the incentive effect is particularly strong in low-income countries.

---

[7] Note also that while our main measure of human capital formation (the change in the proportion of highly educated among natives) accounts for return migration of skilled migrants, school enrolment indicators do not, which could also go part of the way towards reconciling the two approaches.

At this stage and within the limits of a cross-sectional analysis, the empirical results point to a robust, positive, and sizeable effect of skilled migration prospects on human capital formation in developing countries.

9.2.3 Implications

Relying on their baseline model, Beine et al. (2008) used counterfactual simulations to estimate the short-run net effect of the brain drain for each country and region. The counterfactual experiment consists of equating the high-skill emigration rate to the low-skill rate.[8] We replicate this counterfactual experiment on 148 developing countries using the estimates of column (1) in Table 9.1. Figure 9.2 summarizes the results. The horizontal axis is the skilled emigration rate whereas the vertical axis gives the percentage change in the proportion of tertiary educated induced by our numerical experiment. The latter variable is a good indicator of the cost of the brain drain in terms of human capital.

Comparisons between observed and simulated human capital levels show that the brain drain depletes human capital in 79 countries (53.4 per cent of the sample). These 'losers' include many small and medium-sized countries exhibiting skilled emigration rates above 50 per cent. In particular, the average

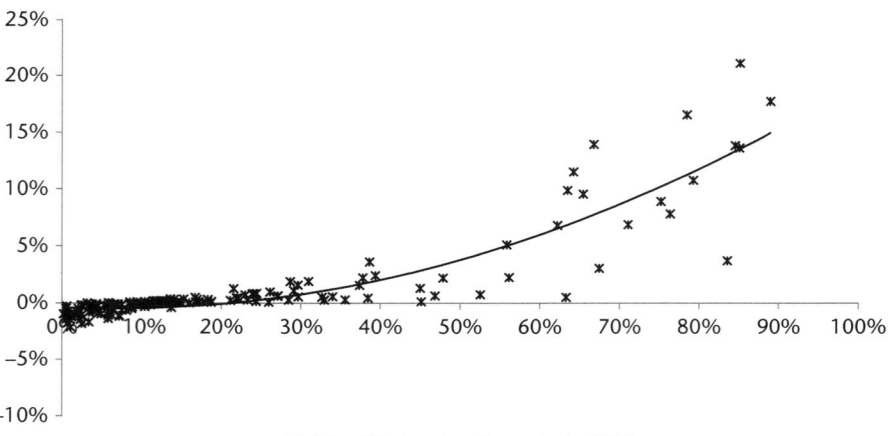

Highly skilled emigration rate in 2000

Figure 9.2. Short-run effect of highly skilled emigration rate (X-axis) on the proportion of educated residents as percentage points (Y-axis).

---

[8] For countries with extremely low low-skill emigration rates, they divide the highly skilled emigration rate by ten.

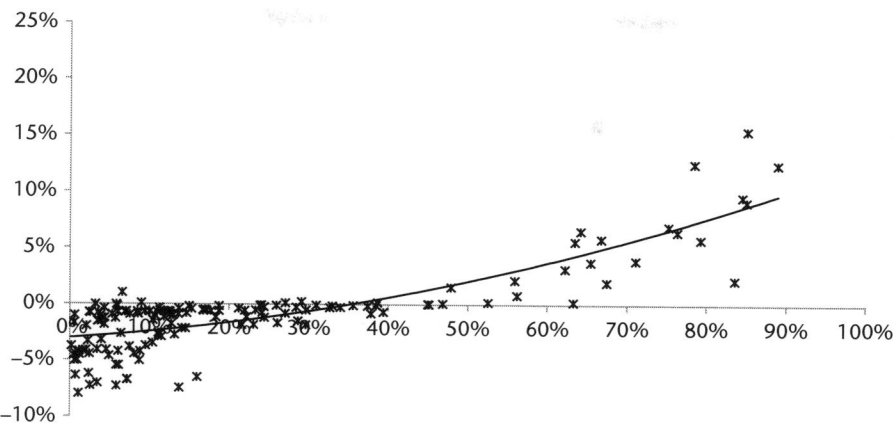

Highly skilled emigration rate in 2000

Figure 9.3. Short-run effect of highly skilled emigration rate (X-axis) on the proportion of educated residents as percentage points (Y-axis).

Note: Change in the proportion of college graduate residents when the emigration rate of college graduates is set at the value of the low-skilled emigration rate.

loss experienced by some Caribbean and Pacific islands can be as high as 15 percentage points (in terms of proportion of the educated in the domestic workforce). Conversely, the brain drain has a positive but moderate net impact on human capital in countries combining low levels of human capital (below 5 per cent) and low-skilled migration rates (below 20 per cent). This group of 'winners' includes the main 'globalizers' (e.g. China, India, Brazil) and other countries such as Indonesia, Thailand, Mongolia, Venezuela, Argentina, and Egypt.

Figure 9.3 gives the long-run impact of our counterfactual experiment. The long-run impact should be taken cautiously since panel data would help in refining the estimate of the convergence speed. Clearly, the number of countries benefiting from a decrease in skilled emigration prospects declines to 29 (19.6 per cent of the sample). The other developing countries would suffer from a decrease in skilled emigration prospects. In our terminology, they experience a net brain gain or a 'beneficial brain drain' (henceforth refereed to as BBD).

9.3 The screening-selection channel

The recent contributions on brain gain all rely on probabilistic migration models in which the probability of migration depends on the achievement of a given educational attainment, which is observable, and not on individuals' ability, which is not perfectly observable. Hence, migrants are assumed to be randomly selected among those who satisfy some kind of prerequisite with informational content regarding their ability—in our case, education. If high-skill migrants are positively selected within the high-skilled population, this mitigates the brain gain arguments of the previous section.

9.3.1 *Theory on screening and economic performances*

As discussed in Commander et al. (2004) or Schiff (2005), the brain gain implicitly arises because foreign firms cannot perfectly screen migrants to distinguish the more able from the less able. A necessary condition for a beneficial brain drain (BBD) to occur is that the marginal educated person must have a positive probability of emigration. Under perfect screening, the government or employers at destination would target the most able individuals and leave a low probability of emigrating for the less able and a BBD would be impossible.

A reasonable counter-argument is that when taking education decisions, agents can hardly anticipate their future position in the distribution of skills. Nevertheless, it is well documented that migrants are positively selected at origin. Among the highly trained, the more able have a higher probability of leaving their country. Consequently, even in the optimistic case where the brain drain generates a net increase in the proportion of educated at origin, the average level of ability of remaining educated workers should decline.

9.3.2 *Empirical evidence*

To the best of our knowledge, there is no systematic study comparing the ability of educated migrants to that of educated residents. However, there is a large sociological and economic literature on network and selection (see Massey et al., 1993). Carrington, Detragiache, and Vishwanath (1996) show that when moving costs decrease with the size of the network already settled in the destination, migration occurs gradually over time. Migration tends to follow geographical, cultural, or political channels and the most able individuals migrate first, due to lower moving costs or higher incentives. Their presence reduces the migration costs of the next group and the process continues as long as the benefits from migration exceed its costs. McKenzie and Rapoport (2010) demonstrate that a decrease in Mexico-to-USA migration costs generally has a stronger effect on low-skill migration than on high-skilled migration. In the same vein, accounting for the usual determinants of migration and addressing several econometric issues, Beine, Docquier, and Ozden (2011) use a bilateral international migration data set to show that larger diasporas increase migration flows and lower their average educational level. In comparing different education groups, these two studies confirm that positive selection increases with migration costs.

Mattoo, Neagu, and Ozden (2007) compare occupational attainment of immigrants to the USA with similar education backgrounds but from different countries. After controlling for age, experience, and education level, they find that highly educated immigrants from certain countries are less likely to obtain skilled jobs. For example, a hypothetical 34-year-old Indian college graduate who arrived 5 years before, has a 69 per cent probability of obtaining a skilled job, whereas the probability is only 24 per cent for a Mexican immigrant of identical age, experience, and education. A large part of this country-level variation can be explained by certain country attributes, such as quality of education or English proficiency. Other attributes leading to a self-selection include the GDP per capita, the distance to the USA, and the openness of US immigration policies to residents of a given country.

Although the empirical literature focuses on selection between groups, there is a strong presumption that these selection patterns also apply within the educated group. The most able among the skilled migrate first. Suggestive empirical evidence pointing to this phenomenon, however, is scarce. The only study we are aware of that directly tackles this issue concerns the self-selection of medical doctors out of Ethiopia. De Laat and Jack (2009) took advantage of a feature of the recruitment process of physicians in the public sector of Ethiopia to estimate the extent of adverse selection in that sector. More precisely, physicians' first placements occur through a lottery, leading to self-selection into the lottery while non-lottery participants apply mainly to private institutions. The authors argue that such random placement does not allow for efficient signaling of individual ability and therefore leads to adverse selection into the lottery, which is indeed what they find using career and wage records of physicians who remain in the public sector. They also find that within the group of lottery participants, the most able tend to leave and are likely to account for a substantial part (one third) of the physician brain drain out of Ethiopia.

9.3.3 *Implications*

The literature reveals that the quality of diplomas varies across countries and individuals. This means that i) diplomas acquired in different countries are heterogeneous, and ii) the average skill of educated emigrants differs from that of remaining educated workers.

Regarding the first source of heterogeneity, Dumont and Lemaitre (2007) illustrate the gap in employment rates between natives and immigrants in OECD countries. This gap increases at higher levels of schooling, revealing a problem of non-transferability of human capital across countries. The authors estimate that one third of this gap is explained by differences in real abilities. This is confirmed by Coulombe and Tremblay (2007) for Canada. They evaluate that the average ability gap between immigrants and natives with identical levels of schooling amounts to 3.2 years of schooling. However, it varies a lot across countries (from 1 to 7 years) and decreases with the home country's development level.

In our framework, we first assume that the average ability of workers depends on the level of development of their country, reflected by the proportion of educated among natives. This assumption is not essential for our numerical experiment since we concentrate on the relative change in ability when emigration decreases. More importantly, we assume that the level of ability varies across individuals, and that skilled migrants are those at the top of the ability distribution. The distribution of abilities is uniform, with a conservative ability differential of 30 per cent between the least and the most productive workers.

Box 9.3 describes the analytics. If the most talented are leaving first and abilities are uniformly distributed, it shows that the average ability of the remaining skilled workers is a linear decreasing function of the highly skilled emigration rate. Let us come back to our counter-factual experiment. Equating the highly skilled emigration rate to the low-skilled rate reduces the brain drain and the screening of talented workers. Consequently, the average ability of the highly skilled is likely to increase in origin countries.

Figure 9.4 shows the percentage change in the average ability of domestic college graduates resulting from this experiment, as a function of the high-skilled emigration rate. Clearly, in the most open countries, screening is likely to play a significant role in the average performances of high-skill workers at home. With a conservative 30 per cent ability differential between the least and most productive workers, the brain drain reduces by 12 per cent the average ability of college graduates left behind.

Box 9.3 BRAIN DRAIN AND THE SCREENING CHANNEL

The screening-selection channel implies that the average level of ability of remaining educated workers declines with emigration. We have:

$$q_t = q(m_t) \text{ with } q'_m < 0. \tag{9.9}$$

Under screening and quality changes, the condition (9.8) for a net 'qualitative brain gain' becomes more restrictive. Indeed, $q_t h_t$ increases if

$$\Theta'_3 \cdot (1 - m_t) \cdot \left(1 - \frac{w_{H,t}}{w^*_{H,t}}\right) > \Theta_t - \frac{q'_m}{q_t} > \Theta_t \tag{9.10}$$

In our partial equilibrium framework, we assume that the average ability of workers depends on the level of development of their country, reflected by the proportion of educated among natives. Assume a linear function with a maximal ability difference of 20 per cent between developing (with extremely low levels of human capital) and leading countries (with proportions of tertiary educated around 50 per cent). We have $q_t^{\max} = q^{\max}(h_t) = 0.8 + 0.4h_t$. This assumption is not essential for our numerical experiment since we concentrate on the relative change in ability when m_t increases.

Regarding the second source, the level of ability varies across individuals. To simulate (9), let us denote by $\bar{q} = q_t^{\max}(1 + \vartheta)$ and $\underline{q} = q_t^{\max}(1 - \vartheta)$ the highest and lowest levels of ability for skilled workers born in the origin country and assume that the individual ability level is uniformly distributed between these two bounds. Hence, the average ability of skilled natives q_N is normalized to unity:

$$q_N = \int_{\underline{q}}^{\bar{q}} q U(q) dq = \frac{\bar{q} + \underline{q}}{2} = q_t^{\max} \tag{9.11}$$

In the case of screening, skilled migrants come from the top of the ability distribution. As m_t is the skilled emigration rate, the ability $\hat{q}$ of the highest remaining in the country is such that $(\hat{q} + \underline{q})/(\bar{q} + \underline{q}) = 1 - m_t$. The average ability of remaining skilled workers is:

$$q_t = \frac{1}{1 - m_t} \int_{\underline{q}}^{\hat{q}} q U(q) dq = \frac{(\hat{q} + \underline{q})(\hat{q} - \underline{q})}{2(\bar{q} + \underline{q})} = q_t^{\max}(1 - \vartheta m_t), \tag{9.12}$$

It is a linear decreasing function of the skilled emigration rate.

Obviously, a stronger impact would be obtained by increasing the range of the ability distribution. For example, assuming that the most able is twice as productive as the least able, the brain drain would reduce by almost 30 per cent the average ability of college graduates left behind. On the one hand, this 'selection-screening' cannot be neglected; on the other hand, in the absence of empirical evidence, it should not be overstated. Our conservative assumption seems a good compromise.

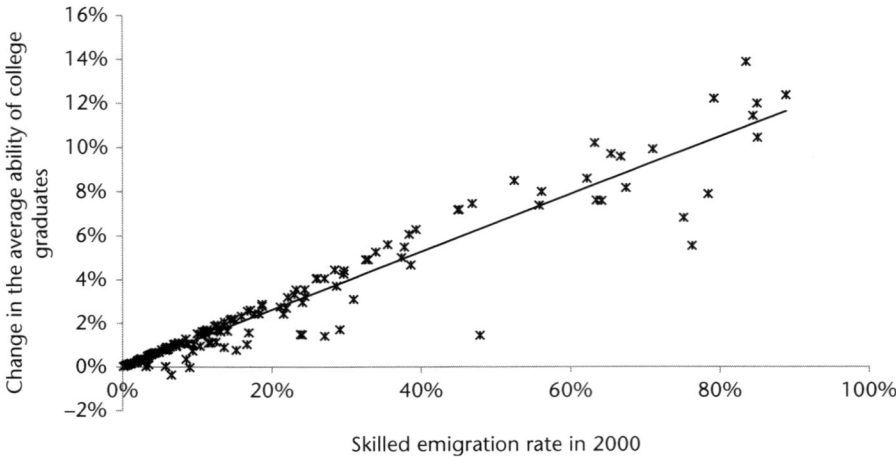

Figure 9.4. Brain drain and the relative ability of highly skilled residents.

Note: Percentage deviation in the average ability of college graduate residents when the emigration rate of college graduates is set at the value of the low-skilled emigration rate.

9.4 The productivity channel

If skilled migration affects total factor productivity, it is likely to have a strong impact on economic performance. Indeed, the elasticity of GDP per capita to total factor productivity in our GDP equation is around 1.5. In this section, we review the literature on highly skilled emigration and productivity growth.

9.4.1 Endogenous productivity with diaspora externalities

The new growth literature has stressed the existence of strong externalities related to human capital and education, showing the social return to human capital exceeds its private return (see Lucas, 1988; Azariadis and Drazen, 1990; and Klenow and Rodriguez-Clare, 2005 for a theoretical and empirical survey). However, the role of human capital is closely linked to the level of development of the origin country. Human capital is key to a country's innovation and adoption capacity, but the various stages of the education system play different roles in this process: the adoption of foreign technologies requires individuals with strong technical and professional skills developed through secondary or specialized higher education, while innovation is research based and requires the presence of high level scientists and engineers. Innovation plays a minor role in most developing countries, where adoption is the main source of technological progress.

Benhabib and Spiegel (2005) formalized productivity growth as a function of the country's capacity to innovate and adopt modern technologies. First, productivity gains resulting from innovations are assumed to be a non-decreasing function of human capital, with possible threshold effects accounting for the fact that innovation requires human capital to exceed a certain critical mass (which is unlikely to be reached in most developing countries). Second, the speed of adoption of leading technologies is an increasing function of human capital and depends on other country characteristics such as private R&D expenditures, public subsidies, degree of openness, foreign direct investments, and so on.

The recent literature shows that the size and composition of foreign diasporas abroad may affect technology diffusion, that is can be included in the set of determinants of adoption. The importance of expatriate networks has been emphasized against the background of the successful examples of the Indian and Chinese diasporas which are said to have greatly contributed to growth of the information technology sector in India and Taiwan (see e.g. Biao, 2006; Saxenian, 1999, 2001, 2002; Opiniano and Castro, 2006; or Pandey et al., 2006). These examples show that diasporas can foster productivity growth by strengthening trade and investment linkages, increased technology transfers and adoption, and knowledge circulation. Meyer and Brown (1999) and Meyer (2001) provide anecdotal evidence on knowledge diffusion and 'brain circulation'. It is worth noticing that the case studies refer to countries with large diasporas.

More recently, the role of scientific diaspora networks has been identified using patent citation data, notably by Agrawal et al. (2011) and Kerr (2008). Kerr (2008) uses patent citation data to examine the international transfer of knowledge between the USA and the home countries of USA-based diasporas, with scientists being assigned to a particular diaspora by a name recognition software. He finds strong evidence of knowledge diffusion along the ethnic diaspora channel, especially for the Chinese diaspora, and evidence that such transfers have a direct positive effect on manufacturing productivity in the home countries, especially in the high-tech sector. Similarly, Agrawal et al. (2011) developed a model in which innovation depends on knowledge access, and knowledge access partly depends on membership in both co-location and diaspora networks. A necessary condition for the movement of an innovator to the diaspora to increase knowledge access of the home country (India in their case) is that the diaspora knowledge-access effect is stronger than the co-location effect,[9] which could happen if emigration is associated with positive productivity effects combined with continued strong ties with those

---

[9] To undertake this, the authors have developed an original data set allowing for identification of Indian inventors by their last names.

Box 9.4 BRAIN DRAIN AND TOTAL FACTOR PRODUCTIVITY

How does high-skilled emigration affect total factor productivity in the origin country? Following Benhabib and Spiegel (2005), the growth of total factor productivity may be written as a function of the country's capacity to innovate and adopt modern technologies. Let us denote by $\mu(q_t h_t)$ the function which measures the productivity gain resulting from innovations. It is assumed to be a non-decreasing function of human capital, with possible threshold effects accounting for the fact that innovation requires human capital to exceed a certain critical mass (which is unlikely to be reached in most developing countries). The function $\gamma(q_t h_t, X_t)$ measures the speed of adoption of leading technologies. It is an increasing and concave function of human capital and depends on other country characteristics X_t such as private R&D expenditures, public subsidies, degree of openness, foreign direct investments, and so on.

In light of these studies, it can reasonably be assumed that the skilled diaspora abroad M_t stimulates the speed of adoption, that is $\gamma(q_t h_t, M_t)$. Consequently, developing countries productivity growth can be modelled as

$$\ln\left(\frac{A_{t+1}}{A_1}\right) = \mu(q_t h_t) + \gamma(q_t h_t, M_t) . \ln\left(\frac{A_t^*}{A_t}\right) \tag{9.13}$$

In the rich world, only innovation matters

$$\ln\left(\frac{A_{t+1}^*}{A_t}\right) = \mu(q_t^* h_t^*) \tag{9.14}$$

Combining these two equations allows us to characterize the dynamics of $\ln(A_t/A_t^*)$, the distance to the frontier:

$$\ln\left(\frac{A_{t+1}}{A_{t+1}^*}\right) = [\mu(q_t h_t) - \mu(q_t^* h_t^*)] + [1 - \gamma(q_t h_t, M_t)] \ln\left(\frac{A_t}{A_t^*}\right) \tag{9.15}$$

A steady state of this economy, if it exists, is determined by

$$\ln\left(\frac{A_t}{A_t^*}\right) \underset{t\to\infty}{\to} a_{ss} \equiv \frac{\mu(q_{ss} h_{ss}) - \mu(q_{ss}^* h_{ss}^*)}{\gamma(q_{ss} h_{ss}, M_{ss})} \tag{9.16}$$

The numerator is negative if origin countries innovate less than the leader. This is especially the case if there is no innovation at origin, $\mu(q_t h_t) = 0$. The denominator is ambiguously affected by high-skill emigration. On the one hand, skilled migration can boost or reduce human capital at origin; on the other hand, it induces diaspora externalities which are potentially important if the distance to the frontier is large.

---

remaining at home. While on average the co-location effect is found to be much larger than the diaspora effect (hence the inference of a net loss), the latter appears to be much stronger for the most cited patents, which are presumably the ones with the highest social and economic value. This mitigates the pessimistic conclusion about a net loss for the source country and opens the door to a potentially beneficial overall effect.

In the light of these studies, it can reasonably be assumed that the skilled diaspora abroad stimulates the speed of adoption. Hence, the long-run value of the productivity ratio between origin and leading countries becomes endogenous. First, highly skilled migration can boost or reduce human capital at origin. Second, it induces diaspora externalities which are potentially important if the distance to the frontier is large. These mechanisms are analytically developed in Box 9.4.

9.4.2 Empirical evidence

Vandenbussche, Aghion, and Meghir (2006), henceforth VAM, estimated a neo-Schumpeterian model of this sort using panel data on OECD countries. Recently, Lodigiani (2009) extended their framework by adding a diaspora externality: skilled emigrants living in rich countries increase the capacity to adopt modern technologies. She re-estimated the model on a larger sample of countries (92 countries, including developing countries) during the period 1980–2000 (one observation every five years). She follows VAM and computes the log of total factor productivity as the residual of a standard production function. Then, the productivity growth is regressed on the lagged proximity with the technological frontier (total factor productivity in the USA), the level of human capital (proportion of college graduates in the labour force), the log of the skilled diaspora residing in the USA, some interaction terms, and country and time fixed effects.

In such a framework, the distance to the frontier is by construction correlated with the lags of the dependent variable. To avoid endogeneity problems, it is instrumented using the two-period lagged values of the log of distance, human capital, and of the log of skilled emigrants and interactions. Table 9.3 shows a selection of the most interesting results obtained in a GMM framework with correction for heteroscedasticity.

Column (1) provides estimates without country fixed effects. Interaction terms and the diaspora externality are not significant. In column (2), country fixed effects are introduced without interaction terms. The diaspora externality becomes significant. The best specification is presented in column (3) which provides estimates with fixed effects and interaction terms. All key variables are significant and have the intuitive signs. Hence, the best and most parsimonious estimated equation governing productivity growth is the following:

Total factor productivity growth
= Country – and time – specific constant term
+ 0.285 *times* the lagged TFP level expressed in percentage of the leader
+ 1.486 *times* the proportion of college graduates (human capital)
− 0.103 *times* the stock of high – skilled expatriates in OECD countries (diaspora)
+ 0.878 *times* an interaction between human capital and the lagged TFP level
− 0.055 *times* an interaction between the disapora and the lagged TFP level

Table 9.3. Explaining TFP growth with diaspora externalities.

	(1)	(2)	(3)
Proximity with frontier (log)	−0.019	−0.695***	−0.285*
	(0.039)	(0.147)	(0.200)
Human capital	0.266*	0.198	1.436**
	(0.138)	(0.473)	(0.707)
Skilled emigration (logs)	0.009	0.0298*	−0.103*
	(0.010)	(0.0164)	(0.052)
Proximity × Human capital	0.346***		0.878*
	(0.112)		(0.476)
Proximity × Skilled emigration	−0.001		−0.055***
	(0.004)		(0.018)
Dummy 1995	−0.001	−0.0499***	−0.0370**
	(0.019)	(0.0167)	(0.018)
Dummy 2000	0.038**	−0.049**	−0.031
	(0.017)	(0.0243)	(0.026)
Constant	−0.105	−1.626***	−0.616
	(0.099)	(0.272)	(0.505)
Country fixed effects	No	yes	yes
Underid./IV relev test			
Chi-sq(.) P-value		0.000	0.000
Anderson can. corr LR stat	779.38		
Chi-sq(.) P-value	0.000		
Hansen J stat		eq. Ex	0.961
Chi-sq(.) P-value			0.6185
N		276	276
R2		0.693	0.693

Robust t statistics in parentheses
* significant at 10%; ** significant at 5%; *** significant at 1%

where the technological level of the leading countries is the TFP observed in the USA.

Confirming VAM, the interaction effect between proximity and the proportion of workers with tertiary education is positive, meaning that skilled workers are more important for growth in economies closer to the frontier. Conversely, the interaction effect between proximity and the log of skilled emigrants is negative, implying that skilled emigration has a depressing effect on growth when a country is closer to the frontier. Backward countries, that rely more on adoption, can benefit more from a skilled diaspora as it facilitates technology and knowledge transfers from abroad.

Given the specification above, the rate of productivity growth increases with human capital when the economy is not too far from the frontier. Moreover, productivity growth increases with the highly skilled diaspora when the economy is far from the frontier.

An important limitation of Lodigiani's study is that it only considers technology transfers from the USA to origin countries. The bilateral dimension of technology diffusion is better accounted for in the recent work by Papageorgiou and Spilimbergo (2009). They estimate the effect of foreign education on country-specific productivity growth. They show that technology adoption is greatly facilitated by the expertise acquired by students trained abroad. Their analysis is based on panel data on sectoral multi-factor productivity. Their specification is similar to (15) in Box 9.4 except that the frontier is replaced by a weighted average of productivity observed in 50 destination countries, with weights equal to the bilateral fraction of students trained in these destinations.

9.4.3 Implications

The empirical literature on diasporas and productivity is still in its infancy and obviously needs further development. In this section, we start by exploring Lodigiani's model, derive its implications and weaknesses, and compare it with alternative scenarios.

First, the above equation of productivity growth can be used to predict how changes in skilled emigration impact the distance to the frontier in the short run. Assuming that the leading economy grows at a rate of 1.5 per cent a year and that the country- and time-specific fixed effects for 2000 are time invariant, we can also predict the long-run effect.

Remember Figures 9.3 and 9.4 above gave the short-run and long-run responses of the proportion of the tertiary educated in the labour force. It is also straightforward to estimate the change in the stock of skilled workers abroad. Then, plugging these two variables into productivity growth equation gives the predicted change in the distance to the frontier in the medium term (after 10 years) and in the long run.

Figure 9.5 shows the long-run impact (the short-run impact is very similar, with 60 per cent of the long-run change occurring in the first 10 years on average). The change in the distance to the frontier is represented as a function of the observed distance to the frontier in 2000. Clearly, countries which are far from the frontier (relative TFP level below 0.17) would experience a decline in their relative performances, due to lower adoption capacities. On the contrary, 65 countries (44 per cent of the sample) closer to the frontier would benefit from a lower brain drain.

This literature is still in infancy and its predictions should be taken cautiously. Indeed, a first unfortunate corollary of this model is that the decrease in adoption is particularly strong in Swaziland, Malawi, Guyana, Ghana, Guinea-Bissau, Gambia, and many other sub-Saharan African countries. In other words, the predicted impact of a marginal migrant on adoption capacity is greater for small states. This is quite at odds with case studies indicating that diaspora-induced technological spillovers are mainly obtained for larger countries. This counter-intuitive result is probably due to the log-specification of the diaspora externality and the absence of threshold size effects.

To avoid this problem, we consider a variant of Lodigiani's model in which network-based externalities only operate for countries with high-skill diasporas above 300,000,that is countries with very large high-skill diasporas such as the Philippines, India, Mexico, China, Vietnam, Poland, and Iran. For other countries, the diaspora terms enter the fixed effect (i.e. becomes a constant term). Under this scenario, changes in productivity are much lower than those reported in Figure 9.5: the ratio now varies between 0.9 and 1.1. The highest decreases in total factor productivity are observed in the larger countries of the world as well as in poor small states experiencing a large brain drain (Guyana, Jamaica, etc.). Indeed, consistently with VAM, Lodigiani's model predicts that increasing the proportion of the tertiary educated is detrimental to adoption if the initial distance to the frontier is large (secondary educated workers would be more efficient). Some could consider this result as a second inauspicious corollary of the model.

For these reasons, we can consider a third scenario assuming that productivity is a concave function of human capital as in Lucas (1988), and the elasticity of total factor productivity to human capital is equal to 0.4. We used the same hypothesis in Section 9.1 when we presented the traditional view (see Fig. 9.2). The difference here is that human capital formation is endogenized and brain gain effects are factored in. Figure 9.6 gives the long-run change in productivity under this scenario as a function of the high-skill

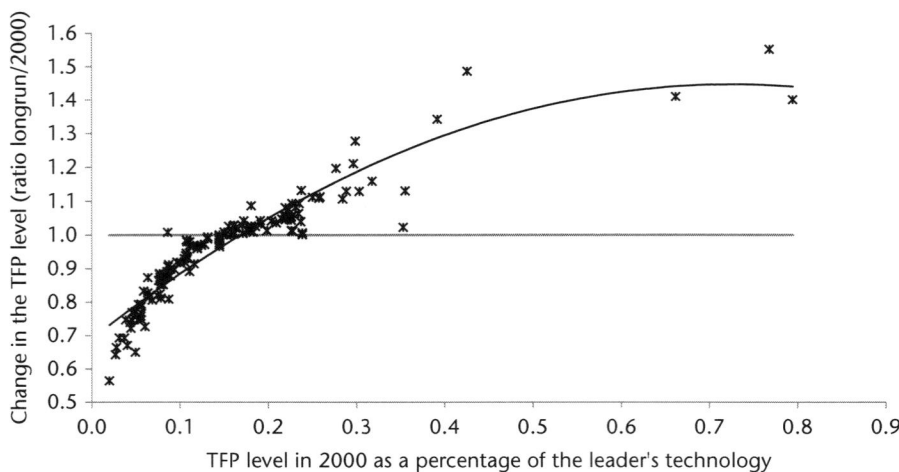

Figure 9.5. Longrun TFP response (Lodigiani's specification)

Note: Ratio of longrun TFP to 2000 observed TFP when the emigration rate of college graduates is set at the value of the low-skilled emigration rate.

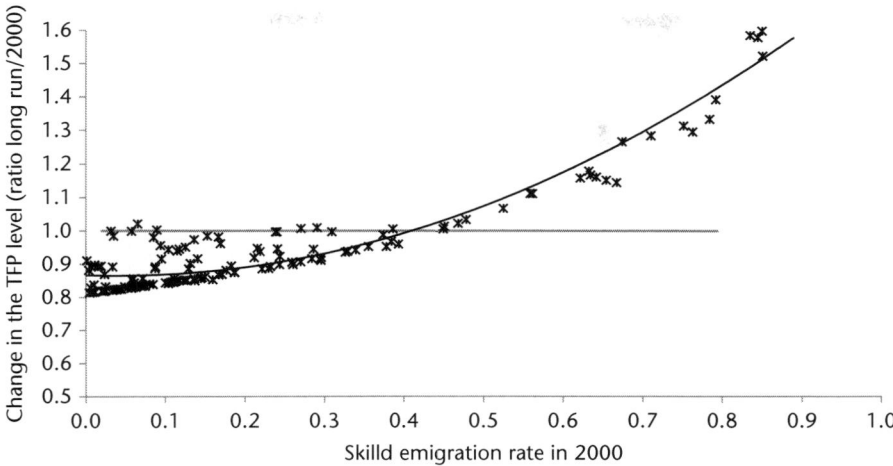

Figure 9.6. Long-run TFP response (Lucas' specification).
Note: Ratio of long-run TFP to 2000 observed TFP when the emigration rate of college graduates is set at the value of the low-skilled emigration rate.

emigration rate. Unsurprisingly, the pattern is identical to Figure 9.3, with productivity changes varying between −20 and + 50 per cent.

We will come back to these three scenarios in Section 9.6 when computing the global impact of the brain drain on GDP per capita.

9.5 The institutional channel

The hypothesis that migration diasporas may generate positive externalities on the sending country is not only valid for technology adoption. For example, migrants to relatively democratic societies may have a positive impact on social, economic, and political institutions at home. Since better institutions usually translate into higher total factor productivity, those institutional channels are partly captured by the productivity responses quantified in the previous section. However, as demonstrated in an increasing number of studies, diaspora networks also help reduce international transaction costs and thus promote bilateral trade and FDI between the migrants' home and host countries.

9.5.1 *Endogenous transaction costs and institutions*

The importance of diasporas in facilitating trade has been the focus of many recent studies, from both the theoretical (Greif, 1993; Rauch and Casella,

2003) and empirical perspectives (Gould, 1994; Rauch and Trindade, 2002; Head and Ries, 1998). For example, Rauch and Trindade (2002) estimate a global bilateral trade model for 63 countries in 1980 and 1990, investigating whether the presence of large numbers of ethnic Chinese residents in the partner country is associated with more trade. They computed the product of ethnic Chinese population shares for each trading partner and add this variable into a gravity equation. Using this extended gravity model, they find that country pairs with higher concentrations of ethnic Chinese residents trade more with each other. In his seminal paper on US trade with 47 trading partners during 1970–1986, Gould (1994) also finds that the stock of immigrants increases US trade. Both studies finally find that immigrant networks induce less effect on trade in more homogeneous products, for which prices can effectively convey the relevant information, than on trade in more differentiated products, for which matching the multifactor characteristics of buyers and sellers is more important. Along these same lines, Head and Ries (1998) estimate an extended gravity model of Canadian import and export patterns using panel data from 1980 to 1992 on bilateral trade with 136 trading partners. They find that a 10 per cent increase in the number of immigrants increases exports by 1 per cent and imports by 3 per cent.[10]

On the whole, these studies provide evidence that networks are important in overcoming informal trade barriers. Rauch (2003) stresses two major channels through which these diaspora effects operate. First, a diaspora creates (or substitutes for) trust in a weak international legal environment. Co-ethnic networks provide community enforcement of sanctions to deter opportunism and violation of contracts. If a party acts opportunistically, then its reputation suffers within that network. Second, the diaspora may provide market information as well as supply matching and referral services. Co-ethnic networks can promote trade, because they are familiar with the market needs in the origin country. They can provide important information to foreign investors that may otherwise be difficult or costly to obtain. In addition, they reduce communication barriers; migrants know the language, the culture, the values, the law, and the practices of their home country. They know their compatriots' ways of thinking, and they better understand who is trustworthy with regard to potential business partners.

As stated above, most of the diaspora externalities discussed in this section are captured in the Solow residual representing total factor productivity. However, there is an additional effect which is likely to complement the

---

[10] However, Schiff and Wang (2009) find that 'the brain drain reduces productivity growth both directly [*via a lower human capital stock*] as well as through its interaction with trade-related technology diffusion, with a greater reduction for small than for large states'. Their finding is consistent with a view where most developing countries experiencing negative net brain gains, as found by Beine et al. (2008).

productivity response. Many recent studies investigated whether FDI and migration are substitutes (as one would expect) or complements. Docquier and Lodigiani (2010) find evidence of significant network externalities in a dynamic empirical model of FDI-funded capital accumulation. Their analysis confirms that business networks are mostly driven by skilled migration. Using bilateral FDI and migration data, Kugler and Rapoport (2007) also found strong evidence of a complementarity between FDI and skilled migration with a similar elasticity. By impacting governance, corruption, rent-seeking, and ethnic discrimination, by reducing communication and information barriers between countries, diasporas also impact on the incentive of foreign investors to invest in the migrants' home countries. In our neo-classical framework (5), this will affect the level of the risk premium. The effect on economic performances is potentially high since the coefficient associated with the risk premium in our GDP equation is a value around 0.5. The effect of migration on institutional quality may be channeled through a negative effect of highly skilled emigration stock on the risk premium.

9.5.2 Empirical evidence

Several empirical studies focus on the empirical relationship between brain drain and governance. Although causality is obviously questionable, the stylized facts presented in Mariani (2007) suggest a strong relationship between skilled migration and the allocation of talents. Spilimbergo (2009) shows that foreign-trained individuals promote democracy in their home countries, but only if foreign education is acquired in democratic countries. The potential for diasporas to affect institutional development at home has long been recognized in political circles.[11]

Coming back to FDI, it is noteworthy that the first studies to look at the migration–FDI relationship did so in a bilateral setting. Kugler and Rapoport (2007) investigated the migration–FDI relationship for 'USA–Rest of the world' flows throughout the 1990s. They showed that US manufacturing FDI towards a given country are negatively correlated with its current unskilled migration, as trade models would predict, while FDI in the service sector are positively correlated with the initial US skilled immigration stock of that country.[12] In a subsequent paper, they extended the scope of their study to include virtually all pairs of countries analysed in a gravity model with adjustment for selection bias. They again found that past skilled immigration significantly increases

---

[11] Yet, the empirical assessment of these effects is still very preliminary and, as for the productivity growth channel above, limited to just a few working papers. See Li and McHale (2009) or a recent report commissioned by the CIA Strategic Assessment Group (Lahneman, 2005).

[12] Their results are confirmed by and Javorcik et al. (2011) after instrumenting.

the occurrence and magnitude of FDI inflows in the subsequent period (Kugler and Rapoport, 2006). Their results were shown to be robust to the use of sub-samples of developed/developing FDI receiving countries only and to different education classifications (skilled/unskilled v. primary/secondary/tertiary).[13]

Docquier and Lodigiani (2010) estimated a beta-convergence model govern-ing the dynamics of the stock of FDI-funded capital per worker. Obviously, there is no data set providing series of capital stock (a fortiori, FDI-funded capital stock) by country. They collect flow data on foreign direct investments and the gross formation of physical capital from the World Development Indicators for 114 countries in 1990 and 2000. Using an inventory method, they estimate the stock of FDI-funded capital stock. Hence, the dependent variable is the average annual real growth rate of the capital stock per worker funded via FDI inflows rather than the levels of FDI. To address the question of whether the amount of FDI is influenced by the stocks of migrants abroad, they regress the growth rate of the FDI-funded capital stock on the log of the initial stock, the log of the diaspora size, the educational structure of the diaspora, and several control variables capturing the labour market character-istics of the country. They first use Docquier–Marfouk's data set on emigration stocks and rates in 1990 to estimate the determinants of FDI in a cross-country setting. Then, they use Defoort's data set on emigration stocks and rates from 1975 to 2000 in a panel regression with four observations per country. Table 9.4 shows the results obtained in the parsimonious specifications.

Columns (1) and (2) describe the cross-section setting. In (1), the estimated coefficients of the log of the stock of total expatriates and of the share of highly skilled migrants are positive and highly significant. It could be argued that the migration stock is the only significant variable capturing the size of the country. However, alternative specifications including both the size of the labour force and the stock of expatriates give similar results despite a strong correlation (0.68) between these variables. The proportion of skilled migrants is also an important source of business externality. This suggests that business networks are mostly driven by skilled migration. In column (2), diaspora effects are constrained to transit through skilled workers. The short-run elas-ticity of capital per worker to highly skilled migration amounts to 0.019. The long-run elasticity amounts to 0.46 (0.019/0.041). A 10 percentage point rise in the number of skilled migrants increases the stock of capital per worker by 0.2 per cent after one period, and by 4.6 per cent in the long run.

---

[13] Interestingly, Buch et al. (2006) show that immigration can also attract FDI from the migrants' home to host country; using regional differences for the origin-mix of immigrants to Germany, they show that the presence of immigrants from a given country significantly affects the spatial bilateral pattern of FDI to the German Lander.

Table 9.4. Skilled migration and FDI accumulation.

	(1)	(2)	(3)	(4)
	OLS	OLS	Panel	Panel
	1990–2000	1990–2000	1980–2000	1980–2000
Initial FDI-funded capital in logs	−0.042	−0.041	−0.032	−0.033
	(4.21)***	(4.06)***	(3.34)***	(3.08)***
Labour force growth rate	−0.043	−0.022	0.064	0.005
	(0.24)	(0.12)	(0.29)	(0.02)
Initial total migration stock in logs	0.017	–	0.025	–
	(2.51)**	–	(1.72)*	–
Initial share of skilled migrants	0.174	–	0.22	–
	(2.04)**	–	(1.97)*	–
Initial skilled migration stock in logs	–	0.019	–	0.025
	–	(2.52)**	–	(1.80)*
High-income dummy	0.090	0.088	–	–
	(2.33)**	(2.29)**	–	–
Initial democracy score	0.082	0.077	−0.156	−0.179
	(1.95)*	(1.74)*	(2.04)**	(2.27)**
Democracy × High-income dummy	–	–	0.181	0.232
	–	–	(2.10)**	(2.43)**
Initial trade in logs	0.034	0.036	0.050	0.068
	(2.13)**	(2.27)**	(2.44)**	(2.75)**
Trade × High-income dummy	–	–	−0.030	−0.046
	–	–	(1.27)	(1.84)*
Initial GDP per capita in logs	–	–	0.024	0.021
	–	–	(1.07)	(0.75)
Constant	−0.040	0.013	−0.399	−0.291
	(0.34)	(0.13)	(42.69)***	(2.34)**
Country and time dummies	No	No	Yes	Yes
Nb of observations	109	109	332	332
Nb of countries	109	109	83	83
R-squared	0.53	0.52		
Hansen test—Pr > Chi2			0.512	0.225
Arellano–Bond test for AR(1)—Pr > z			0.083	0.082
Arellano–Bond test for AR(2)—Pr > z			0.413	0.411

Such cross-sectional results can be biased and inconsistent given the dynamic nature of the growth equation and the bias of omitted variables. In order to obtain more accurate results, Docquier and Lodigiani extend their analysis in a panel setting using a more sophisticated econometric method which accounts for the possible endogeneity of explanatory variables and unobserved heterogeneity. There is a large debate about the most accurate methodology to estimate growth equations (see Islam, 1995, 2003; Caselli et al., 1996; Bhargava and Sargan, 1983; Bhargava et al., 2001). In column (3) and (4), we report the GMM system estimator for a dynamic panel data model. This technique exploits both the cross-sectional and the time dimension of the data. It accounts for unobserved fixed effects. It controls for the potential endogeneity of all the explanatory variables and allows for the inclusion of the lagged dependent variable. The period of analysis is divided into four sub periods of five years each (1980–85, 1985–90, 1990–95, 1995–00). The sample includes 83 countries for a total of 332 observations in a balanced panel data set. One of the most difficult issues to apply the above dynamic panel technique is to identify the nature of the explanatory variables (they can be endogenous, exogenous, weakly exogenous, or predetermined). Several specifications were tried. Given the Hansen and serial correlation tests, we finally retain a specification with the time dummies and the high-income dummy as exogenous variables; all the other time-varying explanatory variables are considered as predetermined (instrumented with their one lagged and earlier values).

The estimated coefficient of the log of the stock of the total number of expatriates and the share of highly skilled workers is positive and statistically significant. The magnitude of the coefficient, at least for the log of the total stock of migrants, is in general higher than in the cross-section analysis (0.025 to 0.03, instead of 0.02). Also, the log of the highly skilled migration variable is positive and statistically significant. In model 4, the short-run and long-run elasticities of the FDI-funded capital stock to skilled migration amount to 0.033 and 0.75, respectively. A 10 percentage point rise in the number of high-skill migrants increases the stock of capital per worker by 0.3 per cent after one period, and by 7.5 per cent in the long run. This supports the results of the cross-section analysis, and is in line with results from empirical studies in a bilateral setting (Kugler and Rapoport, 2006, 2007).

9.5.3 *Implications*

How could these empirical results be incorporated in our numerical setting? In our GDP equation, the country risk premium can be modelled as follows:

> Log of one plus the risk premium
> = Country – fixed effects
> $-\phi$ *times* the log of the highly skilled emigration stock

where ϕ is the elasticity of the premium to the skilled diaspora size.

The country-specific constant term can be calibrated so as to match the risk rating observed in 2000. We use data available from the OECD for country-specific risk (CSR), which in turn relies upon the Knaepen Package methodology. Countries are ranked from 0 (no risk) to 7 (maximal risk). Assume that the maximal premium is equal to 40 per cent for country with CSR = 7. We rescale the CSR by using the following formula in the following way: *Risk* = 1+.4 × *CSR*/7. This is compatible with Caselli (2007) who shows that on average, the returns to capital are comparable between advanced and developing countries. The average return to capital in poor countries is 1.6 times higher than in advanced countries after correction for natural capital, and 1.25 times

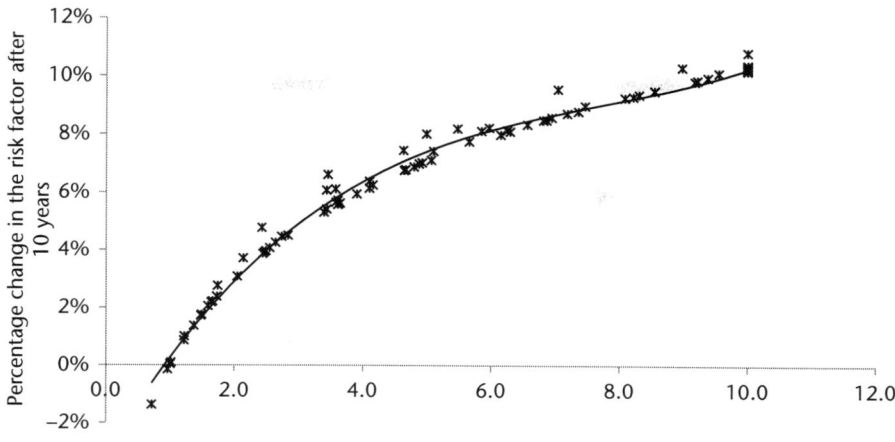

Figure 9.7. Brain drain and the risk premium on returns to capital

Note: Percentage deviation in the risk factor (one plus the risk premium) when the emigration rate of college graduates is set at the value of the low-skilled emigration rate.

higher after correction for price differences. Then, we use the elasticity presented in column (4) of Table 9.4, that is a long-run elasticity of the FDI-funded capital stock to skilled migration equal to 0.75. Relying on the fact that foreign direct investments represent less than 10 per cent of total investments in developing countries, the calibrated value for ϕ is around 0.05. Figure 9.7 shows the impact of a reduction in skilled emigration on the country risk premium in the long run.

By reducing the size of the skilled diaspora, equating highly skilled and low-skilled emigration rates would increase communication and information barriers between host and origin countries. The premium would increase by 12 per cent in the countries experiencing the largest change in their diaspora (countries for which our experiment consists of dividing the skilled emigration rate by ten). Note that the short-run impact is very similar. Indeed, 85 per cent of the change happens in the first decade after the shock.

9.6 Summing up: brain drain and economic performance

In the previous sections, we reviewed and assessed the impact of the brain drain on the different determinants of GDP per capita, that is human capital, average ability of remaining college graduates, total factor productivity, and the risk premium. We can now plug these predictions into the GDP equation and simulate the effect on GDP per capita in the short run (after 10 years) or in the long run.

Obviously, the novelty and weaknesses of the empirical literature prompt us to consider empirical elasticities with caution. The empirical literature on the brain gain and institutional channels has been rapidly growing since the late 1990s and delivers more and more mature predictions. On the contrary, the effect of diasporas on productivity growth and technology adoption is still understudied and deserves further investigation. Hence, we consider three scenarios regarding productivity externalities:

- *Scenario 1* is based on Lodigiani's model.[14] Figure 9.8 shows the global impact on GDP per capita. On average and contrary to the traditional view, the brain drain is beneficial below 45 per cent (i.e. the cost of the brain drain is negative) and the optimal high-skill emigration rate is around 25 per cent. In addition, the cost for small states is limited to 30 per cent of GDP (with a few exceptions). Most of the beneficial effect of the brain drain is channelled through the impact on adoption capacity. Out of 148 countries, we detect 91 beneficial cases in the short run and 112 in the long run. This includes large countries with low emigration rates. Nevertheless, as stated previously (see Section 9.4), the group of main beneficial cases also includes sub-Saharan African countries such as Swaziland, Malawi, Mozambique, Zambia, Mali, Madagascar, Ghana, and so on. This counter-intuitive result could be due to misspecification problems in the modelling of total factor productivity.

- *Scenario 2* is based on the variant of Lodigiani's model where network effects only operate for countries with high-skill diasporas above 300,000 people. The global impact on GDP per capita is given in Figure 9.9. On average, the brain drain is beneficial for origin countries below 35 per cent and the optimal high-skill emigration rate is around 10 per cent. The effect is much more limited than in the previous scenario. Out of 148 countries, we detect 108 beneficial cases in the short run and 125 in the long run. The 15 main beneficial cases are India, China, Philippines, Vietnam, Argentina, Venezuela, Iran, Mongolia, Maldives, Brazil, Thailand, Costa Rica, Botswana, Egypt, and Paraguay. Conversely, among the countries where the short-run cost of the brain drain exceeds 2.5 per cent of GDP, we have El Salvador, Mexico, Suriname, Lebanon, Cape Verde, Haiti, Fiji, Guyana, Belize, Jamaica, and so on.

- *Scenario 3* is based on a Lucas-type technological externality (with an elasticity of total factor productivity to human capital equal to 0.4).[15]

---

[14] See Figure 9.5 for the simulation of the change in total factor productivity.
[15] See Figure 9.6 for the simulation of the change in total factor productivity.

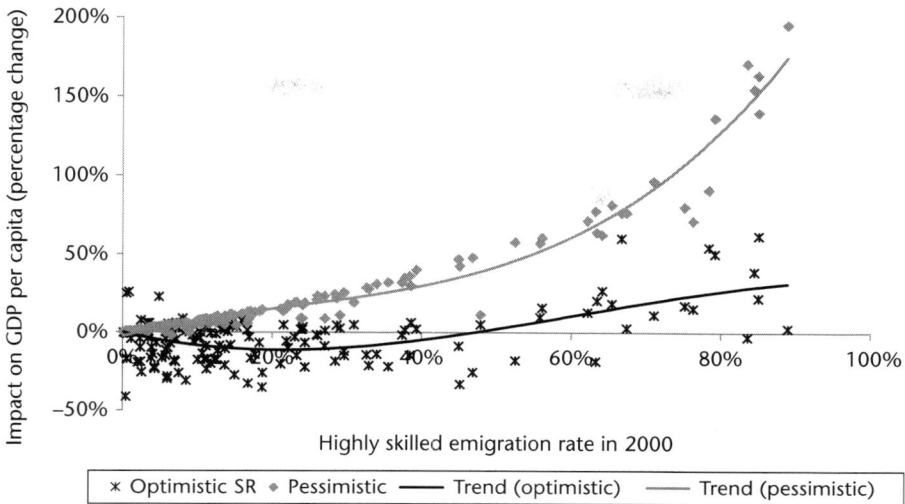

Figure 9.8. Short-run brain drain cost under traditional and modern views (Scenario 1).

Note: Percentage deviation in GDP per capita when the emigration rate of college graduates is set at the value of the low-skilled emigration rate.

The global impact on GDP per capita is given in Figure 9.10. On average, the brain drain is beneficial below 20 per cent (i.e. the cost of the brain drain is negative) and the optimal high-skill emigration rate is around 5 per cent. Conversely, the costs are very large for small states and follow the prediction of the traditional view. Out of 148 countries, we detect 85 beneficial cases in the short run and 123 in the long run. The 15 main beneficial cases are Maldives, Bhutan, Thailand, Brazil, Venezuela, Mongolia, Indonesia, Argentina, Chad, Burkina Faso, Paraguay, Namibia, Botswana, China, and India. Conversely, among the countries where the short-run cost of the brain drain exceeds 20 per cent of GDP, we have Kenya, Laos, Lebanon, Mozambique, Liberia, Ghana, Sierra Leone, Gambia, Fiji, Belize, Cape Verde, Haiti, Jamaica, and Guyana.

Figure 9.11 plots the short-run and long-run impacts under Scenario 2, which account for most feedback effects emphasized in the recent literature. Since the elasticity of human capital formation to migration prospects is much larger in the long run, it is not surprising that more beneficial cases are obtained in the long run. A very similar pattern is obtained under Scenarios 1 and 3.

In sum, there is a great deal of uncertainty about the magnitude of the losses experienced by the most affected countries, especially small states. However, for countries exhibiting low skilled emigration rates (below 20–30 per cent),

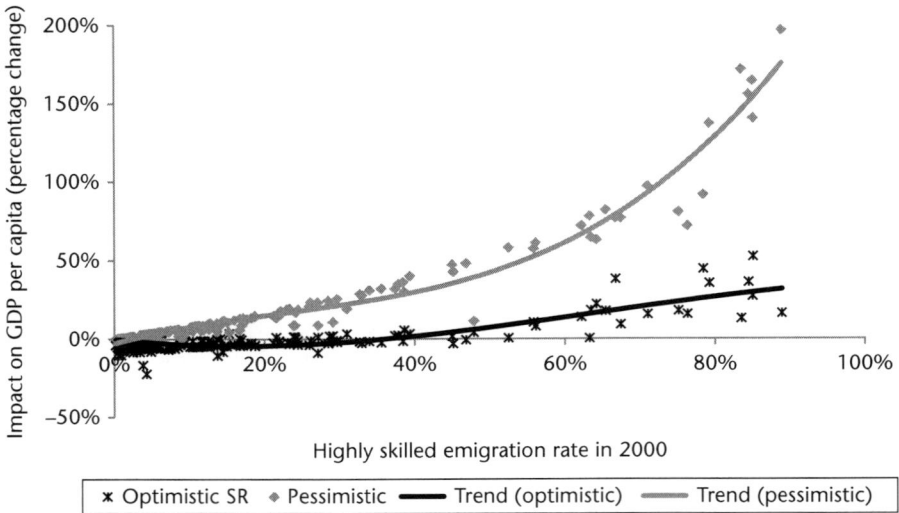

Figure 9.9. Short-run brain drain cost under traditional and modern views (Scenario 2).

Note: Percentage deviation in GDP per capita when the emigration rate of college graduates is set at the value of the low-skilled emigration rate.

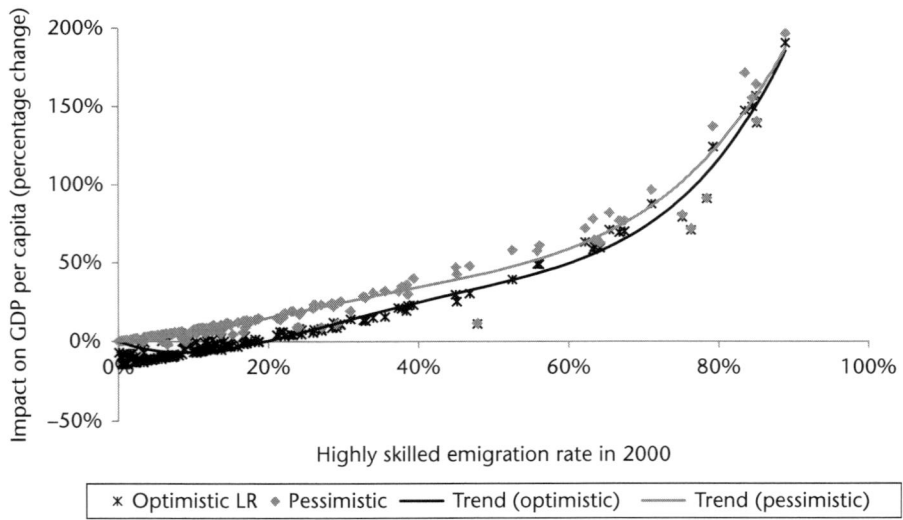

Figure 9.10. Short-run brain drain cost under traditional and modern views (Scenario 3).

Note: Percentage deviation in GDP per capita when the emigration rate of college graduates is set at the value of the low-skilled emigration rate.

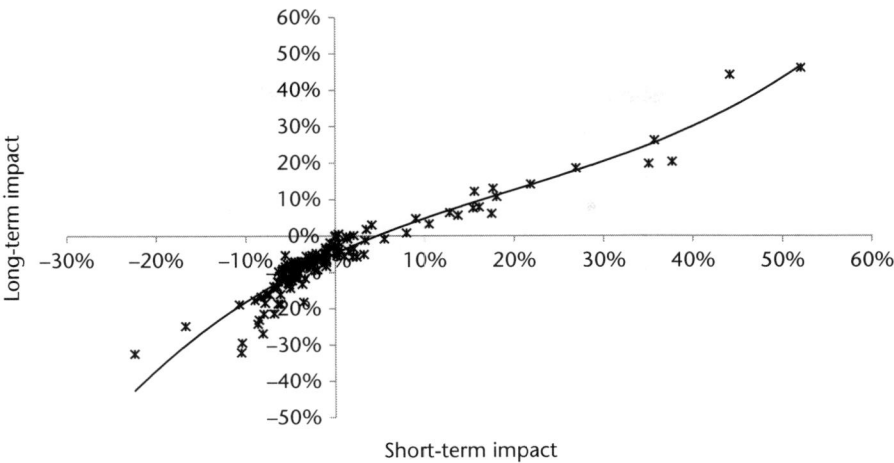

Figure 9.11. Short-run and long-run impacts (Scenario 2).

Note: Percentage deviation in GDP per capita when the emigration rate of college graduates is set at the value of the low-skilled emigration rate.

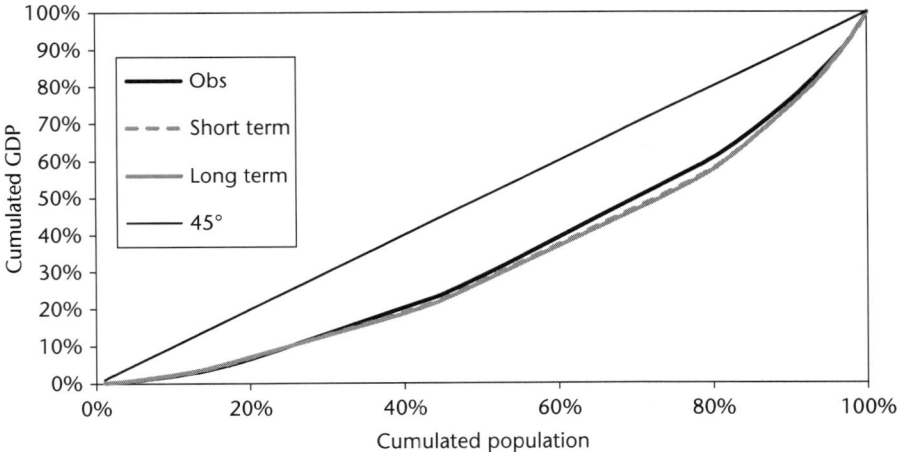

Figure 9.12. Brain drain and the between-country inequality (Scenario 2).

Note: Lorenz curve based on GDP per capita with observed emigration rates and when the emigration rates of college graduates are set at the value of the low-skilled emigration rate.

gains are very likely to be observed. This pertains to the vast majority of developing countries. The 2000 average level of GDP per capita in developing countries is equal to US$3,782.2 (in PPP). Under the traditional view, it would increase by 5 per cent in the short run. Under the modern view, it would decrease by 9.8 per cent in Scenario 1, 10.3 per cent in Scenario 2, and

7.7 per cent in Scenario 3 after 10 years. The long-run impacts would be −16.5, −17.8 and −32.2 per cent, respectively. In addition, lowering the brain drain could raise between-country inequality across developing countries. Abstracting from within-country inequality, Figure 9.11 represents the effect of our numerical experiment on the Lorenz curve. Under the traditional view, the new Lorenz curve (not represented) perfectly coincides with the observed one. Under the recent view, the Lorenz curve slightly shifts downward in the short run and in the long run. The simulation is based on Scenario 2 but similar patterns are obtained under the Scenarios 1 and 3.

9.7 The transfer channel

Besides its direct effect on the domestic output level, migration also induces international transfers. Migrants' remittances constitute an important channel through which the brain drain may generate positive indirect effects for source countries. Workers' remittances often make a significant contribution to GNP and are a major source of income in many developing countries. Recorded remittance flows to developing countries increased almost fivefold from US$57 billion in 1995 to US$240 billion in 2007, now representing roughly the same amount as FDI and about three times as much as official development aid (World Bank, 2008).

Migrants' remittances impinge on households' decisions in terms of labour supply, investment, education, migration of relatives, occupational choice, and fertility, with potentially important aggregated effects on poverty rates, income distribution, and a variety of other economic outcomes. This is especially the case in poor countries where capital market imperfections (liquidity constraints) reduce the set of options available to members of low-income classes. However, as rich countries increasingly pursue skill-selective immigration policies and migration, as we have seen, is increasingly of the brain drain type, this has given rise to questions about whether the increasingly highly skilled nature of emigration from developing countries will hamper the rise in remittances. We address this question theoretically and empirically, before reframing it in within an accounting framework.

9.7.1 Do skilled migrants remit less? Theory and macro-evidence

Theoretically there are several reasons to believe that there will be differences between the remitting patterns of highly skilled emigrants and less skilled emigrants.

- On the one hand there are several factors which would tend to lead highly skilled migrants being more likely to remit and/or to send a larger amount of remittance. First, highly skilled individuals are likely to earn more as migrants, increasing the potential amount they can remit. Second, their education may have been funded by family members in the home country, with remittances providing a repayment of this family investment. Third, skilled migrants are less likely to be illegal migrants, and more likely to have bank accounts, lowering the financial transactions costs of remitting.

- On the other hand there are several factors which may lead highly skilled migrants to be less likely to remit or to remit less. First, highly skilled migrants may be more likely to migrate with their entire household, so will not have to send remittances in order to share their earnings abroad with other household members. Second, they may come from richer households, who have less need for remittances to alleviate liquidity constraints. Third, they may have less intention of ever returning to their home country, reducing the role of remittances as a way of maintaining prestige and ties to the home community.

A priori then, it is not clear which direction will dominate, and thus whether the highly skilled will remit more or less on average. The only empirical evidence to look at this issue across a range of countries are two recent papers (Faini, 2007, and Niimi, Ozden, and Schiff, 2008), which use cross-country macro-economic approaches to claim that the highly skilled remit less. Faini (2007) shows that migrants' remittances decrease with the proportion of skilled among emigrants; he takes this as suggestive evidence that 'the negative impact of the brain drain cannot be counterbalanced by higher remittances'. Faini's results are confirmed by Niimi et al. (2008) after instrumenting. Such analyses can at best tell us whether countries which send more (or a larger share of) highly skilled emigrants receive less or more remittances than countries that send relatively less skilled emigrants. However, there are very many other ways that countries differ, and so any correlation between remittances and the skill level observed across countries may be spurious. For example, a richer country characterized by a higher proportion of educated natives will send more educated migrants while also keeping more educated workers. If the correlation between emigrants and residents' human capital is large, one should not be surprised that low amounts of remittances go together with a high proportion of highly skilled emigrants. Moreover, these studies suffer from the fact that they use migration data for emigrants to the OECD area only while the remittances data are for remittances sent from the rest of the world, not just the OECD, which creates important potential sources of bias.

9.7.2 An accounting framework

To assess how the brain drain impacts remittances, we calibrate an accounting model using cross-country data on remittances and GDP per capita. Highly skilled and low-skilled migrants remit specific fractions of income earned abroad. For the theoretical reason explained above, we can reasonably expect the fraction remitted by highly skilled workers to be smaller than or equal to that of the less educated.

Our parametrization method is described in Box 9.5. We construct estimates of migrants' per capita income per education level in 33 destination countries (30 OECD members + Singapore, Saudi Arabia, and South Africa), accounting for imperfect assimilation on the foreign labour market. Then we calibrate the propensity to remit of college graduate and less educated migrants so as to match data on aggregate remittances in the recipient countries. The parametrization shows that the fraction of income remitted by college graduates is reasonably equal to 0.5 to 0.75 times the fraction remitted by the less educated. A lower fraction would require unrealistically large value for the propensity to remit of the less educated. As highly skilled workers are likely to earn more than twice low-skilled workers' wage, it is hard to believe that remittances decrease with the average skill level of emigrants in many recipient countries. This is in

---

Box 9.5 BRAIN DRAIN AND REMITTANCES

Assume high-skilled and low-skilled migrants remit fractions γ_h and γ_l of income earned abroad. From the empirical literature, we have no idea about the difference between γ_h and γ_l. For theoretical reasons, we can reasonably expect γ_h to be smaller or equal to γ_l. Let us define by $\gamma_0 = \gamma_h / \gamma_l$ the ratio of propensities to remit ($\gamma_0 < 1$). The amount of remittances received in developing countries can be written as

$$R_t = \sum_d \gamma_l (M_{d,t}^h \gamma_0 y_{d,t}^h + M_{d,t}^l y_{d,t}^l) \qquad (9.17)$$

where $(M_{d,t}^h, M_{d,t}^l)$ are the numbers of highly skilled and low-skilled migrants in destination country d, and $(y_{d,t}^h, y_{d,t}^l)$ are the income per capita of highly and low-skilled migrants at destination.

We need estimates for $(y_{d,t}^h, y_{d,t}^l)$. Restricting the set of destinations to high-income countries, migrants' income per capita by education level can be estimated for each destination. We consider 33 high-income destination countries (30 OECD members + Singapore, Saudi Arabia, South Africa). In all these destinations, we assume the average return to an additional year of schooling is 10 per cent and average years of schooling of workers are equal to 6 (for primary educated), 12 (for secondary educated), and 16 (for college graduates). Hence, workers with tertiary and secondary education earn respectively 2.6 and 1.8 times more than workers with primary education. Using data on the structure of the labour force, we can proxy the levels of income per capita of highly skilled and low-skilled workers in each high-income country. Due to assimilation problems, immigrants earn on average less than native workers. Following Dumont et Lemaître (2007) or Coulombe and Tremblay (2007), we consider that assimilation is a concave function of the ratio of GDP per capita between

---

origin and destination countries, with an elasticity equal to 15 per cent. Hence, Ethiopian workers in the USA earn 45 per cent less than US natives.[16]

Using these predicted income levels at destination and data on remittances R_t in 2000, we use (19.17) to calibrate γ_I for 10 possible values of γ_0 (ranging from 0 to 1). Figure 9.13 shows the calibrated propensity to remit of unskilled workers for ten important recipient countries (where remittances represent 13 to 30 per cent of GDP). The fraction γ_I obviously decreases with γ_0. In some cases (Jordan or West Bank and Gaza), the propensity to remit exceeds 1 when γ_0 is too low. A value of γ_0 between 0.5 and 0.75 seems quite realistic.

As highly skilled workers are likely to earn more than twice low-skilled workers' wage, it is hard to believe that remittances decrease with the average skill level of emigrants in many recipient countries.

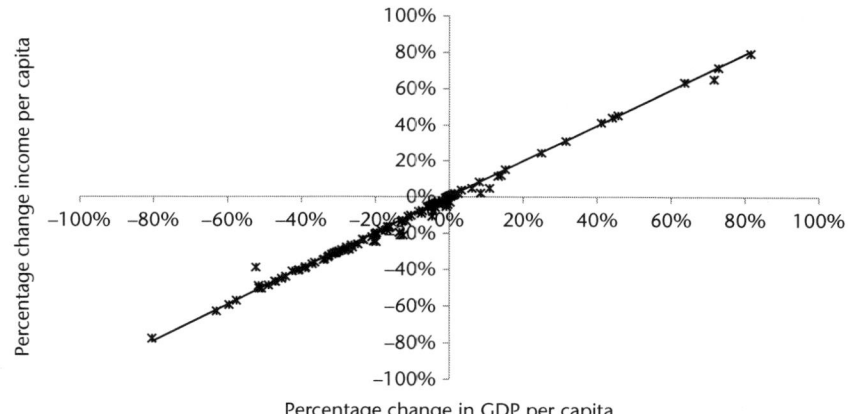

Figure 9.13. Brain drain impact GDP per capita and income per capita (Scenario 2).

Note: Percentage deviation in GDP per capita and income per capita when the emigration rate of college graduates is set at the value of the low-skilled emigration rate.

line with Bollard et al. (2011) who use micro-data on remittances and migrants' level of schooling from various sources and countries. They obtain a strong positive relationship between education and the amount remitted conditional on remitting. Combining the intensive and extensive margins, they conclude an overall positive effect of education on the amount remitted.

On this basis, we can compute the change in the amount of remittances which would be observed if highly skilled migration rates were reduced to low-skilled rates. The shock reduces the number of skilled emigrants to high-income countries. We suppose that the percentage change is identical across

[16] Ethiopian and US levels of GDP per capita are US$800 and 48,000 in PPP. The 'assimilation rate' is given by $(48,000/800)^{0.15} = 0.541$.

destinations. For example, the shock reduces the Cambodian high-skill diaspora by 87.7 per cent after 10 years and by 91.2 per cent in the long run. These percentages are homogeneously applied to the Cambodian diaspora in the USA, Europe, Singapore, and so on.

Figure 9.14 compares the results obtained for GDP per capita and income per capita. It focuses on the long-run impact computed using Scenario 2 but similar patterns emerge in the short run under other scenarios. The impact of remittances appears to be very limited. It shows that responses in income per capita are perfectly correlated and almost equal to changes in GDP per capita. The two reasons are the following: i) the ratio of remittances to GDP is low in many countries, and ii) the proportion of highly skilled in the diaspora is low for many developing countries. In conclusion, the 'transfer' channel is likely to be minor and, with a few exceptions, does not significantly impact the gains and costs of the brain drain.

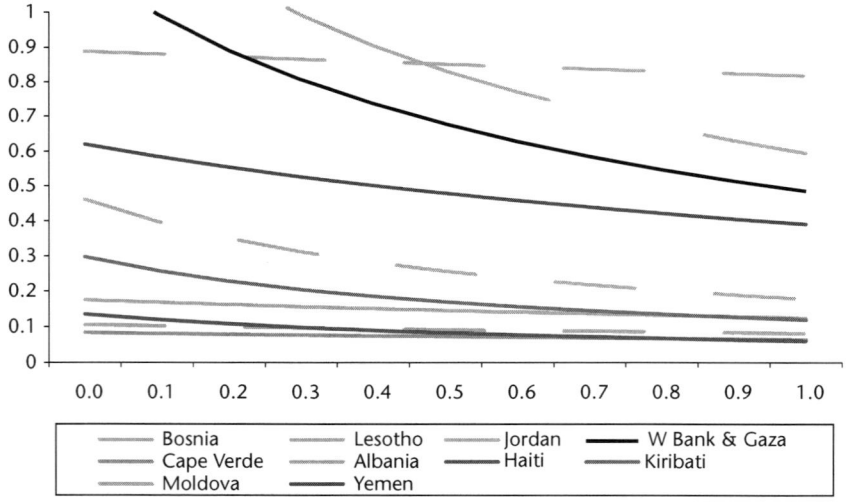

Figure 9.14. Calibrated propensity to remit of low-skilled migrants (Y-axis) for selected recipient countries as a function of γ_0 (X-axis).

10

Policy Issues

In this we evaluate the policy implications of the brain drain. To make progress on this front, we will be guided by the main results of the previous chapters, and notably by the facts that: i) a country's stock of human capital is endogenous to the prospect and realization of migration; ii) migrants keep affecting their home countries after they have left as they generate flows of goods, capital, and ideas, be it directly, through remittances and return migration, or indirectly, through participation in migration and diaspora networks; and, iii) both ex-ante (e.g. brain gain) and ex-post (e.g. diaspora externalities) channels affect different countries differently, and so there is no 'one size fits all' optimal policy response to the brain drain.

Policy discussions of brain drain and development generally recognize ii), sometimes i), but usually ignore iii). There are certainly sound general policies that can help developing countries take greater advantage of the financial, human, and social capital embodied in the diaspora. Examples include improving governance and the investment climate,[1] favouring more circulation by making emigration and re-migration easier (e.g. through dual citizenship agreements)[2] and, ultimately, by creating domestic networks that allow for quality interactions with the expatriate networks. While this is easier said than done, there seems to be a strong commitment at the bilateral and multilateral level to favour such institution building aimed at 'harnessing the diaspora'.[3] In what follows we will focus on policies that specifically address the causes and consequences of the brain drain. In particular, we will ask whether sending countries should rethink their education policy in the face of the brain drain, whether immigration policies in receiving countries are at

---

[1] Obviously, such policies are desirable in and of themselves and their potential interaction with brain drain issues is second order.

[2] See e.g. Leblang (2009), who shows such dual citizenship agreements are associated with more remittances, capital flows, aid flows, and return intentions.

[3] See for example the Global Forum on Migration and Development (http://www.gfmd2009.org/) for a list of policy initiatives in this direction.

odds with their aid and development policies, and whether international tax cooperation is required (and feasible) in order to allow for a better sharing of the surplus from international skilled migration. Finally, we discuss the likely effects of the current crisis on the future of international skilled migration from developing to developed countries.

10.1 Implications for education (and other) policies in sending countries

Given that the social return to education is higher than its private return, education subsidies can in theory (and are in practice) used to address human capital externalities. However, one may wonder whether education subsidies remain an appropriate policy response in a context of brain drain. Stark and Wang (2002) explore how migration and education subsidies may substitute one or the other and be optimally combined as policy tools in the hands of home country governments.[4] Docquier, Faye, and Pestieau (2008) refine this argument: they show that in case of beneficial brain drain, migration prospects stimulate human capital accumulation and can be seen as a substitute for education subsidies; in the case of detrimental brain drain, however, each dollar invested in the public education system generates lower social returns (the number of remaining skilled decreases) and induces higher perception costs (less educated fiscal contributors); they also provide empirical evidence showing that it is indeed the case that public expenditures on education are lower in high-skilled emigration countries, including after controlling for possible reverse causality. Finally, Poutvaara (2008) proposes a theoretical model where the possibility of brain drain distorts the provision of public education away from internationally transferable education (e.g. exact sciences, engineering, economics, medical profession) and towards country-specific skills (e.g. law), with the source country possibly ending up training too few engineers and too many lawyers; he then demonstrates that such a negative outcome could be avoided by introducing graduate taxes or income-contingent loans for students to be (re)paid also in case of emigration.

---

[4] In the same spirit, Docquier and Rapoport (2009b) use a simple brain drain model allowing for introducing (lump sum) taxes and education subsidies. In this specific setting and under a balanced budget constraint, the fiscal loss of the brain drain entails a fiscal adjustment through either higher taxes or lower subsidies. Reducing education subsidies lowers the proportion (less efficiency) and income (less inequality) of skilled workers, while increasing taxes stimulates education investments but disproportionately harms unskilled workers. Hence, providing that liquidity constraints are not binding and human capital externalities are not too strong, the choice between a fiscal adjustment through taxes or through subsidies raises an efficiency–equity trade-off, with the optimal policy mix depending on the social objective (welfare function) of the government.

More generally, governments can and should react to the departure of the highly educated by adjusting the public supply of higher education. We just briefly discussed the case of education subsidies and that of public education provision in particular fields. Other possible routes include promoting foreign education, adjusting education quality, or having an export strategy of skilled professionals. Should local governments instead free ride on destination countries' foreign education programmes, and encourage their students to learn abroad? Such a strategy induces positive and negative effects. On the one hand, it would certainly represent a source of fiscal gain, at least in the short run (especially for small countries suffering from high emigration rates), is also likely to raise the average quality of tertiary education, and could allow for reallocating the saved budget to other, maybe more productive, investments.[5] On the other hand, as emphasized by Rosenzweig (2005), foreign education provides its owners with a much higher probability of finding a job in the training country (due to better recognition of diploma, knowledge of the culture and language, better quality of education, and network ties), meaning that students' mobility is likely to further increase the brain drain in the longer run.[6]

If enforceable at reasonable cost, conditional scholarships to study abroad and return upon completion of studies could help in avoiding a massive flight of foreign-educated students. This has been suggested as a possible component of aid and development assistance, for example in the case of health-care workers (Barnighausen and Bloome, 2009). OECD countries (e.g. the EU) often discriminate against students from developing countries in offering scholarships or in tuition fees while there should be room for a well-designed policy of selection, training, and incentives to return, at least for completion of internships, fieldwork, and practical training. Such scholarship programmes can also be decided upon unilaterally, as the Turkish Ministry of National Education did by encouraging Turkish students (the programme includes an average of 1000 students per year) to attend master or doctorate programmes abroad. Students are selected via a central examination system which is managed by the Higher Education Association. Selected students are offered a scholarship (covering tuition and living expenses) but contractually commit to return after training and to work in national universities or other national entities. As a rule of thumb, students must work twice the years they have spent abroad with the scholarship. In other words, if a student finished his/her doctoral studies in five years, s/he must work at least ten years in a

---

[5] A possible endogenous policy response in source countries is to adjust the supply of public infrastructure (Grossmann and Stadelmann, 2011).

[6] Students' mobility and skilled workers mobility appear to be strongly correlated. Using UNESCO data on foreign students in 2004 and the Docquier and Marfouk (2006) skilled emigration rates, we obtained a correlation of .48 between the two.

predetermined job place. Students also commit to pay the scholarship back in the event of no return.[7]

Should local governments instead increase education expenditures and try to improve the quality of home-country higher education institutions in order to retain more students at home? One possible answer is to design quality-assurance programmes (i.e. certification of the quality of higher education by national or international agencies) aimed at reducing uncertainty about education quality while at the same time making it more transportable internationally, as has been done in a number of Asian and Latin American countries.[8]

Which route is preferable certainly depends on the extent to which the quality of public education impacts on the international transferability of human capital and on the extent to which having foreign education increases the probability of staying in the country of training, not to mention the role of home country characteristics such as geographic, linguistic, and cultural proximity with the leading nations. It also depends on the social welfare function of the government since the fiscal adjustment to a detrimental brain drain generally raises a trade-off between efficiency and social justice (see Docquier and Rapoport, 2009b).

Unfortunately, all these issues are currently largely under-studied and, therefore, policy recommendations in this area should be taken with great caution as they are not evidence-based enough. At the least, policy recommendations should not be uniform as countries with different characteristics are affected differently by the brain drain. As we have seen, certain countries at an intermediate level of development and with not too high skilled emigration rates can take advantage of migration prospects and of having a skilled diaspora abroad. Such countries should invest in public education quality in order to provide students with internationally transferable human capital. They should also let the substitution between migration prospects and education subsidy operate by allowing for private provision of higher education in certain fields with high international demand (e.g. nursing, engineering). On the other hand, the poorest countries (with binding liquidity constraints and poorly transferable education) with high skilled emigration rates should largely outsource higher education training and rely on development cooperation programmes (of the 'training and return' type) except for very specific needs (e.g. local teachers and civil servants at intermediate levels).

---

[7] For more details, see http://bologna.yok.gov.tr [accessed 10 Feb 2012].

[8] See Lien (2008) for a few examples and a theoretical discussion of the effects of such programmes on the demand for local and foreign higher education and the conditions (depending on the distribution of abilities, the initial (pre-programme) demand levels, and return rates) for such programmes to be welfare improving.

10.2 Immigration (and emigration) policy

In this book we have emphasized the distributional effects of the brain drain both within and (mostly) across countries. In particular, we showed that certain home-country characteristics in terms of institutional quality, technological distance, and demographic size, are associated with the ability of a country to seize the benefits from skilled diaspora networks and, similarly, that a 'beneficial brain drain' is more likely where skilled emigration rates are sufficiently small and human capital levels are not too high. The implications for migration policy are far reaching.

From the perspective of developing countries, the main implication is that for a given developing country, the optimal migration rate of its highly educated population is likely to be positive. This is shown formally by Docquier and Rapoport (2009b) in a simple model where wage differentials and credit constraints combine to generate an inverse-U shape pattern between optimal skilled emigration and level of development.[9] Whether the current rate is greater or lower than this optimum is an empirical question that must be addressed country by country. In many instances, countries that would impose restrictions on the international mobility of their educated residents, arguing for example that emigrants' human capital has been largely publicly financed, could in fact decrease the long-run level of their human capital stock.

From the perspective of receiving countries, the main implication is that selective immigration policies aimed at attracting the highly educated and skilled may or may not contradict the goals of their aid and development policies depending on where the additional skilled migrants come from. The difficulty then is to design quality-selective immigration policies that address the differentiated effects of the brain drain across origin countries without distorting too much their immigration system. Frequently suggested options include designing specific incentives to return migration to those countries most negatively affected by the brain drain, and promoting international cooperation aiming at more brain circulation. It has also been suggested that in coordination with national and supra-national development policies, quality-selective immigration programmes could also include a blacklist of high-risk occupations and/or origin countries (e.g. physicians and nurses originating from high medical brain drain countries with less than 0.5 healthcare professionals per 1,000 people). However, there is little a host country can

---

[9] In their setting the optimal migration rate is zero for relatively rich countries, that is, for countries with a low foreign wage premium, it then increases with the foreign wage premium as long as liquidity constraints are not binding, and then decreases for poor countries where liquidity constraints are binding.

do to alter the origin mix of its immigrants. Empirical analysis on the determinants of the brain drain (e.g. Mayda, 2010; Docquier, Lohest, and Marfouk, 2005) show that networks (diasporas) and invariant bilateral variables (such as geographic and linguistic distance, colonial ties, etc.) largely explain the size and skill composition of migration. Recalling that selective immigration policies can only select immigrants among a pool of self-selected candidates, the main (but still limited) effect of such policies is to alter the skill composition of immigration from given countries rather than sparking new migration chains. A corollary is that some receiving countries may implement quality-selective immigration policies which happen to be beneficial to origin countries, while others may promote the same policies with adverse effects on development.

For the sake of illustration, let us briefly analyse the origin mix of skilled immigrants to Western Europe (EU15). Europe is currently less selective than the USA and other traditional immigration countries such as Australia and Canada. For example, while Europe's net skilled migratory balance was basically zero in 2000 (outflows of skilled Europeans to the rest of the OECD area are more or less compensated numerically by inflows of skilled immigrants from developing countries), it was largely positive for the USA, with a net inflow of skilled immigrants representing 5.4 per cent of the labour force, and even more so for Canada (10.7 per cent) and Australia (11.3 per cent). This means that Europe also has the greatest potential for more selectivity, and we are actually witnessing such a tendency in many EU counties. Given what we know from cross-country analyses on the push and pull factors of migration, a change in European migration policies (such as the introduction of point-systems or similar selection devices, or the European blue card project) is likely to primarily affect the traditional suppliers of skills to the European economy. However, in spite of its lower selectivity, Europe disproportionately attracts migrants from demographically small, economically very poor (less developed), and institutionally disadvantaged countries, especially African ones (see Figure 10.1).[10] These countries are typically those negatively affected by the brain drain (see Section 9.2) and which lack the characteristics and institutional environment which help in realizing the potential gains from diaspora networks. Recent policy changes in Europe, if confirmed, are therefore likely to increase the brain drain from these countries without generating any sizeable brain gain or compensating feedbacks.

From the analyses above we can also conclude with some confidence that the optimal immigration and development policy mix will be different for

---

[10] For example, the share of skilled immigrants opting for Europe is more than twice the share of Europe in the OECD's population in the case of 22 countries out of 127 countries in our sample, and nearly all of them are located in Africa.

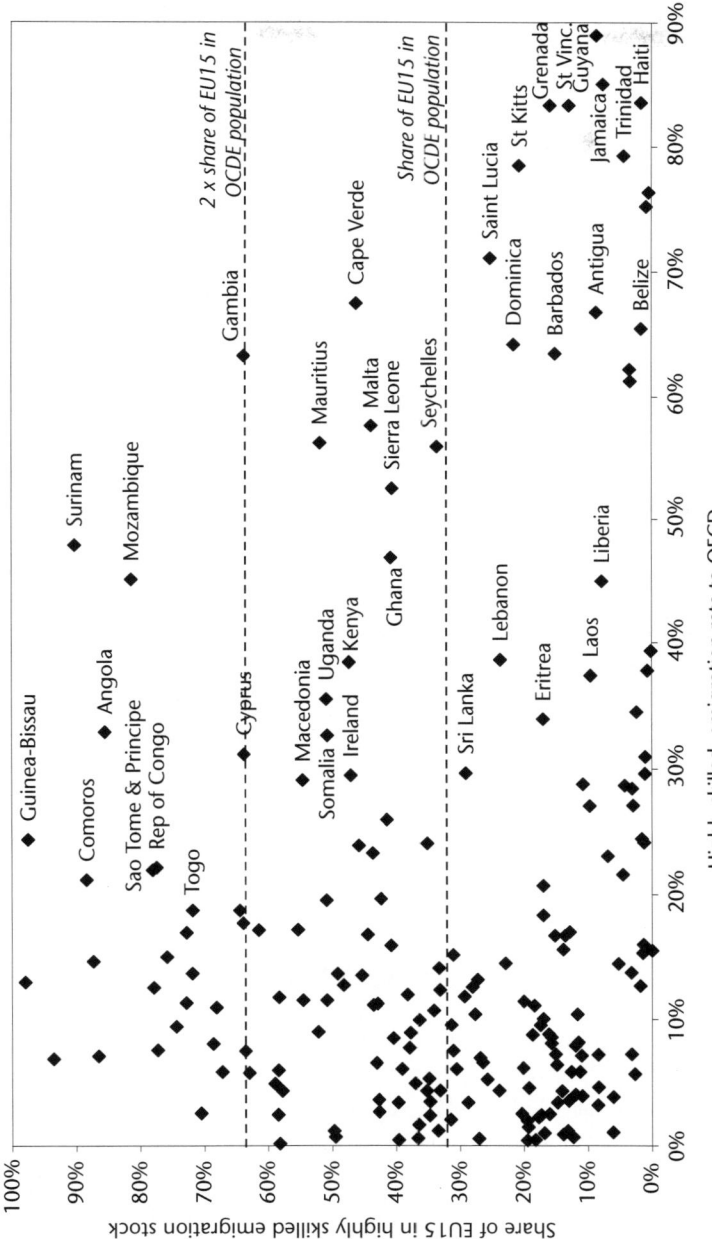

Figure 10.1. Europe's (EU15) share in the brain drain from developing countries.

different host countries. Selective immigration policies in countries such as Canada, Australia, and, to a lower extent, the US and the UK, are broadly consistent, and in some cases may even be seen as adjuvant to source countries growth and development goals (with the exception of Caribbean and Central American countries). In contrast, continental Europe's situation raises a trade-off between immigration and development policy: more selectivity, which may be required from a nationalistic viewpoint, would penalize further Europe's main suppliers of skills. To attract more skills and talent, Europe should first try to become more talent-friendly to try to get back some of its many skilled expatriates and curb the exodus of European researchers.[11]

Our second recommendation is to oppose creating blacklists of professions or source countries from which it would be forbidden to recruit skilled professionals. Economists tend to dislike distortions, which often solve a problem by creating a bigger one. In the context of brain drain, this is supplemented by a moral argument as the countries generally cited as candidates for being blacklisted are precisely those where emigration is quite often provoked by political and racial conflicts and/or oppressive and corrupted governments. Constituting such blacklists would deprive many developing countries individuals from their basic right to escape oppression and extortion, and could even lead to higher political and economic repression (Docquier and Rapoport, 2003). Finally, such blacklists of countries and professions could be subject to protectionist lobbying and based on changing, and quite often erroneous, appreciation of the role of migration in explaining professional shortages in developing countries. For example, a proposal to ban recruitment of health professionals from Sub-Saharan Africa has gained wide support in many health-care and media circles; however, it is doubtful whether the medical brain drain is detrimental to Africa in general; in many cases, it appears to be beneficial, especially for countries with poor medical infrastructure.[12]

10.3 Taxation policy: the case for a Bhagwati tax

The idea of introducing a 'tax on brains' (later coined 'Bhagwati tax') was first proposed in the 1970s by Jagdish Bhagwati, according to the following principles: i) it is an income tax paid by skilled emigrants on top of their regular income taxes, the tax revenue being transferred by the tax authorities of the host country to the government of the home country; ii) the rationale for the tax is double: compensation (of those left behind, for the externality imposed

---

[11] See our second case study in Docquier and Rapoport (2009a)
[12] See our first case study in Docquier and Rapoport (2009a).

on them, and of home country governments for their public financing of education costs), and equity (through redistribution of the rents earned by skilled emigrants as a result of international restrictions on labour mobility); and iii) the tax is basically a tax on retained citizenship (in its last version).

Given the dramatic rise of the brain drain during the last two decades and the current trend toward increasingly selective immigration policies, one may ask whether the time has come to think afresh about such a tax on expatriated brains. Or, in the words of Bhagwati (2009, pp. 10–11): 'Now that the incomes of the skilled migrants have reached exceptionally high levels, and even a small surcharge levied on US income of Indian citizens in the USA would raise sums of money that could add significantly to the Indian budget, for example, the issue has come back into economic research and public debate.'

In its current format, the Bhagwati tax proposal comes part of the way towards addressing the various objections raised at different stages of its formulation. For example, to be consistent with a 'rent' rationale, the proceeds of the tax must be administered by some international authority, which raises political feasibility issues and does not guarantee any direct or proportional compensation for home countries. As seen, the proposal now states the proceeds should be used to compensate those (public and private) left behind, that is, households and governments at home. As noted by Bhagwati, another objection was that there need not be compensation in the first place as in many instances education is privately financed and/or acquired abroad. In addition, many skilled emigrants would be unemployed or employed ineffectively at home, while many others (or the same ones) emigrate to escape corruption, violence, or economic discriminations which should by no means be encouraged by fiscal compensations.[13] Finally, it was argued the tax was equivalent to an exit tax and represented a form of extortion; again, as far as the last version is concerned this is easily refutable as one can always voluntarily forfeit citizenship.

How would such a tax work, and which form should it take? As acknowledged by Bhagwati (2009), the many iterations and changes finally led to something very close in practice to the US tax system; he writes: 'I discovered accidentally that this was in fact what the United States was doing: taxing by citizenship, not by residence (as the Europeans did). The US practice was the one that finally fitted neatly my thinking; and so the Bhagwati Tax took the final form of extension of income tax jurisdiction to nationals abroad.'

---

[13] On the former point, Bhagwati (2009, p. 10) notes: 'Today, that objection seems far less cogent as several highly-skilled migrants, whether temporary or permanent, come with exceptional education from leading educational institutions in key exporting countries such as India and South Korea, with that expensive education fully financed by the governments.' On the latter point, see our discussions on the brain waste in Section 9.2 above.

Nevertheless, a number of issues may be raised against the Bhagwati tax proposal: some have to do with legal and administrative feasibility (see McHale, 2009), others with the rationales for taxing skilled emigrants, which can be re-appraised in the light of the new economic perspectives on the brain drain developed in this book. Last but not least, and notwithstanding time-consistency issues, the 'tax on retained citizenship' argument may limit the scope of the tax to just a few countries and individuals. To put it simply, the US tax system cannot be extended worldwide because the threat of losing citizenship does not operate for most origin countries. Regarding the other rationales for the tax, it seems the 'rent' argument can easily be reversed once one adopts a new growth theory perspective: in a world of increasing returns and agglomeration effects, restrictions to international mobility of the highly skilled, if anything, decrease the migration premium earned by skilled emigrants. The compensation argument can also be challenged as many developing countries appear to actually benefit from the interaction with their skilled diasporas as well as from the additional incentives for people to invest in mobile human capital, as we have seen.[14] In contrast, the countries for which emigrated citizens would not try to retain citizenship are exactly those whose characteristics are conducive to a detrimental brain drain: poor institutions, very low income, and low growth prospects.

There are, therefore, many good reasons to object to a tax on brains, and as many reasons to go for it on both efficiency and equity grounds. Docquier and Rapoport (2009b) discuss this issue within their simple theoretical framework. They show that in terms of efficiency, a Bhagwati tax is detrimental unless credit constraints on education investment are binding. In both cases, redistributing the tax revenue as an education subsidy is more efficient than a lump sum transfer. In terms of social justice, however, taxing migrants and redistributing the proceeds from the tax as a lump sum transfer is preferable as long as spillover effects (human capital externalities) are not too large.[15] There is a growing consensus that the rationale for such a tax should be a surplus sharing one, and that it should be based at least partly on a voluntary mechanism: retained citizenship, as advocated by Bhagwati, or an insurance-upon-return tax cut, as suggested by Wilson (2008).

However, the magic formula that would gain wide support from all the sides involved has yet to be found. In our view, a revised Bhagwati tax proposal should follow the following principles:

---

[14] Still, the relative losses of the losers may be substantial, and in any event the receiving countries and most of all the migrants themselves appear to be the main beneficiaries.

[15] See also Wilson (2011), who shows that a tax on brains could benefit the home country even if home country governments are malevolent.

1. The rationale for the tax is a surplus sharing one; in case compensation is needed, then the proceeds from the tax serve as partial compensation and mitigate the risks of seeing home country governments disinvest in higher education, which would result in a global inefficiency.

2. The tax is on top of the regular income tax paid to the host country government, and levied according to a matching principle: for example, a 1 per cent tax paid by the skilled expatriate (defined as someone who left his home country after age 18) would be matched by an equivalent amount paid by the host country government.

3. The migrant can choose whether the proceeds from the tax should be transferred to a bilateral fund, a global fund, or a NGO/charity of his choice. This prevents rewarding oppressive home country governments and should spark efforts on their side to induce migrant opting for the first option.

10.4 Migration flows and immigration policy in times of crisis

In the second half of 2008, most industrialized countries entered a recession sparked by the financial crisis and experienced rising unemployment and a prolonged economic slowdown. While things seem to have stabilized by 2010, most industrialized nations have not got back yet to their pre-crisis unemployment levels and many analysts believe the revival of the labour market could be delayed until 2012. How does an economic crisis affect migration flows (especially skilled ones) from developing to developed countries? The rest of this chapter suggests that the outcome will result from the interaction between migrants' self-selection decisions and receiving countries immigration policy responses to the crisis. The current episode, therefore, offers an interesting exploration ground to observe such interaction.

Let us first focus on the supply side, that is, on migration (and return migration) decisions. Obviously, some migrants may choose to return home after losing their jobs, or because they expect lower benefits from staying over. On the other hand, the economic recession in the Western world may transmit itself to developing countries through a number of channels, including decreases in trade flows and prices, lower inflows of remittances,[16] lower foreign investments or official assistance, which could in turn exacerbate migration pressure. This is not certain though as wage differentials may

---

[16] The World Bank says global remittances are expected to fall by 0.9 per cent in 2009, but could fall by as much as 6 per cent if the economic situation worsens. See also Frankel (2009) for a study of how remittances react to business cycles both at origin and destination.

actually be reduced and, in addition, lower income at home may make migration more credit constrained (see e.g. Rotte and Vogler, 2000). While the credit constraint argument would seem less relevant in the case of highly skilled workers, they may be more sensitive to the gloomy employment prospects and concerned about future restrictions on immigration in destination countries. In any event, it is difficult to predict which effect will dominate, be it for low-skilled or highly skilled workers.

So far, there have been no signs of massive returns, maybe because migrants are unwilling to return, fearing that they may not be able to re-enter because of tighter immigration controls. In the case of skilled workers, however, this assessment may be less relevant and is contradicted by media reports and anecdotal evidence of skilled return migration to the Philippines or Poland. At the same time, the number of applications for high-skill visas seems to be decreasing, as exemplified by the fall in the number of applications for H1B visas in the USA, to the point that for the first time since their creation it was only by year's end that the cap on the number of H1B visas was reached both in 2009 and 2010.

On the demand side, there have been strong political pressures to adjust immigration policies. This was expected. In February 2009, the USA enacted a new law imposing strict restrictions on the hiring of skilled immigrant workers by companies receiving government bailout money.[17] In Spain, the Zapatero government decided that in the face of rising unemployment, all non-EU immigrants should be offered the chance to cash in their unemployment benefits in exchange for leaving Spain for at least three years. The Czech Republic implemented a similar programme, while Ireland or Italy also came out with their own restrictive immigration policy proposals. Finally, Malaysia and Saudi Arabia directed national companies to lay off foreign workers first if they needed to downsize.

It is worth being reminded that immigration policy has essentially long-run objectives. In the case of skilled migration, these objectives have to do with the global competitiveness of the economy, its ability to invest in research and development and take advantage of the human and social capital skilled migrants bring in. The objective of dealing with occupational shortages may be relevant for both high- and low-skill workers; however, this is a short-term objective, which should not be central when designing immigration policy. Certainly, economic crises affect labour demand and the magnitude of employment mismatch in many sectors and occupations. However, preventing firms from hiring qualified personnel in times of skill shortages, as enacted in the USA, is likely to delay recovery. Encouraging current migrants to go

---

[17] American Recovery and Reinvestment Act of 2009 (H.R. 1), final version published on 10 February 2009.

back home with social benefits is likely to attract a new wave of migrants who will be less integrated and increase negative public attitudes towards immigration. Malaysia and Saudi Arabia have often used immigrants and minorities as scapegoats in times of economic distress, and the latest decisions on immigration follow that tradition. More generally, it is simply wrong to try to solve short-term problems by using long-term policy tools.

11

Conclusion

In this book, we have largely demonstrated that the impact of highly skilled emigration on sending countries need not be detrimental. In terms of human capital formation, the brain drain becomes clearly detrimental only when skilled emigration rates exceed a certain threshold that we estimated at around 20 per cent. If one accounts for other feedback effects in terms of technology diffusion, better institutions, screening-selection of skilled migrants, remittances, and induced trade and FDI, this threshold can reasonably be pushed to 35 per cent. A corollary of this is that between 0 and 20 to 35 per cent, the optimal skilled emigration rate is certainly positive and, based on our computations, could be conservatively set at about 15 per cent in many developing countries. Obviously, these numbers should be taken with caution. First, the optimal brain drain rate is likely to be extremely heterogeneous across countries, depending on their size, economic and institutional development, and on whether the brain drain is concentrated in certain sectors that are essential to TFP growth and human capital formation. Second, the empirical literature remains relatively poor to guide policymaking. In particular, due to data limitations, existing empirical studies are mostly based on cross-sectional regressions, which is an inherent limit as this precludes capturing the complex dynamics of migration and human capital formation.

A more precise quantification of the effects of skilled emigration on developing countries, therefore, first requires extending the geographic (to include South–South migration) and time (to include a panel dimension) coverage of the existing data sets on international migration by education level. It also requires obtaining better comparative data on immigration policies in order to be able to obtain more precise estimates of the effects of skilled emigration on the type of outcomes detailed in this book (e.g. trade, FDI, technology diffusion, institutional dividends) and to understand whether specific dimensions of immigration policies (such as their general restrictiveness and selectivity), or specific policies (e.g. dual citizenship laws) affect these outcomes both directly and indirectly, through their effects on migration flows.

References

Acemoglu, D. (2002), 'Technical change, inequality, and the labor market.' *Journal of Economic Literature* 40, 7–72.

Adams, R. (2003), 'International Migration, Remittances and the Brain Drain: A Study Of 24 Labor-Exporting Countries', World Bank Policy Research Working Paper No. 2972.

Agrawal, A.K, Kapur, D., McHale, J., Oettl, A. (2011), 'Brain drain or brain bank? The impact of skilled emigration on poor country innovation.' *Journal of Urban Economics* 69, 1, 43–55.

Angrist, J. (1995), 'The economic returns to schooling in the West Bank and Gaza Strip.' *American Economic Review* 85, 1068–87.

Azariadis, C., Drazen, A. (1990), 'Threshold externalities in economic development.' *Quarterly Journal of Economics* 105 (2), 501–26.

Baernighausen, T., Bloom, D.E. (2009), 'Conditional scholarships for HIV/AIDS health workers: educating and retaining the workforce to provide antiretroviral treatment in Sub-Saharan Africa.' *Social Science and Medicine* 68, 3, 544–51.

Barro, R. J., J. W. Lee (2001), 'International Data on Educational Attainment: Updates and Implications', CID Working Papers 42, Center for International Development, Harvard University.

Barro, R. J., Mankiw N. G., Sala-I-Martin, X. (1995), 'Capital mobility in neoclassical models of growth.' *American Economic Review* 85 (1), 103–15.

Batista, C., Lacuesta, A., Vicente, P.C. (2012), 'Testing the "brain gain" hypothesis: micro evidence from Cape Verde.' *Journal of Development Economics* 97 (1) 32–45.

Beine, M., Defoort, C., Docquier, F. (2011), 'A panel data analysis of the brain gain.' *World Development* 39 (4), 523–32.

Beine, M., Docquier, F., Ozden, C. (2011), 'Diasporas.' *Journal of Development Economics* 95(1), 30–41.

Beine, M., Docquier, F., Rapoport, H. (2001), 'Brain drain and economic growth: theory and evidence.' *Journal of Development Economics* 64(1), 275–89.

Beine, M., Docquier, F., Rapoport, H. (2007), 'Measuring international skilled migration: new estimates controlling for age of entry.' *World Bank Economic Review* 21 (2), 249–54.

Beine, M., Docquier, F., Rapoport, H. (2008), 'Brain drain and human capital formation in developing countries: winners and losers.' *Economic Journal* 118 (4), 631–52.

Beine, M., Docquier, F., Rapoport, H. (2010), 'On the robustness of brain gain estimates', *Annales d'Economie et de Statistique* 97–98, 143–66.

Benhabib, J., Spiegel, M.M. (2005), 'Human capital and technology diffusion.' In: Ph. Aghion and S. Durlauf (eds), *Handbook of Economic Growth*, Amsterdam: Elsevier, Vol 1, Chapter 13, pp. 935–66,

Bhagwati, J.N. (2009), 'Overview of issues.' Chapter 1 in J. Bhagwati and G. Hanson, (eds) *Skilled Immigration: Problems, Prospects and Policies*, Oxford: Oxford University Press, pp. 3–11.

Bhagwati, J.N., Hamada, K. (1974), 'The brain drain, international integration of markets for professionals and unemployment.' *Journal of Development Economics* 1(1), 19–42.

Bhargava, A., Jamison, D., Lau, L., Murray, C. (2001), 'Modeling the effects of health on economic growth.' *Journal of Health Economics* 20, 423–40.

Bhargava, A., Sargan J.D. (1983), 'Estimating dynamic random effects models from panel data covering short-time periods.' *Econometrica* 51(6),1635–60.

Biao X. (2006), 'Promoting knowledge exchange through diaspora networks (the case of the People's Republic of China)', in C. Wescott and J. Brinkerhoff (eds), *Converting Migration Drains into Gains Harnessing the Resources of Overseas Professionals*, Manila: Asian Development Bank.

Bollard, A., McKenzie, D., Morten, M., Rapoport, H. (2011), 'Remittances and the brain drain revisited: The microdata show that more educated migrants remit more.' *World Bank Economic Review* 25 (1), 132–56.

Boucher, S., Stark, O., Taylor, E. (2008), 'A Gain with a Drain? Evidence From Rural Mexico', Working Paper, UC Davis.

Buch, C.M., Kleinert, J., Toubal, F. (2006), 'Where enterprises lead, people follow? Links between migration and FDI in Germany.' *European Economic Review* 50 (8), 2017–36.

Carrington, W.J., Detragiache, E. (1998), 'How Big is the Brain Drain?' IMF Working paper WP/98/102.

Carrington, W.J., Detragiache, E. (1999), 'How extensive is the brain drain.' *Finance and Development* 32 (2), 46–9.

Carrington, W.J., Detragiache, E., Vishwanath, T. (1996), 'Migration with endogenous moving costs.' *American Economic Review* 86 (4), 909–30.

Caselli, Franceso (2007), 'The marginal product of capital.' *Quarterly Journal of Economics* 122 (2), 535–68.

Caselli F., Esquivel G., Lefort, F. (1996), 'Reopening the convergence debate: a new look at cross-country growth empirics.' *Journal of Economics Growth* 1, 363–89.

Chand, Satish, Clemens, M. (2008), 'Skilled Emigration and Skill Creation: A Quasi-Experiment', Center for Global Development Working Paper No. 152, September.

Clemens, M.A., Pettersson, G. (2006), 'A New Database of Health Professional Emigration from Africa', Working Paper, 95, Center for Global Development.

Cohen, D. Soto, M. (2007), 'Growth and human capital: good data, good results.' *Journal of Economic Growth* 12 (1), 51–76.

Commander, S., Kangasniemi M.,Winters, L.A. (2004), 'The brain drain: curse or boon? A survey of the literature', in R. Baldwin and L.A. Winters, (eds) *Challenges to Globalization*, Chicago: The University of Chicago Press, Chapter 7.

Coulombe, S. , Tremblay, J.F. (2007), 'Migration and skills disparities across the Canadian provinces.' *Regional Studies* 43 (1), 5–18.

De la Fuente, A., Domenech, R. (2006), 'Human capital in growth regressions: how much difference does data quality make.' *Journal of the European Economic Association* 4 (1), 1–36.

De Laat, J., Jack, W. (2009), Adverse Selection and the Brain Drain, Mimeo., Georgetown University.

Defoort, C. (2008), 'Tendances de long terme en migrations internationales: analyse à partir de 6 pays receveurs.' *Population-E* 63, 285–318.

Docquier, F., Bhargava, A. (2006), 'Medical Brain Drain - A New Panel Data Set on Physicians' Emigration Rates (1991–2004).' Report, World Bank, Washington DC.

—— Faye, O., Pestieau, P. (2008), 'Is migration a good substitute for subsidies.' *Journal of Development Economics* 86, 263–76.

—— Lodigiani, E. (2010), 'Skilled migration and business networks.' *Open Economies Review* 21(4), 565–88.

—— Lohest, O., Marfouk, A. (2005), 'Union Européenne et migrations internationales: l'UE 15 contribue-t-elle à l'exode des travailleurs qualifié?' Revue Economique 56, 1301–30.

—— Lowell, B.L., Marfouk, A. (2009), 'A gendered assessment of highly skilled emigration.' *Population and Development Review* 35 (2), 297–321.

—— Marfouk, A. (2006), 'International migration by educational attainment (1990–2000)', in C. Ozden and M. Schiff (eds) *International Migration, Remittances and Development*, New York: Palgrave Macmillan.

—— Marfouk, A., Salomone, S., Sekkat, K. (2012), 'Are skilled women more migratory than skilled men?', *World Development*, 40(2), 273–90.

—— Rapoport, H. (2003), 'Ethnic discrimination and the migration of skilled labor.' *Journal of Development Economics* 70, 159–72.

—— Rapoport, H. (2009a), 'Documenting the brain drain of "la crème de la crème": three case-studies on international migration at the upper end of the education distribution.' *Jahrbucher fur Nationalokonomie und Statistik* 229(6), 679–705.

—— Rapoport, H. (2009b), 'Skilled migration today: the perspective of developing countries', in J. Bhagwati and G. Hanson, (eds) *Skilled Immigration: Problems, Prospects and Policies*, Oxford: Oxford University Press, Chapter 9, pp. 247–84.

Dumont J.C., Lemaître, G. (2007), 'Enjeux et limites des politiques migratoires sélectives à des fins d'emploi', Actes du 17e congrès des économistes belges de langue française, Cifop: Charleroi.

Dumont, J.C., Martin J.P., Spielvogel, G. (2007), 'Women on the Move: The Neglected Gender Dimension of the Brain Drain.' IZA Discussion Paper, n. 2920.

Easterly, W., Nyarko, Y. (2009), 'Is the brain drain good for Africa?' In J. Bhagwati and G. Hanson (eds) *Skilled Immigration: Problems, Prospects and Policies*, Oxford: Oxford University Press, Chapter 11, pp. 316–60.

Epifani, P., Gancia, G. (2008), 'The skill bias of world trade.' *Economic Journal* 118 (530), 927–60.

Faini, R. (2003), 'Is the Brain Drain an Unmitigated Blessing?' UNU-WIDER Discussion Paper No 2003/64, September.

Faini, R. (2007), 'Remittances and the brain drain: do more skilled migrants remit more?' *World Bank Economic Review* 21, 177–91.

Frankel, Jeffrey (2011), 'Are Bilateral Remittances Countercyclical?' *Open Economies Review*, 22(1), 1–16.

Gibson, J., McKenzie, D. (2011), 'The microeconomic determinants of emigration and return migration of the best and brightest: evidence from the Pacific.' *Journal of Development Economics* 95(1), 18–29.

Gould, D. (1994), 'Immigrants links to the home countries: empirical implication for U.S. bilateral trade flows.' *Review of Economics and Statistics* 76(2), 302–16.

Greif, A. (1993), 'Contract enforceability and economic institutions in early trade: The Maghribi traders' coalition.' *American Economic Review* 83 (3), 525–48.

Grossmann, V., Stadelmann, D. (2011), 'Does international mobility of high-skilled workers aggravate between country inequality?' *Journal of Development Economics* 95 (1), 88–94.

Head, K., Reis, J. (1998), 'Immigration and trade creation: econometric evidence from Canada.' *Canadian Journal of Economics* 31, 47–62.

Islam, N. (1995), 'Growth empirics: a panel data approach.' *Quarterly Journal of Economics* 110 (4), 1127–70.

Islam, N. (2003), 'What have we learnt from the convergence debate?' *Journal of Economic Surveys* 17 (3), 309–62.

Javorcik, B.S., Ozden, C., Spatareanu, M., Neagu, I.C. (2011), 'Migrant networks and foreign direct investment.' *Journal of Development Economics* 94(2), 151–90.

Kauffman, D., Kraay, A., Mastruzzi, M. (2005), Governance Matters IV: Governance Indicators for 1996–2004, Mimeo. World Bank.

Kerr, W.R. (2008), 'Ethnic scientific communities and international technology diffusion.' *Review of Economics and Statistics* 90 (3), 518–37.

Klenow, P.J., Rodriguez-Clare, A. (2005), 'Externalities and growth.'In P. Aghion and S. Durlauf, (eds) *Handbook of Economic Growth*, Amsterdam: Elsevier-North Holland. Vol. 1A, Chapter 11, pp. 817–61.

Kossoudji, S., Cobb-Clark, D. (2002), 'Coming out of the shadows: Learning about legal status and wages from the legalized population.' *Journal of Labor Economics* 20(3), 598–628.

Kugler, M., Rapoport, H. (2006), 'Migration and FDI: complements or substitutes?' CEPR/ ESF conference on 'Outsourcing, Migration, and the European Economy', Rome.

Kugler, M.,Rapoport, H. (2007), 'International labor and capital flows: complements or substitutes?' *Economics Letters* 94(2), 155–62.

Lahneman, W.J. (2005), 'Impact of Diaspora Communities on Global and National Politics. Report on Survey of the Literature.' CIA Strategic Assessment Group and University of Maryland, July.

Leblang, D. (2009), 'Harnessing the Diaspora: The Political Economy of Dual Citizenship.' Working Paper, University of Virginia.

Li, X., Mc Hale, J. (2009), 'Does Brain Drain Lead to Institutional Gain? A Cross Country Empirical Investigation.' Mimeo, Queens University.

Lien, D. (2008), 'Quality-assurance programs and the brain drain.' *Education Economics* 1 (1), 59–73.

Lodigiani, E. (2009), 'Diaspora Externalities and Technology Diffusion.' Mimeo. University of Luxembourg.

Lucas, R.E. (1988), 'On the mechanics of economic development.' Journal *of Monetary Economics* 22 (1), 3–42.

Lucas, R.E.B. (2004), 'International Migration Regimes and Economic Development.' Report for the Expert Group on Development Issues (EGDI), Swedish Ministry of Foreign Affairs.

Mariani, F. (2007), 'Migration as an antidote to rent-seeking?' *Journal of Development Economics* 84 (2), 609–30.

Massey, D.S., Goldring, L., Durand, J. (1994), 'Continuities in transnational migration: an analysis of nineteen Mexican communities.' *American Journal of Sociology* 99 (6), 1492–533.

Mattoo, A., Neagu, I.C., Ozden, C. (2008), 'Brain waste? Educated immigrants in the US labor market.' *Journal of Development Economics* 87 (2), 255–69.

Mayda, A. M. (2010), 'International migration: A panel data analysis of the determinants of bilateral flows.' *Journal of Population Economics* 23(4), 1249–74.

McCullock, R., Yellen, J.T. (1977), 'Factor mobility, regional development and the distribution of income.' *Journal of Political Economy* 85 (1), 79–96.

McHale, J. (2009), 'Taxation and skilled Indian migration to the United States: revisiting the Bhagwati tax.' In J. Bhagwati and G. Hanson (eds) *Skilled Immigration: Problems, Prospects and Policies*, Oxford: Oxford University Press, Chapter 12, pp. 362–86.

McKenzie, D. Rapoport, H. (2010), 'Self-selection patterns in Mexico-US migration: the role of migration networks.' *Review of Economics and Statistics* 92 (4), 811–21.

McKenzie, D. Rapoport, H. (2011), 'Can migration reduce educational attainment? Evidence from Mexico.' *Journal of Population Economics* 24 (4), 1331–58.

Meyer, J.-B. (2001), 'Network approach versus brain drain: lessons from the Diaspora.' *International Migration* 39 (5), 91–110.

Meyer J. B., Brown, M. (1999), 'Scientific Diasporas, a New Approach to the Brain Drain', Discussion Paper no. 41, Management of Social Transformation, UNESCO, Paris.

Mountford, A. (1997), 'Can a brain drain be good for growth in the source economy?' *Journal of Development Economics* 53 (2), 287–303.

Niimi, Y., Özden, C., Schiff, M. (2008), 'Remittances and the Brain Drain: Skilled Migrants Do Remit Less!' Working Paper, World Bank.

Opiniano J., Castro, T. A. (2006), 'Promoting knowledge transfer activities through diaspora networks: a pilot study of the Philippines.' In C. Wescott and J. Brinkerhoff (eds) *Converting Migration Drains into Gains Harnessing the Resources of Overseas Professionals*, Manila: Asian Development Bank, Chap. 3.

Ottaviano, G., Peri, G. (2008), 'Immigration and National Wages: Clarifying the Theory and the Empirics.' Mimeo, UC Davis.

Özden, C., Parsons, C.R., Schiff, M., Walmsley, T. (2011), 'Where on Earth is everybody? The evolution of global bilateral migration 1960–2000.' *World Bank Economic Review* 25(1), 12–56.

Pandey, A., Aggarwal, A., Devane, R., Kuznetsov, Y. (2006), 'The Indian diaspora: A unique case?' In Y. Kuznetsov (ed.), *Diaspora Networks and the International Migration of Skills*, Washington DC: The World Bank, Chap. 4.

Papageorgiou, Ch., Spilimbergo, A. (2009), 'Learning Abroad and Technology Adoption.' Mimeo., IFM, Washington DC.

Poutvaara, P. (2008), 'Public education in an integrated Europe: studying to migrate and teaching to stay?' *Scandinavian Journal of Economics* 110 (3), 591–608.

Rapoport, H. and Docquier, F. (2006), 'The economics of migrants' remittances.' In S.-C. Kolm and J. Mercier Ythier, (eds) *Handbook of the Economics of Giving, Altruism and Reciprocity*, Amsterdam: North Holland, Chapter 17.

Rauch, J. E. (2003), 'Diasporas and Development: Theory, Evidence, and Programmatic Implications,' Department of Economics, University of California at San Diego.

Rauch, J. E., Casella, A. (2003), 'Overcoming informational barriers to international resource allocation: prices and ties.' *Economic Journal* 113 (484), 21–42.

Rauch, J. E., Trindade, V. (2002), 'Ethnic Chinese networks in international trade.' *Review of Economics and Statistics* 84 (1), 116–30.

Rosenzweig, M.R. (2005), 'Consequences of Migration for Developing Countries.' Paper prepared for the United Nations Expert Group Meeting on International Migration and Development, Population Division, July 6–8, New York.

—— (2008), 'Higher Education and International Migration in Asia: Brain Circulation', in F. Bourguignon (ed.) *ABCDE World Bank Conference*, Oxford University Press.

Saxenian A. (1999), *Silicon Valley's New Immigrant Entrepreneurs*, San Francisco, Calif: Public Policy Institute of California,

Saxenian, A. (2001), 'Bangalore, the Silicon Valley of India?' CREDPR Working Paper No 91, Stanford University.

Saxenian A. (2002), *Local and Global Networks of Immigrant Professional in Silicon Valley*, San Francisco: Public Policy Institute of California.

Schiff, M. (2005), 'Brain gain: claims about its size and impact on welfare are greatly exaggerated.' In Caglar Özden and Maurice Schiff (eds) *International Migration, Remittances, and the Brain Drain*. Washington DC: The World Bank and Palgrave Macmillan.

Schiff, M., Wang, Y. (2009), 'North South Trade related Technology Diffusion, Brain Drain and Productivity Growth: Are Small States Different?' World Bank Policy Discussion Paper No 4828), January.

Spilimbergo, A. (2009), 'Democracy and foreign education.' *American Economic Review* 99 (1), 528–43.

Stark, O., Helmenstein, C.,Prskawetz, A. (1998), 'Human capital depletion, human capital formation, and migration: a blessing or a "curse"?' *Economics Letters* 60 (3), 363–7.

Stark, O., Wang, Y. (2002), 'Inducing human capital formation: migration as a substitute for subsidies.' *Journal Public Economics* 86(1), 29–46.

Vandenbussche, J., Aghion, Ph., and Meghir, C. (2006), 'Growth, distance to frontier and composition of human capital.' *Journal of Economic Growth* 11(2), 97–127.

Vidal, J. P. (1998), 'The effect of emigration on human capital formation.' *Journal of Population Economics* 11 (4), 589–600.

Vogler, M. Rotte, R. (2000), 'The effects of development on migration: theoretical issues and new empirical evidence.' *Journal of Population Economics* 13 (3), 485–508.

Wilson, J. (2008), 'A voluntary tax on brains.' *Journal of Public Economics* 92 (12), 2385–91.

Wilson, J.D. (2011), 'Brain drain taxes for non-benevolent governments.' *Journal of Development Economics* 95(1), 68–76.

World Bank (2008), *Migration and Remittances Factbook 2008*. Washington DC: World Bank.

Comments

by Antonio Spilimbergo

Background

Flows of ideas are key to economic development and ideas often move with people. This explains why scholars and policymakers have been interested in the migration of skilled people for a long time. Since ancient times, countries have restricted (or favoured) the migration of skilled workers as a way of protecting (or absorbing) the latest techniques from other countries. In the Middle Ages, the Republic of Venice restricted the movement of artisans who knew the art of glass-blowing. In modern days, Soviet rulers heavily restricted the movement of people with particular information on nuclear technology.

Even though economists long ago recognized the importance of highly skilled migration for development, the empirical study of the effect of migration has lagged for a long time because reliable data on highly skilled migration were not available. In the absence of comprehensive data on skilled migration, economists have been free to conjecture many mechanisms through which highly skilled migration may have an impact on development.

In this context, the ambitious report by Docquier and Rapoport in Part II of this volume performs three tasks: i) reviewing the main theoretical arguments behind the main channels proposed in the literature; ii) briefly discussing the empirical evidence of these channels; iii) calibrating the total effect of migration on economic development in sending countries using the best estimates from the empirical literature. Before focusing on these contributions, it is worth giving an extremely brief (and necessarily extremely partial) introduction to the research on highly skilled flows.

The literature on skilled migration can be roughly divided into two waves. The first wave of literature in the 1960s and 1970s stressed the negative effects of migration of skilled workers from the South—a developing country in which human capital is scarce—to the North. The flow of skilled people interested economists mainly for two reasons. First, the flow from South to North seems to go against what trade economists would have *prima facie* expected (i.e. resources tend to move to the places where they are relatively scarce so skilled labour should move South and not North). Second, the effect of this flow could be very detrimental to growth because skilled workers are not only a factor of production but also the main machine behind technological progress. Focusing on the negative aspect, skilled migration was called 'brain drain.' Unfortunately, these observations could only be answered with theoretical speculations given that large comparable cross-country data sets were not available. Given this, the relevant policy questions were: How do poor countries stop this flow? With a tax on brain movement? If yes, would such a tax be enforceable? Do we need the collaboration of receiving countries? Is there need for international coordination? Curiously the Soviet policies to restrain skilled migration were based on similar arguments so potential emigrants were supposed to pay back the human capital received. Probably also for this reason an international tax on skilled labour migration never had the chance to be seriously considered. In addition, the most serious problem of this first phase of research was conceptual due to the fact that skilled migration was mostly considered a flow of a factor of production, forgetting that a brain belongs to a human being, and had a static aspect.[1]

The second phase of the literature on skilled migration put back the 'human factor' into the 'brain drain' through several channels: individuals invest in human capital, individuals abroad are also conduits for technological transfers and a broader range of ideas, including institutions, and, finally, individuals come with different abilities and brighter individuals could have higher propensity to move.[2]

These channels could overcome the first clear policy implication of the old literature that skilled migration is unequivocally bad. However, the theoretical possibility of overthrowing the presumption was not enough to necessarily change the policy advice if there was no quantification of these effects. The main contribution of this report is to use data from available research to quantify these different effects.

The task of quantifying the human factor, which is the hallmark of the second phase of the literature, is heroic and has to be commended. After all,

---

[1] Interestingly, the terminology on skilled migration is borrowed from physics of fluids as often happens in economics at least since the *Tableau Économique* of the physiocrats. So, for instance, we speak of flows and, derogatively, of brain drain when referring to skilled migration. While this metaphor has been helpful to conceptualize the issue, it also limited the understanding of a complex phenomenon for a long time. It is not a case that when during the second phase of the literature on skilled migration the human factor was introduced the fluid metaphor disappeared.

[2] Some of these mechanisms have been described in previous surveys (see for instance, Commander, Simon, Mari Kangasniemi, and Alan Winters, 2003, 'The Brain Drain: Curse or Boon?' IZA Discussion paper No. 809.).

few economists dare to 'stick their neck out' and to attach numbers to the human factors such as the distribution of innate abilities.

Brain drain and human capital formation

Probably the most important contribution in the new literature on brain drain is the intuition that the possibility of moving abroad increases the return on human capital and so induces ex-ante more investment in education; in such a way, almost paradoxically, the possibility of a flow out of the country increases the amount of education in the country. This effect was shown to be not just a theoretical *curiosum*, but an effective possibility in some poor countries by Beine, Docquier, and Rapoport (2008).[3] This effect should not come as a surprise to people familiar with developing countries in which education is often the only ticket to upper mobility, which in many cases implies migration abroad. While this is surely a plausible and important channel for many countries, it seems improbable that roughly 50 per cent of countries would increase their human capital endogenously as a consequence of skilled migration, as the authors imply in Section 2.2.

Screening-selection

Not all individuals (and skilled emigrants) have the same abilities. This simple fact was ignored by the first phase of the literature in which there was no differentiation within a flow (all water is the same, after all). If better skilled workers tend to emigrate more, the effect of endogenous human capital formation discussed above is partially offset. This could be an important effect and, in the spirit of calibration, Docquier and Rapoport pose an equation describing the distribution of skills within educated individuals. Taking 'plausible' values from other studies on heterogeneity (hats off to them for the inventiveness in finding and using these studies), the authors find that this effect is relatively unimportant: the average ability of the remaining workers decreases by only 4 per cent when 30 per cent of the skilled workers emigrate.

Productivity and other 'non-liquid' channels

Probably the main drawback of the first wave of literature on skilled migration is that it identified movement of people with movement of ideas. Being

---

[3] 'Brain Drain and Human Capital Formation in Developing Countries: Winners and Losers' by M. Beine, F. Docquier, and H. Rapoport. *The Economic Journal*. Vol. 118. pp. 631–52.

implicitly prisoner of the fluid metaphor, all research posited that a skilled worker who emigrated abroad must be a body loss for the domestic economy. However, flows of ideas and people are sometimes dissociated: a skilled worker abroad can propel domestic innovation at home. For instance, many high-tech enterprises in India were started by skilled Indian émigrés who followed the companies even from abroad. The transfer of technological progress does not require the physical presence of workers. On the contrary, empirical studies have shown that the catch-up with countries at the technological frontier is facilitated by skilled workers abroad.[4] The authors confess that there is vast uncertainty on this effect and give a range of possible effects. However, as a rule of thumb these effects could be as important as the effects of endogenous human capital formation. I share their judgement, especially given the relative novelty of the empirical studies in this field. In the future, as more accurate estimates become available, this particular parameter in the calibration will probably be fine-tuned.

The skilled workers abroad also facilitate contacts, which are important for trade and foreign direct investment. Docquier and Rapoport incorporate this effect as a decrease in the interest rate faced by the home economy. While I appreciate the need to incorporate this effect in the integrated framework, I think this is a very first cut and future calibration of this effect will use other parameters, for instance including trade explicitly.

Policy implications

What are the policy implications of the second wave of literature on skilled migration? A first very important contribution of this book is to show that the endogenous human capital formation and the productivity/institutional channels can overthrow the results of the old literature for some countries for plausible values of parameters.

Does this mean that countries should encourage out-migration of skilled workers? Probably not. We still do not know enough to give such strong recommendations. We have learned that it is dangerous to quickly jump to policy conclusions based on easy metaphors, as during the first wave of literature.

Are there general policy lessons that we have learned from the second wave of literature? Yes, we have learned that people do not move forever to one place and a policy to persuade skilled nationals who move abroad to come back could be more effective than trying to dissuade people from

---

[4] 'Diaspora externalities and technology diffusion' by Elisabetta Lodigiani, 2009, and 'Learning abroad and technology adoption' by Chris Papageorgiou and Antonio Spilimbergo, 2009.

going abroad. As Docquier and Rapoport have shown for the productivity/ institutional channel, we sometimes just need to make sure that *ideas* come back even if the *brains* remain abroad.

Another issue that is still unexplored is that in many countries good superior education can only be obtained abroad. For instance, many Caribbean or Pacific islands typically are not large enough to afford a first-rate university in many fields. In this case, brain circulation is the only realistic option to increase human capital at home.

Overall, Docquier and Rapoport have done a superb job to show that the channels studied in the recent skilled migration literature are economically relevant. Future research should pursue this line of enquiry further.

Comments

by Alessandra Venturini

Migration has always been a highly selective process. In the past, when work was manual, being in good health was an asset for migration, which meant that migrants often had longer life expectancy than non-migrants.[1] Today, when work is more closely related to technology, being educated and skilled improves the chance of emigrating, which in general produces more educated migrants than educated non-migrant workers.

The expression 'brain drain' has a twofold meaning: on the one hand, it refers to *educated migrants* and it was used for the first time in Great Britain after World War II to denote British scientists emigrating to the USA;[2] on the other hand, it refers to *needed migrants*, which means the most talented workers with or without a formal education. It was frequently used, for instance, in the case of Italian emigration to the USA at the beginning of the last century, or to North Europe, which deprived the Southern regions of their best and most talented workers, though frequently illiterate, and reduced the potential growth path of the area of origin.

Today, the connotation of brain drain combines both meanings—educated and needed—in the production processes of the origin country.

The report by Frédéric Docquier and Hillel Rapoport and their many other papers on the subject are key references on the issue, and the data set they have constructed is very important and unique. They have now extended the observation to the non-OECD countries, providing a more comprehensive

---

[1] Sermet C., Laurier D., Khlat M., 1998, La morbidité dans les ménages originaires du Maghreb, sur la base de l'enquête Santé de l'Insee, 1991–1992, *Population*, vol.53, n.6, pp.1155–84, cited also by Philippe Fargues 2009 CARIM Call on Highly Skilled Migration.
[2] Reference C.Brandi 2001, The Evolution in theories of brain drain and the migration of skilled personnel, Studi Emigrazioni, n.141, cited also by Michael Clemens 2009, Skill Flow: A Fundamental Reconsideration of Skilled-Worker Mobility and Development, Human Development Research Paper n.2009/08.

and reliable picture of educated outflows and more robust results. This extension is also vital for understanding the African and Middle East migration on which myself and the CARIM focus.[3]

Part II is divided into three sections: the first on data, the second on interpretation, and the third on policies.

Even if in general the conclusions seem convincing, the following comments counsel caution in using the numbers of the empirical exercise.

1. A first problem arises from considering all tertiary educated workers abroad as constituting a single group: some of them are success stories, while others are not. The tertiary educated migrants in the data set and in the subsequent empirical analyses do not necessarily hold tertiary educated jobs. Many examples of *brain waste* or of *unskilled occupation* are documented: for instance the Algerian migrants in Canada,[4] who even if educated, generally have unskilled jobs. According to a survey cited in the World Bank report (2009),[5] the probabilities of obtaining a skilled job in the USA for immigrants with a BA range from 24 per cent for a migrant from Jordan, 30 per cent for a migrant from Morocco, Algeria, and Egypt, to 44 per cent from Lebanon, whilst for a migrant from India it is 70 per cent. The same disparities are apparent among migrants with master degrees, in which case the probability of getting a skilled job is 47 per cent for MENA (Middle East and North Africa) workers and 80 per cent for Indian ones. A recent OECD (2007)[6] report also stresses the over-education of immigrants in all the destination countries, albeit with a very large variation. Only for specific professions—medicine, nursing, HT engineering—is there a closer correspondence between the education and the job skill level, while in many other cases there is not. According to our analyses, scientific education reduces the education/job mismatch by 40 per cent.[7] While longitudinal studies provide clear answers, cross-sectional analyses compare educated migrants with skilled jobs with those who hold unskilled jobs. The heterogeneity implies different wages, different integration patterns, and also different prospects of return, and therefore confuses the picture. The weak results in the remittances section may be due to this mismeasuring.

---

[3] CARIM is a project on migration in the Mediterranean at the Robert Schuman Center for Advanced Studies, at the EUI in Florence.

[4] Khelfaoui H., (2006), La diaspora algérienne en Amerique du Nord: une resource pour son pays d'origine? CARIM Research report 2006/4.

[5] World Bank (2009), Shaping the Future, A long term Perspective of People and Job Mobility for the Middle East and North Africa, p.48.

[6] OCDE (2007) Matching Educational Background and Employment: A Challenge for Immigrants In Host Countries, by Dumont J.C. and Monso O.

[7] CARIM, Venturini A., (2009), Highly Skilled Migration, Rapporteur paper.

2. With the revised version of the data set, which now covers non-OECD countries, a different type of skilled emigration has been included, and the heterogeneity among the emigration patterns of the educated has increased as well. Better understanding of whether educated migration damages or benefits the origin country would require at least a *control for the destination area*, because 'migration processes' are very different around the world.

Migration to some of the Arab countries by either skilled or unskilled workers is by definition *temporary* because not all the Arab countries allow family reunification and permanent settlement. Migrants, either skilled or unskilled, therefore have as their point of reference the country of origin, to which they return at the end of migration. Moreover, numerous Egyptians in the Arab countries are employed in public administration or in the educational sector. Do they bring back knowledge? Are they agents of social change? Are they able to increase business or trade? Probably the answer to the first two questions is negative, while for the last there is more room for improvement.

Migration to the USA, Canada, Australia, and the UK is different in its nature. Skilled migration is an intrinsic part of the points-based system that these countries have developed over many years. Hence skilled migrants who want to move to one of them know that education is useful for entry. In addition, these countries have important foreign student programmes, which again favour the creation of educated workers connected with the country where the education has been completed, at least for the language spoken. Lastly, these countries have large wage premiums, which attract skilled migrants from other destination countries.[8] These factors tend to explain the greater concentration of skilled migrants in science professions in the USA and positive feedbacks in the science field for some of the origin countries (particularly India). This, however, is not a return pattern common to all types of skilled emigration.

Continental Europe is different. It has been unable to attract as many skilled migrants as it has wanted because it does not have an efficient points system, because it is not able to attract large numbers of foreign students, and because there are not enough high-skilled job openings for foreigners. Skilled migrants in Continental Europe are frequently employed by multinationals and if they do not have linguistic barriers, they frequently re-migrate to more rewarding places.

---

[8] According to the OECD data on earnings distribution, the dispersion between the first and ninth earning deciles in 2007 was, for instance, 4.85 in the USA, 3.59 in the UK, and 3.75 in Canada, while it was 2.91 in France, 3.26 in Germany, and 2.31 in Sweden.

Thus not only does selection differ among destination countries but so does what the migrants bring back home besides human capital and technologies. They bring back some of the social norms prevailing in the destination country,[9] so that not controlling for the area of emigration does not help clarify the picture of the effects of emigration.

3. The idea that migration is a permanent phenomenon has been recently reversed with the explosion of research on temporary migration and *return migration*. The brain drain stops being detrimental if migration is temporary. Research on Europe, which is the research that I know, has found that the average duration of stay in Germany is eight years.[10] But the decision to return is also a function of economic trends in the sending countries, and it increases the more the income in the sending country grows.[11] Return migration is very frequent: after two years of migration 85 per cent of Moroccans declare that they would like to return; the longer they stay in the destination country, the less they would like to return.[12] But return migration is also a highly selective project. Assimilation studies in Germany,[13] Sweden and Finland,[14] and Italy, for instance, have shown that workers who perform better in the destination labour market in terms of wages are those who are more likely to leave the country in order to return home or to move elsewhere. Those workers who remain are the worse, while the best ones leave. Hence if the aggregate stock of educated migrants is used, the risk arises of controlling for the worst in the group. Moreover, cross-sectional analyses, which use changes in the stock variables, consider as equal a small increase due to a small inflow and large inflows and returns, which have different impacts on the growth path of the country of origin.

4. There is likewise the role of *migrant networks* in favouring productivity growth and positive externalities. A large body of sociological literature shows that returning migrants may be agents of change if they come back from more socially advanced countries. There is a general consensus on this phenomenon, but it is distributed very unevenly. In some

[9] Fargues P., (2007), The Demographic Benefit of International Migration: A Hypothesis and Its Application to Middle Eastern and North African Contexts, in Oxden C., Schiff M. (eds) *International Migration, Economic Development and Policy*, Palgrave Mc Millan and World Bank.

[10] Dustmann, C., (2003), Return Migration, Wages Differentials and the Optimal Migration Duration, *European Economic Review*, 47, pp. 353–67.

[11] Venturini A., and Villosio C., 2008, Assimilation of Migrants in Recent Immigration Countries: The Italian Experience, OXREP, vol.24, n.3, pp. 518–42.

[12] Carim database.

[13] Constant, A., and Massey, D. S. (2003), 'Self-selection, earnings, and out-migration: A longitudinal study of immigrants to Germany', *Journal of Population Economics*, 16 (4), 631–53

[14] Roof D-O., and Saarela J., (2007), Selection in migration and return migration: Evidence from micro data, *Economic Letters*, p. 90–5.

destination countries, migrants become part of the society—they vote and so on—while in others they remain at the margins of social life (the Arab countries versus the USA or Australia). But also important is the role of the country of origin and its efforts to maintain contacts with the migrants abroad. The Moroccans and the Algerians in Canada, both of whom are skilled migrants doing unskilled jobs, provide examples of these different behaviours. Moroccans maintain strong links with the country of origin, for example by being involved in the Tokten programme to train natives, while the Algerians in Canada rarely return and have very few forms of contact with the national government at home. Thus, although the theory of the effect of the community abroad is convincing, the use of migrant stocks abroad is much less so, and it should be weighted at least with some indicator of contact between two areas, such as the number of direct flights, the amount of per capita remittances, or any other measure which highlights the presence of contacts between the destination and the sending country.

5. Does skilled migration really damage the sending country? *Brain waste* does not take place only abroad but in many cases also *at home*. Skilled migrants frequently emigrate for unskilled jobs abroad because they cannot find skilled jobs at home. In the CARIM area, the unemployment of university students is higher than the average (21 per cent against 15.4 per cent in Morocco, 17 per cent against 13.8 per cent in Algeria, 19 per cent versus 14 per cent in Tunisia, 14.4 per cent versus 8.3 per cent in Egypt, 11 per cent versus 9.2 per cent in Lebanon, 27.2 per cent versus 25 per cent in Palestine, and 15.5 per cent versus 13.8 per cent in Jordan).[15] Use of the production function is standard, but it does not account for supply and demand mismatches although it is this that is documented in the Mediterranean countries: a higher unemployment rate among the more educated workers and its recent increases. If these potential workers remained in the origin country, it is unlikely that they would enter a production function as skilled labour.

Of course, this evidence is in line with the incentive to pursue education for emigration (the brain drain/brain gain model implies educated unemployment), but it is also in line with the search for employment in the *public sector*, which attracts workers and requires formal education. There are two contrasting examples among the MENA countries: only 10 per cent of Morocco's labour force is tertiary educated, while the proportion in Egypt is 30 per cent; but in Egypt the public employment

---

[15] See Ivan Martin (2009) 'Labour Markets and Migration Flows in Arab Mediterranean Countries. A Regional Perspective', and Background national papers RSCAS, Florence.

is three times higher than in Morocco: 30 per cent against 12 per cent.[16] The high education rate among females in Egypt, together with the higher unemployment rate among the more educated, is also driven by the search for a job in public administration, which grants more social security and more flexible working hours. This finding is corroborated by the type of tertiary education pursued by migrants, which is concentrated in the humanities and social sciences. These subjects are the best options for migration but they do not favour the country's development. The share of university students specializing in these fields ranges from 76 per cent in Egypt to 50 per cent in Tunisia,[17] while it is less than 30 per cent in China.

As a concluding comment, we would like to emphasize that pointing out the above weaknesses is not to question the general approach of the authors but to adapt a general interpretation to a more specific reality and to propose a more tailor-made framework in which appropriate, and therefore viable, policies can be devised.

---

[16] See Ivan Martin (2009) 'Labour Markets and Migration Flows in Arab Mediterranean Countries. A Regional Perspective', and Background national papers RSCAS, Florence.
[17] World Bank Shaping the Future, 2009, p.44.

Index

Index

Printed and bound by CPI Group (UK) Ltd, Croydon, CR0 4YY